Best wishes to

from your friend —

Frank "Junior" Coghlan

SHAZAM —

They Still
Call Me Junior

To Letha, for her patience
in putting up with me
while I was writing this book,
and to our daughter Judy
who first suggested that I write it

They Still Call Me Junior

AUTOBIOGRAPHY OF A CHILD STAR; WITH A FILMOGRAPHY

by

Frank "Junior" Coghlan

with a foreword by
WILLIAM C. CLINE

McFarland & Company, Inc., Publishers
Jefferson, North Carolina, and London

British Library of Congress Cataloguing-in-Publication data are available

Library of Congress Cataloguing-in-Publication Data

Coghlan, Frank.
They still call me Junior : autobiography of a child star; with a filmography / by Frank "Junior" Coghlan.
p. cm.
Filmography: p.
Includes index.
ISBN 0-89950-762-X (lib. bdg. : 50# alk. paper) ∞
1. Coghlan, Frank. 2. Motion picture actors and actresses—United States—Biography. I. Title.
PN2287.C557A3 1993
791.43'028'092—dc20
[B] 92-50432
CIP

Manufactured in the United States of America

McFarland & Company, Inc., Publishers
Box 611, Jefferson, North Carolina 28640

Acknowledgments

I am especially grateful to William C. Cline, author of the fine book on serials, *In the Nick of Time* (published by McFarland in 1984). Bill and I first met at the Western Film Fair in Raleigh, North Carolina, in 1990. When he learned I was writing this book he offered to help me with his publisher. He told me if I would send my manuscript to him he would take it to McFarland personally. I did and he fulfilled his promise and I had a contract in the return mail. Bill kindly consented to write the introduction to this book and in return I am writing the introduction to his newest book. If it sounds like mutual admiration, it is.

I am also grateful to William Witney who directed me in the serial *Adventures of Captain Marvel* at Republic Pictures in 1941. When I told him I was having trouble recalling some of the dates and particulars in connection with the serial, he referred me to Jack Mathis, author of the great book on serials, *Valley of the Cliffhangers.* Jack is now working on his next effort, *Republic Confidential,* and is without a doubt the leading historian on this great old studio. Jack reviewed the chapter on Captain Marvel and corrected many mistakes that my memory had mislaid in the fifty years since I played Billy Batson.

I appreciate the help in research I received from Mary Housel, the chief librarian of our Los Alamitos–Rossmoor Branch Library and her assistants Toni Sawyer, Kate Dolan, Sandy Lamoureux, Edith Sheffield, and John Madigan. John is a longtime member of SPERDVAC, the Society to Preserve and Encourage Radio Drama, Variety, and Comedy, and he was most helpful on the chapter about my career in radio.

Many thanks to Laura Masoner, the senior reference librarian at the Garden Grove Regional Branch Library for putting together a fine group of reference books on the motion picture industry. And to Carol Cullen, Sam A. Gill, and the excellent staff in the reference section of the Margaret Herrick Library of the Academy of Motion Picture Arts and Sciences.

I wish to thank my good friend Robert Parrish for his encouragement and for the help he gave me on the chapter about John Ford. Bob and I were kid actors together in the 1920s and 1930s. He became an Academy Award–

winning film editor and then a fine motion picture director. Bob served in John Ford's motion picture unit of the OSS during World War II and gave me much information on Ford's wartime activities and the Field Photo Farm.

And thanks to Leonard Maltin for his kind words on "Entertainment Tonight" and to Leonard and his assistant Ben Herndon for their help in tracking down titles and cast members of some of the very old films in which I appeared.

I appreciate the loyalty of fans like Jim Shoenberger, Michael Fitzgerald, Gregory R. Jackson, Jr., Boyd Magers, Glenn Shipley, Steve Wichrowski, Norman Radford, Corky Savely, Alvin Naifeh, and others who call or write whenever they see me on the late show. Some have even taped many of my old films and sent me VHS copies. Their efforts have been a big help to me in putting the filmography of this book together. I especially appreciate the help Mike Hawks of Larry Edmunds Bookshop in Hollywood has given to me by checking titles and cast members for the filmography.

Contents

Foreword

(by William C. Cline)

There is a fantasy in which most devoted fans of the movies usually indulge: that the actors and actresses we see in motion pictures are the same in real life as we see them on the screen; that we will some day meet the ones we like best; that we will immediately like each other and become good friends. For most of us, it remains a fantasy; for some, the fantasy changes to disillusionment (when we finally do meet an idol and discover he has feet of clay); but for a few lucky ones the fantasy actually becomes reality.

Ever since 1941, when I saw him play Billy Batson in *Adventures of Captain Marvel,* I have sustained the fantasy that Frank Coghlan, Jr., would be the same open, friendly, sincere, and straightforward kind of person he appeared to be on the screen. When a chance to meet him in 1974 did not materialize, I was disappointed but continued to harbor the belief that the guy who had helped to immortalize the word "Shazam" would be the kind of person it would be a pleasure to know.

That belief was confirmed, and the rest of the fantasy made real, when we finally met at the Western Film Fair in Raleigh, North Carolina, in 1990, at which time Frank revealed that his autobiography was nearly done and almost ready for publication. During the three days at the Film Fair, Frank's outgoing personality and unconditional friendliness were at the same time refreshingly welcome and unexpectedly disarming. He seemed almost too good to be true, and it challenged those with whom he came in contact to likewise be themselves, whatever that was in each case. He seemed so good, in fact, it was tempting to think that he might be putting on an act for everybody; but time has verified that he was just being himself, no more nor less. To complete the fantasy, Frank and I have indeed become good friends and, even though it has been for a comparatively short time, it seems much longer—almost as if we have known each other for years.

Part of that has come from reading Frank's manuscript. Told in the same straightforward, forthright manner he employs in personal communication, it is a triple-faceted narrative that is a love story, a dramatic saga, and an adventure epic all rolled into one. Now that may seem a little high sounding, and I am sure Frank did not write the book with all that in mind; but I do not retract any of it. In putting in writing the events of his life to date, Frank has revealed his love affair with life itself—and his zest for living it, the dramatic evolution of the motion picture and television industries—of which he was, and is, a very visible part—and details of the greatest epic adventure of the century, World War II and its aftermath, in which he played a vital and significant role.

Seldom will you see so much of life's history and drama recounted in such a simple, matter-of-fact way by a person who was there and accepted all that was happening as just events of his life—no big deal. But that's the way Frank Coghlan writes, and the way he is. You know you are reading the truth, because it is too understated to be fiction. The story of Frank Coghlan is a capsule account of American life and ways for the past seventy years: reflected in his personal career, the evolving entertainment business, and America's changing national involvement. But, most important, it is enjoyable to read.

I would have been satisfied to have met any good serial hero and become his friend: the fantasy would have been realized. It would have been all right if the star of *Adventures of Captain Marvel* had turned out to be just a nice guy when I met him, and not a disillusionment: the fantasy would not have been damaged. Since everyone knows that Billy Batson can't *really* turn into Captain Marvel by yelling Shazam, it would have been OK to learn that the man who played him didn't have magical power and was no hero at all: the fantasy would still be a fantasy.

But the strange thing is that Frank Coghlan turned out to be a hero after all—just a different kind of hero. One dictionary defines "hero" as "a man noted for his special achievements." By that definition, this movie extra at age three, DeMille star at age ten, all-around actor during his teens, creator of a screen legend in his early twenties, U.S. naval aviator and U.S. naval activities entrepreneur during his mature years, and character actor and television spokesman in his golden years is, without a doubt, a hero. And he personifies the heroic trait that exists in all of us who are known as "the common man." He makes us think that, if a nice little guy like him can do it, then so can we.

Frank "Junior" Coghlan makes it all look so easy. And that is the mark of a true professional. A hero? No doubt about it.

Preface

This is the story of my now 71 years in the motion picture and television industries, from my first role in 1920 at the age of three, to being a featured player in "The Republic Pictures Story" that ran on the American Film Classics cable network in 1991 and the 1992 PBS special *Shirley Temple—America's Little Darling.*

Many of my contemporary kid actors have written, or coauthored, a book about their years as a child performer. Too many of them fill countless pages bemoaning the fact that they never had a normal childhood and were forced to work by parents seeking riches and the glory to satisfy their own egos. I don't feel that way about my early days since I cherish those memories. At age nine I spent two weeks at the Grand Canyon working for Cecil B. DeMille in *The Road to Yesterday* where I even had the fun of riding a burro deep into the canyon each day to reach our location site. Because I had to shoot a bow and arrow in this film, the ever meticulous C.B. had me to the studio daily taking archery lessons for two weeks before production started.

This role led to a five-year contract where I attained stardom at age 11. Imagine the joy as a ten-year-old spending six weeks at sea in a real three-masted, square-rigged sailing vessel in *The Yankee Clipper* with my idol William Boyd.

In my very next film I spent four weeks on the playing field with the 1927 New York Yankees when I played their bat boy in *Slide, Kelly, Slide.* I even got to meet Babe Ruth and Lou Gehrig. Then I lived for three weeks in a tent city our studio built on the Navaho Indian Reservation near Monument Valley in Arizona working in *The Last Frontier*, again with William Boyd.

Later I played a jockey in three films and did my own riding in *Racetrack, Kentucky Blue Streak,* and *Charlie Chan at the Race Track.* Then I worked in three serials. I played Uncas in *The Last of the Mohicans* with Harry Carey and was Jackie Cooper's pal Ken in *Scouts to the Rescue.*

In 1941 I played the role that still has me invited to film festivals, when I was Billy Batson in the classic action serial *Adventures of Captain Marvel,* now considered by most fans and critics to be the finest serial ever made. There I was, the young radio reporter who was granted the right to utter the magic word "Shazam" and be transformed into Captain Marvel, "The world's mightiest mortal." Now, how can you top memories like that?

You will read that I became a naval aviator during World War II and served 23 years on active duty. Even these years should be interesting for in eight of them I headed the navy motion picture cooperation program. From 1952 to 1954 I was in charge of the movie section in the Office of Information in the Pentagon. There I monitored what I consider to be three of the finest navy films ever produced. They were *The Caine Mutiny, The Bridges at Toko-Ri,* and *Mr. Roberts.*

Then during my final five years in the navy I was in charge of the Hollywood office. There I was in the studios almost daily and even had the pleasure of helping my good friend Jackie Cooper on his television series, "Hennesey." I handled the cooperation on *PT-109,* the film about our late president John F. Kennedy when he was a PT boat skipper in the Pacific. My final film on this great tour of duty was *In Harm's Way,* starring John Wayne, Kirk Douglas, and Patricia Neal.

When I retired from the navy I was able to get back into motion pictures playing supporting roles. On the side, I also worked as a public relations executive, including three years as director of PR at the Los Angeles Zoo and seven years at the Port of Los Angeles. I also began working in television commercials and for seven years was the spokesman for Curtis Mathes, a Texas-based television manufacturer. All in all it has been an interesting and rewarding life, and I want to say my childhood was the greatest.

In 1975 Richard Lamparski came to our house and interviewed me in depth for two hours. This led to a nine-page profile in the next issue of his book series, *Whatever Became of. . .?* (Bantam Books). As he was leaving the house he said he thought I was the best adjusted and happiest of all the former child stars he had ever interviewed.

I hope this book leaves you with the same impression.

1

The Beginning

The toughest thing about writing this book is getting it started, so I'll just begin at the beginning.

The question I'm asked most often is, "How did you get started in the movies?" I always say it was easier in 1920 than it is today because there weren't so many kid actors.

It really all began early in the morning of March 15, 1916. It seems rather prophetic, but my mother and father were walking down the stairs from the balcony of the old Bijou Theater in New Haven, Connecticut, when my mother's water broke and she began having labor pains. This was about two weeks earlier than I was expected or she certainly would not have climbed those stairs. She and Dad rode the streetcar home, he put her to bed, then called the doctor. I was born a few hours later.

My father, Frank E. Coghlan, had a high school education and worked as a clerk for the New York, New Haven, and Hartford Railroad. He also picked up additional income as a professional boxer. Only 5′ 3″ tall and weighing 118 pounds, he was recognized as the bantamweight champion of Connecticut. The boxing scene in those days was not the healthiest of environments and he became involved in a rough crowd. Mother said her friends referred to him as a "tough."

My mother, Katherine V. (Coyle) Coghlan, was truly a saint. She too had a high school education and also worked for the railroad, then one of New Haven's leading employers. She met Dad at work and romance soon flared. Her family and friends tried to talk her out of marrying this man who they claimed was beneath her station, but love does not always listen to reason.

After their marriage my mother tells me she was in a sprint race and a high jump event at a railroad picnic while carrying me, so I guess I got any acting ability I have from my dad and what athletic skills I have from both of them.

Shortly after my birth Dad showed his first signs of instability when Mother happened to look into a closet to find that he was all packed for a fast getaway. When he came home Mother confronted him with her findings. He tearfully told her he was deeply in debt to gamblers and had borrowed $200 on the furniture. He said his creditors did not consider that enough payment and they were going to beat him up. Sure enough, my dad did run away that night and was at sea for nearly a year as a seaman and cook on a merchant freighter.

Mother and I moved in with her parents, John J. Coyle and Bridget (Gaffney) Coyle, at the family home at 479 Orange Street in New Haven. My mother returned to her former position at the railroad to support us and pay off the debt on the furniture.

The Coyles were a marvelous Irish couple. Both were born in Ballyjamesduff, in County Cavan, about five miles from each other. Grandpa came to New Haven in his youth and began working as a carpenter. He earned $6 per week and from that he saved enough money to send for his younger brother Phil who settled in New Jersey.

Grandma came to New Haven, by coincidence, and worked as a domestic before meeting Grandpa. This marriage was blessed with seven children and they celebrated their 68th wedding anniversary before they both passed away within one week of each other.

Grandpa was quite a clever guy and, in addition to his carpenter work, he became an expert clock repairman. He worked on the clocks for the railroad and also for Yale University.

He told the story of the clock in the main rotunda at Yale that kept losing one minute a day. He tried everything known to clock making to correct this deficiency to no avail. Several days later he happened to notice an empty whiskey bottle sitting on the gigantic concrete pendulum that swung three floors below the main floor. Some overexuberant student had evidently set it there as it swung near him and just this slight weight riding off-center was the culprit! Grandpa carefully removed the bottle and time returned to normal at Yale University.

On April 6, 1917, the United States declared war on Germany and soon Congress passed a law calling for a draft. This brought my dad hurrying home from sea expecting Mother to take him back so he could be exempt as head of a household. To his surprise she refused and soon he was in khaki and on his way overseas.

He lucked out as the Armistice was declared while he was crossing the Atlantic. On hearing the good news the happy doughboys tossed their rifles, helmets, mess kits, and anything else loose overboard. To their disappointment they spent the next few months paying for the missing equipment out of their meager paychecks. My dad's time at sea as a cook served him well and he came home a year later with the rating of mess sergeant.

The first memory I have in life is of my dad returning home in uniform and giving me a set of toy soldiers and a flagpole with a miniature American flag that could be run up and down.

My dad's father, George K. Coghlan, had died when my father was just a boy. His mother, Mary (Flynn) Coghlan, had raised him and his older brother Harry and younger sister Josephine by scrubbing office building floors on her knees at night after feeding the three children and putting them to bed. I'm sure that overwork and just plain fatigue caused this lovely lady to have a crippling stroke while still a relatively young woman.

Uncle Harry was draft exempt, being the sole support of his invalid mother and Josephine. Grandma's left side was completely paralyzed. That arm hung limp and she dragged that leg, though she could get around by supporting herself with a chair which she pushed forward as she walked. Through it all she remained a delightful person and never complained. Harry had great faith in her recovery and during the war moved her and Josephine to California to escape the harsh New England winters.

When Dad was released from the army we packed up and followed them to the West Coast. This was a tearful departure for my mother as she had never been away from New Haven and her close family ties.

2

California

We settled in the Echo Park section of Los Angeles and moved into a boarding house until we could find a larger home to house all the Coghlans.

I was only three but I'll never forget that boarding house. It was high on a hill with about thirty steps down to the street. The owners had a parrot which they kept in a cage on the front porch. Several times a day my mother would come out on the porch to check on me as I played in front of the house. If she couldn't see me she would call an elongated "Junioooor" and I would come running. It only took a few days before that darn parrot started imitating her to perfection. Many times a day I'd hear the familiar "Junioooor" and hurry home, only to find it was the bird calling me and not my mother.

Uncle Harry soon found a pleasant home on Glendale Boulevard that had a smaller house in the rear. He, Grandma, and Josephine moved into the front and we took the little house in the back. The main house was a two-level duplex and a few years later, when Josephine married, she and her husband moved into the upper story. It was a great family complex with a good yard between the houses where I spent many happy hours.

With my father's previous experience he was able to get a job with the Southern Pacific Railroad and only had to walk one block to Sunset Boulevard to catch the streetcar to his office in downtown Los Angeles.

We lived about one mile south of what was then known as Edendale, where many of the original movie studios were located. Mack Sennett and Charlie Chaplin were there as were many of the other pioneers in the mushrooming film industry. All have long gone from Edendale, but in 1919 that was where things were happening.

My dad was always a "ham" at heart and started hanging around these studios on his days off. Finally he was hired to play a bit part in a film and a new sideline career developed. Being small in stature he was a natural for playing bellboys, as I did so many times in my career. Though my shy, sweet mother objected at first, Dad got her involved and soon she was also working as an extra in some of the early films.

This was early 1920 and Jackie Coogan had just gained fame as the first important child star due to his role with Charlie Chaplin in *The Kid.* His "Dutch" bobbed haircut was famous at the time and my mother fashioned my hair in this popular mode. People would see me on the street and ask Mother if I was in the movies. Though she and Dad were playing extra roles, never did she intend to put me to work at such a tender age.

Uncle Harry had now decided on a medical career and was attending night classes at the Los Angeles College of Chiropractics, then located on Vermont Avenue in what had once been the mansion of Jack Dempsey. Dad wanted to follow his brother in this profession but money was short.

It was finally decided that if so many people thought I looked cute, maybe there was a career for me in the movies. Reluctantly Mother took me to one of the nearby studios and registered me as a potential child actor. This studio was owned by the then big star Clara Kimball Young and they were casting for her next motion picture, *Mid-Channel.* I was cast as one of the kids in the charity bazaar scene and, as the youngest child on the set, I was pushed and pampered so much I finally ran off the set crying. My mother and the director calmed me down and I completed my first film assignment without disgrace. I was paid $3 for that first day's work.

Having the still three-year-old Junior bringing in an additional $3 a day looked pretty good to my father. At his insistence Mother took me around to all the studios and registered me for employment.

"Registering" meant leaving a photo at the casting office with the child's name, age, height, weight, coloring, telephone number, address, and any other pertinent information, such as athletic ability and other special skills or talents. She also signed me up at Central Casting, an employment agency for extras that was supported by all the studios. A call to them each afternoon would tell you if there was a job for the next day, or you would hear the disappointing, "Try later."

Extras still use this same system and you see them lined up at the studio pay telephones at 4 P.M. to see if they have a job for the next day. Established actors have agents instead who cover the field for their clients. Most agents subscribe to a daily service that lists the upcoming roles so the agent can contact studio casting offices to arrange interviews for the players in their stable of performers.

3

Kids in Early Movies

Soon I was working frequently and I can honestly say that in the next four years my earnings put my father through Chiropractic College. After my first near debacle in *Mid-Channel,* I began to take naturally to this new experience. I looked forward to working in different films and really enjoyed going on studio sets and especially on location calls to interesting places. Though the adult performers probably groaned at them, I relished the box lunches we always received on locations. They usually consisted of a ham sandwich, a piece of chicken, an apple, orange, or banana, a slice of cake or a piece of pie, with coffee for the grownups and milk for the kids. It seemed like being on a picnic to me.

Box lunches have now been replaced by finely catered hot meals due to union regulations. These meals are now served at exact five-hour intervals, or the producer suffers a costly fine. If they don't provide the cast and crew with hot meals on schedule they are charged a meal penalty of triple the hourly scale.

The state of California now has strict laws regarding the use of children in motion pictures but in the early 1920s the regulations were not so stringent. Now a licensed teacher must be on the set at all times when minors are working. The law insists that the child have three hours of schooling and one hour of recreation during the eight-hour working day. Lunch is considered the ninth hour. A child cannot work past this ninth hour and the teacher can shut the set down if this is about to happen.

I remember an early costume film directed by Herbert Brenon for Paramount in 1921. It was *The Spanish Dancer* starring Pola Negri. It was here that I first met the lovely Anne Shirley whose boyfriend I was to play many years later in RKO's *Make Way for a Lady.* Anne was then known as Dawn O'Day and she played the little princess in this period film. I was one of the many other children of the court.

Part of the film was shot in Brookside Park in Pasadena. Anne was to ride a feisty Shetland pony which was supposed to shy and run away with her. This led to a big chase and a rescue. Anne was doubled by Jimmy House, then four years old and the youngest of the House family. Jimmy was

The comedy *Rookies* for Century Productions. Directed by Alf Goulding. I'm on the right.

already an accomplished rider. The Houses had a stable and provided horses and riders to the studios for years. Later the eldest son Newton became a cowboy star in his own right. His sister Dorothy married Andy Devine and Jimmy became a studio makeup man. I didn't mean to digress—what I was getting at is that the studio allowed the young Jimmy to double Anne. Today that would be a jockey-sized man or woman wearing a copy of Anne's costume and certainly not another child.

On another "day" of this same film we went into the studio to a costly palace scene. There must have been two hundred extras working and when the sequence was not finished by the end of the working day we went right on filming until 12:30 A.M.

We kids were dead on our feet, but we were given a call back for 8:00 A.M. that same morning. That would be a double violation by today's rules. Now we would never be permitted to work that many hours in a row and would have to be allowed a break of at least 12 hours before returning to the set for the next day's work.

Another meal violation that I vividly recall was during my only experience of working with Charlie Chaplin. I never had the pleasure of working with this genius as a fellow actor but I did work for him in a film he directed. It was *A Woman of Paris,* starring his then lady friend Edna Purviance.

My memory of him at the time was of a friendly but fussy little man who insisted on taking the same scene over and over again. In it Edna Purviance was riding, facing backward, on the tailgate of a horse-drawn wagon with me and two other youngsters sitting beside her with our legs dangling over the rear of the cart. Chaplin with his camera crew followed closely, riding a platform built on the front of an auto.

In fairness it was a tough scene to photograph. In a case like this distance and speed must be maintained to perfection if the actors are to be properly framed and in focus. We began rehearsing this simulated French countryside scene around 9:00 A.M. and it was 2:30 P.M. before Chaplin approved a finished take. Naturally, we kids were in pain from hunger by then but Charlie wouldn't break for lunch until he was completely satisfied. That could never happen today as the teacher would have braved the Chaplin wrath at the proper lunch hour.

4

Universal Studio

I have so many memories of these early movies. Most of them seem funny now but at the time they were quite serious. We couldn't afford a car yet, so we were fortunate that Los Angeles then had such a fine public transportation system, now long gone to the freeways. In those days, with the help of transfers, you could cover most of the city and the studios by streetcar.

Universal Studio was one of the hardest to get to. Mother and I would walk the short block to Sunset Boulevard, take the streetcar to Cahuenga and Hollywood Boulevard, then hitchhike over Cahuenga Pass to the San Fernando Valley where Carl Laemmle had built his studio on a 420-acre plot of land.

Cahuenga Pass was then a two-lane road—now it's a ten-lane freeway. Actors with cars were very good about giving rides to their fellow thespians. It was a good thing because I worked at Universal frequently in those early days and had long runs in two serials there. One, *The Great Circus Mystery*, starred strongman Joe Bonomo, and the other, *Winning His Way*, featured then heavyweight boxing champion of the world Jack Dempsey.

Universal Studio is located in Universal City and is the only studio to have a city named in its honor. It had, and still has, a gigantic back lot filled with lakes, rivers, forests, city streets, foreign villages, and even a replica of Notre Dame Cathedral. Much of the back lot is now covered in the highly popular Universal Studio tour.

I remember going to Universal Studio one day and seeing a lion loose on the front lawn. The owner-trainer was showing how tame the beast was in hopes of landing it a job in a coming picture. It was quite a surprise to see this large cat on the loose, but then, after all, this was show biz.

Though I was to become a naval aviator during World War II and served 23 years on active duty as a career naval officer—during which time I married and became the father of five children—I must confess in those early days I frequently played "sissy" roles. This was mainly due to my small stature and, of course, that darned bobbed hair which I came to hate.

Not only did I play sissies, once I played an angel. It was in what must

William Carleton and Wanda Hawley in *Bobbed Hair*. Whose child am I?

have been a hilarious dream sequence in a Larry Semon comedy *The Suitor* for Vitagraph and was directed by a brash 20-year-old Norman Taurog at the helm of his first film.

I wore a flowing chiffon gown and wings and had a long red wig that reached to my waist. I was suspended on wires and drifted into the scene where I shot the sleeping Larry Semon with an arrow, causing him to awaken and fall in love with the next girl he saw. Norman Taurog and I became good friends in later years and we joked many times about my days as an angel.

Probably because of my hair I received a good part in a picture called *Bobbed Hair.* It was pretty far out for its time as it took place in an art colony and all the male players wore togas and the females flowing Grecian gowns. The leads were character actor William Carleton, the lovely Wanda Hawley, and the leading man was the newcomer William Boyd. Bill Boyd and I were to team together in four films in later years while both of us were under contract to Cecil B. DeMille and long before Bill became the legendary Hopalong Cassidy in the long-running series of western films. (Strangely enough, Warner Brothers released aother film titled *Bobbed Hair* in 1925.)

Being a reddish complexioned Irishman, the California sun soon had my face covered with freckles. This became a problem and the makeup men used to cover my face with a darker greasepaint to neutralize the sun spots before applying the normal skin shade. In later years these same freckles became part of my trademark in the "all–American boy" image that I brought to the screen.

They say you can't fool mother nature, but my mother tried by having me wear a wide-brimmed straw hat when I played outside. One night my father brought home a baby goat that someone at work had won and could not keep where they lived. This goat and I became real pals and he used to follow me around like a puppy dog, but he sure sabotaged the freckle effort. That goat just loved my straw hats and he ate the brim off several of them before we also had to get rid of him when he grew larger and became mean and started butting the mailman and other visitors to the yard. One day we received a telephone call from our local grocery store. The goat had wandered up onto Sunset Boulevard and was eating vegetables off the produce counters. That was the end of the goat.

5

Bits and Small Parts

I broke out of the extra ranks while only five years old when Goldwyn, later to become part of Metro-Goldwyn-Mayer, cast me to play the boy Richard Dix and Leatrice Joy wanted to adopt in *The Poverty of Riches.*

Things did not change overnight but gradually the word of my dependability spread through the studios and I began receiving more and more calls directly from the studio casting offices for specific bits and small parts. Our dependence on Central Casting for work grew less and less and eventually the daily telephone calls and the disappointing "Try later" was a thing of the past.

I met Frankie Darro for the first time while working on the Joe Bonomo serial at Universal in 1921. I was then five and a half and Frankie had just turned four. (Frankie will be mentioned many more times in later pages.)

Mother and I used to visit other sets to see and be seen when time permitted between scenes of my own picture. This particular day we dropped in on a gypsy theme film *A Prince of a King* being directed by Charles "Chuck" Riesner. Chuck was a former actor and gag writer who went into directing and received credit as associate director on some Charlie Chaplin films, including *The Kid,* which sprung Jackie Coogan to fame.

On this film Chuck was trying to make a star out of his own son Dean who was burdened with the unbelievable stage name of Dinky Dean. This was probably Dinky's first and last starring vehicle but it did get Frankie Darro established on a long and successful acting career. In all fairness to Dinky Dean, he did go on to become a well-known screenwriter using his real name of Dean Riesner and spent several years writing under contract to Twentieth Century–Fox.

I called him on July 8, 1982, to confirm the accuracy of this scene in *A Prince of a King* and was pleased to learn he was then under contract to Rastar Productions and was writing the screenplay for a sequel to *Blue Lagoon* which had brought Brooke Shields to stardom. We spent at least half an hour on the telephone reminiscing about the old kid actor days and we both had vivid memories about Frankie Darro in later years. Dean told me something I hadn't known before. The year prior to making *A Prince of a King* he and his dad had toured for a season in vaudeville with Jack Dempsey. Chuck Riesner did songs and some patter with Dempsey and Dean did an impersonation of Jackie Coogan in *The Kid,* complete with the oversized cap. At the end of the act Jack Dempsey took on all challengers from the audience.

In *A Prince of a King* Dinky Dean played a young prince who had been kidnapped by gypsies and taught to become a performing acrobat. An actor he was but an acrobat he was not, so in this scene he was being doubled by Frankie Darro who was working in his first motion picture.

Frankie at the age of four was already an accomplished tumbler. His father had been a circus performer and Frankie could stand on his head and on his hands soon after he learned to walk. He could already do a round-off and back handsprings the length of the set followed by a beautifully arched back flip, ending in the traditional "ta-da" pose of circus acrobats.

Frankie's own father was also doubling for one of the actors in the scene. The setting was a run-down tavern where the gypsies were putting on their act. One cue Frankie's dad held his arm out at full length over one of the tables. Frankie jumped to the top of the table and then did a handstand on his father's outstretched arm. After holding the handstand for about ten seconds, Frankie eased himself gracefully down to the tabletop where he performed the stunt that was to become one of his trademarks through the years. This little tyke placed his head on the table and rose to a perfect headstand. Then he spun himself, making two complete rotations while still balanced on his head with his arms outstretched. This seems incredible for a four-year-old, but I saw it happen.

When we arrived home that night I decided to try this trick I had seen a boy nearly two years younger than me perform. I didn't tell my parents but went into my room, rose to a shaky headstand, and then tried to spin myself. I heard all kinds of funny noises in my neck as my head remained stationary and only my body twisted. Needless to say, I had a very sore and stiff neck for a few days but my parents never knew why!

6

Comedies and *Our Gang*

In my second and third years in films I became involved in lots of kid comedies. Again, usually as the sissy or foil for the leader of the pack. Several producers were experimenting with kids, including Mack Sennett, Larry Darmour, Julius Stern at Century Studios, and, of course, Hal Roach.

I was pushed, shoved, tripped, dunked, and beaten by such kids as Buddy Williams and Jack McHugh, and the *Our Gang* comedy bunch.

It seems funny to me, but to this day I am asked which kid I played in *Our Gang* or *The Little Rascals.* I always answer truthfully that when *Our Gang* was getting started in 1922 I worked in a few of them. I was never a lead in the series and only filled in when they needed additional members. I was a guest at a birthday party, in the audience at a backyard circus, and played center field in a ballgame where I backed into the fence, fell down, and then was hit on the head by the baseball.

When I tell people that I left the kid comedies and became a featured player and starred in many silent full-length films, starred in my own high school age comedy series, and costarred in the serial *Adventures of Captain Marvel* among many other lead parts, they still think it most important that I was once an *Our Gang* comedy kid.

I consider this strange as *Our Gang* and *The Little Rascals* that followed ran for over 20 years with at least eight or nine turnovers of kid actors. With certain exceptions, like Jackie Cooper, Johnny Downs, Dickie Moore, Mary Ann Jackson, Darla Hood, and Robert Blake, few are remembered by their own given names. There were many nicknames like Freckles, Fatty, Farina, Buckwheat, Stymie, Wheezer, Spanky, and Alfalfa, but can you recall these clever kid actors' real names? It doesn't seem to matter since these kids still have a special place in the hearts of the public and reruns of their uniquely funny exploits show almost daily on television in most cities.

Alfalfa did make several feature films under his given name of Carl Switzer, the most important being *Going My Way* with Bing Crosby, where he played the choirboy with the black eye. Jackie Cooper is still famous as an actor-producer-director and Robert Blake was the star of *In Cold Blood* and later his own television series "Baretta."

With Tom Santschi in *Sin Buster* for Universal in 1920. My mother is Vera Sisson.

Many of those fine kid actors are gone now. Bobby "Wheezer" Hutchins was killed in a training accident during World War II; Billy "Froggy" Laughlin died in a motor scooter crash in the early 1950s; Mary Kornman, the original leading lady, died of cancer in 1973 at the age of 56; after many scrapes with the law for drunk driving, bad checks, and drugs, Scotty Beckett passed away from an apparent drug overdose; and Allen "Farina" Hoskins and Matthew "Stymie" Beard both died of natural causes in the late 1980s.

The most violent death was that of Carl "Alfalfa" Switzer. In lean years between acting jobs, Carl became a professional hunting guide. For one trip he borrowed a friend's dog and it was lost during the expedition. Carl advertised for the animal and paid a $50 reward to the man who returned it. When the dog's owner came to Carl's house to retrieve his pet, Carl asked for repayment of the $50. An argument followed, a knife was drawn, then a gun, and Carl "Alfalfa" Switzer ended up dead on the floor.

I didn't mean to bring unhappiness into this book while writing about former *Our Gang* comedy kids, but if you hadn't heard these stories you might as well learn of them now.

Jackie Lynn Taylor who was a leading lady in the closing years of the series has written a book *The Turned on Hollywood 7*. On page 75 under

***Our Alley* with Bobby Dunn. An obvious take-off on *The Kid* which starred Charlie Chaplin and Jackie Coogan.**

In Memoriam she lists Frank Coghlan. Far be it from me to contradict a lady, but I'm happy to say she was a bit premature in this case. She most likely confused me with Junior Durkin who was killed in the tragic automobile accident that also took the lives of Jackie Coogan's father and Robert Horner.

In this same time span the old bobbed hair probably had lots to do with my being cast in what was obviously a take-off on the great Charlie Chaplin–Jackie Coogan film *The Kid.* This two-reel comedy *Our Alley,* had me playing the son of Bobby Dunn, who went on for many years playing small parts and doing stunts. I have several stills from this short but, unfortunately, my mother didn't list the studio, producer, or director on the back of the still as she usually did.

Bobby Dunn played a happy little tramp who panhandled for a living. Our humble home was a piano box at the end of "our alley." We both wore baggy hand-me-down clothes topped off by ill-fitting derby hats. Due to our capricious activities we were under the constant surveillance of the neighborhood cop played by Glen Cavender. Glen also went on for years playing small bits and parts.

While my father was completing his chiropractic education—which my earnings were financing—we moved from the Glendale Boulevard complex to the Hollywood Apartments. It was a nice place to live and many young movie aspirants used it as a place to reside while seeking their claim to fame.

One of the regulars was a handsome young fellow named Charles Farrell. He spent much time in the lobby during the evenings and taught me how to play checkers. We played many games before Charley Farrell was signed by Fox Studio to costar opposite Janet Gaynor in *Seventh Heaven.*

I used to see Charley Farrell through the years at the Racket Club in Palm Springs which he founded with Ralph Bellamy. After he sold the club Charley still served as host there for many years and he and his wife, silent-day film star Virginia Valli, lived in a bungalow on the property.

About this time (1922) I met Jackie Coogan for the first time. Mother and I had joined the Catholic Screen Actors Guild and were attending our first communion breakfast. Jackie was then just turned eight and I was still six. We were the only children at the breakfast, we both had bobbed hair, and we were wearing almost identical blue sailor suits.

During the speeches Jackie left his table and was sitting on a window seat playing with a game he had brought with him. I wandered over and stood next to him. He ignored me and continued playing with his game so I returned to my seat. I saw his father go over to him and scold him and soon he appeared at our table and invited me to join him at the window seat and share his game with him.

7

Hugh Dierker

After three years in California Mother was getting homesick, so the two of us boarded the Super Chief and headed east. We had a fine visit and I enjoyed seeing my grandma and grandpa, my six aunts and uncles, and meeting my many cousins who I hardly remembered due to leaving New Haven when I was only three.

The cross-country trip both ways was a real education for me as I didn't recall much of our first trek west in 1919. I especially liked seeing the Indians who met the train at several stops and eating in the Fred Harvey dining rooms on days we didn't have a dining car attached.

On the return trip we met Hugh Dierker who was to have an important effect on my career. He was an independent film producer-director who was returning from the East where he had arranged for the financing and release of a film he planned to make. He was impressed with me and asked mother to contact him when we were back in Hollywood.

She did and as a result he cast me to play the son in his new production, *Cause for Divorce.* My father in the film was played by David Butler and my mother was Fritzi Brunette.

Cause for Divorce covered a two-year time span in the lives of our little family and in it I supposedly progressed from six to eight years of age. During production, what seemed like a tragedy happened when I lost my two front teeth. Instead of being furious, Hugh Dierker was delighted. He sent me down to the dental clinic of the University of Southern California where the student doctors made me what must have been the smallest dental plate of all time. For the rest of the film, when I was supposed to be eight I wore the plate. While playing myself at six, I took it out and the vacant spots in my smile made everything seem more realistic.

Cause for Divorce gave me my first screen credit as a lead actor in a feature-length film and if we hadn't met Dierker on the Super Chief it probably would never have happened. David Butler went on to become one of Hollywood's top directors and Twentieth Century–Fox chose him to direct some of Shirley Temple's most memorable classics, including *The Little Colonel, The Littlest Rebel,* and *Captain January.*

He later became Bing Crosby's favorite director and Bing had him at the helm on many of his best films. In Bing's 1936 release of *East Side of Heaven,* I played a Western Union messenger boy. Knowing I would see my two good friends Bing and Dave, I brought stills from *Cause for Divorce* to the set. When Bing saw the young, handsome, svelte David Butler in these stills he really gave his director a bad time. By now Dave Butler was weighing nearly 300 pounds and no longer looked like the young leading man who played my father in the stills. He took it in good nature, of course, as a Dave Butler–Bing Crosby set was always a fun set to work on.

While it is out of context here, I might as well mention Western Union now that I have brought it up. By this time all the major studios had large wardrobe departments and could fit the actors in almost any costume imaginable. If they did not have the required clothes on their racks, they sent you to Western Costume Company, a firm sponsored by all the studios to fill the needs not available in their own wardrobe departments.

One of the few exceptions to this system was if you were to play a Western Union messenger. Then the actor had to go to their company headquarters in downtown Los Angeles to be fitted in one of those distinctive olive drab uniforms. This was their own peculiar rule and they would not release any of the ill-fitting outfits with the billed hats and puttees to the studios or to Western Costume Company.

I delivered so many Western Union telegrams in films in the 1930s and 1940s that the nice man in charge of the uniform department finally set aside a new uniform altered to fit me that he kept cleaned and pressed with my name on it. The only other juvenile actor given this special status was my good friend William Benedict. During those years I'm sure Bill and I delivered more telegrams than all the rest of the kid actors combined.

8

Marshall Neilan and *Mike*

In 1923 my father and Uncle Harry received their chiropractic degrees and licenses and opened an office together. We all moved to a neat upstairs duplex on Carlton Way in Hollywood. The house served as our living quarters as well as their offices. There were bedrooms for my parents and Grandma Coghlan and a gigantic sun porch that ran the entire width of the house. This they partitioned into four treatment rooms and Harry and I slept at opposite ends of this sun porch. We were to live there for six years.

A big bonus to that house was that Tom Mix lived in the same block with us. He was the top cowboy in the business, earning a reported $21,000 a week, but he still lived in this middle-class neighborhood. His garage held a Rolls Royce, a Locomobile, and a Pierce Arrow, but he lived here for a while before moving to a mansion in Beverly Hills. His cars had pistols for door handles and one had the horns of a Texas longhorn on the hood.

The first Christmas we lived there a neighbor friend of mine and I both found cowboy suits under our trees. We put on our boots, chaps, bandanas, western hats, and gun belts and went down and rang Tom's doorbell. He answered the door himself and we pulled out our cap pistols and said, "Stick 'em up Tom." He laughed and his wife said, "That's cute. Give the boys some money for ice cream Tom." He reached into his pocket and handed us a $5 bill. Needless to say, we had our fill of ice cream for that day.

One of Uncle Harry's first patients was the mother of film director Marshall Neilan. He was a very talented, young writer-director and at the time was married to the silent-day film star Blanche Sweet. Mrs. Neilan told her son about me and I was invited to the studio he then owned in Edendale for an interview. This worked out well for me as I had parts in the next three films that Neilan made.

The first was *The Skyrocket* made at Neilan's own studio in Edendale in early 1924. It starred Peggy Hopkins Joyce. She was an international beauty and former Ziegfeld Follies' showgirl. She was best known for her penchant of acquiring rich husbands and expensive jewelry. One of her husbands made her a countess and one of her diamonds was rated at 127

With Jack Pickford in *Garrison's Finish.*

carats. There is conjecture that she was the prototype of Anita Loos's famous showgirl Lorelei of *Diamonds Are a Girl's Best Friend.*

Neilan then moved to MGM where he wrote and directed two films and, bless him, he gave me big parts in both of them. The first was *The Great Love* with Viola Dana, Robert Agnew, ZaSu Pitts, and Frank Currier. The real star of the picture was an elephant named Norma, which I got to ride in the film, and Chester Conklin was hilarious as her patient keeper.

The second film was *Mike,* a delightful family story that became my first important screen credit at a major studio. It was also the first starring vehicle for two of MGM's young contract players, William Haines and Sally O'Neil.

Mike was a railroad story and our family consisted of Charlie Murray as our widower father who was a brakeman on the train. Sally O'Neil, then 18 years old, was the oldest child. I was the oldest brother at eight, Muriel Frances Dana, seven, was next in line, and Frankie Darro at six was the younger brother.

Our family lived in a converted caboose at the end of a long freight train. William Haines was a radio telegraph operator who became smitten with our sister Sally. Most of the movie was shot on location on railroad lines

Form 554—Trip

Goldwyn Producing Corporation
Goldwyn Pictures
Studios
Culver City, California

No. 1438

METRO-GOLDWYN-MAYER
~~GOLDWYN PRODUCING~~ CORPORATION, hereinafter called "The Corporation," hereby employs Junior Coghlan (Name)

(Address) , (Phone)

hereinafter called "the Artist," for production No. 224 "MIKE" for part of Boy

The Artist accepts such employment and the Corporation agrees to pay the Artist as compensation $75.00 per week commencing on or about the .... day of .... 19...., for the period of time required by the Corporation to complete that part of a motion picture for which the Artist is hereby employed, upon the following terms and conditions:

Compensation by the week shall be paid pro rata only for the number of days the Artist is actually engaged immediately preceding the completion or suspension of work upon the motion picture in which the Artist is engaged, if after the beginning of a new week. A week shall consist of seven actual working days. Compensation shall not accrue to the Artist for services to be rendered at a place distant from the studio until such place is reached and the Artist actually commences work, and shall cease when actual work by the Artist at such place is completed or suspended, and the Artist is directed to return therefrom. Should the Corporation desire the services of the Artist in making retakes or taking added scenes for the said picture, the Artist agrees to work in such retakes or added scenes, at the same compensation as herein provided, pro rata for less than a week or fraction of additional week, after the completion of the term hereof.

Compensation at a daily rate shall accrue only for the days the Artist actually works.

The Artist agrees to act, pose and appear as directed by the Corporation in and for the production of motion pictures and to perform and render such services to the full satisfaction of the Corporation and at the times and places required and as the Corporation may direct or find necessary or convenient for the staging of plays and scenes for the purposes of producing motion pictures.

It is agreed that the ability of the Artist is unique, peculiar and extraordinary, and that the services contemplated hereunder cannot be duplicated elsewhere by the Corporation.

The Artist ~~Corporation~~ agrees to furnish all modern wardrobe required in the performance of his ~~her~~ duties hereunder which modern wardrobe shall belong to and remain the property of the Artist ~~Corporation~~. The Corporation agrees to furnish all costumes other than modern that are required for the Artist's use in the picture, which costumes remain the property of the Corporation.

The Artist expressly consents that his ~~her~~ name, portrait or picture may be used by the Corporation for advertising purposes or for the purposes of trade.

In the event that, by reason or sickness or otherwise, the Artist should become incapacitated and prevented from performing the services contemplated hereunder, or in the event that the Corporation should be hindered or prevented, by riots, fire, flood, strikes, internal or external disturbance, national epidemic or calamity, or the act of God, or of a sovereign power, or the public enemy, or other cause or causes beyond the control of the Corporation, from carrying on its business in the usual and ordinary course thereof, or in case the Corporation hereafter decides to suspend or abandon the making of said production referred to above, this agreement shall be suspended both as to services and compensation, and the Corporation shall have the right, at its option, to forthwith terminate and cancel this agreement.

During term of contract, Artist agrees to communicate every afternoon with the Casting Director, by telephone or in person, on days not called.

Dated February 17th, 1925

METRO-GOLDWYN-MAYER
~~GOLDWYN PRODUCING~~ CORPORATION

By .... ~~Casting Director~~

....
Artist

My contract for *Mike*. I guess $75 per week in 1925 wasn't all too shabby. I was still eight years old when this was signed.

in Southern California, mainly in El Cajon Pass near San Diego. This film also featured funny men Ned Sparks and Ford Sterling. (In later years Charlie Murray costarred with George Sidney in the very funny Cohens and Kellys series of motion pictures.)

In the story we had a pet duck living in the caboose with us. One tough day when we were out of food, Sally decided that our duck had to be the main course at a dinner she had planned to impress Bill Haines. She ordered our dad to butcher the poor bird but, as kindhearted as he was, he just couldn't do it. Instead, he hid it and produced another one that he conned from the chef of a nearby passenger train dining car. At the meal none of us kids felt hungry until Charlie released our duck to prove that the pièce de résistance of the meal was not our pet.

On the set Charlie invented some dialogue that Neilan agreed to and it went into the printed titles seen on the screen of this silent film. As Murray was ceremoniously preparing to carve the bird, he asked each of us individually which part we wanted. In close-ups each of us said we wanted a leg. On hearing the fifth request for a leg, Murray, with his famous arched eyebrow expression said, "What do you think this is, a centipede?"

In another wild sequence, we kids decided that dad was drinking too much and planned a ploy to scare him into sobriety. At that time our train was hauling a circus and we cajoled the elephant trainer to help us.

Between shows he allowed us to paint several elephants in outrageous stripes, plaids, and polka dots. Can't you just imagine the hilarious facial reactions of funny men Charlie Murray, Ford Sterling, and Ned Sparks coming out of a saloon to see these apparitions passing before them? We did it very cleverly. When one drunk would go back in to tell the others what he had seen, we would change elephants to compound their disbelief. Though this film was made in black and white, Neilan employed a form of animated color additive to show the audience what these painted monstrosities really looked like to the three drunks: maybe another first for this creative man.

Making the movie was a real ball for us three kids. Can you imagine living in Pullman cars on railroad sidings and then going on to moving flatcars and other railroad equipment for the day's work? The finale to this film was as exciting as any chase sequence in modern-day films.

Our caboose became disconnected from the train of freight cars while moving on a long upgrade; it began rolling downhill on the same track with an approaching fast passenger train; when William Haines became aware of this he began sending out telegraphic messages; when they did not help, he commandeered a nearby engine and by carefully backing to slow our car, now speeding uncontrollably downhill, he pushed us back uphill just as the limited came roaring by. Wow! Where can you find more drama and suspense than Marshall Neilan staged in this 1924 film?

While writing about the incredible Neilan, who not only wrote and directed some memorable motion pictures and also wrote the beautiful song "My Wonderful One," I must report that on the set, while tender and creative in directing, he was a madcap between scenes.

He was the first director I ever saw use the "goose" as a form of diversion on the set. Webster's definition of the goose is "to prod suddenly and playfully in the backside so as to startle." Neilan did this playful prodding several times a day.

Though he didn't need it, Neilan frequently carried a cane. He would come up behind some unsuspecting actor or crew member and flip the cane up into their anal area and roar in laughter at their reaction. I definitely believe he kept certain crew members on the payroll and habitually hired a few certain actors just because he enjoyed their humorous and boisterous antics when goosed.

Needless to say, this was a bad influence on us three young kids and we started goosing each other at every opportunity when out of sight of the grownups. We would giggle and make funny faces and movements but I know we never really had any idea what it was all about.

One day our company was being honored by a railroad community town and we kids were going to be part of the entertainment. While waiting in the passageway between two Pullman cars we started goosing each other with more gusto than usual. As a result we made poor Muriel wet her pants just as she received the music cue to go out and sing her solo.

While dissertating on the goose, I repeat that I am sure that certain crew members and actors used it as a means of gaining popularity and promoting employment in the studios.

One actor I knew had a reputation for shouting out whatever was on his mind when goosed. I was on a set with him one day when he was watching our leading lady walk by. Someone goosed him just then and he yelled out, "beautiful legs, beautiful legs." I'm sure on other occasions his blurtings were much more entertaining.

There was a black actor who went by the single name of Snowflake. He was a very funny man in the old wide-eyed, quaking tradition of many negro actors of the time. His reactions to the goose were the most famous in Hollywood. He would put on a display that sometimes lasted nearly a minute. Whether feigned or not I'll never know, but this man was dangerous to be near at times. Once while he was playing a waiter and balancing a tray full of dishes, someone gave him the prod and he tossed the loaded tray of food and dishes high into the air. This brought a huge amount of laughter to the set—but I'm sure the propman didn't think it was very funny as he was cleaning up the mess.

With the completion of *Mike* my bobbed hair days were over. As part of our characterization as rough, tough railroad kids, Frankie Darro and I

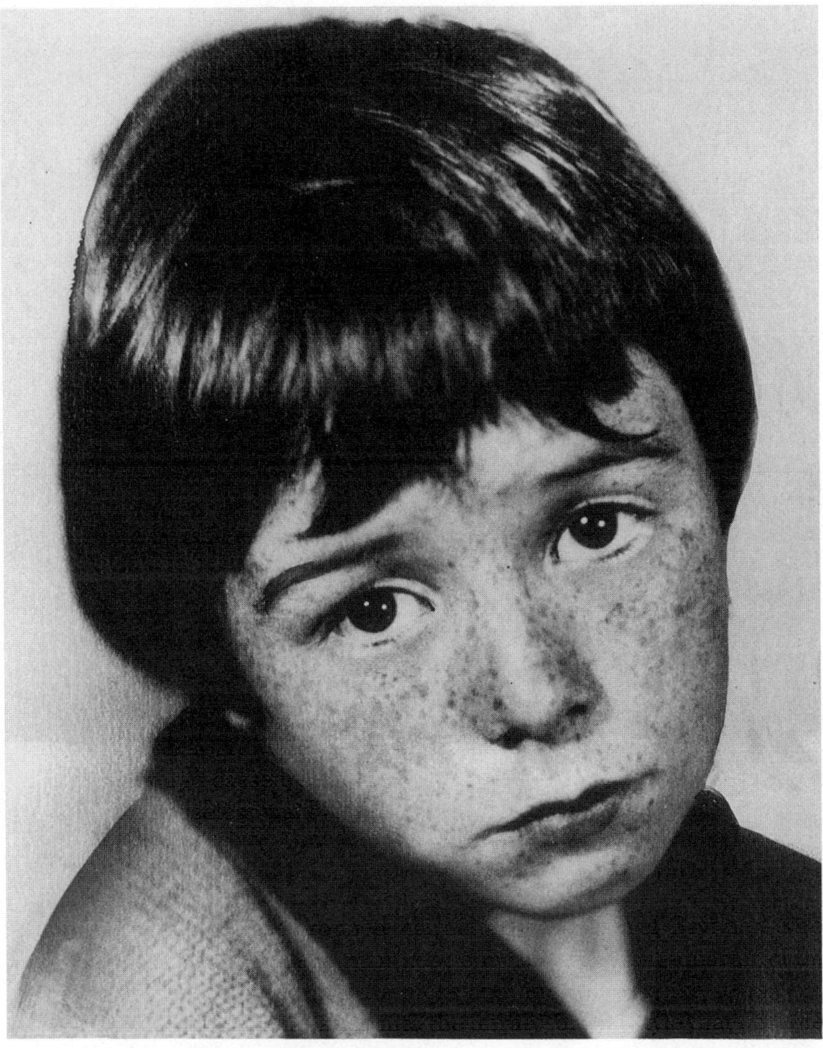

The first publicity still on my five-year contract with Cecil B. DeMille. This still caused DeMille to declare, "Junior Coghlan is the perfect example of a homeless waif."

had to submit to a close-cropped hairdo. It wasn't a Yul Brynner–type shave, but close. The makeup man kept our hair about one-quarter of an inch long and even shaved in little nicks and lines to look like scars.

When my hair grew out it fell into the unruly, urchin style that became my trademark and caused Cecil B. DeMille to describe me as "the perfect example of a homeless waif."

9

I Meet Cecil B. DeMille

I can't imagine the free-swinging Marshall Neilan and the staid, proper, sometimes despotic Cecil B. DeMille being friends. Maybe they weren't socially friendly, but at least they respected each other professionally. In any event, DeMille was preparing his big film *The Road to Yesterday*. There was a good part for a nine-year-old boy in it and C.B. asked Neilan if he had any suggestions as C.B. knew Neilan was working with a group of youngsters. Neilan told DeMille about me and I ended up with the part.

My friend William Boyd from *Bobbed Hair* was the leading man, Vera Reynolds was the love interest, and Joseph Schildkraut the heavy. It was a typical DeMille production with flashbacks to medieval days with sword fights and all. I was to be in the modern-day portion and had to be an excellent archer. DeMille never did things halfway, so for two weeks before production started I went on salary and had to report to the studio for a daily archery lesson.

In the modern-day portion William Boyd played a minister taking some boys from his church on a hunting trip with bows and arrows. I supposedly spotted a pheasant and shot an arrow at it. The rub was I actually shot a gaily feathered hat off the head of the lovely Miss Reynolds who was resting against a fallen log in the forest. She of course was irate, Boyd was apologetic, and things went on romantically from there.

When DeMille wanted a forest, he wanted a big one, so we went to the Grand Canyon to shoot this hunting sequence. We spent two weeks at the beautiful El Tovar Hotel on the south rim of the canyon and rode burros down narrow winding trails to the location site each day. My old friend Dick Winslow played my hunting companion and we had a marvelous time on this trip.

The Grand Canyon is so impressive and changes appearance hourly as the sun moves across it during the day. I especially enjoyed seeing the Hopi Indians who performed ceremonial dances on the hotel grounds, gave demonstrations of blanket weaving and made beautiful jewelry out of silver, turquoise, and petrified wood.

A few weeks after my part in *The Road to Yesterday* was completed we were called to the studio for a meeting. There we were told that DeMille and other studio executives were impressed with my work and I was offered a five-year contract. Agents were not very prevalent in 1925 so Mother handled the salary negotiations alone and we now know she settled for much less than an experienced agent would have achieved.

Be that as it may, it was still a good contract and I rode it out for the entire five years. In those days options came up at the end of each calendar year and the actor was on salary for all 52 weeks. In later years contracts usually had six-month options and the actor only received pay for 40 weeks a year and went on lay-off between pictures.

The timing of *The Road to Yesterday* was lucky for me as DeMille was forming his own studio and was building a slate of contract performers along with writers, producers, and directors. He had acquired the studio in Culver City from the estate of Thomas H. Ince after Ince had died mysteriously following a shooting on board the yacht of newspaper tycoon William Randolph Hearst. In later years this same studio would be known as Pathé, RKO, Selznick International, Desilu Culver, Laird International Studio, and is now known as Culver Studio.

During the five years of my contract I was part of a fine group of players consisting of Constance Bennett, Ann Harding, Gloria Swanson, Carole Lombard, Ina Claire, Sally Eilers, Vera Reynolds, Marie Prevost, and a buxom 20-year-old dancer named Sally Rand, to name a few. On the male side were William Boyd, Rod La Rocque, Lew Ayers, Robert Armstrong, Louis Wolheim, Rudolph and Joseph Schildkraut, Morton Downey, Alan Hale, Sr., Eddie Quillan, and the family of James, Lucille, and Russell Gleason. Through all those years I was the only child under contract on the lot and I am the only kid actor C.B. ever did have under a long-term contract.

The studio was located about one mile east of MGM and about the same distance west from the Hal Roach Studio on Washington Boulevard in Culver City.

The main administration building was a striking replica of George Washington's home, Mount Vernon. It had a large back lot, lovingly referred to as "the Forty Acres." I worked on the Forty Acres many times during my contract years and again many years later when I worked in *Gone with the Wind*. Another pleasant feature was that the studio had a swimming pool.

10

Under Contract

Being under contract to a studio in the old days was really a pleasant experience. In addition to a guaranteed steady income, it meant you worked with many of the same cast and crew members much of the time and it was like being part of a large and happy family. Our studio was small compared to the giants like MGM, Fox, Paramount, Warner Brothers, and Universal, so our family was even more closely knit and a much more friendly group. I was "their kid" and everyone took it upon themselves to look after me. Swearing in front of me became an absolute no-no on the set.

My mother was a marvelous "movie mother" and she was liked and respected. She kept me well behaved and never bothered the directors and other technicians. Many movie mothers were ogres on the sets and consistently interfered with production to promote the interests of their little darlings. I do believe that my dear mother was respected through the years as the best of all the movie mothers of the era.

Cecil B. DeMille, of course, was the king on our lot and his epics took priority over everything. Now that I was a member of the studio team it became the responsibility of producers and writers to work me into their pending films.

The first one I made under my new contract was a western, *Whispering Smith,* directed by George Melford. It starred the fine English actor H. B. Warner who two years later played Jesus Christ in one of DeMille's best films, *The King of Kings. Whispering Smith* was remade years later by Paramount as a starring vehicle for Alan Ladd.

Smith was a railroad detective who came to the rescue of Lillian Rich when crooks were trying to swindle her out of her ranch. Other cast members were the gravel-throated Eugene Pallette, the striking Lilyan Tashman, and John Bowers. I became an accomplished horseman during the making of this film, which was to be an advantage to me later when I was able to ride my own races in the three films where I played a jockey.

My mount in *Whispering Smith* was a feisty little Shetland pony that Frankie Darro was riding on a regular basis in the series of westerns in which he costarred with Tom Tyler and a German Shepherd dog.

I guess I was just enough heavier than Frankie to make the pony resent me. This mean little critter tried several times to sweep me off by running under low-hanging branches. He didn't succeed in throwing me and I eventually earned his respect. This may sound like something funny, but several years later cowboy actor Jack Randall died from head injuries received when he rode under a low-hanging tree limb.

My second production for the studio was *Her Man o' War*, starring Jetta Goudal and William Boyd. It was a World War I story with a German locale. Jetta played my older sister. We were orphans, trying to maintain a small farm to provide for ourselves and also help feed the German army. Because there were just the two of us, the local officials assigned an American prisoner of war to us as a live-in farmhand.

I played Peterkin, a crippled ten-year-old who was not much help on the farm due to his affliction. Like Hugh Dierker had done earlier for my two front teeth, our studio sent me to the Children's Orthopedic Hospital where I was fitted with a metal brace for my leg.

The American prisoner assigned to our farm was my dear friend William Boyd and he became "her man o' war." This was our third film together after *Bobbed Hair* and *The Road to Yesterday* and I literally adored the man.

In later years I even adopted his unique, parted-in-the-middle hairstyle. I think Bill thought of me as the son he never had and he gave me the nickname of "Jugie," which he pronounced "jew-gee."

Bill became the workhorse on our small German farm and even pulled the plow with an across-the-chest harness, much like the one he later used in his most famous starring role for DeMille, *The Volga Boatman.* In that memorable film he played a Russian peasant who helped pull the barges upriver and the calloused scars across his chest were vividly displayed in closing scenes.

Jetta Goudal was a good actress and very pleasant to me on the set; but from her I saw my first exhibitions of a temperamental actress. Our director was Frank Urson, one of the kindest men alive. He had worked his way up in the DeMille hierarchy, finally receving codirector credit on some of C.B.'s films.

This was Urson's first full directorial assignment and Jetta made life unbearable for him on the set. She would make demands and argue with him on the set in front of the entire company over her least little displeasure. Maybe she didn't like having a first time director on her starring vehicle. Good old Bill Boyd would just sit there until she was through with her tantrums and then he would take his place and go on with the day's work.

In later years as head of the Navy Public Affairs Office in Hollywood, I was asked to invite the local admiral to be guest of honor at the championship matches at the Los Angeles Tennis Club on Armed Forces Day. There I again saw Jetta, now a retired matron of the arts. She was very cordial to me when I told her who I was.

My visits to the Children's Orthopedic Hospital for the metal leg brace fittings started a happy association, and for years I visited the hospital every Christmas and on other occasions to talk to and entertain the children confined there.

11

Rubber Tires

My next outing was rather a lightweight compared to some that followed but it was a good family story and fun to make. It was called *Rubber Tires* and told of a family crossing the country in an open touring car. My father, Erwin Connelly, had lost his job in the East and figured our only hope for survival was to get to California where he had relatives with property. My mother was the marvelous character actress May Robson and my sister, the real backbone of the family, was Bessie Love. The leading man was Harrison Ford (the original actor with that name) who we kept running into on our cross-country trek, and who saved my father from even more financial disaster when we reached California. There is now a famous young actor with this same name (*Raiders of the Lost Ark* and others) but I have yet to learn if this modern-day star is related to my old friend or has just taken that as a screen name.

Rubber Tires was the first directorial effort for Alan Hale, a dynamic young actor in the DeMille stable. He went on to great fame as a character actor at Warner Brothers playing supporting roles with James Cagney, Pat O'Brien, and other stalwarts of the Warner Brothers stock company.

His son, Alan Hale, Jr., also did well as an actor. Young Alan dropped the Jr. after his father's death and is probably best remembered for his role as the skipper in "Gilligan's Island," a popular television show that is still in reruns daily. Alan, Jr., or Bud, as his friends called him, was a much better actor than "Gilligan's Island" let him be. But I know he laughed as he went to the bank with his almost daily residuals.

Meanwhile, back to *Rubber Tires.* My father in the film was a real loser and if Harrison Ford didn't keep catching up with us when we had a flat tire or a broken radiator hose we never would have completed the cross-country trek. I remember one funny scene when our car broke down for lack of water and I climbed up on a railroad water tower and got stuck straddling the long, metal spout used to fill the train's tanks. My father ordered me to pull the cord attached and of course he was doused with the full down force of the water pressure in the tank.

Much of the movie was shot in the scenic area of California's Monterey

Bay. We spent a week working out of a resort at Ben Lomand, near Santa Cruz, where I played tennis with Bessie Love each evening after work. I'm sure she could have found a more skilled opponent, but she kindly taught me the game and put up with my many wild shots. We refreshed ourselves between sets by picking and eating the crisp, yellow delicious apples the area is famous for right off the nearby trees.

Next we moved down the coast to Carmel, near Monterey, where we stayed a week at the beautiful Del Monte Inn, one of the real showplace resorts of the era. It was taken over by the navy during World War II and is still retained by them as a post-graduate school.

Then we moved south to locations around Los Angeles. We played one sequence in a small hamburger-chili stand operated by an exvaudevillian named Dave Chasen. It was his first venture into the restaurant business and it had a counter with ten stools. This is still the location of Dave Chasen's, probably the most famous of all the dining places frequented by the upper Hollywood set. His chili is now world famous and I know you have heard of Elizabeth Taylor, and even J. Edgar Hoover, having gallons of his chili flown to them. Liz even had it sent by air to Rome when she and Richard Burton were working on *Cleopatra.*

After Los Angeles we drove farther south to work in the hills above San Diego. There we stayed in a picturesque mountain resort, where in complete innocence, I played a dirty trick on the dear May Robson.

That night during dinner the lights went out at the resort due to an electrical storm. The management quickly set up candles on our tables. Following dinner Miss Robson and I went to a card table to play our evening games of double solitaire. Attendants set a candle at each corner of our table and we had played several games when Miss Robson left the table for a few minutes. While she was away one of the company members came over to me and said, "Hey, Junior, if you want to have a good laugh, blow out one of the candles when May gets back."

After she had been seated for a few minutes I casually leaned over and blew out one of the candles. I had no idea that just blowing out a candle could cause the reaction that it did. I thought poor May Robson was going to have a heart attack. She let out a shriek and almost violently extinguished one of the remaining tapers. I soon found out that Miss Robson, like many others from the New York stage, was highly superstitious. To her, three burning candles meant death.

I felt bad for causing her such displeasure and could have shot the thoughtless clown who put me up to this cruel stunt. I apologized and pleaded ignorance of her superstition. I never did admit that I had been led into the act by a company prankster. I know he was also glad I didn't spill the beans on him because I'm sure she would have made things very embarrassing for anyone she thought guilty of such a nasty trick.

12

The Yankee Clipper

Can you imagine a ten-year-old kid being told he would have to spend the next six weeks at sea on board a real three-masted sailing ship? That's exactly what happened to me on my next film, *The Yankee Clipper.* This is still my favorite memory of my entire movie career.

In the story, our ship *Yankee Clipper* was pitted against its British rival, *Lord of the Isles,* in a race from Foo Chow, China, around the Horn to Boston to see which nation would win the lucrative tea trade.

The skipper of our ship was my idol William Boyd who played Captain Hal Winslow, son of the builder of *Yankee Clipper.* Elinor Fair played Lady Jocelyn Huntington, daughter of the owner of the British ship, and in real life she was then Mrs. William Boyd.

I played Mickey, an orphan, who had been raised by two mean old aunts and, as a result, I hated women. To escape them I stowed away in a potato sack and was discovered by crew members soon after the ship left Boston on the first leg of the journey. When I was brought before the surprised Captain Winslow he ordered me to climb to the top of the mainmast to haul down a cap that one of the sailors had left up there. Instead of being frightened at this challenge I jumped with joy and headed for the rigging. The captain was amused at my lack of fear and said, "How would you like to help me boss this ship?" It wasn't long before the ship's crew taught me how to chew tobacco, and I'll bet I ate more than 30 pounds of licorice during the 12 weeks we were in production. This tobacco chewing was an important part of my characterization as you will learn later.

Our director was Rupert Julian, a very pleasant but strange man, who had the obsession that he looked like Kaiser Wilhelm of Germany. We thought this rather odd because in most eyes the kaiser was the villain of World War I who led his nation to defeat. In spite of this, Julian was proud of the resemblance and wore his hair close-cropped and sported a mustache that he kept waxed and twirled upward at the ends to further enhance the similarity. To this day he is the only director I have ever known whose wife joined him daily on the set. She was pleasant and never interfered but she was there every day.

Rupert Julian had come to our studio to direct *The Yankee Clipper* straight from Universal Studio where he had just completed directing Lon Chaney in *The Phantom of the Opera.*

The three-masted, square-rigged ship that we used was the *Indiana,* one of the last real clipper ships still in service in 1926 and she was sail propulsion all the way. With the exception of a generator to provide lights, the only power on board was a "donkey engine" used to raise and lower the sails and the anchors. The original capstans, once used for this purpose, were still in place and were often used to good effect in our movie rendition of life at sea in the clipper ship days.

The Yankee Clipper is considered to be one of the all-time classic films of the sea. As late as the 1970s it was still being shown in theaters that ran silent films and was shown several times on the once popular television show "Silents Please." I have a videocassette of it that was released by Video Yesteryear in which I do a five-minute live introduction filmed here at my house by my son on his minicam. My grandchildren just love seeing their grandpa climbing the rigging and chewing tobacco at the age of ten!

There is one very funny sequence when our crew is in China waiting for the big race to start. I am seen stripped to the waist while a local tattoo artist is, as I told our crew, "Tattoottlin' a ship on back." I am being observed by a group of young Chinese girls who I drive away while telling the tattoo artist, "I hate wimmin." When the Chinaman holds a mirror up to show me his work, I am horrified to find he has actually tattooed a mermaid on my back. I exhibit a look of horror and proclaim, "Now I'll have to keep my shirt on for the rest o' my life." Then I beat him over the head with the mirror and completely wreck his shop.

The day the race was to start from Foo Chow Harbor, Lady Jocelyn and her fiancé, Paul de Vigny, played to perfection by master villain John Miljan, visit our ship to pay their farewell respects to Captain Winslow. Their timing was bad and they were still on board when the cannon was fired announcing the start of the race. They demand to be put ashore, but *Lord of the Isles* was upping anchor and getting underway and Captain Winslow refuses to delay *Yankee Clipper*'s start in the all-important contest.

Their presence on board was a major story line. I naturally hated her, Bill Boyd fell in love with her, and John Miljan led part of the crew to a mutiny after the ship was caught in a typhoon and developed a shortage of drinking water.

The typhoon sequence was one of the picture's best. The miniatures were very believable and the storm scenes aboard ship were frightening. For this sequence our ship was tied alongside a wharf at that time used for storm effects by all the studios of that era. It had gigantic tanks atop spillways that sent tons of water cascading down onto the deck in a realistic storm-like illusion. While filming these scenes our cameramen had their

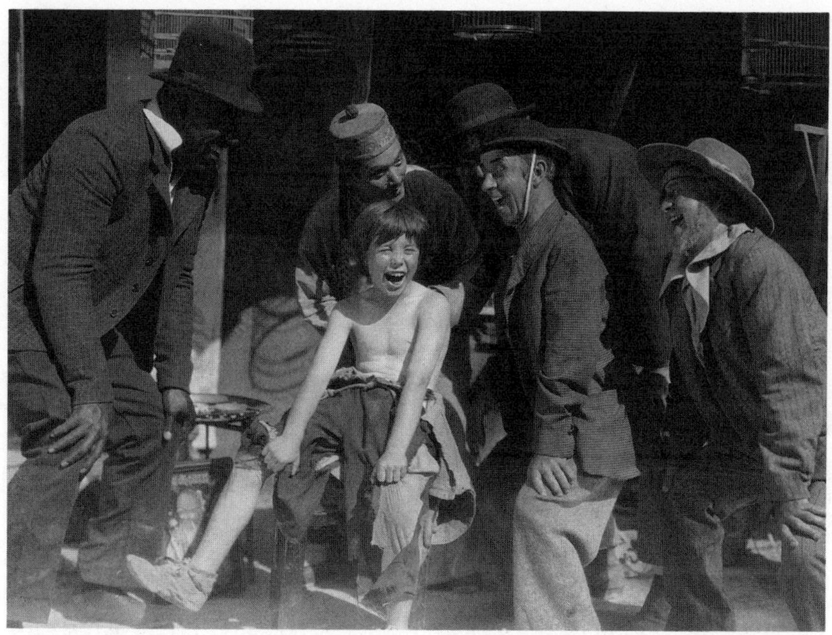

In *The Yankee Clipper* I tell our crew members that this Chinaman is "tattoottlin' a ship on my back." I hated "wimmen" in the film and find to my horror that he has marked me for life with a mermaid. This causes me to say, "Now I'll have to keep my shirt on for the rest o' my life."

cameras stationary, but mounted on pendulums that gave an accurate imaginary roll to the ship.

We spent five very wet nights working on this sequence. At the height of the storm, when sailors were being knocked down by the waves and heavy wind, Mickey was seen having the time of his life riding around the deck in a large wooden washtub. Bill Boyd braved the elements and pulled me out of the tub just before a wave washed it overboard.

The next morning, John Miljan, as de Vigny, who had been seen praying on his knees during the worst of the storm, was now wearing a bandage on his head. When Lady Jocelyn asked him why he failed her during the typhoon, he claimed he was struck by a falling spar and was unconscious most of the night. Captain Winslow tells Lady Jocelyn that four good men were lost to the seas that night and he orders de Vigny to join the crew in mending the badly torn sails. She believes de Vigny's story of his injury and calls Captain Winslow a "merciless bully" for ordering de Vigny to work in his condition. When the captain tears the bandage from de Vigny's head he is shown to be unmarked. When de Vigny reluctantly goes to work, Lady Jocelyn shows the first doubts about the man to whom she is betrothed.

The lady's only dress had become torn at the shoulder during the storm. In dialogue (printed titles) the captain says to Mickey, "Why don't you go mend Lady Jocelyn's topsails." When I impishly, and with great pleasure, jab her in the arm with the needle, the captain says, "Better luff your needle a little to port." It may read a bit corny now, but these terse, well-written lines were very important to the story line in silent films.

One thrilling episode during the mutiny was when Ironhead Joe, played menacingly by Walter Long, takes advantage of the confusion, using it as a perfect diversion for his planned seduction of the hapless Lady Jocelyn. Mickey catches him in the act and bops him on his bald head with a belaying pin. While Ironhead Joe is still dazed, Mickey leads Lady Jocelyn into the rigging to climb to safety above.

This proves to be a tactical error as Ironhead Joe soon follows them up the rigging with a knife between his teeth. Mickey and the lady stop at the first platform of the mainmast and, looking down, are dismayed to see Joe coming after them. Mickey leads Lady Jocelyn to the far side of the platform and then inches himself out to the very end of the yardarm that supports the mainsail.

When Joe reaches the platform he glowers at Jocelyn and then starts following Mickey out on the long spar. Mickey reaches the end of the yardarm and straddles it to await the arrival of Ironhead Joe. There are excellent close-ups of Mickey waiting, Lady Jocelyn clinging to the platform, and Ironhead Joe approaching menacingly with the knife gripped firmly between his teeth.

When Joe nearly reaches Mickey he takes the knife out of his mouth and prepares to make the fatal stab. As Joe lunges, Mickey lets him have it right between the eyes with a well-aimed mouthful of tobacco juice. The startled Joe lets go of his hold on the yardarm to wipe the painfully blinding juice out of his eyes. He then loses his balance and falls to his death in the ocean 75 feet below.

This sequence was well planned and at no time was I in any great danger. A strong wire was strung the length of the yardarm and I wore a harness around my waist with a metal ring securely encasing the wire. If I were to slip off the cable used by the sailors as a foothold for furling the sails, my only indignity would have been the embarrassment of hanging there until crew members came out to lift me back to my original position.

The stuntman who doubled Walter Long in his fall to the water did a beautiful job with his arms and legs flailing the air in spectacular fashion. He was quickly rescued by a powerboat standing by out of camera range and back on board in a matter of minutes. Unfortunately, as he pushed off from the cable, it swung out from under him and he landed flat in the water, breaking an eardrum on impact with the water.

As I now look back on this scene I realize that the real heroes were the

Showing that I hate "wimmen" in the mutiny sequence in *The Yankee Clipper*.

camera crew who went out on the yardarm with us. First they went out to shoot the close-ups of me waiting for Ironhead Joe's arrival. Then they had to assume my position at the end of the yardarm to film close-ups of Joe approaching, leering at me, as he slowly takes the knife out of his mouth to make the final attack.

Of course everything turned out right by the end of the story. *Yankee Clipper* made up the time and distance it lost in the typhoon and, at the approach to Boston Harbor Light, Captain Winslow ordered the crew to rig the weather stunsails to catch more wind. The first mate warned him that this might break the masts, but the captain was determined. He even sent crewmen aloft to wet down the sails so they would draw more wind. As a final ploy, he had the crew bring out their blankets and hold them into the wind. This last effort paid off and *Yankee Clipper* crossed the finish line the winner by a bowsprit.

The evil de Vigny had been done in by his cohorts at the end of the mutiny when they found he had hidden away two water kegs for his personal use. By now Lady Jocelyn knew that de Vigny was really a craven coward. Besides, she had fallen in love with Captain Winslow.

When Mickey sees them embracing at the end of the race he figures it is time for him to go. He packs up his worldly possessions in a single

My mother was with me on board the ship for the six weeks we were at sea on *The Yankee Clipper*.

bandana and bids farewell to the captain. When Captain Winslow protests his leaving, Mickey bursts into tears. He puts his head on his arms at the railing and sobs his heart out. Lady Jocelyn goes over to him and puts her arms around him saying, "Why Mickey boy, you're not going to leave us?" At this Mickey wipes his eyes and, grinning through is tears, says, "I guess women aren't so bad, it's just aunts." Aunts of the world, please forgive me.

13

Slide, Kelly, Slide

Mother and I were hardly unpacked from our six weeks on the *Yankee Clipper* and getting rid of our sea legs when we were notified that I was being loaned to MGM to play the batboy of the New York Yankees in the baseball film, *Slide, Kelly, Slide.*

Wow! After six weeks at sea on that wonderful clipper ship, I was now to spend a month or so on the playing field with many greats of the baseball world.

Slide, Kelly, Slide reunited me with William Haines and Sally O'Neil from the earlier MGM film, *Mike.* Haines played Kelly, a cocky bush-league pitcher who came unannounced to the New York Yankee spring training camp in Florida and made it into the big leagues. Sally was the daughter of the team's aging catcher, played by the former cowboy star Harry Carey. Our director was Edward Sedgwick, who I learned also broke into the business as a kid actor at the age of three, but on the legitimate stage. This charming Texan was a real delight to work for.

The assistant director was Edward Brophy. Ed already had credits as an actor and why he was now working as an assistant director I'll never know, unless it was as a favor to Edward Sedgwick. Brophy went on to recognition in later years as one of the tough but kindhearted comedians. (Forty-five years later in 1972 when I was working in a Champale malt liquor television commercial, the director said to me, "Give it a sort of an Ed Brophy approach"; so he certainly left a lasting impression on the industry.)

Other performers in *Slide, Kelly, Slide* were Warner Richmond, as the team manager, and such stalwarts of the day as Karl Dane, Paul Kelly, and Guinn "Big Boy" Williams. There was also a new young actor, Johnny Mack Brown, playing his first role in a motion picture. Johnny was an All-American football player from the University of Alabama who had starred in the Rose Bowl game that year. He scored three touchdowns and received so much publicity that MGM signed him to a long-term contract. When his MGM contract ended he later became a well-known cowboy star.

I again was a homeless orphan whom Kelly finds one night sleeping on

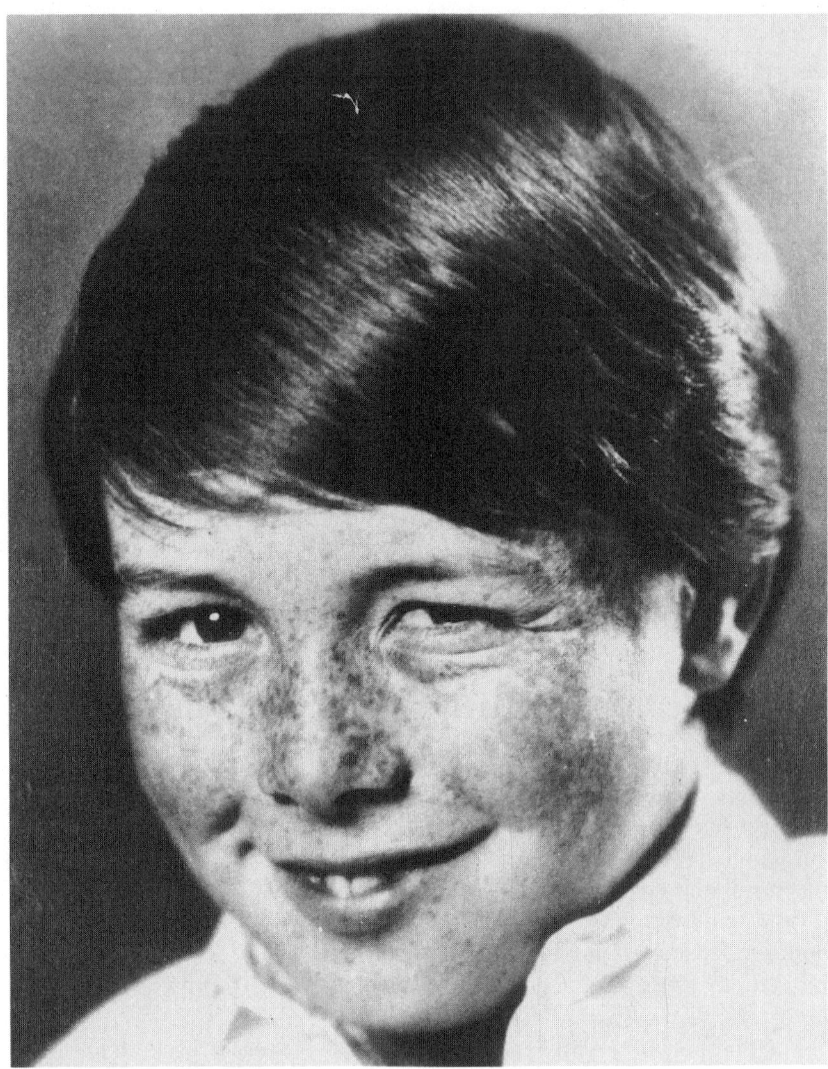

This publicity still caused me to be called "The All-American Boy" by many writers.

a bench with old newspapers as my only cover. He takes me to his hotel room, feeds me, and gives me a clean bed. I eventually become the Yankees' batboy.

For the playing field scenes we used the old Wrigley Field in downtown Los Angeles, then the home park of the Los Angeles Angels, a Pacific Coast League Triple A farm team owned by the Chicago Cubs.

Can you imagine the thrill experienced by an 11-year-old kid walking

With William Haines in *Slide, Kelly, Slide* for MGM in 1927. I played the batboy of the New York Yankees.

out on the field that first day in his little New York Yankee uniform to meet players like Tony Lazzari, Bob and Irish Meusel, Fred Haney, Larry French, Vic and Ernie Orsatti, Hollis Thurston, Lew Fonseca, Wally Hood, and others from the big leagues and the Pacific Coast League.

Bill Haines went back to New York City and Yankee Stadium for special scenes with Babe Ruth and Lou Gehrig. I met them later that year when they came to Los Angeles on an off-season barnstorming tour with their special teams, the Battling Babes and the Larruping Lous. I still treasure a single baseball they both autographed for me that day. I have another baseball signed by all the players who worked in the picture.

The technical director on the film was Mike Donlin. The lead umpire was Beans Reardon who was famous among other things for his salty language on the field.

Mike Donlin invited me to his home one day to see his vast array of awards and trophies, including the gold bat received the year he was the league batting champ. Beans Reardon later invited me to Catalina Island to watch him umpire at the Chicago Cubs spring training camp.

Late in the film, as the Yankees were going into the World Series, I was hit by a car while riding my bicycle to the ballpark. There was a tearful vigil by the entire team in the hospital hall while they waited to see if their batboy was going to pull through.

On the day of the final game of the series I was taken to Yankee Stadium in a wheelchair with my head all wrapped in bandages. In the bottom of the ninth inning with the Yankees one run behind, Kelly comes to plate with a runner on first base. He makes a hit which he tries to stretch to an inside-the-park home run. As he rounds third base heading for home and the ball is being relayed to the plate there is a big head close-up of me yelling, "Slide, Kelly, Slide." He does, of course, he is safe, and the Yankees are the world champions. Needless to say, there was great joy in Mudville that night.

Looking back, after my wonderful experience in *The Yankee Clipper, Slide, Kelly, Slide* has to be my second best all-time memory film. For several years I was welcome in the dugout of the Los Angeles Angels when they played their home games in Wrigley Field and I spent many happy hours with my new friends from the baseball world.

I was now earning $250 per week on my contract with DeMille and we were surprised to learn that MGM had paid our studio $750 per week for my loan out for *Slide, Kelly, Slide.* My sweet little mother, again without benefit of an agent, went to the front office and requested a pay raise. She reasoned that if I was worth $750 to MGM, why wasn't I worth that much to my own studio? When they said no, she asked if we could not at least split the difference at $500 per week. Again she was turned down.

That same night, the man who made the refusal was heard bragging in a restaurant, "We have the biggest bargain in Hollywood. Junior Coghlan at $250 per week, and just today I talked his mother out of a pay raise."

14

The Last Frontier

My next film was also memorable for me. It was *The Last Frontier* and again featured me with my dear friend William Boyd. It was a wagon train story and the entire film, less studio close-ups, was shot on the Navajo Indian Reservation about 150 miles north of Flagstaff, Arizona. Our director was George B. Seitz, who in later years was to direct me in several of the *Andy Hardy* series with Mickey Rooney at MGM. The leading lady was Marguerite de La Motte. Supporting players were cowboy actor Jack Hoxie as Buffalo Bill Cody, J. Farrell MacDonald as Wild Bill Hickok, and Gladys Brockwell played my mother.

We traveled to Flagstaff by train, where studio cars met us and we were driven through beautiful rock formations to an Indian settlement and trading post near Tuba City and The Gap. This was to be our home for the next six weeks. The studio had built an entire tent complex, complete with a mess hall and outhouses. Mother and I shared a tent with a wood burning stove as it was cold at that elevation at that time of year.

Bill Boyd played a trail scout who agreed to lead our wagon train through Indian country. My contribution to the defense of this caravan was my marksmanship with a slingshot. In the big "wagons in a circle" finale, I rendered several of the attacking Indians hors de combat with well-aimed rocks from my trusty weapon. I didn't really hurt any of them badly, but distracted them enough so others in the circle could attack them with their rifles and pistols. It may seem farfetched but it brought a welcome comedy relief to the suspense and brutality of the big battle.

When we were finally victorious and the wagon train reached its destination, Marguerite de La Motte became the schoolmarm, Bill Boyd hung up his spurs and six-shooters and married her, and they adopted me as I had been orphaned in the big fight.

Navajo braves from the surrounding area became actors in our film and rode their own pinto ponies into the battle sequences. The old-timers taught the younger braves how to apply war paint, but our wardrobe men had to outfit them in battle garb as the blue jeans most of them wore were from a more modern era.

Each morning our propmen would check out the rifles, bows and arrows, and lances to be used in the battle and at the end of the day the braves would return them to the prop tent adjacent to our mess tent.

One night while we were having dinner we heard an explosion and ran next door to see what had happened. The Indians were returning the weapons and one brave handed his rifle to a propman muzzle first. The busy propman took the rifle with his hand over the barrel. As he set it down stock first, a blank still in the chamber went off and he received a very severe blast burn. He was in great pain and had to be driven the 150 miles to Flagstaff to receive proper treatment. We had a doctor and a nurse with us, but this poor fellow was in danger of losing his hand, so the drive to the hospital in Flagstaff was a must. Ten days later he rejoined us with his hand in a cast. I assure you he was more careful after this incident when he took back the rifles from the Navajo braves.

While we were on the reservation we witnessed a gigantic wedding celebration when one of the chief's daughters was going to take the big step into marriage.

Things went on normally during the day, but around 9:00 P.M. for three nights in a row about 300 men and women formed a large circle and danced until 5:00 A.M.—for three seemingly endless nights.

They alternated man, woman, man, woman, locked their arms together, and took tiny steps to the right, making the large circle rotate slowly in that direction. All the while they chanted in a monotonous song the lyrics to which sounded like, "Ho-oh-oh, Ho-oh-oh." It made sleeping very difficult for us.

On the third night things became more festive and individual dancing commenced. Now the noise was so loud that we just gave up and stood around observing. We were told that this was a form of courting among the unmarried pairs and if a boy accepted a girl's invitation to dance it was considered pretty serious.

On this third night one of our stuntmen rigged up one of his buddies by making it known to one of the girls that this fellow really wanted to dance with her. She came over and stood in front of him and wasn't about to leave until he accepted her invitation. The fellow just sat there, but the girl wouldn't take no for an answer and tried to pull him into the circle of dancing couples. The stuntman really started sweating and I guess had visions of a tomahawk wedding, or whatever the Navajo equivalent of a shotgun wedding is. Things were getting rather sticky so the perpetrator finally made it known to the chief that it was all a gag so he very sternly told the girl to knock it off and go back among the other single girls.

During the second day of celebration I was standing near the trading post when an Indian led a young steer into the courtyard. Without any warning, another Indian who was near me drew a pistol from its holster and shot the poor beast right between the eyes. It fell in a heap and two braves drew their knives and started dressing it right on the spot.

When they were through, the carcass was hung by its hind legs on a hook hanging from the roof of the trading post. It was right out in the open and in almost no time it was literally covered with flies. When the animal was barbecued at the wedding feast it was probably tender and delicious, but our studio doctor told us not to eat any of it.

I had another strange experience on this location trip. One day when I was not working I asked the location manager if I could go horseback riding. He took me over to one of the hogans, the strange earth and timber dwellings in which the Navajos lived. He spoke to the old man who was the obvious leader of the family group and gave him a few dollars and rented a horse for me to ride.

When I was up in the saddle this grizzled patriarch came over to me and reached up and pinched me right on the penis. Then he said something out loud in his Navajo dialect to the nearby group. They all laughed uproariously. To this day I don't know what the old chieftain said, but it sure must have been funny.

15

My Father and Booze

Things were going so well for me and now all of a sudden my father started acting up. My success and steady income had enabled him to expand his chiropractic practice. Uncle Harry had married and moved to a new home and office and we had the entire upper floor at Carlton Way to ourselves. My father felt he should improve his community relations and joined the Hollywood Athletic Club.

This was a great idea on the surface. He moved into a group of influential men and played handball and squash and swam with them several days a week. The bad thing was he then went up to the card room and drank and gambled with them. Unfortunately, most of the new acquaintances were much richer than we were and the stakes were over his head.

Though we were living under Prohibition, there always seemed to be liquor available and in a short time my father became addicted. I remember one weekend when I wasn't working my dad drove miles out into the country where with great pride he introduced me to the man whom I learned was his bootlegger. My father bought a gallon of what must have been real rotgut and we drove back home.

In addition to the athletic club gambling, he started having weekly poker games at the house where he always served booze. The guests usually drank with moderation but by the end of the evening my father would be drunk and, too frequently, deeply in debt.

One day he told my mother he wanted to establish a credit rating at our local bank. He said it was important to his business and had her cosign a note for $5,000. It seemed harmless at the time, but this note was to cause me great embarrassment in later years.

My father was a really fine doctor and seemed to have magic hands. One night at the old Orpheum Theater in downtown Los Angeles one of my films was playing and the studio asked me to make a personal appearance with it. At that time the Orpheum ran a feature film, a two-reel comedy, a newsreel, and eight acts of vaudeville all for the admission price of 65 cents.

My folks and I were backstage waiting for my introduction while a team of tumblers were performing. It so happened that the under-stander, the man assigned to catch the flipping acrobat on his shoulders, caught him off balance and received a painful neck injury. My father went with him to his dressing room where he applied hot towels and gave him an adjustment. The man was able to perform when their act came up again later that night.

At the Hollywood Athletic Club Dad met several professional boxers who worked out there. He began treating some of them and soon was recognized as a miracle man among the local prizefighters. With his patients from the sports world and the many studio people that I had brought to him, his practice was full and very profitable. For a while Charlie Chaplin was a regular patient.

He was now matching my $250 per week, so there was no reason for my money ever to be touched. Unfortunately, that was not the case. There was no Coogan Law in existence at the time and all of my earnings were available to my father. It soon became apparent that by the end of each week his income and mine had all been blown on his drinking and gambling. When my mother finally left him about one year later, all we escaped with was my paycheck for that week.

One night while all boozed up my father fell and broke his leg. We drove him to the hospital in the middle of the night where he had the break set and a plaster cast applied. The cast and crutches slowed down his medical practice for a few weeks but not his drinking.

By now he had a steady bootlegger who made frequent deliveries to the house. One night Dad was worse than usual. He couldn't manipulate the crutches and was crawling around on the floor. He was getting to the bottom of his bottle so he made a telephone call and ordered a new one. I don't know where I got the nerve but I decided to take some action. When the bootlegger came to the lower front door I pushed the button that unlocked it and he started up the stairs. I was standing at the top landing with a baseball bat in my hands. The man saw me and kept climbing the stairs until I said, "Okay mister, one more step and you get this bat right across your teeth." He looked up at me trying to figure if an 11-year-old kid would really hit him. Then with real bravado, I said over my shoulder, "Mother, call the police and tell them some bootlegger is trying to make a delivery here." That did it and the guy made a hasty retreat down the stairs. I was strictly bluffing as I knew mother would not make that call. The farthest thing from her mind was to call in the police and cause bad publicity for me.

Of course, my dad was furious. He shouted after the bootlegger and swore at Mother and me but he didn't get his bottle. In his frustration, he tore off his plaster cast that night and this foolish gesture was to cause him to lose that leg in later years.

Things got even worse after that. My dad was half drunk most of the time and embarrassed us several times in restaurants. He would wake up so badly hung over that he missed many of his early morning patients and his once fine practice started going downhill.

Worst of all, he began getting mean and roughed up my mother pretty badly on too many occasions. Finally, one night she woke me up with an overcoat on over her nightgown and told me to throw some clothes on, saying, "We're getting out of here. I can't take any more of this." We spent a few nights in a hotel until Mother found a cute bungalow up in the Hollywood hills where we spent a happy year.

After Grandma Coghlan died, Harry married and moved to a nice home in Hollywood where he lived and conducted his practice. After we left, my father couldn't handle the Carlton Way house by himself, so Harry, with a new bride who hated my father, reluctantly let him move his practice in with them. Dad took up residence on the fourth floor of an apartment building directly across the street and seemed to be shaping himself up. Being the great actor that he was, he tearfully convinced Mother that he was through with his old ways and patsy that she was, she decided to give him another chance. She told me at the time that I was growing up and she felt I should have a father. This reconciliation lasted about a month before Dad went back on the bottle.

When I reached the age of 12, I joined the Boy Scouts of America. This was well received by the BSA organization as I was then the leading kid actor in the business and I had chosen scouting. I was good at it too and in less than two years I was a Life Scout with 14 merit badges and closing in fast on the coveted rank of Eagle Scout.

Our troop was sponsored by the American Legion Post 43 in Hollywood and met behind the old fight stadium run by the post. I guess due to my success in scouting my father wanted to affiliate in some form, so he had himself voted a commissioner of the troop. This gave him the privilege of attending meetings and going to camp with us and other benefits the ordinary parents did not enjoy.

One meeting night as we were lining up in formation my father staggered on the scene. He saw me standing in front of my patrol and shouted, "Hi Junior. I decided to come to the meeting." Then to my horror and shame he fell flat on his face. I burst into tears and ran all the way home where I cried myself to sleep. Unfortunately, that was my last night of scouting.

That same night I was awakened by the sounds of a loud argument and saw my dad, completely nude, beating my mother and tearing her nightgown off. She was scratched and bleeding, so I stepped in between them. My dad brutally shoved me aside knocking me completely over the kitchen table. He then went back at my mother with even renewed violence. When I recovered from my fall, I found a baseball bat and again came between them with the bat held high. I guess he was sure I wouldn't hit him so he tore the bat out of my hands. Then he picked up a shoe and began hitting me on the head with it. (Thank God he didn't use the baseball bat.)

Mother had stood his beatings before, but when she saw him finally turning his fury on me she decided that was the last straw. She was in the torn nightgown and I was in pajamas, but again she said, "Let's go," and we went for the door. We picked up what clothes we could and ran down the hall with my father, naked as the day he was born, shouting and staggering after us. We couldn't wait for the elevator so we ran down all four flights of stairs. Though my dad still had the gimp leg from that earlier break, he had his adrenalin flowing and only remained about one floor behind us, screaming at us all the way.

When we reached the lobby he was still only one floor above us and shouting at the top of his lungs. We went through the locked front door just as an elderly couple was using their key to enter. We sped past them and a few seconds later so did Dad. We ran to our car parked at the curb in front of the building and sped away. As I looked back I saw my dad, naked as a jay bird, standing at the curb shaking his fist at us. I also saw the elderly couple going into the apartment building and locking the front door behind them. To this day I still wonder how my father got back to our apartment, undressed as he was and of course without a key.

After we left this time I guess my dad rarely ever drew a sober breath. His practice ran downhill fast and finally Uncle Harry was forced to ask him to leave his office. Dad had a small $40 a month pension from an injury received in World War I and with that as his main source of income he finally deteriorated into a skid row wino living in cheap hotels in the worst part of Los Angeles.

One day I received a call from the Veterans Administration Hospital telling me that my father was a patient there and wanted to see me. I found him in bed in the orthopedic ward with his leg in a cast. I was told that with the hard drinking and little or no food his condition had declined and osteomyelitis had set in where the broken leg had never knit properly. The doctors tried for months to save his leg but it was too far gone and eventually had to be amputated just below the knee. He was provided with an artificial leg which he never did use, preferring to hobble along on crutches. He was released from the hospital when the stump had healed and returned to his life on skid row.

One day years later, while in Los Angeles on leave from the navy, I asked the Veterans Administration for the address where they were sending his pension checks. They gave me the address of one of the sleaziest hotels on skid row where I finally found him.

Here I was, a navy officer in full uniform, calling on my father in what amounted to a seedy flophouse. When the desk clerk came to realize that I truly was looking for my father and not trying to check in with some broad, he finally said, "You must be doc's son" and gave me the room number.

I walked back to his room and knocked. He hobbled to the door and opened it and it was obvious that I had awakened him from a wine-induced nap. The room was a single, without bath, and a very depressing place in which to find one's father.

We chatted and he told me he was doing fine. He said in addition to his pension he picked up occasional fees for giving treatments to his new friends, the whores, pimps, and bartenders of the area. He proudly said, "They all call me doc."

After a while he asked me if I would walk down to the corner and buy him a bottle of wine. I didn't want to, but I figured what the heck, he'd only hobble down and get it later anyway, so I ran the errand for him.

If you've never been to a liquor store in skid row, it's something different. The shelves are lined with the cheapest of wines and what hard booze is on display is mostly in pints and half pints. I selected a fifth of the best brand of muscatel wine they had and brought it to my dad. He was impressed with the size of the bottle and the quality and thanked me very much.

As we talked he took little sips right from the bottle and soon was drowsing off, so I left. As I think back on this sad scene, I wonder if he ever remembered me being there.

16

Pathé Studio and *The Country Doctor*

I realize in those last few unhappy pages I covered a span of years that put my story out of context, but I wanted to tell of my father's deterioration in a single chapter, so if you don't mind, now I'll go back to 1927 and continue the narrative.

Rudolph Schildkraut, the great Austrian actor and father of the Cecil B. DeMille favorite Joseph Schildkraut, was now under contract to our studio and big things were planned for him. While his son was a very self-important, rather snobbish fellow, his father was a cuddly old sweetheart and we got along great together.

His first starring vehicle at our studio was the original version of *The Country Doctor* and I received second billing in it. (In the mid–1930s the fine Danish actor Jean Hersholt was to make a series of films where he was called the Country Doctor. In this series he was known as Dr. Christian. As luck would have it, I played a running character of the drugstore soda jerk in two of them.)

Our country doctor was a lovable old general practitioner in a rural farm area who made his house calls in a horse drawn buggy. Most of his fees were on the barter system, like a dozen eggs for a sick call in the middle of the night, or a baby pig for delivering a child. His likable nurse-housekeeper was Jane Keckley who tried to keep his practice on a moneymaking basis, but the kindhearted old doctor just couldn't say no to a patient who didn't have the cash.

My widowed mother was played by the fine character actress Gladys Brockwell, now acting as my mother for the third time. In the beginning of the film she was dying of consumption, which now is better known as tuberculosis. When she was on her deathbed and we were out of food, I was caught stealing eggs from the barn of the villain, played by Sam de Grasse.

When my mother died, he insisted that I be sent to the local orphanage but the kind old doctor interceded and I was placed in the care of a childless young couple played by Virginia Bradford and Frank Marion, two new contract performers at the studio.

With Rudolph Schildkraut in the original version of *The Country Doctor* at DeMille Studio in 1927. The kindly old doctor tells me, "This won't hurt a bit."

In one sequence Frank Marion is seen chopping down a pine tree for firewood and I was standing in the path of the tree as it was about to fall. He sees me and runs to push me out of the way and the tree falls on him instead. He is pinned to the ground and Virginia and I cannot possibly pull him out from the heavy weight of the tree.

This was supposed to be in the winter time and I was dressed in snow boots, a wool muffler and cap, a heavy overcoat, mittens, and the whole works. The artificial snow was up to my knees as I plodded through it to the doctor's house. (No telephones of course.) The film was made in the summertime and with all the lights and no air conditioning, the set temperature was in the high 90s. Needless to say, even for an 11-year-old kid it was very hot and uncomfortable. We finished those scenes one afternoon and to my surprise I was told we would repeat them the following afternoon.

Though Cecil B. DeMille owned our studio he was considered to be an independent producer. He did not have the advantage of a large chain of theaters so he had to send his output to the theaters through a releasing organization. The first year I was with him it was Metropolitan and for the next two years it was Producers Distributing Corporation (PDC). Before this year would end PDC and Pathé were to merge and soon Joseph P. Kennedy was to buy out DeMille and we became known as Pathé Studio.

Well, it so happened that the heads of Producers Distributing Corporation were in town for their national convention and they and their families were invited to the studio to watch us work. It was not until after I had finished wading through the knee-deep snow and they had left the set that I learned we had worked the entire afternoon with no film in the camera just to provide them with an interesting scene to watch. I sure earned my pay that day.

Each lunch hour when we worked on the back lot the crew would have a baseball game and they kindly let me play shortstop. One day I dipped to field a grounder. The ball took a bad hop and hit me right in the mouth. Fortunately I didn't lose any teeth but I sure developed a fat lip. For the next two days we were shooting the scenes of my mother's death. In them our director (Rupert Julian from *Yankee Clipper*) had me holding my clenched fist to my mouth supposedly holding back tears. What he really was doing was having me hide my swollen lip!

Something else happened during this picture that showed me what the crew thought about me. There was a young fellow working with us for the first time and during one lunch break he was bragging about his achievements of the night before and using some words I had never heard before.

Suddenly our property master Bob McCreedy grabbed this guy by the front of his shirt and stood nose to nose with him. Then McCreedy, through clenched teeth, said, "Listen you jerk, we don't swear in front of our kid. Do you understand?"

That didn't impress me much at the time, but as I look back it was quite a compliment. In their eyes I really was "their kid" and they were protecting me from hearing things I shouldn't.

17

Marked Money

Our studio was now known as Pathé and from then on all of our films were preceded by the familiar Pathé white crowing rooster. Cecil B. DeMille had finished his final production at our studio, *The Godless Girl,* and had moved to MGM. The Joseph P. Kennedy influence was being felt more and more. He had bought not only the studio property but the contracts of the actors and all the other key personnel. Fortunately, I was still in his plans and the final four films I made on the original five-year contract were all starring vehicles for me.

Our studio writers now came up with an excellent script written expressly for me entitled *Marked Money.* This film proved to be prophetic as in the final scenes I wore the uniform of a naval aviator, complete with the wings of gold that I wore so proudly during the 23 years I spent on active duty in the navy.

Marked Money was directed by Spencer Gordon Bennet, who later became known as one of the finest of the action-packed serial directors. Again I played an orphan and the opening scenes were made on board the *Indiana,* the clipper ship that had been my happy home for six weeks during the filming of *The Yankee Clipper.*

In the first scenes I am shown leaving the ship with my pet monkey on a leash. I am accompanied by a tall sailor who is carrying my duffel bag over his shoulder. He is also carrying a mysterious paper-wrapped, shoe box–sized package under his arm. As we go down the gangplank we are being followed by another sailor who is obviously tailing us for reasons of his own.

The friendly sailor takes me to the office of an attorney whose name and address are written on the paper-wrapped box. While the sailor is looking for the attorney's office, I am seen peeking through the keyhole of an adjacent office. After my first peek I turn and look right into the camera with an unbelieving but very pleased look on my face. It is obvious that this 12-year-old kid has seen some hanky-panky going on behind that door and the pleasure I showed at what I had just seen was really very suggestive for films of that day; especially in that it involved someone so young.

When we are admitted into the attorney's office we see that he is preparing to leave on a fishing trip and has a box filled with lures and hooks on his desk. At the sailor's direction the attorney unwraps our box and is surprised to find that it contains $25,000 in currency. There is also a letter from my father specifying that I am to be delivered to the home of his old sailing master and the money is for my expenses and education.

The lawyer and I then go down to his car. He packs the gear for his trip, my duffel bag, and both boxes on the back seat of his open touring car and he drives me to the old sea captain's house. When we arrive in front of the house the attorney is attacked by two men and we see that the sailor who was following me is driving the getaway car. One of the hoods struggles with the attorney, shoots him, and makes off with the box. A crowd gathers, the police arrive, and the lawyer tells one of them to take me into the house and deliver me to Captain Fairchild. At the sound of the commotion the old captain's cook and handyman, played by the very funny Tom Kennedy, comes out to see what the ruckus is all about.

The policeman and I tell him what has happened and he takes me in to meet Captain Fairchild. My pet monkey precedes us and jumps up on the table and completely scatters the chess game the captain has been working on. As a result he is furious when we enter. The captain, played by Burt Woodruff, soon settles down when I hand him the box. He sees the cash and learns from the letter that he now has a former shipmate's son to raise. Then there is a cutaway line to the villains in their car as they gleefully open their box, only to find it is filled with nothing but fishing gear.

For the rest of the movie there are many attempts made to steal my money but we always foil the efforts. In one scene Tom Kennedy frosts the box to make it look like a freshly baked cake. He leaves it in plain view and the bad guys walk right past it when they break in.

While I am watching Tom Kennedy frost the box I notice he has the head of a snake tattooed on his throat and he can make the reptile's mouth open and close by flexing his Adam's apple. He removes his shirt to show me that the snake entwines clear around his torso and the tail enters his trousers straight down from his navel. When I ask him where the rattlers are he blushes and whispers in my ear and I giggle at what he tells me. Also pretty risqué for a film of that era intended for the family trade.

Captain Fairchild has a lovely niece, played by Virginia Bradford, who is in love with a naval aviator played by George Duryea. This was Duryea's first film. DeMille scouts had seen him playing the romantic lead in the road company of *Abie's Irish Rose* and signed him to star in DeMille's next film, *The Godless Girl.* It was still a few months away from production and George was on salary so they decided to give him some experience in front of the cameras in *Marked Money.* George later became better known as the western star Tom Keene.

I don't want to bore you with all the plots and counterplots, but the conclusion of the film is exciting. It seems that the old captain hated aviators and when he finds out that Duryea had been teaching his niece how to fly he banishes him from the house. As a result, the couple plan to elope. As she is sneaking out of the house the villains kidnap her and decide to hold her for the ransom of my money. I see them making off with her and jump onto the spare tire of their car to find out where they are taking her.

When I see they have taken her to a hangar at the old airport, I run back into town to tell Duryea where they are. Due to the long distance, I steal a horse-drawn milk wagon and drive it into town. As luck will have it, as I approach the house, I am sideswiped by Duryea in his car and I direct him to where the girl is being held.

In the meantime the kidnappers have sent the bad sailor to climb a telephone pole to call the captain and demand that he bring the money to the airport. When I lead Duryea to their hideout, we find they have already forced the niece into the front cockpit of the airplane and are waiting for the money to arrive to make their getaway. Duryea gets into a fight with the hood who is to fly the plane and beats him up so badly that he is unable to pilot the aircraft. When villain number two sees that Duryea is a naval aviator, he orders him to fly the plane. The hood climbs up into the front cockpit where the girl is tied up and forces George into the rear cockpit and orders him to take the plane into the air.

When I see the plane rolling I run alongside and try to prevent it from becoming airborne. As a result I end up being taken aloft with it and I cling to the fuselage just forward of the tail and ride it like a jockey.

Once in the air, Duryea gets in a fight with the bad guy and both fall out of the plane and come to earth, suspended by the villain's parachute. There are some funny scenes where I slide fore and aft with the plane's gyrations with no one at the controls. I finally slide forward and climb into the rear cockpit. The girl tells me to cut her bindings and we change cockpits. Fortunately, Duryea has taught her how to fly and she brings the plane in for a landing.

At the conclusion Duryea and the niece get married and fly off on their honeymoon. That is where both my pet monkey and I are each seen wearing navy uniforms. I tie a "Just Married" sign and a string of Tom Kennedy's shoes to the tail of the airplane and he berates me for making him lose all his extra shoes.

A very strange thing happened to me during the production of this film. When I was working in *The Yankee Clipper* one of the ship's crew made me a beautiful two-foot-long sailboat. To pass the time between scenes on *Marked Money* I used to sail my boat in the swimming pool at our studio. In *Marked Money* I wore a rather unusual costume. It had blue sailor pants and a unique pullover sweater with long, striped sleeves. It was customary to always have a backup set of wardrobe, but this sweater was so different that the studio could not find a double for it. Every night at the conclusion of shooting I would remove the costume and leave it in my dressing room. The wardrobe man would then have it dry-cleaned for me, so I had a fresh outfit to put on each morning.

One day I was sailing my boat in the pool when one of our new crew members came out to watch me. He was a very likable young fellow named Allen Smiley and due to his pleasing personality and happy appearance was called "Smiley" by all. He watched me for a while and when I was kneeling over beside the pool to retrieve my boat he just couldn't resist the urge and put his foot to my rear and pushed me into the pool.

There was no danger because I was a good swimmer but he didn't know that. I emerged from the water just as the assistant director came out to call me for the next scene. When he saw me dripping wet, he shouted, "Junior, what in hell happened to you?" Smiley was standing nearby and I knew if I told the assistant that he had pushed me into the pool he would be fired on the spot. I made up a white lie and told him that while bending over I lost my balance and just fell into the pool.

The assistant reported this to the director and then rushed me to wardrobe where they stripped me down and put my costume in the dryer. I held up the company for over an hour while my clothes dried, but I never told on "Smiley."

Allen Smiley finally left the studio for what I suppose he felt were greener pastures. Soon we started reading his name in the newspapers for various infractions of the law and for being associated with known gangsters. The charges against him became more and more serious and the names of his acquaintances were soon among the top echelon of the local crime mob.

The syndicate kingpin on the West coast was then a former New York hood named Benjamin "Bugsy" Siegel. He had talked the Eastern mafia families out of an advance of six million dollars with which he built the first posh hotel and gambling casino on the Las Vegas strip. He named it the Flamingo which was the nickname of his girlfriend Virginia Hill. Due to wartime travel restrictions and for other reasons, the Flamingo became a white elephant and the mob wanted Siegel to return the money. They also suspected Siegel of skimming off a large part of the construction costs and of dipping into the gambling revenues. At the syndicate's famous Havana Convention in 1946 it was decided that "Bugsy" Siegel had to go. On June 20, 1947, while Siegel was sitting on the sofa in Virginia Hill's mansion in Beverly Hills, parties unknown pumped nine slugs from a .30 caliber carbine into him. Three hit him in the head, killing him instantly. The killer, or killers, who fired through the front window, were never discovered and this is still one of gangland's unsolved crimes.

Now, who was sitting on the sofa right next to "Bugsy" but Allen Smiley! His name was then in the papers daily and for a long time there was speculation that he had set "Bugsy" up for the execution-type killing.

In doing research on "Smiley" for this book I learned that he was born Aaron Smehoff in Russia and his parents moved to Canada when he was a child. He grew up a Canadian citizen and entered the United States illegally in 1923. I suppose that due to the notoriety he received from the Siegel killing he was charged with illegal entry and for falsely claiming U.S. citizenship. For these offenses he served a year in prison in 1948. I also found out he was acquitted in 1944 on charges of knifing actor Jon Hall in what was called a "Hollywood fracas" and acquitted again in 1963 of attempting to extort $60,000 from Palm Springs hotel man Ray Ryan. Despite all this bad publicity, he was granted U.S. citizenship on July 2, 1966, over the objections of the U.S. Immigration Service. As late as 1974 his name was in the papers as an accomplice of known gangsters and from repeated charges of being involved in illegal gambling and attempted extortion.

Looking back on the swimming pool incident it makes me wonder how anyone could have such a total disregard of values and the utter lack of self-control as to push the star of a film into a swimming pool in his only change of wardrobe just as he was needed on the set, and on top of that, not even knowing if the kid could swim or not.

Maybe I should have told on "Smiley."

18

Let 'er Go Gallegher

My next film was *Let 'er Go Gallegher*, a newspaper story, where the studio bought the screen rights to the Richard Harding Davis book, *Gallegher*, especially as a starring vehicle for me.

Again I played an orphan and was joined by Harrison Ford from *Rubber Tires* and Elinor Fair from *The Yankee Clipper*. Ford played the cocky reporter Callahan and Miss Fair was a columnist on the same newspaper. This little film was directed by Elmer Clifton, who had received acclaim for his direction of *Down to the Sea in Ships* and *The Wreck of the Hesperus*. A new Lithuanian actor, Ivan Lebedeff, played the dastardly villain, "Four-Fingered Dan."

The picture opens with scenes of me and my dog Watson living in an old wrecked automobile in a junkyard. Early in the movie it is revealed that Gallegher's great ambition is to become a famous detective. That explains the rather unusual name for his faithful dog.

One night Watson and Gallegher are prowling the neighborhood when Watson chases a cat down the coal chute of a mansion on the street. Naturally I follow Watson down into the basement to rescue him. While there I hear a loud argument between two men and peer through an open door just in time to hear gunshots and see that the man who fired the shots has the index finger missing on his right hand. Though scared to death, I wait until the murderer leaves and then run to the newspaper to tell my friend Callahan what I had just seen.

My description of the killer gives Callahan the story of his life and he names him "Four-Fingered Dan." The newspaper runs a picture of me on the front page as the only witness to the shooting. When the murderer sees the newspaper he searches for me. For protection, Callahan takes me home to live with him and gets me a job as a copy boy on the paper.

Later in the story there is a hilarious scene where I see a man I think is Four-Fingered Dan in a railway station. I notice he is using a cane and wearing gray suede gloves and the index finger of his right hand is pointing straight down from the handle of the cane. I sneak up behind him and with a look of real fear on my face I squeeze that finger. My suspicion is confirmed

In *Let 'er Go Gallegher* the villain, played by Ivan Lebedeff, is showing me just how sharp his knife is before he slits my throat.

when I realize that the finger of the glove is stuffed with cotton. I stay behind him until he buys his ticket, then I buy one for the same destination and follow him onto the train. As I board the train my faithful dog Watson boards right behind me.

When we arrive at the station I call Callahan from a telephone booth to tell him where I have followed Dan. I tail him out into the country where I get trapped alone with him in an old deserted house. Watson barks at Dan, giving away my hiding place. He catches me up in the attic of this spooky old house and takes me to a sleazy looking roadhouse where he orders dinner for both of us. At the table he takes out the newspaper with my photo on the the front page and accuses me of being the only witness to his crime. To stall for time I remark that the steak knife I am using is about the sharpest I have ever seen. He takes it from my hand and says it would be just perfect for slitting a throat. To my relief, at that very moment Callahan arrives with the police.

The cameraman on this film was Lucien Andriot who later received many honors in his profession. Some of his shadow effects in *Let 'er Go Gallegher* were really frightening and certainly added to the suspense.

When Callahan and the police save me, there is a sequence where in the best tradition of the classic newspaper film *The Front Page,* Callahan wants to take the killer to his newspaper office to turn him in.

Callahan forces the 12-year-old Gallegher to drive the car and the chase that follows is as good as those seen in modern-day films. There is one set of scenes where Gallegher is trapped betwen two fire engines. When they order the young kid to get out of the way, Gallegher says, "You get out of the way. I don't even know how to stop this thing."

That is proven when Gallegher could not stop the car and drove it right into the lobby of the newspaper building.

19

A Harp in Hock

Apparently, in *The Country Doctor* Rudolph Schildkraut and I showed some chemistry together because the studio now costarred us in our next film, *A Harp in Hock.* This strange title did have a meaning: I was an Irish orphan (a harp) and Schildkraut was a Jewish pawnbroker and ran a hock shop. When my mother died he adopted me and I became "a harp in hock."

The opening scenes showed me arriving in this country from Ireland and being brought to the tenement where my mother lived only to learn that she had just passed away.

Her neighbor was May Robson, who had played my mother in *Rubber Tires,* and her daughter was Bessie Love, who had been my sister in that same film. In *A Harp in Hock* May Robson had a son about my age, but much larger than me and quite a bully. When he laughed at my funny clothes and my Irish accent, I poked him in the nose. That had me heading for the orphanage when May Robson pressed charges against me for beating up her little darling.

Here again, Schildkraut interceded for me and then "took me in hock" so to speak. I was on probation in his custody, but when I beat up May Robson's bully son a second time she did have me put away. I later escaped from the orphanage and returned to the hock shop and was finally placed in his permanent custody. This was a real tearjerker and the old man and I had many tender scenes together.

Our director was the wonderfully thoughtful Renaud Hoffman. He was such a realist that, even though this was a silent motion picture, he made me talk with an Irish brogue throughout the entire production. I felt silly doing it but he was so nice to work for that I tried hard to please him. Hoffman was also the first director who ever gave me a gift at the completion of a picture. When the final scene was finished he presented me with a beautiful Elgin pocket watch. I was really impressed.

While *A Harp in Hock* was originally developed under the DeMille regime, it was released by Pathé. By now Joseph P. Kennedy had completely taken over our studio and many changes were being made. Kennedy

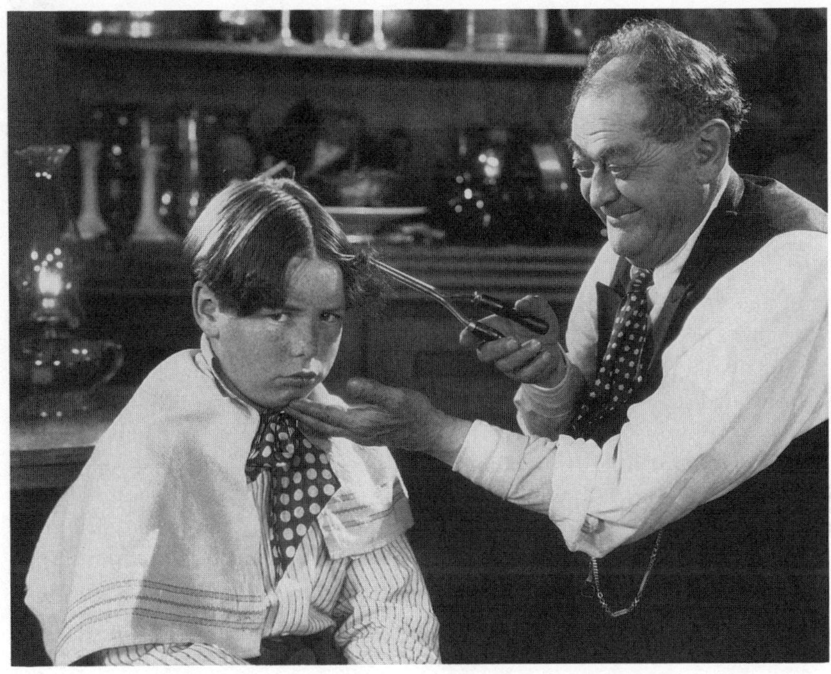

My next starring film, *A Harp in Hock*, with Rudolph Schildkraut. I was the Irish orphan and he was the Jewish pawn shop broker who adopted me; so I became "a harp in hock." Here he is trying to make me look better for a neighborhood function. I don't seem to appreciate the new hairdo he is planning for me.

brought many important players into the studio like Ann Harding, Carole Lombard, Lew Ayres, Robert Armstrong, and Kennedy's own favorite, Gloria Swanson. Though I was just a 12-year-old kid, I remember seeing old Joe Kennedy frequently climbing the long flight of stairs to the dressing room suite he had built for his ladylove.

I was still the only child player in the new slate of performers. One of the first to go in the new regime was DeMille's protégé, the buxom, overweight, 20-year-old dancer, Sally Rand.

However, a few years later at the Chicago World's Fair, Sally learned how to use a pair of feathered fans, so I guess her career was not ended by her being fired by Joe Kennedy.

20

Square Shoulders

It was now late 1929 and I was in the closing months of my five-year contract. I was now 13 years old and for the past two years I had been having my teeth straightened. Each time I would start a new film my kindly, patient orthodontist, Dr. Matthew Conner Lasher, would remove my braces and fix me with a retainer brace on a removable plate to keep my teeth from returning to their old snaggle-toothed appearance. As a result of all these interruptions, this normal four-year process took six years to complete.

I was now cast to appear in *Square Shoulders* costarring with the fine actor Louis Wolheim, in what was to be the final film of my contract. If you recall Louis Wolheim, he had a flattened nose that made Karl Malden look like an extremely good-looking boy.

Wolheim's very next role was probably his best remembered: he played the grizzled sergeant in the original version of *All Quiet on the Western Front* with Lew Ayres. There were many rumors on how he received the nose but he said it was from playing football in college. The nose made him look like a hoodlum, but actually this nice man was highly educated and had taught English and dramatics on the college level before embarking on his own career on the stage and in motion pictures.

In this film I had my first leading lady. She was the lovely 11-year-old Anita Louise, who later went on to stardom while under contract at Warner Brothers in such films as *The Story of Louis Pasteur, Anthony Adverse,* and *A Midsummer Night's Dream.*

She was born Anita Louise Fremault and had appeared on the New York stage before coming to Hollywood. She had the cutest little mother, who couldn't have been taller than 4′ 10″. She fussed around Anita on the set and watched over her like a hawk.

I had two rivals for Anita in this film. They were Philippe de Lacy and Erich Von Stroheim, Jr. I don't have to tell you who Erich's father was and in later years Erich, Jr., became a very good and well-liked assistant director.

Philippe de Lacy has an interesting background. He was a World War I

French war orphan, found near death from rickets and malnutrition by a British army nurse. She brought him to health, adopted him, and then took him to her home in England and later to the United States.

Philippe was an absolutely beautiful child and his entry into motion pictures is not surprising. Despite his extremely good looks, he was all boy and I enjoyed working with him. When *Square Shoulders* was completed Phil and I used to visit children's hospitals and orphanages together. We would run the film and then do a skit in which we duplicated the knockdown fight we had in the movie. This was to show the kids that we were really good friends and did not hurt each other in our mock battle.

When Phil left the motion picture industry he entered the advertising field and for years represented Disneyland for the J. Walter Thompson agency. He is now living in retirement in Carmel, California.

In this film my mother, on her death bed, pins a medal on the lapel of my coat. It was the Distinguished Service Cross (only second to the Congressional Medal of Honor) that my father had earned for heroism as a soldier in World War I. She shows me his initials on the reverse side of the medal, then tells me he is dead when she really knew he was in prison. I was much impressed by this medal and from then on I wore it proudly at all times.

After her death I became a ward of a newsboys' home and contributed toward my upkeep by selling papers on the street. I was the leader of my gang and used to drill them on an open field near our home. During these marching drills I always wore the medal, my father's army cap that my mother had given to me, and a wooden sword to show my leadership over the group.

One day as I was drilling my "troops," the scene fades to a freight train where three bums are seen hopping off as the train is approaching the railyard. The leader of the trio smiles when he sees where they are and says it is his old hometown and he has lots of memories and scores to settle there. The three bums part company and the leader trudges off into town. He walks past where I am marching my gang just as a big limousine drives up and parks in front of the building bordering the field. The owner of the building steps out of his expensive car, accompanied by his son who is resplendent in the uniform of a stylish military academy. The kid watches me drilling my shock troops and giggles at my mistakes. His father also laughs and suggests that his son go over and show me how to properly conduct close order drill.

The fancy dressed kid approaches my gang and makes a few good-natured comments which I immediately resent. Words lead to hotter words and soon we are in a real fistfight. Though I have all the spunk needed in a fistfight, this kid is a skilled and highly trained boxer and soon has me down and out.

The bum walks up at this time and shouts encouragement for the underdog. When the military school kid rejoins his father we find that the rich man recognizes the tramp as someone who had served under him in the army. He welcomes the tramp back to town and offers him a job in his factory. The bum resents this as a put-down and tells the rich man what he can do with the job.

When the limo drives away the tramp walks over and chides me for letting a fancy dan beat me up. In the heated conversation that follows I tell him to shove off and that I can take care of myself. To prove it, I show him my medal and tell him what a hero my father had been. The bum takes the medal in his hand and in turning it over he sees his own initials. He asks me where I got the medal and soon realizes that I am his son. Without telling me who he is, he learns from me that my mother is dead, that I live in a newsboys' home, and that I love the military because of my father's heroism.

When he learns all this he decides to do something about it. That night he rounds up his two cronies and they break into the building owned by his former commanding officer and empty the safe. When the job is completed the three of them break up, leaving the money with my father as he assures them he knows of a place to hide it until they can meet again and divide it up. However, we soon see that my father has other plans for the loot.

A few days later an officer from the military academy shows up at the newsboys' home with a letter for me. The director of the home instructs the nearest boy to go find Tad and tell him he has a letter. Then ensues a great series of scenes as one newsboy relays the information to the next boy by shouting on the street, "Tad's got a letter." The boys' faces and the written titles keep getting bigger until finally the face of the last boy fills the screen as he shouts to me, "TAD, YOU'VE GOT A LETTER!"

I race back to the home, followed by all the other kids, to find out what the letter says. I read it with tears in my eyes when I find that a benefactor has left me an endowment, paying for my education at the military academy clear through to graduation.

The transition to the strict routine of the academy is tough for Tad to make but he is determined to make good and feels he owes it to the memory of his hero father. This is a big change for him as his background is very different from the rich kids he now rubs elbows with daily. The boy he had fought with ridicules him at first; but they eventually become friends.

The commandant has a cute daughter who flirts with the cadets and Tad soon finds a new interest in life. His biggest rival for her affections, of course, turns out to be the rich kid he had fought with, but when she jilts both of them for another cadet, they drown their sorrows in ice cream sodas (literally).

The jilting takes place at a soda fountain where Tad and the other boy

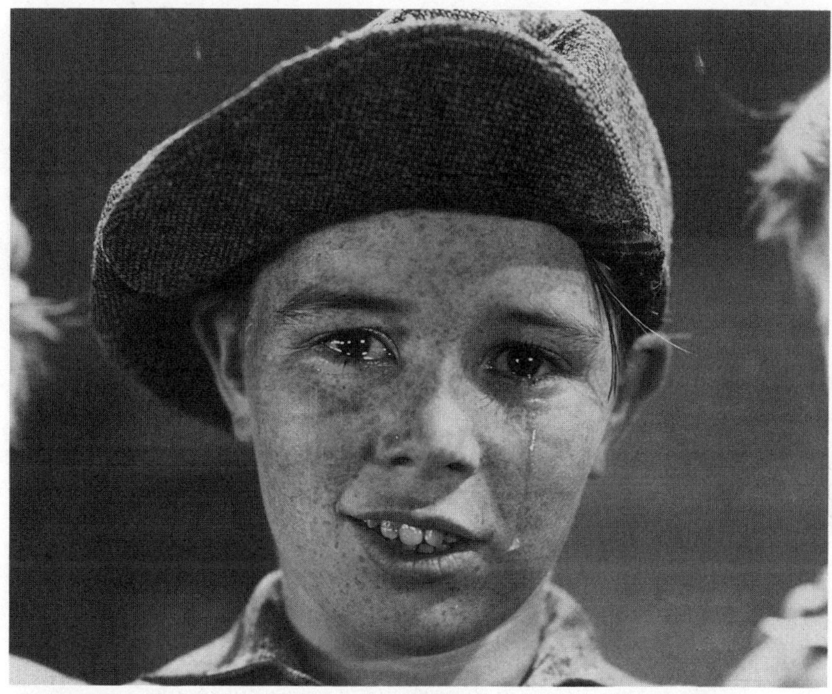

In *Square Shoulders*, the last film on my DeMille contract. I have just been told that I have received a full scholarship to a military academy because of my father's heroism in World War I.

were trying to impress her by seeing who could order the most exotic ice cream concoction. When the cadet, played by Erich Von Stroheim, Jr., outdoes them both and she leaves the confectionery store on his arm, Tad and the rich boy shake their heads in disbelief at her fickleness.

Now a strange thing happens. Slag, the bum who is really Tad's father, shows up at the military academy. He applies for and receives the position of stable hand at the academy stable, which holds about thirty fine riding horses. At their first meeting Slag handpicks a horse for Tad to ride that he says is the finest horse in the stable.

Tad isn't much of a rider yet and the spirited steed throws him. It is a real embarrassment to Tad because it happens at a big horse show with many parents and friends in attendance. This leads to a scene where Tad accuses Slag of purposely trying to show him up in front of the young girl and the other cadets.

Eventually the two make up and become friends. One day Slag produces his old army bugle and persuades Tad to learn to play it. Then follow some funny scenes as Tad does his best while Slag winces at the many blue

As I said, "I blow in so sweet and it comes out so sour."

notes until Tad becomes proficient with the horn. His patience pays off and soon Tad becomes the regimental bugler and a popular member of the student body. At the many military formations that follow, Tad's bugle calls set the pace for all events.

One night as Tad approaches the barn area for his nightly visit with Slag, he hears a large commotion taking place in the stable. The horses are whinnying and neighing and angry shouts are heard. It seems that Slag's two cronies had found out where he lives and had shown up, demanding their cut of the safecracking. Of course, Slag didn't have the money as he had paid it to the military academy for Tad's education. He couldn't tell them this and they were furious with him.

One bum has a wicked looking metal hook where his hand had once been and he slashes Slag from his cheekbone to his jaw in the fight that follows. The other bum draws a pistol and mortally wounds Slag. As he falls, Slag wrestles the gun away from him, and Tad finally drives both bums from the stable while shouting at them and jabbing them with a giant pitchfork. After the bums had fled, Tad runs back to Slag and tearfully nestles his head in his arms as the man dies.

The final sequence is a real tearjerker as Tad is seen blowing taps over Slag's grave in Potter's Field. As a last tribute to the man he has grown to love, Tad unpins his cherished Distinguished Service Cross from the underside of his lapel and buries it in the dirt on Slag's grave, never knowing that the man was really his father.

This was one of the many films made that year in which the final reel was reshot with sound and dialogue for release to the theaters that were now showing "talkies."

This was a real experience. Sound equipment was still pretty primitive. The microphones then in use were not very directional and they were hidden all over the set. Many were suspended overhead, but others were placed in flower pots and other choice places where they could pick up the dialogue. Also, the newly invented camera motors were noisy and the poor camera crews were encased in a soundproof booth about six feet square with the camera filming through a thick plate of glass. Air conditioning was still not in use and the unfortunate cameramen really suffered from the heat.

I now own a silent 16mm print of *Square Shoulders* that I acquired in a rather unusual manner. About 1965 Harry Jenkins, a former theater organist, invited my wife and me to attend a meeting of the San Fernando Valley Elks Club. He said he was going to show my film and accompany it on the Hammond Organ as he said he had done a hundred times in the theaters. As the film was running, Jenkins played music to match every mood of the action. In the final scenes he made the Hammond play taps and when the film ended there wasn't a dry eye in the hall.

He repeated his performance about two years later and then asked me if I would like to have the print. Jenkins's ability to follow a film is a lost art and these fine organists brought much pleasure to theatergoers in the era of the silent movies.

21

New Haven

The year 1929 came to a close and my five-year contract terminated. I think the main reason was the studio heads just didn't know what to do with a young kid approaching adolescence. Those in-between years continued to be a problem for the studios until Mickey Rooney proved them to be probably the most interesting years of all in his highly successful *Andy Hardy* series.

For the first time in five years I was now off salary with no prospect for the future. Being at the same studio for five years is wonderful but when they discontinue planning for your future, you are really out on a limb as no other studio is ready for you to move into their production plans. Mother decided we both needed a change of scenery so we went back to New Haven for a three-month family visit.

This was a neat experience for me. After 11 years in Hollywood knowing not much else but life in the motion picture industry I now settled into a quiet life with the large group of relatives I had barely known. We stayed in the big, family, three-story home with Grandpa and Grandma Coyle. The first floor was now occupied by my aunt Agnes and her husband Joe Close. Aunt Ado, as I called her, was about six months pregnant with her first child. Grandma and Grandpa and my uncle Jack Coyle lived on the second floor and mother and I had an apartment on the third floor that had been built into part of the attic to be used as a rental unit for Yale students.

I met aunts, uncles, and cousins I had never met before and really enjoyed being part of a large, happy family for the first time in my life. After the Christmas holidays I enrolled in the eighth grade at the Orange Street School where Aunt Agnes taught the third grade. I always had a tutor on the set when working in a film but in between pictures I went to public schools; however, this was very different.

In Hollywood I was accepted as a movie actor while in school but it was no big deal for the other students as every school I ever attended also had several other kid actors enrolled and we were just taken for granted as part of the Hollywood scene.

At Orange Street School I was really an oddity. I was at the height of my film popularity and everywhere I went I was pointed at and stared at and at first most of the other students were reluctant to even talk to me. Fortunately, I had a great teacher who was an old friend of Aunt Agnes and she set a good pace by treating me just like one of the gang with no favoritism. By the time I left there three months later, I'm pleased to be able to say, I was one of the best liked kids in the school.

At that time being a celebrity in Hollywood was nothing as the town was filled with them and you could walk down Hollywood Boulevard and be almost ignored. But being a hometown celebrity, back visiting in that town, was completely different.

When I walked down the main streets of New Haven people respectfully stepped aside to let us pass. They were friendly but their reaction at seeing a well-known Hollywood face was far removed from what I had been used to.

My family had a friend named Eddie Quinn who had gone to school with my uncle Joe Close, Aunt Agnes's husband. Eddie had been a goalie on the New Haven Eagles, the local ice hockey team that was a farm club for the New York Rangers. Eddie was at our house frequently and one night he asked me if I would like to see a hockey game. I jumped at the offer as I had never seen a real hockey game and was just learning to skate on shaky ankles at a lake near our house. Eddie not only took me to the game; he also brought me into the Eagles' dressing room where he was still popular. He introduced me to the coach and all the players. Most of them were Canadians and I liked them immediately. From that night on Eddie took me to every game when the Eagles were in town. I became a favorite with the team and ended up sitting on the bench with them as a kind of mascot.

I'll never forget one night the Eagles were playing the team from Providence, Rhode Island, and a fight broke out on the ice. There are frequent little personal clashes between individual players but this was one that cleared both benches. The fight started right in front of the Eagles' bench. The Providence players tore across the ice and soon both teams were throwing punches and swinging hockey sticks and I was right in the middle of it. I stood up on the bench and was shouting encouragement for my friends on the Eagles. The fracas went on for several minutes and finally a big policeman grabbed me around the waist and carried me up to where our family was sitting. I think that was the most exciting thing that had ever happened to me up to that point in my life and I loved every minute of it.

While we were visiting in New Haven, mother and I made a few trips into New York. We didn't have a car with us so we'd take the 90-minute ride on the New York, New Haven, and Hartford Railroad. I loved that ride. The Connecticut countryside was beautiful and I especially liked the entry into New York City. The train was on elevated tracks there and you could look right into the windows of the brick tenements as we passed by. New

York Central Station was a real thrill to me with its immense size and people hurrying in every direction. The subways were also exciting and we had to learn to step quickly or be left standing on the platform.

My good friend Mitzi Green was in New York at that time making a personal appearance at the Palace Theater and we went backstage to visit her and her mother Rosie. I had made personal appearances with my pictures many times, but this was the Palace, the top theater in all of vaudeville. I had appeared at the Orpheum Theater and Lowes State Theater in Los Angeles and also theaters in San Francisco and San Diego, but nowhere to match the quality of the acts that "played the Palace"—the very cream of the crop.

Backstage with Mitzi I met a brash 22-year-old comic named Milton Berle and also Leon Errol, who did a hilarious, rubber-legged, drunken act with unbelievable movements as he lurched and tripped across stage and up a flight of stairs. Milton Berle and I have had a friendly acquaintance through the years and about six years later I had the pleasure of playing Leon Errol's son in some of the two-reel comedies he made at RKO.

That night Mitzi's mother and father took Mitzi and me and my mother to a Broadway nightclub. It was during Prohibition and no liquor was served or I guess Mitzi and I would not have been admitted.

In the floor show that night I saw my first bare-breasted chorus girls and also my first female impersonator. He was a big man, a transvestite I imagine, and he was wearing a gorgeous formal gown and was painted and padded in the proper places and sang in a fine contralto voice. His name was Jackie May and the Greens invited him, her, or it, over to our table at the finish of his act.

The chorus girls were beautiful and I suppose I was staring wide-eyed and open-mouthed at their jiggling breasts. I must have been, because I remember Mitzi's father, Joe Green, leaned over to me and, with a smile on his face, whispered in my ear, "Can you hear all right Junior?"

22

The Panama Canal

Mother gave me a pleasant surprise on our return trip to Los Angeles when she booked passage for us on the SS *Pennsylvania* of the Panama Pacific Line for a two-week cruise home through the Panama Canal.

This pleasure cruise was quite a luxury for us, especially as I was now off salary. To save money, mother had us billeted in economy class and we shared our cabins with others. The ship's purser did a nice job for us as he placed mother in a stateroom with two schoolteachers and I shared a cabin with two Catholic priests.

I was recognized by just about everyone on board and got along great with the other passengers and the crew. The ship's printer took an exceptional liking to me and made me welcome in his print shop. It was on the deck even with the waterline in the forwardmost part of the ship. There he printed all the ship's announcements and the three daily menus among other things.

I was down visiting him on the second day out as we were passing the Carolina coast. It was very rough and his shop was extremely warm as he could not open his porthole due to the heavy seas. I had been a fine sailor during the six weeks at sea during the filming of *The Yankee Clipper* and had no fear of seasickness. However, the combination of the rough sea and the extreme heat in the print shop started to get to me and soon I began to feel nausea coming on. I ran up on deck and just made it to the rail in time to part with my lunch. Unfortunately, the attack hit me so fast I didn't have time to remove my orthodontic retainer plate and it went over the side with all that was in my stomach. As my printer friend later said, I not only fed the fishes, I gave them a plate to eat it on.

Our first port of call was Havana, Cuba, and believe me, Havana in 1930 was a beautiful city to visit. Its wide boulevards were lined with well-constructed buildings and spectacular monuments and graceful statues were everywhere.

One interesting sight to me was a tour through Morro Castle, the fort built in the sixteenth century by the Spaniards as protection from the

French, English, and Dutch buccaneers of the period. It was later used as a prison and fired its guns for the last time during the Spanish-American War. Morro Castle overlooks the entrance to Havana's harbor and from their vantage point its gunners must have made the early invaders pay dearly.

Next we went to what was then Havana's most famous tourist attraction, a bar called Sloppy Joe's. There mother had one of its famous rum creations while I had something tall, cool, sweet, very fruity, and, of course, nonalcoholic.

Outside the bar was another of Havana's oddities, a man who could blow smoke out of his ears. That is no joke. I saw him do it and even took a picture of him performing his claim to fame. This fellow, for a fee of course, would take a deep drag on a cigarette, inhale it, then hold his nose and soon smoke would emit in a billowing stream out of both of his ears. With all you read about the dangers of smoking these days, I wonder if this poor fellow finally died of cancer of the eustachian tubes?

The next interesting event was our passage through the Panama Canal. Early one morning halfway through the cruise our ship was standing off the cities of Colón and Cristóbal on the Atlantic side of the Canal Zone. The *Pennsylvania* made its way slowly to the Gatun Locks where two vehicles called "mules" were hooked to us by cables to pull us into the three sets of locks where we were raised 85 feet for our passage through Gatun Lake. After a few hours we came to the Pedro Miguel Locks where we were lowered 31 feet and then to the Miraflores Locks to drop another 54 feet to the level of the Pacific Ocean where we went ashore to see Panama City.

Mother and I rented a car for sightseeing and shopping. While we were cruising through the city, I was spotted by some of the natives and soon a group of them began following our car and shouting my name out loud. Finally, there were about 50 of them and they began banging on the windows of our car and it became very frightening. Eventually, some motorcycle police came alongside and escorted us through the city and back to our ship. Thank heaven the natives were friendly!

That evening we ventured back into the city for dinner and to see the floor show at the leading nightclub of the city, Panama Hattie's. We had a fine dinner and the show was excellent with lots of exciting South American music and singing and dancing.

At the close of the entertainment the show's leading lady came to our table and took me by the hand, leading me to the center of the floor where she invited me to dance with her. The 14-year-old Junior was a lousy ballroom dancer, but she was so good and led me so well that she kept me from making a fool of myself. I decided right then and there that I had to take dancing lessons, but that will be a later story.

One night after the Canal passage the ship held a costume ball. Mother decked me out in an outrageous getup consisting mainly of an attractive Spanish shawl she had bought in Panama City. She draped it around me and covered my hair with a smaller matching kerchief she had bought with the shawl, giving me a sort of gypsy dancer appearance. Under it she put one of her bras on me (they called them brassieres in those days), and padded me seductively with many sheets of toilet tissue. She borrowed a pair of high-heeled shoes that fit me from one of her schoolteacher roommates and, of course, painted me up with lipstick, rouge, and eye makeup to go along with the charade. A pair of dangling earrings and a long cigarette holder completed the illusion.

At the judging ceremony I hammed it up a bit, winking at the male judges, kissing the lady judges, and then sitting on the captain's lap. Would you believe it, I won first prize for the most original costume and still have the trophy to prove it.

The rest of the cruise was uneventful and we docked at the port of Los Angeles 14 days after our departure from New York Harbor.

23

Dialogue and Crying

When I am invited to film festivals around the country I am frequently asked by fans, "Did you have to memorize lines when you worked in silent films?" Strangely enough, the answer is yes. We had a script and were supposed to follow it as closely as we could because if we said something far afield from what the titles later said on the screen it looked ridiculous. If we missed a word or two it usually did not cause the director to demand a second take like it does today in talking films. Now a single word of deviation will cause another take if the story line is broken.

When you see the credits on a silent film you will see that recognition is given to a writer, or team of writers, for the screenplay and then a different writer receives credits for the titles. When the picture is all completed and leaves the cutting room, then the title writer goes to work. There would be no point in him writing titles for scenes that were later deleted.

I remember a scene in *The Yankee Clipper* where I enter the cabin of Lady Jocelyn after she was caught on board our ship at the start of the race from Foo Chow Harbor to Boston. She had just been seen stepping out of the hoop skirt petticoat she was wearing beneath her outer dress. I see that she is uncomfortable and I ask her, "Why don't you wear pants like a man?" She answers, "I haven't any." Then I start to untie the rope I am wearing for a belt and say, "I can loan you mine." She then says in mock embarrassment, "I'm afraid they wouldn't fit." I then say, "Aw, wimmin ain't got no sense" and walk out of the room. In viewing this film now you can see that the title writer followed our spoken words precisely as it is obvious that our lips are saying exactly what the titles indicate.

On another occasion, in *Rubber Tires,* Harrison Ford sees our car broken down at the side of the road. He parks his car and runs across the highway to see if we need help. It was a long shot and you could not really see what he was saying to us. I presume our director Alan Hale told him to just ad-lib a greeting to us, so I remember he came up to us and said, "Geef geef geef. Geef geef geef. Geef geef geef." The camera didn't know the difference and no harm was done. However, in the close-up that followed, he had some printed words to say and he read them as written.

Any kid actor who gained a foothold on the ladder was able to cry when required. Some admit that it was difficult at times, but most of us could work up the emotions and the tears would flow. Of course, there were some days when scene after scene and take after take caused any good child actor to become cried out and emotionally drained. Those kind of days were tough and to be emotionally tired is really something all to itself.

Crying was easier in the silent days because any film of importance had what was called "mood music" on the set. This was usually a small musical group who played music in keeping with the theme of the scene. At our studio we usually had a trio consisting of an organ, a violin, and a cello. Later we had a trio that featured an accordion. Our accordionist was Frank Yaconelli who later went on to be a comedian in many western films.

The song that made crying easiest for me was the sorrowful ballad, "Boy of Mine." After Al Jolson made his first talking feature, *The Jazz Singer*, I began using the sad song he sang in that film, "Sonny Boy."

Some directors were easier to cry for than others and it also was easier for me to cry with certain actors than with some others. I had scenes with William Boyd in *The Yankee Clipper*, Rudolph Schildkraut in *The Country Doctor* and *A Harp in Hock*, William Haines in *Slide, Kelly, Slide,* Louis Wolheim in *Square Shoulders,* and Charles Bickford in *River's End* where I broke up the whole set with my tears.

Michael Curtiz, who directed *River's End,* was known as a hard, sometimes crude, and often profane tyrant on the set. Yet in certain scenes with me in *River's End* he was as tender as any director I ever worked for. This film was a talking picture so "mood music" was out of the question. Also, I was now 14 years old and tears were more difficult to produce.

I won the role in *River's End* after a demanding screen test. I say demanding because it was my first screen appearance after about a six-month layoff and I was at Warner Brothers where the first talking films were made. They were real professionals with sound and the days of the camera crew being encased in a small booth were over.

I was at a studio that was new for me with a crew and director I had never met before. The scene selected for my test was one I would later play with Charles Bickford. During this test Michael Curtiz was standing beside the camera reading the lines that Bickford was supposed to be saying. If you didn't know, Curtiz had a thick Austrian accent and it was difficult for me to even understand him, much less react to his words.

It was a large head close-up of me in one of the most emotional scenes in the film where I accuse Bickford of being a liar and I was supposed to burst out in tears as I raged at him at the scene's conclusion.

Despite the difficulty I had in reacting to Curtiz with his funny rendition of Bickford's lines, by the end of the scene I was sobbing and Mike Curtiz was very much impressed and I won the role.

With Charles Bickford in *River's End* for Warner Brothers in 1930. It was my first talkie.

When this scene was actually filmed with Charles Bickford and myself working together, the seriousness of the situation really dug into me, and with the responsive help that Charles Bickford's compassionate performance was giving me, I ended up completely sobbing with tears running down my cheeks.

When the scene was over it was obvious that Curtiz was pleased as he nearly shouted, "Cut. Print it," which was the signal to all that the scene was perfect as far as he was concerned. Then Bickford put his arms around me and I finished the sobbing with my face crushed to his chest. As Bickford held me, he whispered in my ear, "That was great kid, just great." My mother later told me that she heard Curtiz say to one of his assistants, "God that kid is good. He can cry quarts on demand."

"Crying quarts" was a compliment assigned to many fine kid actors. I have enjoyed watching Jackie Coogan, Jackie Cooper, Mickey Rooney, Shirley Temple, Frankie Darro, Bobs Watson, and a few other kid performers just wring your heart out with their tears and great emotional expressions. I'm happy to say many connected with the film industry add Junior Coghlan to that exclusive list.

In *Let 'er Go Gallegher* Elinor Fair and I cry over our fears of what is to happen to the cocky reporter played by Harrison Ford.

While children could usually cry with relative ease, it was tougher for the adult performers. We all have seen films where the great actresses and a few of the male actors produced tears. I have worked in films where I witnessed adults resorting to tricks to bring tears to their eyes.

Gladys Brockwell, who played my mother in four films, was a remarkably fine actress, but I have worked with her on days when her proficient tear ducts became dried out and could produce no more. On these occasions she would resort to artificial means. She had a menthol inhaler rigged up with a rubber tube and just before the scene was to start she would blow the stinging menthol fumes into her eyes. Needless to say, in just a few seconds moisture would be flowing because of the irritation to her eyes. But with her acting ability these tears were soon followed by some of her own and the audience was never to know.

Another and just as painful trick that could produce copious tears was the placing of pure glycerin into the eye by use of a dropper. I tried both this and the menthol fumes to see what these performers were going through and believe me, it smarted. In later years every good propman had a menthol blower and an eye drop bottle filled with glycerin in his prop wagon just in case of emergency.

I remember another crying trick that I observed, but I'm happy to say I only saw it used once. In *Slide, Kelly, Slide* there was a scene in which certain of the baseball players had close-ups to show their reaction when they heard that their batboy (me) was near death.

William Haines, Harry Carey, and Guinn "Big Boy" Williams cried on their own with the help of the menthol blower, but Karl Dane had his own method. This giant of a comedian, who had such a great role in *The Big Parade* and then made a series of feature length comedies with George K. Arthur, had probably never been asked to cry in a scene before.

Just prior to his close-up he went over to the nearest and brightest klieg light on the set and stared into it. Soon his eyes were brimming with moisture and due to this cruel irritation he continued to produce tears for the length of his close-up and for several minutes after.

This was really crying the hard way because many actors suffered what became known as "klieg eyes" just from working near them. The unnatural rays created by these mercury lamps proved harmful to some people's eyes and they were banned from the business when improved arc and later incandescent filament lights were introduced.

24

Talkies and Agents

Now a completely new and different period in my career started. After having been a contract player at the same studio for five years and having achieved stardom in silent feature films, I was now an unemployed juvenile actor in a business turned exclusively to talking films with the demanding requirement to speak your lines and not rely on the printed title to get the dialogue over to the viewing audience.

As I mentioned earlier, adolescent voices were hard to record with the still primitive sound equipment and kid actors had a difficult time in the early days of talking movies.

I remember the first interview I went to for an all talking motion picture. It was at Paramount and the producer handed me a script and said, "All right Junior, read this for me." I'm afraid I didn't do very well on the reading as I didn't get the part. This made me realize that it was a whole new ballgame from the old silent days.

I began checking out plays from the library and reading them aloud so I could get the proper feeling into the lines. Also we discovered that after being at the same studio for five years, without any worries about being cast in coming films, it was now imperative to have an agent to be properly represented at all the studios.

Very few actors had agents in the silent era, but now, especially for freelance players, an agent was a must. Selecting the right agent is very important. There are the big ones like William Morris and later MCA, and now GCA, CAA, and ICM who won't even talk to you unless you are a big, established star. There are little agents who will take almost anyone they can get, but they usually have no bargaining power and can't get their clients seen by important producers.

We wanted to sign with a hardworking representative who was not too big but still had some clout in the studios. Louis B. Mayer's brother, Jerry Mayer, was forming a new agency with a good list of experienced performers and he was eager to add me to his "stable" as he didn't have any kid players. He had a hardworking, fast-talking leg man named Sol Solinger who was to have an effect on my career for years to come. The sad thing that we didn't learn for several years was that Louis B. Mayer wasn't even speaking to his brother Jerry because of some family feud and what we thought was a great entrée to MGM was in reality a closed door. In spite of this unexpected glitch at MGM, Jerry Mayer soon had me working in important roles at other studios.

The first good part he steered me to was playing the orphan kid in *River's End* at Warner Brothers. I mentioned earlier about testing for this part with director Michael Curtiz and of some of my fine scenes with its star Charles Bickford. The leading lady in *River's End* was the lovely Evalyn Knapp. The rest of the fine cast included ZaSu Pitts, J. Farrell MacDonald, David Torrence, Walter McGrail, and Tom Santschi.

This film was a memorable experience for me and we went on location to the Sacramento River where we filmed for two weeks along the river and on an old side-paddle-wheeler riverboat on what was supposed to be the Yukon River in Canada. In *River's End* Charles Bickford played the dual role of a Northwest mounted policeman and his lookalike who was a desperate criminal.

I returned to Warner Brothers later that year where I had the pleasure and real distinction of playing Sam in Booth Tarkington's classic book, *Penrod and Sam.* Leon Janney played Penrod and we remained friends through the years until his death in retirement in Guadalajara, Mexico, in 1980.

Leon was a very talented young actor and entertainer and had a mother who was the role model of a studio mother. She was really a warm and thoughtful person, but boy, did she ever push Leon toward her demanding goal of stardom and complete perfection in every detail!

The first time I ever met them was years before *Penrod and Sam.* He was then using the screen name of Leon (always pronounced Lay-on) Ramon. She had a rear tire cover on the back of their sedan with his name painted on it in letters six inches tall and she forced the poor kid to kneel on the back seat facing to the rear, smiling and waving out of the back window as she drove in traffic. He later told me she had chosen Ramon because at that time Latin names were in favor, but with the demise of Rudolph Valentino and Ramon Navarro she resorted back to the family name of Janney.

Leon's mother was very Jewish, but I don't know about his father whom I never met since they had long been divorced. Leon told me his paternal grandfather was the inventor of the Janney coupler, once used to connect every railroad car in the nation, so I suppose there was lots of money at one time, but Leon and his mother were flat broke until Leon finally hit it big in the 1930s.

Penrod had been produced by First National—the forerunner to Warner Brothers—in the early 1920s and starring Wesley Barry. *Penrod*

With Leon Janney in *Penrod and Sam* for Warner Brothers in 1931. Leon Janney played Penrod and I was Sam.

and Sam was produced by First National in 1925, starring Ben Alexander as Penrod and Joe Butterworth as Sam. Ben went on for years, finally ending up as Jack Webb's sidekick in the popular "Dragnet" series on television where Webb played the laconic Sergeant Friday, of "Just give me the facts, ma'am," fame. (After Ben died, Harry Morgan took over his role.)

William Beaudine directed our *Penrod and Sam* and had also directed the Ben Alexander version. Beaudine went on working for years and ended up directing most of the "Lassie" television series in the 1960s.

Bill Beaudine, Jr., was too young to be associated with *Penrod and Sam* but he broke into the movies on the production side at an early age and joined his father on the "Lassie" series where he shared coproducer status with Bonita Granville Wrather whose husband Jack Wrather now owned the rights to "Lassie."

I met a group of kid actors on *Penrod and Sam* who became my friends for years. One was George Vierra who went on to become a director of television commercials for Filmways. George later married an old girlfriend of mine, Ruby Keeler's youngest sister Margie.

Penrod and Sam was also the first film for Sidney Miller, who became a good friend, and we worked together many times later—including *The Little Red Schoolhouse* and my pal in the entire series of comedies I made for Educational called *The Frolics of Youth,* of which I will write about later in greater detail. Sid was also with me in *Men of Boys Town,* the serial *Scouts to the Rescue* with Jackie Cooper, in some of the *Henry Aldrich* films, and again with Mickey Rooney and me in four of the *Andy Hardy* series. Sid also wrote songs with Rooney, but is probably best remembered from the many television skits he did with Donald O'Connor where Sid was the zany songwriter.

The sissy in *Penrod and Sam,* Georgie Bassett, was Billy Lord and the bully, Rodney Bitts, was Nestor Aber. Nestor was really a nice guy but he could play with such an arrogant manner that you just loved to hate him. One very funny thing happened in a scene I played in with poor Nestor. I was supposed to deck him in a fight and though I had been in many film fights and could fake a knockout punch as well as anyone, in this particular scene I hit Nestor flush on the jaw with all my might and he really went down in a heap. I looked down at him and though I was sorry for what I had done accidentally, I just couldn't help bursting out laughing. Director Bill Beaudine was furious at me and shouted, "Why in hell did you laugh? You just ruined the scene." I apologized to him and Nestor, but my reaction to the poor guy lying there just broke me up.

There was a great group of adult parents in the film. Penrod's folks were Matt Moore, one of the three Moore brothers (Tom, Matt, and Owen) and his mother was Dorothy Peterson. My father was played by the good character actor Wade Boteler, who had worked with me in *Let 'er Go Gallegher.* Rodney's father was Charles Sellon and Georgie's folks were the great comedy team of ZaSu Pitts and Johnny Arthur. William Beaudine's daughter Helen made her screen debut playing Penrod's sister and Beaudine's nephew Bill Anderson was one of our gang members. A real family effort.

Margaret Marquis was the girl who both Penrod and I were in love with. There was a fight scene at a party where Penrod and I got into a knockdown fight when our jealousy over her came to a boil. I hit Penrod back into a large stuffed chair and then charged into him. My drive made the chair fall over backward and we both landed in a heap on the floor. As I landed on top of him I whispered, "Are you all right?" When he whispered back that he was, the staged fight went on to its conclusion. Beaudine was pleased with the fight which we completed in one take and our concerned whispers were not picked up by the microphones.

An assistant director on the picture raised wire-haired fox terriers and one day brought a litter of his puppies to the set. I bought a male which I named Sam and Leon also purchased one which he naturally named Penrod.

Leon's movie career waned in the late 1930s and he and his mother moved to New York where he worked in several stage plays and became a real mainstay on many radio serials. He had a well-modulated voice and could play all ages and was very good with foreign accents. By disguising his voice he was able to be heard for years as the spokesman for many products in radio commercials.

I think Leon was married four times and I know he had a son named Donny from his first marriage. I don't think he was really a communist but he was a very outspoken liberal and for years was an executive in the New York branch of our Screen Actors Guild. My wife and I visited with him in New York in 1953 while I was stationed in the Pentagon. At that time he tried to describe his short stretch in the army during World War II. As best I could make out his story, he was discharged honorably "for the good of the service" due to his political beliefs.

The last time we met was in the 1970s at a large, joint meeting of all the Screen Actors Guild boards where he was a member of the New York delegation. At the close of the meeting I sought him out and he introduced me to his present wife. She was a lovely lady of his age, or maybe a few years older, and I got the impression she was a lady of great wealth. He told me she was to enter the hospital on their return to New York for her second operation for spinal disk problems and she was in great pain when we met.

I assume they moved to Guadalajara for climatic reasons for her condition. I hope they enjoyed their life there and I was really shocked to read of his passing in 1980. It seems so unlikely that Leon could ever really appreciate life away from the glamor of show business, but I hope he did. I'll bet he really kept things lively in the American retirement community down there before he cashed in his chips.

25

I Move to a New School

I always attended public schools through the years and my education was augmented by a tutor on the set while making a movie. I previously related the problems due to my father's drinking and he never lived with us again after that awful night he chased us down the stairs from our Hollywood apartment while he was naked as a jaybird. After our return from the visit to New Haven, Mother and I moved into a neat little house up in the Hollywood Hills and I went back to Le Conte Junior High School for my final year where I graduated with the class of winter 1931. I'm pleased to report that I was elected president of our graduating class and also played the lead in our senior class play which my homeroom teacher Miss Keefauver wrote and directed with me especially in mind. This was a smashing way for me to leave Le Conte and I was looking forward to moving on to Hollywood High School with my classmates. Then an unexpected turn of events occurred that really changed my life.

In 1929 Mother made what seemed like a good move for my financial future. She put $8,500 down on a four-family apartment building in the Fairfax district which was then very sparsely built up and seemed like a budding community in which to own property. The total price of the building was $19,500. The two upstairs apartments rented for $60 each and the lower two flats for $55. Interest in those days was only 6 percent and after making the payment and paying the low taxes of those days there was a net profit of $120 a month, which was not bad extra income in those days.

After the stock market crash of 1929, however, with the depression setting in, by the time I graduated from Le Conte the rents on the four apartments were down to $25 each and some of the tenants were falling badly in arrears even at that low rental rate. My mother was a real patsy and just couldn't bring herself around to evicting anyone and two of the tenants fell over a year behind in their payments. Now we weren't even taking in enough to make the mortgage payment and it became necessary for us to give up our nice home in the hills and move into one of our apartments when there was a vacancy. As a result, I then transferred to Fairfax High School and had to fit in with an entirely new group of schoolmates.

I liked the kids at Fairfax and got along real well with them. I went out for athletics and joined the Class C football and track teams. I was the second-string halfback in my first year of football and in track I ran the 50-yard dash, the 120-yard low hurdles, and was a member of the four-man, 200-yard relay team.

One of the first films I made in 1932 was *Hell's House* for Bennie Ziedman Productions. I played a reform school inmate with a bad heart and died in the movie due to mistreatment from the cruel reform school guards.

Hell's House was a notable film for three newcomers to motion pictures. Top billing was enjoyed by a fine young actor, Junior Durkin, who came to Hollywood from the New York stage. Billed second was a new leading man, also from the New York stage, named Pat O'Brien. Next came a young 25-year-old actress making her third film. Her name was Bette Davis. Junior Coghlan was billed fourth.

Years later when I was playing a four-day bit in *The Man Who Came to Dinner* I waited to see how Miss Davis, then the reigning star at Warner Brothers, would receive me. She remembered me and was friendly, so on my final day on the picture I brought the press book from *Hell's House* to the set. She laughed that I had once been billed equal to her and showed the press book to our director William Keighley and to Monty Wooley and others on the set. Then she had the publicity man bring a beautiful 11″ × 14″ matte finish portrait to the set which she cheerfully autographed for me.

I now own a videocassette of *Hell's House* released in 1981 by Video Yesterday. It is interesting to see that they have redone the opening titles. It now shows Bette Davis's and Pat O'Brien's names over the film's title. The two Juniors, Durkin and Coghlan, follow in that order. That's show biz.

In mentioning Junior Durkin and Pat O'Brien from *Hell's House,* I feel I should mention Junior Durkin's tragic death. He was killed in a terrible auto accident that also claimed the lives of Jackie Coogan's father, actor Robert Horner, and a ranch hand from the Coogan's ranch. Jackie Coogan was the only survivor. Jackie and Junior had just completed playing the lead roles in *Tom Sawyer and Huckleberry Finn* together and were returning from a few days at the ranch when tragedy struck.

I have happier memories of Pat O'Brien. He and his lovely wife Eloise were friends of mine through the years. I later worked in two more films with Pat. They were *Angels with Dirty Faces* and *The Fighting 69th.* Both were made at Warner Brothers and the jovial Irishman O'Brien played a Catholic priest in both of them.

26

Public Enemy and Frankie Darro

I was next interviewed by director William A. Wellman at Warner Brothers for playing the role of James Cagney's character as a boy in one of his best films, *Public Enemy*. These interviews went on for days and finally I was chosen to play the young Cagney and Frankie Darro to play Edward Woods as a boy.

This sequence is a type of a prologue. It runs for 12 minutes and shows how Cagney and Woods are lured into the life of crime by Murray Kinnell who played the nefarious character "Putty Nose." He owned a pool hall and encouraged the young toughs to steal for him and he would then buy and fence the stolen objects.

This was a very graphic part of the film but unfortunately is often cut when the movie runs on television. This is so it will run within the two-hour time slot demanded by the networks after they have added the sponsors' commercials to pay for the air time.

After the final interview, Darro and I were selected to play the parts and were sent to wardrobe to be fitted for the clothes we were to wear in this film set in the Prohibition days of the 1920s. In the fitting room, the brash 14-year-old Darro asked in his usual demeaning way, "Say kid, do you drive a car?"

When I said I did, he then told me he had a date with two girls that night and asked if I could meet him at the Marcal Theater at 8:00 P.M. to help him with one of them.

Our parts were not to start for a couple of weeks and I didn't have an early call in the morning so I saw no objection to meeting him. Then I had to confess that I did drive but my mother still didn't let me take the car out alone at night.

I told him my mother would drop me off and pick me up later if that was all right. He said that was okay if that was the best I could do and told me to meet him in the double loge section of the theater.

The show was just starting as I walked down the aisle and I spotted Frankie sitting between two teenage girls in one of the double loges. I worked my way across to them and Frankie moved over to the next loge telling me to take his place between the two girls. He made the introductions and we had small talk until the theater was completely dark and the show got underway.

A few minutes later, as if by signal, each girl took my arm closest to her and put it around her shoulder and shoved my hand down inside the top of her dress.

To my amazement, for the first time in my life, my hands were fondling bare female breasts. Not one, but one in each hand. I looked in surprise at both girls and they just smiled at me like nothing unusual was happening.

A minute or so later, again as if by signal, the girls began unbuckling the belt on my trousers. This was such a new and different experience for me and my discomfort was so obvious that Darro broke out laughing. This caused an usher to come down the aisle to see what the noise was all about. His presence caused the girls to stop their probing. They removed my arms from their shoulders and one girl slid over into the other loge with Frankie. The usher reappeared several times so there were no more unusual activities for the rest of the show. When the lights came up I bid an embarrassed farewell and went out front where my mother was waiting for me.

A few days later our parts had still not started and Mother let me take the car into Hollywood to pick up something for her. I was only a few blocks from the apartment where Frankie lived, so I thought I'd drop in on him to ask why he had set me up like he did at the theater. I knocked on the door and Darro opened it wearing the most unforgettable outfit I have still ever seen.

He was stark naked and on his head, like it was a beret, he was wearing a girl's pair of silk panties. He also had a gigantic erection over which he had draped a bath towel which hung suspended there, reaching down to his knees on each side.

I looked over his shoulder and behind him on the sofa was one of the girls from the theater. She was completely nude and didn't seem to mind my seeing her that way as she smiled and waved to me. This little domestic scene was too much for me so I bid a hasty retreat, leaving them to return to their interrupted activities.

Our work on *Public Enemy* began a few days later and, due to crowded conditions at Warner Brothers, they assigned Frankie and me to share a dressing room. It was large enough and had a mirrored makeup table, a closet, and a single sink with running water.

Dressing rooms for supporting players were not too plush in those days and these sinks were too often used for others reasons by male actors who were too lazy to walk down the hall to the restroom. Our sink, like those of many other male studio dressing rooms, had a strong odor of urine and I hardly ever used them.

I will write more about Frankie Darro in following chapters.

Production continued on *Public Enemy* under the direction of William A. Wellman.

This unusual man had the nickname of "Wild Bill," which was pinned on him while he was a World War I fighter pilot in the Lafayette Escadrille, the elite group of American aviators who flew under the French flag before our U.S. Army Air Corps was formed.

I believe his nickname was earned because of his daring exploits in the air and from his equally foolhardy antics at the squadron bar after the fighter planes were in the hangar for the night.

Wellman was credited with being an ace with this group and the wartime experience gained there stood him in good stead when he later directed the blockbuster aviation film *Wings.*

He broke into motion pictures as a juvenile actor working in *The Knickerbocker Buckeroo* with Douglas Fairbanks in 1915. From that single acting role he knew he wanted to be a director. He then went to work for the Fox company as a property man and worked himself up to the position of assistant director in a period of four years. B. P. Schulberg, then producing independently for Paramount, gave him his first opportunity to direct.

This multitalented man also directed such diverse films as *So Big* with Barbara Stanwyck and *The Call of the Wild* with Clark Gable, Loretta Young, and Jack Oakie. In 1937 he wrote and directed the first, and I think by far the best, production of *A Star Is Born.* This was the version that starred Janet Gaynor and Fredric March, for which Wellman won the Academy Award for his collaboration on the original story.

Wellman had a way of looking right through you, with one eyebrow cocked, as he directed, yet at times he could be very tender. In many ways he reminded me of my early days director hero, Marshall "Mickey" Neilan.

Jean Harlow and Joan Blondell had memorable roles in *Public Enemy* as did Mae Clarke in the never-to-be-forgotten scene where she took half a grapefruit to the side of her face when Cagney was tiring of her as his girlfriend.

Our long-suffering mother (Cagney's and mine) was played by the marvelous actress Beryl Mercer and Leslie Fenton was the gangster chief "Nails" Nathan. Fenton played many fine roles after this and went into directing; I later worked for him at MGM.

Because many of the sets used in the early part of the film were also seen in later sequences, on several occasions James Cagney and Edward Woods were on the set, waiting in the wings until Frankie Darro and I vacated the set so they could step in and use it.

James Cagney seemed to like the way I was playing him as a boy and he would cheer me on as he watched me. He would talk to me between scenes and give me tips on his mannerisms so that I could portray him better.

There was one sequence in the early part of *Public Enemey* where Frankie and I went into a big department store to do some shoplifting. For these scenes Warner Brothers rented the Broadway Department Store on a Sunday when it was closed and filled it with their own players as clerks and customers.

There was one funny scene, after we had stolen some goods, where we were trapped at the elevators by the floorwalker. The only escape route open to us was to slide down the area between the up and down escalators. As I led Frankie down the slide, a man wearing a high silk hat started ascending the up escalator. Frankie made quick work of that hat, slapping it off his head as he slid past the startled man.

There is another of these early scenes that I enjoy watching again. That is where my father, a hardworking and honest Chicago cop, finds out I have been stealing. He calls me into the house and goes to the kitchen, takes down his trusty razor strop, and leads me into the bedroom to deliver his usual beating to the seat of my pants. As he sits down on the bed, I stand in front of him and say in real defiance as I start to undo my belt, "How do you want them this time? Up or down?" With that he grabs me and throws me across his lap and starts to administer his best-known form of punishment.

The camera then dollies in to a big close-up of my face as I take each whack, wincing at every blow, but never letting him know how much the beating is hurting me.

Public Enemy began a long-standing friendship between me and the Cagney family. They were a very closely knit group and many of them used to visit the set and watch brother Jim perform.

His lovely sister Jeanne was on the set often and I developed quite a crush on her. She gave me her telephone number and we talked on the phone many times. Though I wanted to, I just never had the nerve to ask her for a date. I was mainly afraid that Jimmy would think I was just using her to gain favor with him. This was a big mistake because Jeanne was my age and she told me a few years later that she was waiting for me to ask her out.

Jeanne was a fine actress in her own right and played Jimmy's real sister when he took the role of George M. Cohan in *Yankee Doodle Dandy*. Between 1960 and 1965 when I was in charge of the navy's Hollywood office, there were several occasions where I had wives of navy men on the show "Queen for a Day." She was the cohostess on the show with its longtime master of ceremonies, Jack Bailey.

We would always have pleasant chats before and after the show and it made me realize what a jerk I was for not getting to know this lovely lady better when I had the chance.

She was then married to a college professor and had two daughters. I was saddened a few years ago to read that she passed away due to cancer.

27

Racetrack

Later in 1932 I was cast to play a jockey for the first time. It was in a film called *Racetrack*, starring Leo Carrillo and produced and directed by James Cruze. At that time he had his own company, James Cruze Productions, and he released through World Wide Pictures.

Leo Carrillo was quite a guy. He was a well-known New York stage actor before coming to Hollywood where he made his first movie in 1929. He played in many important films after *Racetrack*, including *Viva Villa*, and was seen in many of these pictures as a lovable Mexican. This he really was, as his descendants came to Mexico as part of the invading army with Cortés in 1546.

One of his forebears was the first provisional governor of the state of California when it was taken from Mexico by the U.S. government. At one time his family owned vast land grants here and he proudly claimed to be the fifth generation of his family to be born in Los Angeles. The beach that I used to frequent when in high school is now called Leo Carrillo State Beach.

He was one actor who never let dust gather on his feet and between films he took many plays on the road where he was always the star and had a good following around the country.

James Cruze was truly a dynamic director. He broke into show business as a juvenile actor playing in medicine shows and stock companies, including Shakespearean productions. His directing credits before *Racetrack* were impressive.

For Paramount he had directed *Merton of the Movies*, *Ruggles of Red Gap*, *Pony Express*, *Old Ironsides*, and one of the greatest westerns ever made, *The Covered Wagon*. After our film he directed many more, the most noted being *David Harum* for Fox which starred Will Rogers. In 1926 and 1928 he was listed as one of the ten best directors in nationwide polls.

Cruze had a very unusual way of directing that must have driven film editors up the wall. When he handed them a completed scene there was nothing they could do but assemble it as he had shot it. They had absolutely no way to add their own creative touch. Here is the explanation.

In a typical "four shot" (four people sitting or standing while they conversed) most directors would shoot the scene in its entirety from a camera set up far enough back to include all four actors in the frame. Then he would move in for a "two shot" of one pair and most likely again repeat the entire scene. This would be repeated again with the other couple. Now he would shoot individual close-ups he felt were needed. He would order all scenes printed and send these combinations of takes to the film editor to assemble as he thought best.

Cruze did not work that way. He would line the four people up for the long shot and commence the scene. To everyone's surprise he would most likely yell cut at the conclusion of the second or third line of dialogue. Next he would resume the scene commencing with the final line or two of speech. That was all the film editor was ever going to see of the long shot of the four people.

Now Cruze would move in on one pair and have them read the part of the scene he wanted them to cover. While there he would do his close-ups of each actor of that pair, maybe giving each only one or two lines of dialogue. Next he would turn to the other couple and have them perform the portions of the scene in which he wanted them to be featured. He would again shoot the individual close-ups he wanted from that pair and then move on to the next scene.

The film editor would receive the opening and closing of the four shot, only certain lines on each couple in the two shots and the other lines that were covered in the individual separate close-ups. The only way the film editor could end up with a complete scene was to splice it together exactly as James Cruze wanted it to be. He must have saved lots of money on film not expended and in printing costs over the other, more normal form of production.

Cruze was a very homely man with large features and a particularly wide mouth. I remember seeing one cartoon of him where he was depicted as one of the gargoyles on Notre Dame Cathedral in Paris. I had heard stories about what a hard-fisted director he was and maybe on such big epics like *Old Ironsides* and *The Covered Wagon* he had to rule the set like a tyrant, but on our little picture he was a pussycat. He had one "set-side manner" that I really liked. Each afternoon when we were working in the studio, he would stop production promptly at three o'clock while we had a "soda break." He had the local drugstore deliver a huge tray of cherry flavored ice cream sodas and we all sat around enjoying his treat.

I've heard they have daily tea breaks on productions in England, but this was the first and only film where I saw a "soda break." It was proven that Cruze had a very active sweet tooth and these sodas were always so heavily laced with cherry syrup that even I as a 16-year-old kid thought they were too sweet, but I never turned one down.

Racetrack was written by J. Walter Ruben and Wells Root and had a good plot with a moral. Ruben later became one of the top directors at MGM and married actress Virginia Bruce. Root later wrote some noted screenplays for United Artists including, *I Cover the Waterfront*, and adapted *The Prisoner of Zenda.*

Our story opened with Leo Carrillo as a bookmaker around the tracks who had just lost $60,000 due to a frame-up. As a result he is forced to eat in second-class diners.

One night he is amused at watching a young kid struggling with a big plate of spaghetti. He sees the kid stuff a roll in his pocket and then try to leave the diner without paying his check. When the youth is apprehended by the manager, as broke as he was, he pays for the kid's meal and saves him from being arrested. When he learns the kid has no place to stay, he takes him to the apartment he shares with his pal "Horseface," played by comedian Lee Moran. He ends up adopting the homeless waif and tries to raise him as best he can.

The kid's mother, played by Kay Hammond, who had left him with his now deceased father, has come into better times and hires a detective to find the child she had deserted.

When she locates him, she learns that her son has become an apprentice jockey under Carrillo's guidance and she wishes to take him away from what she considers to be a bad influence. Well, Hammond and Carrillo fall in love and she pleads with him to let the boy come with her and get away from the racing environment.

The kid has his big chance to win a major race on a horse named "Warrior" owned by Carrillo. The mother begs the gambler to release the boy and get him out of this style of life. Carrillo reluctantly agrees with her and, though he doesn't want to, he decides he must prove to the kid that the life of a jockey in the 1930s is not the best situation for him.

To make himself look bad, he orders the kid to throw the race and have his horse finish out of the money, even though the horse "Warrior" is the favorite and considered to be a sure winner. The kid idolizes Carrillo, so he reluctantly pulls up on the horse and loses the race.

Now to really get the kid out of racing, Carrillo goes to the stewards and claims that his jockey had deliberately thrown the race. The stewards review the film of the race which proves that the kid had pulled up on his horse and they have him disqualified from racing for life.

There is a big final scene at Carrillo's apartment where the kid criticizes his former idol for framing him and walks out of his life with the lady he now knows is his mother. As he watches his two very favorite people leave his life forever, Carrillo says to his friend "Horseface," "Why don't you mix up a big batch of cocktails?"

For the racing scenes we went on location south of the California border

With Leo Carillo, right, and Lee Moran, left, in *Race Track*, where I rode my first race as a jockey in this James Cruze production.

to Tijuana, Mexico. There we checked into the Agua Caliente Hotel and used their brand new racetrack. This fantastic complex had been built to lure people across the border to enjoy the legalized drinking and gambling before Las Vegas was in vogue.

On the first day of shooting I was asked to simulate the running of the big race. They selected a thoroughbred for me to ride who was as fast as the other horses, but was known to have a good disposition and wasn't too highly strung.

They boosted me up on him in the manner of all jockeys by my bending my left leg in a 90-degree angle, then the attendant lifted me up into the saddle. I walked and trotted the horse around for a few minutes and when we felt comfortable with each other, I rode him to the starting area. In those days they didn't have a starting gate and all races began when a barrier was lifted. All the riders rode their mounts to this starting area and when the barrier went up we were racing at full speed for the rest of the race.

In movies like ours they didn't hire top-rated jockeys but used retired jocks and exercise boys who were on their way up. These men were so helpful to me and gave me many tips, like how to cross and hold the reins so you can control these feisty animals once they get running at top speed; and I'll tell you, full speed is reached in about 20 yards and if you are not ready, these heady thoroughbreds will leave you sitting on air if you are not prepared for their hasty departure.

This first racing scene went on for three-quarters of a mile before we pulled up our mounts and trotted back to the starting area. When this simulated race was over I watched the other jockeys throw their right legs over their horse's neck and then drop to the ground. I followed suit, and to my surprise, I went right down to my knees as my legs were like rubber. Now remember, I was a good horseman and in fine physical condition from playing football and running on the track team at Fairfax; but this was something different. I'd only been on my horse for about 20 minutes, but the unnatural position that jockeys attain in riding places a great stress on the muscles of the upper thigh. It was not like the old joke of having to eat off the mantle after riding horseback. A jockey's rear end never touches the horse once the race has begun and the calves and upper thighs take all the weight from the unusually demanding attitude.

For the racing sequences James Cruze hired Reeves "Breezy" Eason to direct them as a second unit. Eason was well qualified as he had directed the thrilling chariot races for MGM in their 1925 version of *Ben Hur*.

Also for the first time I was to meet Jack "Red" O'Hare who became the most famous of the camera car drivers. Red owned a vintage British Simplex touring car which he turned into the best camera car in Hollywood. It had platforms at front and rear, each capable of holding a complete camera crew. The open area behind the driver's cab was built into a platform that could hold three cameras and their operators.

On these race scenes Red's method of operation was to begin about 200 yards before the starting area so he could reach the required speed as he passed the starting barrier. He then maintained his speed and distance so the camera crews could film the entire race. On our film there were three camera crews, each using different lenses. One was a wide angle to get the entire field, a medium length lens to cover the lead horses, and a close-up lens that stayed on me for the entire race. When the race was over I asked Red how fast he had to drive to keep ahead of us and he told me 37 miles an hour, so I guess we were running pretty fast.

After the racing scenes under Breezy Eason's direction were completed we worked in closer quarters, like the stable and paddock areas, the winner's circle, the stands, and other parts of the track. All this with James Cruze back directing.

One day I was to ride our horse Warrior in a simulated time trial with close-ups of Leo Carrillo timing me as I finished the one-mile workout. To get up a good head of steam I trotted our horse about 200 yards down the track where I found that another movie crew was sharing the track with us. I recognized some of the people as friends from MGM. Just as I received the signal for me to commence my run I heard a little kid shout, "That's Junior

Coghlan." The other company was shooting *The Champ* and the youngster was Jackie Cooper.

The MGM crew was also staying at the Agua Caliente Hotel and that evening Jackie's mother invited my mother and myself to join them at their table to help Jackie celebrate his ninth birthday. We had a pleasant time and I found Jackie to be a nice little fellow and his mother Mabel Cooper was charming.

Though they said it was Jackie's ninth birthday, I now know it was really his tenth; but that was just a studio white lie as it was customary for studios to list their kid stars a year or two younger than they really were. I'm sure DeMille Studio did it for me in their press releases too. It was just a method of keeping kid actors younger in the minds of the fans. Most of us were accused of being midgets much of the time anyway so the studio publicity men just tried to keep us as young as they could for as long as they could.

A funny thing happened during the making of *Racetrack* that I'll relate to close this chapter. We had an associate producer on the film whose value to the company I thought was marginal and Cruze used him mainly as a gofer. This guy was a big, obese slob, who was always perspiring, used too much cologne, and always chewed on a handkerchief while watching a scene being shot.

One day Cruze asked him to interview a young lady for a bit part in the film. Well, this guy's idea of an interview was the old casting couch. He took this poor girl over to the next soundstage where one of our apartment's bedrooms was being readied for the next day's work.

Now it so happened that our head propman was over there checking on what other props might be needed to complete dressing the set. He heard this guy approaching while giving this girl his biggest line of charm. The propman thought he had already heard too much and that he had better remain unnoticed so he stepped behind the wall of the bedroom set and held his breath.

After about five minutes on the bed our hero had the girl under his power and was assuring her she would be just perfect for the job and he promised he would make sure she was hired.

Now on our set it was noticed that the propman was missing and he was urgently needed. The second assistant director went out in the street between the soundstages and began shouting the poor guy's name.

About 20 minutes later the repulsive lothario returned to the set with a satisfied expression on his face and told Cruze the girl would be perfect for the small part. A few minutes later the propman showed up and received a blistering for being away from the set. He took the bawling out in stride as he just couldn't publicly divulge where he had been.

He did later confide his predicament to a few close associates and soon the incident was known and relished by all on the set—except Cruze and the handkerchief chewing slob. No one had the nerve to let them in on the joke.

Can't you just imagine the stress the propman was experiencing! He was standing there, only a few feet away from all the activity, hearing everything that was going on and not daring to make a sound. Golly, what if he suddenly had to sneeze?

28

The Last of the Mohicans

In my second year at Fairfax I was cast to play Uncas in the serial *The Last of the Mohicans* for Mascot Productions. This was based on the book by James Fenimore Cooper. Harry Carey played the scout Hawkeye and my father, Chingachgook, was the venerable old silent-day star Hobart Bosworth.

All Mohican Indians of that era wore their heads shaved with an unusual scalp lock at the very top of the head. My agents permitted the studio to shave my head, but Hobart Bosworth would not stand for it and his handsome white hair was hidden by a cleverly designed chamois skin covering. The leading lady, Cora, was played by Edwina Booth, who also worked with Harry Carey in *Trader Horn* which was filmed in Africa. While working there she was bitten by a tsetse fly and almost died of what was then known as sleeping sickness.

I really enjoyed working with Harry Carey again after my pleasant association with him in *Slide, Kelly, Slide* at MGM in 1927. He was a big star in silent-day westerns and was truly a rancher at heart. He then owned a large spread which was nearly washed away in the tragic flood that hit our area right after we completed *The Last of the Mohicans.*

He was the only actor I ever knew who had his wife with him on the set every day. She was also an actress and they had met when she played his leading lady in some of his early westerns. She took good care of him, pampered him, and protected his interests at all times. They had a son, Harry, Jr., whom they called "Dobie." I think this was a nickname they pinned on him because he had a reddish complexion and it reminded them of the adobe bricks of their ranch house. Harry Carey, Jr., became a well-known actor in his own right, mainly in John Ford movies.

Making a serial for Mascot was really an ordeal. They would have us report to the studio at 5:30 A.M. Then we would be driven about an hour away to the location site. Playing an Indian as I was, I had to strip to the waist while the makeup man slapped bollamania, a brown-colored liquid makeup on me. Ten minutes later I looked like Uncas. Of interest to you dear readers, I called the makeup men's union to ask the proper spelling of bollamania and the young fellow at the desk said he had never heard of the stuff!

Of course, at 6:30 A.M., standing on the shores of Lake Malibu, with no way to heat this brown gunk, I would also be covered with gooseflesh from the chill before I was supposed to go to work.

Mascot would shoot until the sun went down and because they were too cheap to take lights and generators to the set, they used magnesium flares to keep us illuminated until the last vestige of sun was available and they finally had to quit for the day. I'll never forget standing there with those fine ashes falling down on me as I tried to deliver lines of dialogue.

On this serial I worked with the great stuntman Yakima Canutt for the first time. "Yak" as he was lovingly called by all, was of American Indian descent and was absolutely fearless. He was among the first to perform dangerous stagecoach wrecks. Though much larger than me, he believably doubled me on several falls from horses during the serial. In 1939 Yak doubled for Clark Gable in *Gone with the Wind* and also played a shantytown marauder in one sequence of that film.

Yak went on to become a great stunt coordinator and second unit director. His most famous credit in this field was when he staged the thrilling chariot race in *Ben Hur* and his son, Yak, Jr., doubled for Charlton Heston. That race, with its frightening crashes, is still one of the best examples of second unit direction.

The Last of the Mohicans was my first serial and I was surprised to learn that most serials used two directors. While the cast was working with one director, the other one was planning the next day's work. Time was the enemy in serial production and anything to save a day was utmost in the producers' minds.

The two directors on *The Last of the Mohicans* were Ford Beebe and Reeves "Breezy" Eason who had directed my racing scenes on the second unit in *Racetrack.* Ford Beebe broke into movies as a writer in the 1920s and then moved into directing. Eason was first an actor and began directing in 1913. In a strange parallel to Yakima Canutt's later career, "Breezy" gained fame in Hollywood when he directed the second unit chariot races for MGM in their 1925 version of *Ben Hur,* which starred Ramon Novarro in the role later played by Charlton Heston.

Now for a moment, back to Fairfax High School. In my junior year in 1933 I had developed into the top low hurdler on the Class C track team and had hopes of winning that event in the upcoming city meet. I was undefeated in all the dual meets before starting on the serial and had set a school record of 13.8 seconds in the 120-yard low hurdles that stood for many years.

While working on the serial I missed a few dual meets, but I had that gold medal in mind. I checked out two hurdles from the school and brought them to the location site where I skimmed over them at every chance I could. It became a regular event each day as Uncas set up his hurdles at 20-yard intervals and broke from the starting blocks to race over his two barriers. I assure you, the entire company was rooting for me to bring a gold medal back to the set.

On the day of the semi-finals of the city meet we were working on location out in what was then known as Sherwood Forest which is now a part of Westlake Village in Thousand Oaks. The area was named Sherwood Forest since the days that Douglas Fairbanks used it for filming his version of *Robin Hood.* Ford Beebe was directing that day and that kind, considerate man arranged the shooting schedule to give me four hours off. He had a studio driver take me to Los Angeles High School where the meet was being held.

Now remember, I was playing an Indian and my upper body was covered with the dreaded bollamania makeup. On that particular day we were shooting a war sequence, so I also had war paint on my chest, arms, and face. This consisted of a yellow tomahawk on my chest and streaks of yellow paint on my upper arms and on my forehead and cheeks.

The route from the location to the meet passed very close to our apartment, so I begged the driver to take me home first. There I washed my head and arms, but I didn't think my chest would show so I left that much of my makeup on knowing time would be important when I returned to the location. I put my track suit on at home and didn't look too bad, so I went down to the car and said, "Let's go to Los Angeles High School."

Now also remember, I had this funny looking Mohican scalp lock at the top of my head, which I certainly did not wish seen by spectators at the meet. I had set a skullcap aside just for this emergency and halfway to the meet I realized to my horror that I had left it at home. When I made my problem known to the studio driver I begged him to go back so I could get it. He said, "I'm sorry Junior, I have to get you back in four hours or I'll be fired."

Well, I showed up at the meet with this weird hairdo. When I ran my race the scalp lock flew up every time I took a hurdle and by the end of the event all the spectators were giving me the Indian yell by slapping their hands over their mouths while shouting," "Hoo-Hooo," or some other form of Indian yell. Despite the heckling, I won my heat and now would be in the finals to be held three days later.

That day, unfortunately for me, "Breezy" Eason was directing. When I asked if I could be excused for four hours to run in the finals, he said, "No way. We need you to be on hand all day long." Would you believe, I never worked in a scene all that afternoon. I found out later that the fellow who finished behind me in the heat that I won placed second in the finals. I'll never know if I could have beaten the winner of the other heat, who did win in the finals, but I'll always feel that maybe "Breezy" Eason cost me the pleasure of winning the coveted gold medal. From the way things worked out, I'm sure I would have at least won the silver medal for finishing in second place.

I had another unpleasant experience during the production of this serial that will always make me remember *The Last of the Mohicans.* During all the weeks I spent working on the serial I always wore the same costume. I was bare to the waist with the scalp lock which supported a single feather sticking straight up from it. I wore a pair of full-length, deerskin breeches and moccasins and that was the entire wardrobe.

Needless to say, I had very little protection for my upper body and received many scratches from the underbrush we were frequently working in. One day, about halfway through the serial, I had to engage in a real knockdown tumbling fight with one of the hated Huron Indian enemies. This scene was shot at close range and I had to do it without a double. As we fought we rolled over and over down the hillside ending up in a large clump of bushes. As luck would have it, this bush was really a gigantic patch of poison oak. I received some nasty scratches from the bush, but scratches were par for the course, so we thought nothing of it. The first aid man swabbed my abrasions with an antiseptic, the makeup man applied more bollamania to the area and we went back to work. What no one realized at the time was that by being scratched by the poison oak I had in effect been inoculated by the plant and some of its pollen had gone right into my bloodstream. In a day or so I developed an irritating rash and soon half of my back was covered by one solid blister.

Finally the studio sent me to a hospital where the doctor said he had never seen such a severe case of infected poison oak. He gave me a series of injections and after a few days the blister diminished and happily, because of those shots, I have never been bothered by poison oak again.

The serial was winding down to the final days and we were working even farther away from the studio on location. Throughout the production all the actors and crew were required to report to the studio to be driven to the location site by studio drivers. Regardless of where you lived, this was a standing rule and was really a concession to the studio driver's union.

"Breezy" Eason had wangled an exception to this policy and had the privilege of driving himself to the locations in his own car from home so he could better plan the day's work in his mind as he drove alone. On this particular day he drove up 20 minutes late for work. The associate producer met him at his car, suspected him of having a hangover, and told him he was fired.

Unfortunately for me and the rest of the cast and crew, this associated producer assigned one of the writers, Wyndham Gittens, to direct in Eason's place. Gittens was a strange person and I didn't like his approach to directing at all. He was very insecure in his new position and caused us all to submit to many more rehearsals than the more professional Beebe and Eason. This annoyed all the actors and crew, but he was the director and we had to comply.

There was one scene in which I was to be shot and then fall backward off a cliff in the final scene, or "cliffhanger" to one of the episodes. Gittens picked a very steep cliff with a narrow ledge below where he told me he would place two crew members to catch me in a net as I fell. I looked the area over and I was convinced the ledge was so narrow that my weight would pull the men off their perch and all three of us would fall about one hundred feet to certain death.

Gittens was one of those directors who liked to personally demonstrate everything himself before he had you do it, so I said, "All right Mr. Gittens, you show me exactly how you want me to make this fall and then I will do it the same way you did it." With this challenge he looked over the cliff and then decided to move the scene to a safer place.

This type of conduct was so unlike me but this pompous man really had a way of getting under my skin. I learned from others that I was not alone in my feelings and the crew was laughing behind his back when I balked at falling over that steep cliff. The two men who were supposed to catch me thanked me later for my resistance and said they were much relieved as they weren't about to stand on that ledge but were waiting for me to make the first objection. They were afraid to voice a protest, fearing that Gittens would have them fired for cowardice. They thanked me profusely for having the guts to speak up against this unreasonable man.

29

The Frolics of Youth

In 1933 I was called to Educational Productions to test for the leading role in a series of two-reel high school comedies to be known as *The Frolics of Youth.* The tests were directed by Charles Lamont, who was to direct me in several feature films in later years.

It was quite a testing session. In addition to the lead role of Sonny, they also tested several cute girls for the part of Sonny's girlfriend and other juveniles for the part of the villain and for Sonny's pal.

It turned out that I won the lead role, Mary Blackford the girlfriend, Kenny Howell the meanie, and my pal was to be Sidney Miller who I had first met while making *Penrod and Sam.* The part of my father was played by Harry Myers who was best remembered for his role of the drunk who Charlie Chaplin cared for in *City Lights,* where the drunk loved Chaplin while in his cups, but didn't recognize him when sober the next morning. My mother was Virginia True Boardman.

On the first day of production I noticed there was a lovable little girl who was to be my sister. Her name was Shirley Temple and she had not been required to test as she was already under contract to Educational where she had played the lead in another series of their comedies called *The Baby Burlesque.*

This talented tyke was only four years of age and she was something to behold on the set. She still couldn't read so every night while she was taking a bath her mother would read the next day's scenes to her over and over again.

As a result, Shirley would arrive on the set the following morning having everyone's lines memorized. So, if any one of us made a mistake in dialogue, the precocious Shirley in complete innocence and without a trace of pretentiousness, would say, "Oh no. You're supposed to say . . .," and then she would tell us exactly what we were supposed to say. And would you believe, she was always right. At first this came as a shock but it wasn't long before we came to welcome it.

Most of the so-called film historians, including James Bacon in his writing, are wrong about Shirley's ascendancy to stardom. Nearly all claim

Shirley Temple and I in *The Frolics of Youth.*

that she was discovered by talent scouts from Twentieth Century–Fox while working in *The Baby Burlesque* comedies. That is not true, as Shirley played my little sister in the first four of *The Frolics of Youth* series and it was at the preview of this fourth film at the Westwood Theater near UCLA that I saw her parents talking with a pair of men who, it turned out, were from the Twentieth Century–Fox talent department. The rest is film history.

After Shirley left our series they tried three other four-year-olds over the next two years as replacements for her. While they were cute and quite capable for their age, they just didn't compare to Shirley. As they say in show business, she was a tough act to follow.

This makes me wonder about some of those so-called Hollywood historians. They copy something that was wrong in the first place and then rewrite that mistake, either because they are afraid to question the source or just too lazy to dig out the real facts. As a result, these errors, like the Shirley Temple mistake, are carried into perpetuity. I hope I will not make too many errors in this book because I am only writing about personal experiences.

Mary Blackford, who played my girlfriend in the first comedy, was a real doll with a fine personality and a great sense of humor and I hoped things were going to develop between us. I soon found out that this was very unlikely as her agent had the same designs on her. We had to work two nights on this first film and this guy showed up both nights and sat with her in his car every minute we were not actually on the set.

Just before we were to start on the second of the shorts, Mary was involved in a head-on car collision and the last I heard of her she was still confined to a wheelchair with little hope of ever walking again.

Kenny Howell was a handsome fellow with blond, wavy hair and with all his good looks he was perfect for the part of the spoiled, overbearing "heavy." Ken later went on to play a running role in *The Jones Family* series at Twentieth Century–Fox and I later played his stooge in the *Henry Aldrich* series at Paramount where my good friend James Lydon played the lovable, mixed-up Henry.

In Richard Lamparski's eleventh edition of his series of books, *Whatever Became of. . .?*, he reports that Billy Mahan who had worked with Ken in all of *The Jones Family* series, ran into Ken, who had played his older brother in the series, at a marina. When Billy recognized him and introduced himself, and tried to strike up a conversation, Howell was abrupt with him, declaring his film career was a closed chapter in his life and as Mahan tells it, "He cut me off short."

All of *The Frolics of Youth* were directed by Charles Lamont and were written by Ernest Pagano. A few years later I played a small part in the movie about "Wrong Way" Corrigan's flight to Ireland. On the set I was pleased to see Ernie Pagano and to learn that he had written the screenplay to the Corrigan film and was now an established writer at RKO.

Most of the plots in *The Frolics of Youth* series were light family stories in the *Andy Hardy* and *Henry Aldrich* tradition, complete with Model A convertible, but there are three that I vividly cherish.

In one I had a bad cold and was confined to bed with a mustard plaster on my chest and an ice bag on my head to reduce the fever. Meanwhile, outside my bedroom window the baseball game for the neighborhood championship was being played. I'm the star player on our team and dying to get into the game.

With the score tied in the final inning our coach lures me to climb out of the window to pinch hit. I hit the game-winning home run and run around the bases in my nightshirt and then dive head first through the window and back into bed. Unfortunately, Shirley catches me in the act, blabs to our parents, and poor Sonny is in serious trouble and grounded.

Another unforgettable short in the series contained a dream sequence in which I fancied I was the son of William Tell. That would have been all right, except in this dream, my father, the famous Swiss archer, was played by Ben Turpin.

I'm sure you can imagine the humor, with me supporting an apple on my head and Turpin taking aim with the crossbow with his cocked eyes. He didn't place the weapon under his chin as an ordinary archer would. Instead, when he placed his chin on the crossbow his face was 90 degrees from the target, which was my head. However, when he took aim you could see that his cocked eye was really sighting down the arrow.

This led to several near misses around my head with the accompanying scared reactions from me. Finally, he split the apple and the dream came to a happy conclusion.

Turpin was a 64-year-old man at the time and was a very strange man. For years he used to stand in the middle of the intersection of Santa Monica Boulevard and Western Avenue in Hollywood where he would direct traffic. I don't think he ever caused any accidents but I'm sure his presence there made for many near misses.

In spite of his age he was still very athletic. He had a trick he loved to pull on unsuspecting people. He would be walking beside you and all of a sudden he'd do what was known in show business as a "108." This consisted of doing a complete front flip and landing flat on his back. A "108" is as follows: the 1 is the man standing up straight, the 0 is the front flip in the air and the 8 is the position he ends up in on the ground at the end of the maneuver.

It just scared you when he did it but he never seemed to hurt himself and sure got lots of laughs with this caper. Some people in the studios thought he had pulled this stunt a few times too often and maybe that was why he liked to direct traffic at Santa Monica and Western.

The other, and to me the most memorable of the shorts, was *The Little Big Top.* Here Sonny decides to stage a circus to raise money for charity. In typical Rooney-Garland, "Let's put on a show" attitude, all the kids pitch in to make the venture a success.

In the story I have the good fortune of meeting the great equestrian clown "Poodles" Hanneford and he kindly agrees to bring his entire act, horses and all, to perform in our circus.

In my role as ringmaster I inadvertently get mixed up in his act and I end up doing many of the stunts that made "Poodles" famous. I was on a wire, of course, but it didn't show and I rode the horse's neck facing backward and ended up hanging on to his tail as he pulls me around the ring with my legs far from the ground.

This was really fun and I was carefully coached by members of the Hanneford family. His daughter Grace and his niece Ernestine Clarke were in the act on the set with us. They were a few years younger than me and we became good friends.

The Hannefords were a famous circus act in the British Isles and were brought to the United States by Barnum and Bailey in 1915. "Poodles" made his first appearance in the ring at the age of two and his venerable mother,

Nana, served as ringmaster of the act for years after she stopped riding herself.

I showed an interest in the marvelous horses they rode. I was told they were a Percheron type, not necessarily purebred stock, but horses with the broad Percheron back and wide rump area. This circus family looked for well-built horses between six and eight years of age to train and they knew in a couple of months if the horse was going to make it. Once a horse was accepted in the act they were known to continue to the ripe old age of 25.

The horse had to have sturdy legs to maintain the perfectly constant gait for as long as needed. Other unusual requirements were the capability to ignore the many noises and distractions that prevailed around them in the ring and they must not be ticklish to the touch as the performers rode the horses bareback. Also very important was a horse that would not shy, bolt, or stop when encountering something unexpected. Ernestine told me of one horse who shied at a sudden ray of sunlight, causing a serious and painful fall for the rider who was balancing on one foot at the time.

The following year when the Cole Brothers Circus came to town I paid them a visit. The circus was performing in a giant three-ring tent on what was then a large vacant area at the corner of Wilshire Boulevard and Fairfax Avenue. That space has now long been covered by a May Company department store and many other high-rise buildings.

Though the circus was under canvas, the performers and laborers lived in the cars of a railroad train parked on a siding nearby. Ernestine and her mother invited my mother and me to visit with them in their car. They were living in a row of compartments just like those seen on a first class passenger train.

"Poodles" Hanneford invited me to his dressing tent while he prepared to go on. It was cold and had been raining and this tent had a sawdust-covered floor and was very drafty. After finishing his act "Poodles" returned to this tent to sit and cool off. Men brought in buckets of steaming hot water and this was what the circus headliner used to wash and remove his makeup. I'll tell you, those performers who worked under canvas the year round were a hardy lot!

Ernestine Clarke continued riding in the equestrian act and also became a star in her own right as a flying trapeze artist in an act called the Clarkonians. When I asked her about the unusual name she explained that the heads of the circus felt that foreign sounding names added more glamor and imagination in the minds of the audience, so the good old Anglo-Saxon name of Clarke became Clarkonian on the circus billboards. She also told me her mother, Elizabeth Hanneford Clarke, who had ridden for years in the equestrian act with all its risks, fainted dead away the first time she saw Ernestine try a lay-out somersault on the flying trapeze—and miss.

Ernestine is married to my friend, the fine actor Parley Baer. Parley also has a circus background. He started out in 1936 as a press agent with the Al G. Barnes Circus. Next he joined the Polack Brothers Circus as a press agent, and then became one of their performers and toured with them for 30 years. Among other things, he worked in the cage with lions, tigers, and pumas, ultimately becoming their ringmaster and performance director.

In addition to his many motion picture and television credits, Parley had a long and distinguished career in radio. He was the original character of Chester in the radio show "Gunsmoke" in the 1950s when William Conrad played Matt Dillon. Also for the past 20 years or so Parley has been the voice of Ernie, the chief elf in all the Keebler commercials.

My wife and I see Parley and Ernie several times a year at various show business functions and Parley and I meet on interviews for television commercials where we sometimes compete for the same part.

I shouldn't tell this story about myself, but after we had completed nine of *The Frolics of Youth* comedies, Mack Sennett bought the rights to the series and the first thing he did was to fire me. I guess after all the great comedians he had sponsored through the years, I just wasn't his type of comic. Norman Phillips, Jr., played the role of Sonny once and Ken Howell played the lead in two more shorts before the series died.

The Frolics of Youth was one of the last series of two-reel comedies ever made because the era of going to a theater where you saw a newsreel, a short subject, and then a single feature film was fast coming to a close.

30

Pickups, 1930–36

I have purposely glossed over a few films that I worked in between 1930 and 1936. Though they were important roles for me I didn't feel any of them rated a section by themselvess, so I'll group them together in a single chapter.

In 1930 I went back to MGM to play in a good family story called *The Girl Said No.* It starred William Haines, with whom I had worked in *Mike* and *Slide, Kelly, Slide.* It was directed by Sam Wood and written by Sarah Y. Mason and Charles MacArthur. MacArthur had earlier written *The Front Page* in collaboration with Ben Hecht, and was married to the lady often called "the queen of the theater," the lovely Helen Hayes. Their son, James MacArthur is an actor who worked for many years with Jack Lord in the television series, "Hawaii Five-O."

The Girl Said No had a fine supporting cast, which included Lela Hyams, Francis X. Bushman, Jr., William V. Mong, Phyllis Crane, William Janney, Clara Blandick, Polly Moran, and Marie Dressler. This shows the kind of cast MGM could put together from their own contract players for what they considered to be a low-budget "program" feature.

Haines played a returning college hero whose fantastic moneymaking schemes provided spirited fun for his small town, middle-income family. Marie Dressler is credited with stealing the picture with her small role of a drunken millionairess. This great actress, among many other things, could play a marvelous drunk as she had proven the year before in *Anna Christie* with Greta Garbo.

My funniest memories from *The Girl Said No* were provided by the very comical Polly Moran. She was a riot on the set and she always referred to her breasts as her avocados. For instance, if someone bumped into her, she would grab her breasts in mock pain and say, "Watch out for the avocados." She kept the set in stitches with her unusual and often raunchy sense of humor.

In 1931 I worked in a short subject for Warner Brothers that was a pleasure and an honor to be a part of. Bobby Jones, the great golfer, after winning every title that an amateur golfer could attain, decided to leave the tour circuit and cash in on his fame. He didn't want to join the pro ranks but instead accepted the offer by Warner Brothers to make a series of 12 instructional films for what was then the astronomical sum of $250,000.

Jones, wearing his traditional knickers and using the wooden-shafted clubs of the day, at the age of 28 won what a famous sportswriter termed the "impregnable quadrilateral" and from then on has been known as the grand slam of golf. In 1930 he won the U.S. and British Amateur championships, the U.S. Open, and the British Open, an unheard-of and never duplicated feat. No amateur has ever again come close and the grand slam in golf is now the winning of the U.S. Open, the British Open, the PGA Tournament, and the Masters. No modern-day professional has ever achieved that goal, but Ben Hogan and Jack Nicklaus have come close.

In this film I played a 15-year-old golf enthusiast whom Bobby Jones invited out to the links to watch him play. I was allowed to bring some of my teenage friends with me and the humor was provided when my parents insisted that I take my five-year-old brother along. He was naturally bored and kept falling asleep on the golf course.

We spent four days at the Oakmont Country Club in Pasadena working on the film. Each of the shorts showed Jones demonstrating his skill with different golf clubs and ours featured his expertise with the middle irons and how he used them to approach to the green.

Bobby Jones was a successful attorney in Atlanta and was truly a Southern gentleman in every sense of the word. I used to love watching him practice between takes on our movie. In 1933 he gathered a group of investors together and purchased 365 acres outside of Augusta, Georgia, where there had once been a flower nursery. He and the famous Scottish golf course architect Alister MacKenzie, codesigned what is now known as the Augusta National Golf Club where the prestigious Masters Tournament is held annually.

In 1952, when I was a naval aviator stationed at NAS Jacksonville, Florida, I had the opportunity to fly to Augusta and watch the golfers on one day of the practice rounds for the Masters. I was in uniform and learned that Bobby Jones was in residence in the home off the eighteenth green he had built for himself in planning this great golf course.

I mustered all my courage and knocked on the front door. Mrs. Jones came to the door herself and I imagine she was surprised to see a naval officer with the gall to impose on them. When I told her who I was she was really pleased and said she knew Bobby would be happy to see me. She led me to the room where Jones was greeting friends. Unfortunately, this great athlete was now permanently confined to a wheelchair due to an arthritic back condition.

When Mrs. Jones told him who I was he called me Junior and asked me to sit on the sofa next to his wheelchair and he had a maid bring me a coke. We chatted for a few minutes and I know this nice man would have made me welcome for a longer time but I felt uneasy as there were literally dozens of people waiting to talk to him, so I bid a hasty and respectful farewell. I tell you, Bobby Jones was a real class act.

In 1932 I began a productive association with a firm of independent producers who released their films under either the banner of Chesterfield or Invincible Productions. The firm was headed by two real gentlemen, George Batcheller and Herbert Cohen. I became their favorite juvenile actor and they had me starring or gave me featured roles in six films over the next four years.

The first was *The Little Red Schoolhouse,* where I was starred. It was directed by Charles Lamont. My older sister was played by Ann Doran and her leading man was the veteran actor Lloyd Hughes. Our kid brother was the cute, seven-year-old Dickie Moore. My buddy was my friend Sidney Miller from *Penrod and Sam* and the villain was Kenny Howell.

My next for them was *Red Lights Ahead,* where they went all out with a large cast headed by the lovable Andy Clyde as our grandfather. Our parents were Lucille Gleason and Roger Imhoff. Lucille Gleason was the wife of James Gleason and we had been under contract together to Cecil B. DeMille in the late 1920s. Here again my older sister was Ann Doran and the other siblings were Paula Stone and my good friend Ben Alexander, who once played *Penrod* and later played with Jack Webb in the "Dragnet" series on television.

I made four more films for Chesterfield-Invincible, including *Happiness C.O.D.* and *In the Money* and two others of which I am not sure about the titles. They were all good, clean family films with capable casts and fitted in nicely where they were intended to be as the second feature on a double bill.

In 1933 I worked in a western, *Drum Taps,* for KBS at Tiffany Studios and our director was J. P. McGowan. The star was Ken Maynard. His real brother, Kermit Maynard, played his "reel" brother here and I was Kermit's son and Ken's nephew. Kermit was the scoutmaster of our troop of Boy Scouts and I was his senior patrol leader.

In the story Kermit takes our troop to Ken's ranch on our summer vacation. While we were there a murder was committed and our troop helps Ken in capturing the killers. What impressed me the most about Ken was that he flew his own airplane to the location site each day.

We would report to the studio at an early hour and be driven out to Iverson's Ranch, which took about an hour. When we were set up for the first scene, Ken would "buzz" the location site and land nearby, sometimes on a road if no good field was available. His plane was the old, open cockpit biplane the Waco UPF-7 that I later flew in my first stage of navy flight training. They would send a car to pick him up and later return him there when the final scene was completed. I'm sure Ken was home enjoying his first cocktail long before we were back to the studio.

Next, my former studio boss Cecil B. DeMille, now at Paramount, chose me to play a small but important part in *This Day and Age.* This film, like most of DeMille's, had a message. Here a group of high school students, headed by Richard Cromwell, decided they had endured enough of a crooked regime in city hall and opted to take matters into their own hands.

The corrupt mayor was played by Charles Bickford whom I had admired so much while working with him in *River's End.* One day while the mayor was getting his daily shoeshine at my stand, all of a sudden I taped his ankles together. At the same time the two teenagers sitting on either side of him taped his hands to his legs. We then brought him to a deserted brickyard where we suspended him over a pit filled with rats until he confessed to his wrongdoings. As a result, a better city government came into being due to the efforts of these dedicated high school students.

I'm sure you have read the two following famous DeMille stories. First there is the one about the fellow who was supposed to follow the great man at all times with a camp chair at the ready so C.B. could sit whenever he wanted to. One day he decided to sit and the poor fellow was distracted for a moment; so DeMille found himself on the deck in an unceremonious position. They say the last time this unfortunate wretch was seen he was hitchhiking toward Bakersfield.

The even more famous story is that one day DeMille was giving direction over his ever-present loudspeaker when he noticed an extra girl in the rear of the set whispering to a friend. He called this unlucky lady up to the front of the assemblage and said, "All right young lady, what were you saying that was so important that you were talking while I was giving instructions?" He handed her the mike and she said, "I was just saying, I wonder when the baldheaded old bastard is going to call lunch?" As the story goes, DeMille immediately said, "Lunch, one hour."

I too was the victim of a "DeMillism" during the production of *This Day and Age.* It wasn't as funny as the two related above but I'll sure never forget it. As we brought Charles Bickford down to the pit of rats, I was holding him by his left elbow and was supposed to release him at a certain point. On the first take I held on to Bickford's elbow too long and C.B., in all his loveliness, shouted over the loudspeaker, "Junior, (see, he still called me Junior) do I have to send you an engraved invitation to release Mr. Bickford's elbow on time?"

This was minor compared to those others, but it was the only time my old mentor ever yelled at me. Needless to say, on the next take I released Bickford a second or two sooner and all was sweetness and light after that. I tell you, when that old boy called your name out in anger over the bullhorn in front of about 300 people, he sure got your attention.

Here I will add an anecdote about DeMille that I have never seen in print. I base this on the three years I was under contract to him and the nearly three months' association on *This Day and Age.* Despite the bald head and the patrician appearance, DeMille considered himself to be a real fashion plate and had fastidious taste in his wardrobe. His favorite ensemble on the set was a meticulously tailored suit, usually with riding pants, which he set off with high laced boots. He frequently wore colorful shirts, sometimes open at the neck, but more often matched with a handsome, color coordinated necktie. The crowning additive to his attire was always a beautiful ring on the little finger of his left hand. If he wore a light green shirt, on his pinky finger he wore a ring with a jade stone or an emerald. With a tan shirt it would be topaz, with blue an aquamarine or a sapphire. On the few times he wore a white shirt, it was a three- or four-carat diamond. I never saw this procedure fail and his collection of finger rings must have rivaled the best that Cartier had to offer.

In 1935 I worked in *Kentucky Blue Streak* for producer C. C. Burr, which must have been the worst motion picture I ever played in. C. C. Burr had a tremendous film background, producing his first movie in 1919. He founded the successful *Torchy* comedy series starring Johnny Hines, and Burr talked E. W. Hammons into changing the format of his Educational Films from strictly a company releasing training films into one that also released theatrical productions.

During the three years he spent on the *Torchy* comedies Burr is credited with "discovering" Billie Dove, Jacqueline Logan, Dorothy Mackail, Jobyna Ralston, Norma Shearer, Dolores Costello, and Clara Bow among others.

Somewhere in his life Burr lost both of his feet just above the ankle but that didn't slow him down one bit. Ours was a racetrack film and I'll never forget this remarkable man mounting a horse without assistance and riding alongside of me during the racing scenes.

I fear I caught Burr at the low ebb of his production financial status as he approved what I consider to be the worst, or at least the most predictable screenplay I ever became associated with. We were a racing family who owned an unproven horse of great blood lines that we hoped to enter in the Kentucky Derby. When Father died, our mother fought to keep his dreams intact and my sister continued training our horse, Blue Streak, which of course I was to ride in the Derby.

To help pay the bills I was riding for the owner of a sleazy stable who cheated everyone he had dealings with. This nasty man was played by the once well known villain, Roy D'Arcy. He is best remembered for his toothy, mustachioed grin in such films as *The Merry Widow* with Mae Murray at MGM.

One day as D'Arcy was attempting to cheat me out of my riding fee,

The sneering villain Roy D'Arcy is about to cheat me out of my riding fee in *Kentucky Blue Streak.*

another disgruntled stablehand shoots him through the window behind me and then throws the murder weapon at my feet. I pick it up and am caught holding the smoking gun while standing over his body. Naturally I am charged with his murder and taken off to prison. (Isn't that pretty sickening?)

To continue with this unbelievable tale, I escape from the penitentiary and hop a freight train to Kentucky. I stay in hiding in the stable area and at the last minute I mount our horse and win the Derby. In the winner's circle I am apprehended and our horse is about to be disqualified for having a murderer as his rider. At the crucial second the real killer confesses and I am exonerated, our horse continues to wear the roses, and we pay off the mortgage on our breeding farm. Wow, what a story!

The only good memory I have from *Kentucky Blue Streak* was meeting Edward Nugent who played the newspaper reporter who proved my innocence. He was a good actor and a real nice guy and we remained friends through the years.

The final film I will cover in this group is when I went to Twentieth Century–Fox to again play a jockey in *Charlie Chan at the Racetrack.*

Warner Oland was still playing the Honolulu-based Oriental detective and his "number one son" was the fine Chinese actor Keye Luke. Oland passed away in 1938 and the series continued with Sidney Toler playing Chan and Victor Sen Yung moving into the role created by Keye Luke. Victor was a pleasant young fellow and a strange thing about him was he lived in San Francisco and commuted to Hollywood for his film assignments.

I played a jockey, crippled from a serious fall, who was desperately trying to make a comeback. Frankie Darro was a crooked jockey who had agreed to throw the big race but, when he became too greedy, the gamblers did him in. On the eve of the race there was no one to ride the favorite and I begged the owners to give me a chance. The gamblers, who also owned the second-favored horse, made it known around the track that any jockey who rode the favorite would be killed during the running of the race.

These hoods devised a unique plan to stop the favorite by placing a poisoned dart in the timing device at the quarter pole and, if the favorite was in contention at that point, he would be shot by an accomplice who was supposedly controlling the electric eye timer.

The favorite, with me in the saddle, was forging to the front, so the hoodlum shot the dart. In a close-up it was shown that the dart landed, but my horse continued running. It won the race and then fell after crossing the finish line. The owner of the second horse retrieved the dart, but Charlie Chan found it in his pocket after the race and justice was done.

Charlie Chan at the Racetrack was directed by H. Bruce Humberstone who also did several others in the *Charlie Chan* series. Humberstone directed our race sequence from the vantage point of Jack "Red" O'Hare's famous camera car.

We planned the thrilling finale of the big race with the cooperation of a fine team of jockeys. We first worked out the finish of the race on a blackboard like it was a military maneuver. Coming out of the back stretch I was to pass one horse on the outside, then go between two horses, pass another between him and the rail, then pull alongside the second favorite and ride neck and neck with him until I just nosed him out at the finish line. This placed me on the outside so my horse was in a position to receive the poisoned dart as we entered the final stretch.

Everything went fine up to the point where I was to go inside that one horse and pass between him and the rail. As I made that move, the horse outside of me stumbled and bumped into my horse causing him to brush the rail. My horse wasn't hurt and kept on running but, due to the jolt and the precarious position jockeys have on top of their mounts, I was slingshotted over the rail and into the infield of the track. Being in good shape and having experience in tumbling, I rolled into a ball and landed on my back and shoulders.

My old friend from Fairfax High School, Aaron "Rosie" Rosenberg (who later became a famous producer at Twentieth Century–Fox and Universal) was our assistant director. He ran to me after Red O'Hare backed his camera car up to where I was inside the track, uninjured, but rather in a daze. Rosie was petrified with fear for me, and this former All-American football player from USC picked me up like I was a child. I'll never forget him shouting, "All right. That's the end of this. Let's get a double rider."

Humberstone, who had the nickname of "Lucky," maybe from events such as this, asked me how I felt and if I would be willing to try it again. I said I would, and over protests from Rosie, we did the scene once more and all came out to perfection. I'm glad I chose to get right back up on the horse because people with experience told me later that if I didn't I might never want to ride again.

A sideline to this story is that the next day I revisited the location of my fall. We were using the Santa Anita Racetrack in their off season and they had many repairs going on in the infield. Just about 50 yards from where I fell, they had taken delivery of a full truckload of lumber. If I had fallen on or into that, I wouldn't be here writing this book.

Now, for the finish of the race. Of course, a double was to fill in for me as in no way was I expected to be on the horse when it fell at the finish line. A stunt rider was hired and he prepared his landing site with a softened area and a hidden mattress covered with dirt. The method selected for the fall was the "Running W." This was a cruel device used in those days to guarantee that a horse would fall exactly where the cameras were trained. In the dreaded "W," a railroad tie or some other formidable object, was buried about 50 yards from the fall site and a quarter-inch steel cable was fed through a loop on the horse's girth leading down to a cuff on one of his ankles, back up through the loop again and then down to the other ankle. In effect, this formed a letter W. In the stunt, when the horse reached the end of the cable, both of his feet were pulled out from under him resulting in a nasty fall. This cruel device led to the injury of many fine animals and has since been outlawed by the Society for the Prevention of Cruelty to Animals. Now falls are accomplished by horses trained to fall on command and very few injuries result.

In this final scene of the race the horse I was supposedly riding was to cross the finish line, winning by a nose. Then he fell and the rest of the field rushed by him. This is not exactly how it turned out. When my horse came to the end of the cable, the horse fell with such an impact that the steel cable snapped and wrapped itself around the ankles of one of the following horses. This horse also fell and miraculously neither it nor its rider were injured. Consternation reigned where Humberstone was standing beside the cameras. My horse fell exactly as planned, then a few seconds later another horse and rider were laying alongside of him. This was another case when the good old film editor saved the day.

He cut the film as soon as my horse hit the ground. Then he spliced in scenes of Chan, the villain, and several others reacting to seeing the favorite fall. By this time the camera went back to the track to see the final horses streaming past my horse. Boy! Talk about getting more stunt than you bargained for, Twentieth Century–Fox sure got it that day.

I learned something about Warner Oland while making *Charlie Chan at the Racetrack* and it was that the old boy liked his booze and wasn't above drinking on the set. In fact, I found out it was standard procedure for him to take a thermos filled with iced martinis to the studio daily.

The day I was riding my big race, Oland had about three hours off and retired to his dressing trailer to "rest." When my racing scenes were over and the assistant director went to the trailer to summon Oland, the poor man could hardly stand up. Humberstone took one look at him, shrugged his shoulders and said, "We'll shoot those scenes first thing tomorrow morning," and then moved to another setup while the assistant director called for a car to drive Oland home.

Speaking of drinking on the set—in one of six films I made for Chesterfield the role of the not too bright muscleman for the villain was played by that very funny actor Warren Hymer.

He was the son of playwright John B. Hymer and actress Elsie Kent. He was educated in the finest parochial schools in Brooklyn and attended Yale University. Then he appeared on the New York stage and broke into motion pictures in 1928 at the old Fox Studios. All the good education failed to rub off on him as his language was strictly "dees, dems, and dose." Maybe that was just a facade he set up to accompany the dumb gangster roles he usually played.

Hymer had a reputation for being a good man with the bottle and he proved it on the one film I worked with him. Those low-budget companies frequently caused us to work nights to complete the movie on schedule. On this particular film we were still working long after the dinner hour and Hymer was nipping from a pint bottle he had on his hip. At one point in the evening Warren went to the water cooler where he poured a generous belt into a paper cup and then chased it with a gulp of water. The assistant director was getting worried about him and said, "Warren, you'd better take it easy on that bottle." Hymer replied in his typical Brooklynese, "Oh dis stuff don't bodder me none."

My buddy William Benedict tells of an incident at Fox Studio where they were both under contract at the time. Hymer had been nipping all day and in one scene Bill was to open the door and Warren was to enter and deliver several lines of dialogue. The director called for a rehearsal and Hymer came through the door and read his lines perfectly and made every move and reaction exactly as expected. The director then said, "OK. Let's shoot one." When the cameras were rolling and the director called, "Action,"

Benedict opened the door, Hymer took one step into the room and fell flat on his face and his work was over for the day.

I'm sorry to report that with all Warren's education and talent as a comedian, he just couldn't control the bottle. He died in 1948 at the young age of 42 from what was described as "a long illness." It is also known that he spent most of his time in later years on the streets of Los Angeles's skid row.

I heard more than once that producers sent people looking for him to offer film work. The word came back that he was in bad shape but content with his lifestyle and had no desire to resume his film career. Sad.

Another important thing career-wise happened to me in this time period: I changed my screen name. While Jackie Coogan, Jackie Cooper, and Mickey Rooney have kept youthful nicknames all their lives, I felt Junior would forever brand me as a child.

Being Irish and a great admirer of Pat O'Brien, my first choice was Pat Coghlan. (I now have a son with that name.) I asked my Irish friend if he would mind my adopting his first name. He gave me his assent, adding he thought it was a compliment and wished me luck with it.

When I told my agents, they were strongly opposed. Naturally, they were thinking of dollars. They insisted that I keep the Junior associated with my name so producers, directors, and casting people would automatically think of the moppet kid star when they heard my name.

Though I didn't particularly like it, I became known as Frank Coghlan, Jr., and used that name until I went into the navy. Since retiring from the service and resuming acting I have just used Frank Coghlan. Now when I am invited to film festivals around the country and they show films from all stages of my career, they always bill me as Frank "Junior" Coghlan.

31

Blazing Barriers

In 1936 I was chosen by producer Ken Goldsmith to play the lead in a low-budget film, *Blazing Barriers,* at Allied Artists Studio. The unique thing about this movie is that it was about the Civilian Conservation Corps. Much of it was filmed at one of their camps in the Angeles National Forest above the city of Pasadena. We had the full cooperation of this worthwhile group and stayed in one of their barracks while on location. We ate in their mess hall and they assigned U.S. Army personnel to us to give technical advice.

The CCC, as it was called, was an organization formed during the depression to provide jobs for the needy. Their main goal was in the field of reforestation and erosion control.

I played a wayward juvenile delinquent who was given the choice of joining the corps or going to jail. The CCC sounded like the better of the two, but I hated it from the beginning and was a malcontent member until I got straightened out and learned we were really doing important work. I finally became an upright member of the community. This was proven in a big forest fire sequence where I saved some lives and was declared to be a hero.

My buddy at the camp was played by Edward Arnold, Jr., the son of the great character actor, who was working in his first motion picture. Young Ed was a natural with a real flair for acting and he had a laugh that resounded through his corpulent body and made you want to share the humor with him. I'm sure he could have had a distinguished career as an actor if he wished, but the last I heard of him he had turned away from the theatrical life and was a successful businessman. Maybe his resentment of the constant comparison to his father drove him away from show business.

My girlfriend was played by Florine McKinney who was a competent actress with a very lovely singing voice which was used effectively in a camp show sequence. Here I had to sing for one of the few times in my career and the result made me cringe when I heard myself on the playbacks.

With Edward Arnold, Jr., in *Blazing Barriers*.

Working with Florine was strange and there just weren't any sparks between us. Even in the few romantic scenes we had together it was strictly a job and no tingles. Oh well, I was still going steady with my high school sweetheart from Fairfax, so I guess it was just as well.

My rival for her hand was Addison Randall who later became the cowboy star Jack Randall. His real-life brother was the cowboy actor Robert Livingston. Addison was a big, demonstrative fellow who kept the set in laughs. In Chapter 8 I wrote about various actors' responses to the "goose"; he was the one who shouted out, "Beautiful legs, beautiful legs." It was Florine's legs he was referring to, and they were beautiful.

Perhaps the best thing to come out of *Blazing Barriers* was the association I made with Milburn Stone. This talented actor played the sheriff who tracked me down when I escaped from the camp and we had some fine scenes together.

He was the nephew of the fine actor Fred Stone, and his cousin Paula Stone was my sister in *Red Lights Ahead.* Milburn is certainly best remembered for his role of the lovable Doc with James Arness in the long-running television series "Gunsmoke."

Ken Goldsmith was the typical low-budget producer who always had

Florine McKinney was my ladylove in *Blazing Barriers*.

to fight the clock to keep his project on schedule and within his allotted funds. In spite of the pressure he was under, he tried to keep a happy set by kidding and joking and loved to pull pranks on people. He had a near maniacal laugh and I thought a rather perverse sense of humor.

All the male actors and principal crew members shared a large bunkhouse which had at least 24 cots in it. Ken was the top man in the company and should have sought respect, but he thought it was funny after we were in bed at night to get up and pass gas right in some poor guy's face. He would giggle for minutes after one of these windbreakings and all thought of sleep was impossible for quite a while.

He pulled a stunt on me one day that demonstrates the level of his humor. Though there was a makeup man on the set, I always carried my own makeup case and it proved to be handy many times on location. It was a nice black leather case with fitted shelves and a removable mirror that could stand by itself. On the front side, under the handle, were the initials F. C. Jr. in gold letters.

We were working out in the forest and Ken came up to me with my makeup box in his hand and told me I needed some powder. I took it from him, opened it, and, looking in the mirror, I hastily used the puff. Then I closed it and handed it back to him.

He seemed disappointed and handed it back to me, telling me to check the initials. Then I saw he had used a brush and gold leaf paint to add two letters and it now read FUCK Jr. I shook my head in disbelief while he doubled over in raucous laughter and went all over the set showing everyone the trick he had pulled on me.

Our director was Aubrey Scotto whom I learned had performed on the stage and in grand opera where had had sung leading roles with minor opera companies.

He was a film editor at MGM for eight years and had about 20 directorial credits before *Blazing Barriers.* The year before our film he had directed the movie debut of the Metropolitan Opera star Marion Talley. That picture was *Follow Your Heart* for Republic.

After a week at the camp we returned to the studio to complete the film on sets built to resemble interiors of the CCC buildings. At the camp we had the army officers who were giving technical advice. They could not leave their duties there, so they sent a sergeant down to the studio to help us out.

One day I was lying face down on a cot in the simulated bunkhouse while studying my lines for the next scene. This sergeant sat down beside me on the cot while I was reading and engaged me in small talk. He seemed like a nice guy and though he was interfering with my studying, I put up with him. Soon I noticed that he was feeling and caressing my buttocks. I looked up at him and asked, "What's the matter, did you lose something?"

To my surprise he answered, "No, but your little firm rear end just drives me wild." I told him there was nothing about my rear end that could possibly be of interest to him or any other man. He said I was wrong and then made a direct proposition. He told me if I would only let him enter my rectum he would give me pleasure I had never known before. He promised that if I submitted to him he would guarantee that I would have an orgasm at the same time he did and that I would never again want any other form of sexual enjoyment.

His advances were making me mad and I said, "Listen Mac, you take your hand off my ass and gets yours back on the set where it belongs or you'll be heading back up to the mountains in a big hurry."

I didn't tell on the guy but I suppose I should have. This was my first experience with anything to do with sodomy and it really repulsed me. Now that I know more about it, I shudder to think of how many innocent, young kids this pervert might have forced himself upon at the camp where he was in a position of authority.

In a career of more than 400 performances, as I now look back on *Blazing Barriers,* I'm sure I have more "sick" memories from this single film than I have from all the others combined.

32

Scouts to the Rescue and Jackie Cooper

In 1937 I went to Universal to play the role of Jackie Cooper's pal and senior patrol leader under him in the serial *Scouts to the Rescue. Scouts* was based on an original story by Irving Crump who was then the editor of the scout's magazine *Boy's Life.* Crump spent the entire time on the set with us serving as technical adviser.

Scouts was directed by Ray Taylor and Alan James, both seasoned serial directors. Taylor broke into the business as an assistant director to John Ford, and among his many serial credits was *Flash Gordon.* James, among others, had previously directed *Dick Tracy* at Republic. Our associate producer was the colorful Henry MacRae who had headed the serial department at Universal since the Carl Laemmle days.

MacRae was born in Canada and had once studied medicine at Toronto University. He gave that up and later owned stock companies that played in Hawaii, Japan, throughout the Orient, and other parts of the world. He is credited with being a pioneer in the use of artificial lights to make exterior motion pictures at night.

MacRae was colorful in more ways than one. He fretted about his short stature and always wore two-inch heels on his expensive shoes. Being rather corpulent, he always and very obviously, strapped himself up in a girdle. He wore what must have been an expensive, but very obvious, hairpiece and always showed signs of powder on his face. His usual garb was a loud plaid sports coat and slacks, topped off by a homburg hat set at a rakish angle.

The screenplay of the serial was written by a team of four writers headed by Wyndham Gittens, my old nemesis from *The Last of the Mohicans.* Fortunately, due to the ever-present Crump on the set, I never had to come in contact with him.

Scouts to the Rescue led to a long and warm relationship with Jackie Cooper and his wonderful mother Mabel whom I first met at his tenth birthday party at the Agua Caliente Hotel while I was working in *Racetrack* and he was working with Wallace Beery in *The Champ.*

The juvenile heavy was played by David Durand, a kid actor I had known through the years. Dave was a strange guy, I presume due to an inferiority complex, and he always seemed to feel that everybody was down on him. I remember him as a young child being brought to the sets by a little crippled mother and maybe this had something to do with his paranoid attitude.

Cooper's and my buddy, Hermie, was played by Sidney Miller, my old friend from *Penrod and Sam, The Little Red Schoolhouse,* and *The Frolics of Youth* comedies. Bill Cody, Jr., son of the former cowboy star Bill Cody, was the youngest member of our troop and his sister in the serial was a lovely young actress, Vondell Darr. A year or so later Vondell met with a deplorable accident when some pervert hit her on the head with a two-by-four and then raped her right on the sidewalk near her home. I don't think she ever resumed her promising acting career after this traumatic experience.

We went on location for two weeks up to Dardanelle Mountain in the high Sierras near Sacramento, California. It was a beautiful part of the Sierras and we worked as high as the 8,000-foot level. It was fun and we got to ride horseback a lot.

We stayed in a large motor lodge near Sonora at the base of the mountains. Our large company of cast and crew just about filled the lodge. Jackie was now 15 years old and felt he was too big to share a room with his mother, so he begged her to let him stay by himself. She didn't like that idea, so he ended up bunking in a large corner room with three beds with Sid Miller and me. We got along great and this led to a lasting friendship for the three of us in years to come.

One night after dinner the three of us went into the bar for a nightcap, nonalcoholic of course. While sitting together in a booth, we struck up a conversation with a real cute girl who was sitting at the bar. When we returned to the room we got talking about her and decided to call her in the bar. I placed the call and told her we were talking about her and wished she was up in the room with us. To my complete surprise, her immediate response was, "What room are you in?" My mouth must have dropped a foot and I placed my hand over the mouthpiece and whispered, "Oh my God, she wants to come up to the room." We talked it over hastily and decided we'd better not risk having her come up, so I made a weak excuse about having an early call the next morning and brought the conversation to a close. Boy! You never know what to expect from the local citizens when a movie company hits their town. I just wonder what that girl would have done if we had invited her to the room.

I mentioned working at the 8,000-foot level. That led to lots of hairy trips up the narrow mountain road from the motor lodge to the location site each day. Because Sid Miller and I roomed with Jackie, we always rode to work in the same car with him and his mother.

On this long drive Jack and Sid and I used to play silly word games to pass the time and to take Mabel's mind off the scary drive. Some of the games got very suggestive and these Mabel seemed to like the best.

One day we were making up parodies to songs and song titles. Sid Miller won the game outright when he sang, "Yank my doodle it's a dandy."

Another day we were making up things you might hear in a public restroom and what you would call this type of rhetoric. Cooper called it "Can conversation," Sid said, "Toilet topics," but I won that game when I came up with "Lavatory lingo." This must sound silly but it passed the time and took Mabel's mind off the frightening drop off to our right.

It seemed that the higher we went the narrower the road got and the drop-off of 7,000 feet or more was very impressive. One day we were on an extremely narrow stretch of road and going in the up direction and the car was on the very outer edge of the road. This day, in particular, was very frightening and Mabel Cooper just couldn't take it any longer and got out of the car and walked the final half-mile or so.

Most of the location work was safe and uneventful, but we did have one near tragic experience. In it, Cooper, Vondell, and I were speeding downstream in a canoe, supposedly escaping from the Indians. I was in the front of the canoe with a paddle, Vondell was in the middle, and Jackie was in the stern, also with a paddle. We were supposed to pull into a cove and go ashore, but as we approached the cove we found the current had control of us and we couldn't make the canoe turn. To everyone's horror, we were swept past the cameras and into the fast-moving rapids below the cove. Being in front I had the best view and I yelled back to Jack and Vondell, "Stay as low as you can and I think we can ride this out." Though it was scary, we were doing all right and the canoe's natural buoyancy was following the current between the rocks and keeping us afloat. I guess Cooper couldn't stand it any longer and as we swept past one very large rock he stood up and tried to push us away from it with his foot. This changed our low center of gravity and over we went into the near freezing water. I grabbed onto a large rock and was able to catch Vondell as she was going by me. Cooper wasn't so lucky and was swept on downstream and finally made it to shore about 100 yards below us.

He was now safe, but Vondell and I were still in mid-rapids with me clinging desperately to the rock with one arm and to her with the other one. I told her to keep her arms around me and that we would soon be rescued. In a matter of minutes there were crew members on both sides of the rapids and they threw a rope across the river. They told me to release my hold on the rock and rely on the rope to catch us. I finally did release my grip and we were caught by the rope. We went hand over hand on it until we reached shore. Vondell was a jewel and never panicked once during our ordeal. The poor girl was wearing riding boots during this scene and they must have weighed what seemed like a ton while she was in the water.

Soon we were wrapped in blankets and standing in front of a roaring fire while we dried off. Everyone was complimenting me as the hero of the event. I was feeling pretty proud of myself and I remarked to Crump and his assistant, De Groot, "It's a good thing I remembered my scouting." By that I meant that I had prescribed staying low in the canoe. De Groot's snide put-down was, "If you had remembered your scouting this never would have happened." I guess he was right, but in my years as a boy scout I had never been taught canoeing. Really there was no way Cooper and I could have prevented our experience with the river in the place the location manager had selected for us to fight the current with only two canoe paddles.

When *Scouts to the Rescue* was finished, Jackie invited me over to his house to swim. He lived in a spacious, two-story house on Elevado Avenue in Beverly Hills. He lived with his mother Mabel and her second husband, Charles J. "Chuck" Bigelow. Chuck was the assistant production manager at Monogram Productions, an independent studio where I worked many times.

Soon Cooper and I were the best of friends and I was at the house several days a week. Frequently present was Mabel's mother, Mary Leonard, who was nicknamed "Queenie" by Chuck Bigelow and the name stuck. Leonard was her married name, but she was Italian to the core and her maiden name had been Polito. Also often there was Jackie's Aunt Julie who at the time was married to Norman Taurog; he had directed Jackie in *Skippy*, for which he had received the Academy Award for direction in 1931. Norman was there occasionally but usually it was just Julie and their daughter Patricia. My first memory of Norman Taurog was from a Larry Semon two-reel comedy he directed when I was four years old. Norman was a brand new director and wasn't more than 19 or 20 years old. I've always remembered this experience because I played an angel with a long, flowing red wig. I was suspended on a wire as I flapped my wings while shooting an arrow into Larry's heart in a dream sequence of this obviously slapstick comedy.

Norman was a strange man and I'll never forget one day when I was home on leave during World War II and visiting friends at MGM Studio in my uniform. Norman made a point of telling me, "Frank, this business owes you a living. When you come home from the war, just look me up and I'll see that you get started again."

In the six months that I was at home at the close of the war, before going back on active duty, and again after my retirement from the navy in 1965, Norman had many opportunities to give me a few days' work in his films but he never did. On the many times I saw him in the studio he always gave me that old saw, "Let's have lunch some day," but that day never came either.

When Jackie Cooper was writing his book, *Please Don't Shoot My Dog,* Jack's cowriter, Dick Kleiner, tells that he tried many times to contact Norman for input on the book but this bitter man would never answer Kleiner's telephone or written queries. After Norman divorced Julie he married the former secretary to Louis B. Mayer and now, nearly blind, he had no interest in Jackie Cooper or anything connected with this earlier part of his life.

In case you didn't know, Jackie is a professional quality drummer. On many occasions I accompanied him to the Hollywood Palladium where he was always invited to sit in on the drums. I saw and heard him sit in for Gene Krupa with the Bennie Goodman band and for Buddy Rich with the Tommy Dorsey organization and the audience was just as pleased as if the original artists were performing.

Jack worked hard on the drums and knew all the arrangements of the big bands, so when he filled in the regular band members were pleased with his expertise. As a result, when it came time for the regular Krupa or Rich drum solo, Goodman, Dorsey, and later Glenn Miller, gave Cooper the nod and he always astounded the band members and the audience with his ability.

I was present at the Palladium the night Tommy Dorsey was playing and his young singer Frank Sinatra came to our table to tell us he had just that day made his first record on his own with a pickup group of musicians from the Dorsey band. The song was "Night and Day." He also showed us pictures of his new child, his first, a daughter named Nancy. While he was showing us the 8″ × 10″ photo, the girl he was living with while the Dorsey band was in Hollywood was sitting at our table, but that didn't still his enthusiasm over the birth of his child.

It so happened, a few days later, I was on location at Catalina Island filming *Rings on Her Fingers* and this chick was playing an extra role in the same film. Knowing she had been sleeping with Sinatra, I figured she was good for a one-night stand in this romantic locale but she said no. She said she was in love with this new singer and turned me down. I wonder how many other girls had the same problem in later years.

Another funny thing happened on this location trip. I don't know why, but the jockey, William "Smokey" Saunders, was hired to play a small role in this film. I was playing a hotel bellhop and "Smokey" was too. He was very famous in racing circles at the time as just a few years before he had been the jockey on the great horse Omaha when it won the triple crown of horse racing with victories in the Kentucky Derby, the Preakness, and the Belmont Stakes.

For some reason that he never made clear, Smokey had been set down for some racing infringement and was not riding at that time. I can only figure that Darryl Zanuck, who was the head of Twentieth Century–Fox at the time and very heavily into racing, had given him this small part to tide him over during his set-down period from racing.

Remember, I had played a jockey in three movies and I got along really well with Saunders. On the night I was pursuing Sinatra's girlfriend, Smokey had his eye on another cute extra in the cast. In his description, told in his racetrack jargon, he said, "I followed her all the way back from the casino to the hotel, but she always stayed about three lengths in front of me and I never did catch her before we passed the wire." In other words, Smokey also struck out.

The film we were making, *Rings on Her Fingers,* was directed by Rouben Mamoulian and starred Gene Tierney and Henry Fonda with Laird Cregar and Spring Byington in supporting roles. As I said, I played a bellhop and for the entire four days on location I was seen and heard in scenes where I was paging people and delivering messages in a sort of "Calling Phillip Morris" type of voice.

When my part was ended I was sent back to the mainland on the old cruise ship *Avalon* which then plied daily between Catalina and Long Beach Harbor. As the *Avalon* passed near the St. Catherine Hotel where we were working, I went to the rail and called out, "Paging Mrs. Jones," as I had done several times in the movie. It was funny because when I did that about 50 voices from the location shouted back, "Goodbye Frank."

As I said earlier, Jackie Cooper was an excellent drummer and received his greatest pleasure and relaxation from his music. He assembled a five-piece Dixieland-style band and they made fine music together. Besides Jack, there was his good friend Buddy Pepper on piano, Leonard Sues on trumpet, Martha Raye's brother Buddy Raye on guitar, and Jimmy Jack on bass.

Buddy Pepper and Leonard Sues were young actors and Leonard was featured for a couple of years on the Milton Berle television show. For years Buddy Pepper toured with Judy Garland as her accompanist and has written many songs, the best known being "Vaya con Dios." Buddy Raye was a great guitarist who died at an early age from a heart attack. Jimmy Jack was a nonprofessional with whom I had played football at Fairfax High and he strummed a mean bass fiddle.

Nearly every Sunday afternoon Cooper used to have a group of friends over to the house. The feature of the afternoon would be a jam session with his group and having some of the guests filling in. Judy Garland was a frequent attender and always pleased with a medley of songs.

The worst example of boorishness I ever witnessed at those functions was the day Jack invited the Andrews Sisters. Would you believe, they came in a party of 12 people! Each of the three sisters had a date, there were their parents, then their manager and his wife, and another couple that the agent brought. I swear their group ate everything in sight and sat in stony silence while Judy and the others performed. But you should have seen them bounce into action when the Andrews got up to sing. They couldn't contain themselves with their beating on the table and swaying in sheer ecstatic exaltations as the three girls did a few numbers. When they had concluded, they all trooped out of the house, as in their eyes, the show was over. I've never seen such a demonstration of pure favoritism and partiality in all my life.

For the first year of my friendship with Jackie Cooper I wasn't going steady with any girl in particular and I brought many different dates to his Sunday get-togethers. However, at the tender age of 16, Cooper was already keeping steady company with a cute girl named Pat Stewart. She didn't do much in show business as an actress but after the war she married Wayne Morris. Her younger sister Peggy Stewart became a well-known leading lady in westerns and married Donald "Red" Barry and bore him a son.

While mentioning Don Barry I should mention that he was one of those actors who would do almost anything to get better known in Hollywood. One day I heard him boasting on a set that at a time when he didn't have enough money to pay his rent he went in hock to throw a major cocktail party at Mocombo where he invited all the top names in town. His date for that event was Joan Crawford.

What he didn't say was that the evening nearly ended in disaster. Don got very drunk and when things were getting out of control a waiter wrapped two heavy salt shakers in a napkin and hit Don on the head with them. He overshot the mark and the heavy object hit Don in the eye and nearly caused him serious injury. This mixed-up man just couldn't stand not being on top and when his career waned badly he took his own life.

In his 16th year Jackie was plagued with frequent bouts of tonsillitis and it was decided that he should have his offending tonsils removed. Jackie had another problem that bothered him and he brought this to the attention of the doctor, who then planned to make that correction at the same time.

During this time I was becoming friendly with the lovely Bonita Granville. "Bunny" and her mother attended the Blessed Sacrament Catholic Church where I never missed the 12:00 noon mass on Sundays. Many people in the movie business were regulars there and used to congregate out front and chat after mass. Soon Bunny and I sought each other out and one Sunday her mother, "Timmie," invited me over to their apartment. The three of us began going out to dinner together and we used to visit at the home of some friends of theirs, but I was never permitted to take Bonita out on a real date.

After Bonita's 15th birthday in 1938 she began preparing for the Sacrament of Confirmation and I was chosen to be her sponsor. The ceremony took place on a Sunday afternoon and I told Bonita and Timmie that I was invited to Jackie Cooper's house for a swimming and music party. Then I asked Timmie if she would allow Bunny to accompany me to celebrate her confirmation. To my pleasure Timmie said yes and I then took Bonita Granville on her first unchaperoned date.

She enjoyed herself swimming with all the kids that she knew and liked the music session that followed. The gathering was breaking up as usual around 5:00 P.M. and as we were preparing to leave, Coop asked if Bunny and I would join him and Pat Stewart for dinner at a nearby family restaurant and then go to see the movie *Gunga Din.* We called Timmie for permission, then the four of us had a good time at dinner and at the movie and I had Bunny home before 10:00 P.M.

That was my one and only real date with Bonita. It happened that Jackie and Pat Stewart broke up the following week and Jack began calling Bonita on the telephone. They really struck it off and for the next two years they were nearly inseparable. Jack was 16, Bonita was 15, and I was 22 at the time. My feelings for her were more like a little sister than a girlfriend and I was delighted to see this perfect couple get together.

I probably came closer to being jealous of Jackie when he told me about his ride in a Christmas parade. Every year since 1928 the Hollywood Chamber of Commerce has sponsored a Santa Claus Parade with bands, searchlights, and all the Hollywood hoopla. It starts on the Saturday night following Thanksgiving and continues right up to Christmas Eve. Though the route changes occasionally, in the beginning it went down Hollywood Boulevard from La Brea near the Chinese Theater and ended at the famous corner of Hollywood and Vine.

The final float in the parade is a replica of Santa's sleigh, complete with old Saint Nick and his eight reindeer. The guest star of the night rides high on a rear seat of the sleigh behind Santa while other dignitaries ride in open cars between the bands and marching units with their names prominently displayed on the sides of their autos. I had the honor of riding on Santa's float in 1928 and 1929 and then rode in one of the cars for several years following.

Both years I had to sit alone, but on his year on the float Jackie shared the seat behind Santa with a lovely young starlet. The night was chilly so the thoughtful Chamber of Commerce people provided blankets. Cooper was in the enviable position of snuggling close to the young lady as they made the hour-long tour down Hollywood Boulevard, smiling and waving to the thousands of fans lining both sides of the parade route.

To think, I rode the same float alone when I was only 12 and 13 years old. Oh well, I guess I wouldn't have properly appreciated the presence of a lovely feminine companion!

As much as Jackie Cooper liked music, his second love was cars. When we first met he had a good-looking Ford convertible which he kept in meticulous condition and he was very proud of it. At the end of 1939 he received one of the first six 1940 Lincoln Continental convertibles to come off the line. It was dark green with a buff-colored canvas top and was as pretty as any car on the road. As beautiful as it was, Coop wasn't satisfied and he removed the canvas top and had it replaced with a cloth-covered, removable hardtop. In bad weather he kept the hardtop in place while in the summer he removed it and hung it in the garage. He also had a canvas deck made with a removable section just for the driver's seat which he used while driving alone with the top off.

Jack really went first class on this car and as fast as it was, he wanted more. He took it to a racing specialist and had the engine modified. The man milled down the heads to give it more compression and added light-weight pistons and valves to give that engine all the speed he could.

With all that work completed, Jack just couldn't wait to see just how fast it really could go. In those days kids used to drive their hot rods to Muroc Dry Lake where official speed runs were held periodically. Jack started working on his mother days before the next scheduled event up there but she would have no part of it.

When Mabel Cooper gave Jack her final and positive turn down, he looked to me with pleading eyes. Heck, he didn't even have to ask. I was dying (and almost did) to drive that car, especially in the coming speed trials.

On the day of the run, Coop and I left early for Muroc Dry Lake as the runs were to be made before the afternoon heat. Muroc is one of the many dry lake beds in the southern California desert that when the water evaporates after the winter rains they are left completely flat with a baked silt surface so hard you can hardly dig your fingernail into it. It is now known as Rogers Dry Lake, having been renamed after an air force general and is part of the landing area at Edwards Air Force Base. You will have seen it on television as the place where the space shuttle lands when it returns to earth.

The speed tests were by classes according to weight, number of cylinders, and horsepower. They were held at the longest stretch of the lake. Each car had a two-mile run to pick up top speed before passing through a quarter-mile speed trap with electric timers at each end. Once through the trap the cars had about six miles to coast to a safe stop without excessive braking.

When the lighter hot rods were through, Cooper's Lincoln was allowed a special run and I drove it to the starting line. To my surprise, as I sat there waiting for my signal to commence the run, about five of those hot rods lined up on each side of the Continental.

When I received the green light and began accelerating, these darn speed demons dug out on both sides of me. Due to the difference in weight and horsepower-to-pound ratio, they left me far behind. What I didn't expect was that their tremendous rate of dig churned up the silt and I was completely engulfed in fine dust and and left with absolute zero visibility.

I should have coasted to a stop and demanded a new run, but I knew Cooper's time trial was special and feared he might be denied another. Though totally blinded, I kept the throttle to the floor. I watched the odometer and when I knew I had passed the timing area I eased off on the gas pedal and slowed to a stop.

During that run I knew I was doing something dumb, but I wanted so badly to please Jackie that I just held on for dear life and finished the run. I probably wasn't in as much danger as I feared because those hot rods were far in front of me but, who knows, if one of them had turned I would have plowed into him and never known about it.

When the Continental came to a stop I pulled off to the right of the raceway and drove back to where Cooper was standing with the timers. To the disappointment of both of us, we learned that the top speed I had attained was 96.7 miles per hour. After all, that Continental was a heavy car and built for comfort and style and not to break speed records.

I'm sorry to have to end my story on Jackie Cooper with a sad note. Sometime in late 1940 I came to the Cooper (Bigelow) home while Jack's mother Mabel was in the hospital for an exploratory examination. Jack was most distressed and told me that his dear mother was found to have incurable cancer. Jack was in tears and completely devastated by the doctor's evaluation of her condition and he had been told she had about a year to live.

I had never been associated with cancer before and it just tore my heart out watching her decline. I saw her go from a comely, well-built lady of 130 pounds or so, down to a mere skeleton of about 80 pounds at her passing. Though she must have been in great pain, she was cheerful and alert to the end. I would leave the house thinking to myself that the poor dear can't possibly make it through the night, only to come back a week later and see her even more emaciated.

Throughout this depressing period Jackie could not have been a more loving and devoted son. That summer he rented a house at Malibu Beach so Mabel could enjoy the fine weather and the beauty of the ocean. I was there many days as were his other close friends Sidney Miller and Buddy Pepper. Bonita Granville was there frequently, as were Norman Taurog and his wife Julie and daughter Patricia, but due to Mabel's illness it wasn't like the music parties at the home on Elevado in Beverly Hills.

When the summer ended they went back to Elevado where Mabel took to the bed that she never left again. I spent many evenings with her and Jackie and several times I heard her say, "Jackie, I have to go to the bathroom," and this loving son would cradle her in his arms and carry her to the rest room and then bring her back to bed.

Mabel died on November 27, 1941, and I will never forget the funeral. At the wake her mother "Queenie" draped her arms over the casket while sobbing hysterically, kept repeating over and over again, "She was so good to me." Everyone there felt sorry for Queenie, but I felt she was feeling more sorry for herself than for her dear departed daughter. Her fears were true, because after Mabel died Queenie's life changed and she never had it so good again.

After the funeral Jack couldn't wait to get out of the home on Elevado and all the memories it held of his mother. By now he hated his stepfather Chuck Bigelow. He told me he was sure that Chuck had been sleeping with the very attractive live-in nurse hired to care for Mabel in her declining days and he ordered him out of the house soon after the funeral.

Jack was only 19 when Mabel died and he moved into a pleasant apartment in the Sunset Towers on the Sunset Strip. I still saw him a few times while he lived there but he was now acquiring a new set of friends and our once close relationship slowly dwindled.

33

"Moe the Gimp" and Romeo

I'm sorry, but I have done it to you again. By trying to keep my years of friendship with Jackie Cooper together in the last chapter I have bypassed many things. The years between 1936 and 1943, when I went into the navy, were not memorable in my career, except for the serial *Adventures of Captain Marvel,* made at Republic Studio in December 1940 and January 1941. I will cover *Captain Marvel* in greater detail later.

During this period I played mainly bits and small parts, but I had some rewarding experiences while performing in these supporting roles. Many of them were while wearing the uniform of a hotel bellhop, or elevator operator, and I delivered many telegrams during those years.

All the major studios had large wardrobe departments at that time and if I was cast in that form of role I would be sent to wardrobe and fitted in the proper uniform. The independent studios would send you to Western Costume Company for the same purpose. In Chapter 7 I explained about being fitted for a Western Union uniform. To my knowledge, the only other young actor afforded the privilege of having a Western Union uniform set aside for him was my dear friend William Benedict, who probably delivered even more wires than I did.

The telegram most important to a film's plot was the one I delivered to my good friend Pat O'Brien when he was playing the legendary football coach in *Knute Rockne—All American.* It was the wire I gave him while he was on vacation in Florida that sent him to the West coast for an important meeting. The plane he was flying in crashed and burned in a Kansas wheat field with a total loss of life.

One of those jobs in uniform was at Paramount under the direction of the great Ernest Lubitsch. I can't remember the title of the film but I'll never forget working for him. My little part in this movie was unimportant but he directed me like my running the elevator was the most important scene in the entire motion picture. I guess that was why he was so great. To him every scene was a jewel and I'm glad I helped him put one of his masterpieces together.

I delivered a telegram to Bing Crosby in *East Side of Heaven,* which was directed by David Butler, who had been my father in the Hugh Dierker production, *Cause for Divorce* in 1923. Bing was very friendly with me and there were lots of laughs when I related that the now very rotund David Butler had once played my father. I brought stills to the set to show Bing how Dave looked in his days as a slender young leading man.

I was a hotel bellhop in *Love Thy Neighbor,* which costarred Jack Benny and Fred Allen. This Mark Sandrich production had a fine supporting cast with the young Mary Martin, Verree Teasdale, Jack Carson, and Eddie "Rochester" Anderson.

As funny as Jack Benny was on radio, with all his carefully written material, he was not a very humorous person on the set. Maybe this different medium had him worried. Allen, on the other hand, kept the cast and crew in stitches all day long with his countless droll, dry-wit stories.

I'll never forget one tale he told about an old vaudevillian who had toured the country for so many years that when he died on the road his body continued on and played three more weeks before they could stop it and get it to an undertaker.

Then I worked in a group of short subjects at RKO. They were then making many two-reel comedies in their *Average Man* series and they thought I was the perfect son for many of their comics. In successive shorts I played the son of such greats as Leon Errol, Andy Clyde, Jimmy Finlayson, and Edgar Kennedy.

In another one there, *Melody in May,* I worked with the lovely singer Ruth Etting. She liked me and invited me to her home to meet and swim with her daughter who was a very nice teenager. Nothing developed out of this relationship but I sure enjoyed being invited to her home.

At this time Ruth Etting was married to Martin "Moe the Gimp" Snyder, a former hood she had met and married while singing in nightclubs during Prohibition days. Everyone in Hollywood knew he had been a minor gangster and wondered what she saw in this homely, vulgar little guy. Many thought she was afraid to try to get rid of him and he sure didn't improve her image in the film capital.

I don't usually relate things like this, but at the preview of the Ruth Etting short it was obvious from the audience response that I had "walked off" with the picture. It wasn't due to any great acting ability on my part, the script as written just gave my role the most appeal. As good as she was and as sweet as she sang, the teenage character I played had most of the good lines and carried the plot to a happy ending.

In the lobby after the preview I was standing with Ruth and her daughter and all the passersby were complimenting me for a job well done. Ruth was sweet about it, but "Moe" walked up with a scowl on his face. He gave me a dirty look and snarled out of the corner of his mouth, "Well, you sure can tell who the real star of this movie is." He was obviously referring

I played the soda jerk in the drugstore in Ruth Etting's musical short *Melody in May* for RKO in 1936. Margaret Armstrong is listening in on our conversation.

to me and I didn't know if I was in trouble or not. There really was nothing he could do. The filming was over and RKO would not go to the expense of retakes on a short subject, but I had visions of broken legs or some other form of gangster-related retaliations.

My fears weren't so far off base as Moe showed his mettle a year or so later when Ruth left him and began an open relationship with her accompanist, Myrl Alderman. Snyder followed them one night and shot Alderman, for which he went to prison for attempted murder. Alderman recovered and he and Ruth were married in 1938.

This well-publicized event led to the motion picture *Love Me or Leave Me,* made in 1955. In this film version of the triangle, Doris Day played Ruth Etting, James Cagney was Moe the Gimp, and Cameron Mitchell was Alderman. More proof that sometimes truth is stranger than fiction.

Also in 1936 I played a nice part at RKO in *Make Way for a Lady,* which costarred my dear friend Anne Shirley and the fine British actor Herbert Marshall. My part as Anne's high school boyfriend was a much sought-after role and I had to submit to a screen test against several other juvenile actors. I won out and spent about seven weeks working on this delightful film.

My crowning sequence here was when I played Romeo against Anne's

Juliet in the high school senior play. Anne was a beautiful Juliet, but I was a bumbling Romeo. In the balcony scene my tights kept slipping down and I was forced to keep hitching them up at crucial times. As lovely as Anne was in her rendition of Juliet, she just couldn't compete with me as a "baggy pants comic" and, without trying, the laughs I received stole the scene.

Herbert Marshall was a hero in World War I, where he lost a leg in combat. In spite of this handicap, he went on to play many romantic leads. In *Make Way for a Lady* he was as Anne's father who, as a single parent, was trying to rear her into becoming a lovely young lady. Marshall was a real gentleman and brought great dignity to the roles he played.

He was the first person I ever worked with who hosted a party for cast and crew at the completion of the film. On our closing night he provided a catered bar and buffet table for all to enjoy and he was a most gracious host. He mingled with all, thanking them for their contributions toward making this a fine motion picture. Anne and I ate heartily, but we sipped on soft drinks while the grownups went for the harder stuff.

34

Radio

In 1936 I added another dimension to my career and a new source of income when I entered the ranks of the free-lance radio actors. This was a real break for me and came about because I had a friend in an important place.

When Mitzi Green's parents, Joe and Rosie Green, were in vaudeville, their act was known as Keno and Green. It was written by a clever writer named Billy K. Wells. He also wrote the material for many other performers. When Mitzi broke into vaudeville he wrote her act as well.

We met Billy K. Wells several times at Mitzi's apartment and also got to know his son George Wells who was getting his own start as a writer. George worked his way up the ladder, first writing gags for radio comedians, and he eventually became the head writer on the prestigious "Lux Radio Theater."

At the time this was the very top radio dramatic show, with Cecil B. DeMille as host and Hollywood's biggest stars playing the leading roles each Monday night over the CBS network.

One week George saw a fine part for a young voice and suggested me to Frank Woodruff who directed the show. (It was funny to me, but in radio the man who directed the show was usually called the producer.) I was called in for an audition and won the role. This led to at least a dozen other appearances on the "Lux Radio Theater" in the next few years. My reputation as a dependable radio actor soon spread and I subsequently appeared in most of the other dramatic shows of the era.

Cecil B. DeMille was credited with being the director of "Lux Radio Theater." He actually had nothing to do with the show's production and the first time we saw him was at dress rehearsal, while we had already been working on the show for three days. It was quite a production. There were about 48 minutes of play broken into three acts. There was a full-scale, 25-piece orchestra under the direction of Louis Silvers and the golden-throated Mel Ruick was the announcer who opened the show by saying, "Lux presents Hollywood." DeMille then presided by introducing each act and he interviewed the stars at the end of the program.

Working in radio was fun for me and I admired the many good performers I worked with. They used to say that 80 percent of the parts in radio shows were performed by about 20 percent of the actors. This certainly was true and many players worked in several shows a day and frequently read more than one voice in those shows. The way these people could change their voices and speak in dialects was amazing to me.

One of my favorite shows to work in was Gene Autry's "Melody Ranch." Here Gene and his funny sidekick Pat Buttram would enact a western tale with always a song or two from the famous singing cowboy.

Louella Parsons, at the time the most feared of the Hollywood gossip columnists, had an important show, "Hollywood Hotel," that ran from 1934 to 1938. If any of you ever heard it I'm sure you will never forget her sickeningly sweet, whining voice. She never did learn how to act and we used to wonder if she'd make it through to the end of her lines. This "lovely" lady used to intimidate the stars into appearing on her show gratuitously and their studios were afraid to interfere. Finally the newly formed union, the American Federation of Radio Artists, put their collective feet down and dear Louella's clout was over and so was her show.

There were other fine dramatic shows like "Hollywood Playhouse," "Screen Guild Theater," and "Stars over Hollywood." Most followed the format of "Lux Radio Theater" with a host and guest stars and presented a well-acted drama each week. Another good show was "Mr. President" starring Edward Arnold, and I played his son in one episode. It was directed by Tony Stanford who impressed me as one of the most dynamic of all the radio directors I ever read for. He really pulled a heart-wrenching performance out of me.

Other interesting shows I worked in through the years were "My Favorite Husband" with Lucille Ball and "The Kraft Music Hall" with Bing Crosby. Bing's announcer was Ken Carpenter and I played his buddy in a series of military school–type commercials that were featured on the show.

The best-running part I had in radio was in 1940 when Ezra Stone came to Hollywood to star in *Those Were the Days* at Paramount. I will tell you more in the next chapter about meeting Ezra in New York and auditioning for his show.

I hope many of my readers remember the great "Aldrich Family" comedy radio program that ran on NBC for 14 years. It always began with the forlorn wail of Mrs. Aldrich calling, "Hen-Reeee! Henry Aldrich." As John Dunning writes in his book *Tune in Yesterday,* "The cracking voice of adolescence that answered, 'Coming Mother!' was your validated ticket to Mayhem."

It all began when a little-known playwright, Clifford Goldsmith, had his play *What a Life* produced on Broadway with the 16-year-old Ezra Stone playing the lead. This funny play came to the attention of Rudy Vallee who introduced it on his radio show in 1938. The following year Kate Smith featured skits from it on her "The Kate Smith Hour," where it ran for 40 weeks. Then NBC gave the show its own half-hour slot and Henry Aldrich remained a befuddled 16-year-old until the show went off the air in 1953. The "Aldrich Family" aired from Hollywood for six weeks while Ezra Stone was starring in *Those Were the Days.* Henry's buddy through the run of the show was Jackie Kelk who played Homer Brown. Kelk was also appearing in a play on Broadway at this time and could not make the trip west. Ezra remembered me and had me brought into the show as Kelk's temporary replacement. Fortunately, they didn't make me try to impersonate the gravel-throated Homer Brown, but instead wrote in a new character called Red for the few weeks I was on the show.

Radio was something all by itself in show business. If you worked in a play you rehearsed it from beginning to end until the cast had it down perfectly, then you performed it that way night after night. In motion pictures one scene was rehearsed until the director was satisfied and then shot on film. Then you went to the next scene, whether it was in sequence or not, as it is common practice to complete all scenes that take place on a certain set before moving on to the next one. So it is not unusual to film the very first scene and then the very last scene of a picture if they both happen to take place in the same setting.

Radio was completely different. Here a group of actors stood around one or more microphones reading the script from beginning to end as they went along telling the story. The director would cue in sound effects and music and the end result was a perfect blend of pure imagination that kept the listener glued to his radio set. Television does not come close to achieving the same result.

Who will ever forget the Halloween Eve in 1938 when Orson Welles with his "Mercury Theater" presentation of *War of the Worlds* sent people running into the streets in terror in the most famous single radio show ever broadcast. In spite of several announcements by CBS that this was a "Mercury Theater of the Air" presentation of a play by H. G. Wells, people were in a panic all over the United States, really believing we were being invaded by spaceships from Mars.

Looking back on my seven years in radio I have great admiration for the talented people who made their voices create such illusions. Some of the unsung heroes of radio were the marvelous sound effects men who added so much to the fantasy. The way they could make a door squeak on cue, bring in thunder and lightning, or a pistol shot, and duplicate horses hooves in western shows was a tribute to their unique genius.

I belong to the Pacific Pioneer Broadcasters, a group that requires 25 years experience in radio, and or television, as a prerequisite for membership. We meet for luncheons five times a year. It's a real pleasure to rub elbows with such radio veterans as Les Tremayne, who played "Mr. First Nighter" and "The Thin Man," among his many credits. Or Olen Soule, who also played "Mr. First Nighter" opposite Barbara Luddy for six years, was Sam Ryder in "Bachelor's Children" for ten years, and even played the Chinese cook, Aha, in "Little Orphan Annie." Announcers Art Gilmore and Andre Baruch are regulars and funny man Pat Buttram is our perennial master of ceremonies.

Our first chairman of the board was the legendary Edgar Bergen. When Edgar passed away the chair was taken over by the equally legendary Jim Jordan, better known as Fibber McGee. He brought happiness to millions from his and Molly's home in Wistful Vista, with its always overstuffed hall closet, when "Fibber McGee and Molly" were on the air. Jim passed away in his nineties and now our chairman is Ralph Edwards of "This Is Your Life" and "Truth or Consequences" fame.

My wife and I usually sit with my good friend Parley Baer and his wife Ernestine and Frankie Thomas and his wife Virginia. Parley is still active in film work and occasionally makes guest appearances as ringmaster at various charity circus performers. For more than 20 years Parley has been the voice of Ernie, the chief elf, on the Keebler cookie commercials. He was the original Chester on the radio show "Gunsmoke" from 1953 to 1961 when William Conrad played U.S. Marshall Matt Dillon. James Arness later played Matt Dillon for 20 years on television. William Conrad is now better known as the Fatman in his television series, "Jake and the Fatman."

The parents of Frankie Thomas, Frank M. Thomas and Mona Bruns, were noted performers on the New York stage and Frankie made his first stage appearance in 1932 at a tender age. In 1933 he starred on Broadway in *Wednesday's Child.* The screen rights to the play were bought by RKO and he also starred in the film version and followed that at RKO with the lead role in *Dog of Flanders.* Then he moved to Warner Brothers for a major role in *Angels Wash Their Faces* and later played opposite Bonita Granville in the *Nancy Drew* series of films.

In 1937 he starred in the Universal serial *Tim Tyler's Luck.* He is probably best remembered for starring in "Tom Corbett, Space Cadet," which ran on television from 1950 to 1955, and doubled on radio from 1951 to 1952.

There was one great radio show that ran on NBC for 27 years but was never made into a motion picture. It was "One Man's Family," created, written, and directed by Carlton E. Morse. Over the years this saga told of the trials and tribulations of the large Barbour family of San Francisco.

Morse put a great cast together and their voices became as well known as if they were members of the listener's own family. The only problem was, as homogeneous as their voices were, when seen in person as a group nobody would ever believe them to be a family.

I know this for a fact because when one studio wanted to make "One Man's Family" into a motion picture, it was decided that the radio cast just would not do. I was selected to play the youngest son Jack. This part was played for the entire 27 years by Page Gilman who was only 14 years old when he began the show and 41 when the program ended in 1959.

It was finally decided that my face was too well known to ever be accepted as Jack Barbour, as were the other Hollywood actors named to be substitute family members. The studio feared the public would resent seeing other players in the roles of people they had loved for 27 years, so the motion picture idea was permanently placed on the shelf.

35

Joe E. Brown and New York

I had a small but very funny part in *Saturday's Heroes* at RKO in the summer of 1937. This was a college football film starring the then 27-year-old Van Heflin. I played the diminutive fifth-string quarterback who never got into the games.

There was a running gag in the movie where the coach was constantly eating peanuts during the excitement of the games. In the closing minutes of the big game, with the score tied and the conference championship on the line, he suddenly calls out my name. I'm beside myself with joy and jump up and begin stretching and running back and forth to get warmed up and ready for action. When I think I am ready I run to the coach with my helmet under my arm and say, "I'm ready coach." To my chagrin he hands me a coin and says, "Here, buy me some more peanuts."

This game sequence was shot at the Rose Bowl in Pasadena. The football players used were all from the UCLA team who were out of school for the summer. I was then going to UCLA and knew most of the players. At this time, Joe E. Brown's two sons, Don and Joe L., were on the team and Joe was the Bruins' biggest booster. (Don Brown was killed while an air force pilot in World War II and Joe L. became the general manager of the Pittsburgh Pirates baseball club.)

When the film was completed and we all returned to school in the fall, the team made me an honorary manager and I was on the field with them every afternoon and on the bench at all games that year. Joe E. Brown came out to watch his sons practice every chance he got and used to talk to me on the field. He had known me ever since I was a kid and his boys and I were old friends.

One day during practice he told me was going back to New York to star in a revival of *Elmer the Great,* a play he had once performed in on Broadway and then made into a movie at Warner Brothers in 1933. Out of the blue he said to me, "How would you like to play my young brother in it?"

I nearly fell over because here was the star of the play inviting me to appear with him on the Broadway stage. I told him yes in no uncertain terms and he gave me the name and address of the play's producers and told me to meet him at their office in New York on a date about two weeks from then.

Luck was with me as my agent was driving to New York for a month-long vacation and said I could go along and share the driving as his wife didn't like to drive. We took five days to cross the country and I arrived a day early for my appointment with Joe E. Brown.

I contacted my friend Moya Olsen and she said I could stay at their house in Great Neck, Long Island. Her father, Ole Olsen, and his partner Chic Johnson were then starring in *Hellzapoppin!* and Moya told me her dad stayed in an apartment in New York so there was plenty of room for me. I checked in at the big, sprawling family home where I stayed with Moya, her brother J.C., and Ole's younger brother and his wife.

Oddly enough, Ole Olsen's real name was John Olsen and the younger brother was truly named Ole Olsen. Because John had taken the name Ole Olsen early in his vaudeville days, when the younger brother joined the act he became known as Ole Olsen, Jr. When the true son, J.C., became a member of the troupe, he was just called J.C. Olsen. Confusing, but they all knew who they were and it worked out all right for them.

The big day arrived and I appeared at the producer's office where I met Joe E. Brown. Then I was shocked to learn they weren't aware that Brown had offered me the part and had already cast it with a fine young stage actor named Johnny Call. As you can imagine, this was devastating news.

Joe spoke up well for me, but it was too late as they had already signed Call to a run-of-the-play contract. In spite of this disappointment, at Joe's insistence, they let me read a couple of big scenes with Brown. They liked my work and now they were disappointed as my name would have added publicity value to the cast. They told me if for any reason Call didn't work out I could have the part.

They even did something rather unethical. They let me into the theater to watch a rehearsal, but they made me sit in a back row in the dark so Johnny Call would not be alarmed at the presence of another young actor watching him work. When I watched him play "my" role, I knew my chances were zilch as he was a very competent actor and there was no way he would fail and allow me to take over the part.

So here I was in New York, out of work, with four weeks to kill before my agent would make the return trip back to Hollywood. I made good use of my time and went into the big city daily, making the rounds of the stage and radio producers. On one occasion I auditioned for Otto Preminger who was casting a new play. I read for him, but I guess he didn't feel I was right for the part because I never heard back from him.

On one of my radio interviews I read for the producer of the "Aldrich Family." Ezra Stone was playing the lead role of Henry, the part he created on the stage in the play, *Those Were the Days*. I met Ezra while I was there and he recognized me and made me feel very welcome. However, there were no openings on the show, so nothing came of it at the time.

Ezra invited me to read for a part in a new play he was about to star in. It had a racetrack theme and I could have had a small role as one of the jockeys. I was surprised to learn that a minor role in a Broadway play only paid $165 per week at that time. I didn't think I could support myself in New York and still send money home for my mother's care, so I reluctantly declined the part.

Every day after my rounds I ended up backstage at the Wintergarden, where *Hellzapoppin!* was playing. If you never saw it you really missed something, as it was Olsen and Johnson at their zaniest. It didn't really have a plot and was just a series of the best of the funny skits O. and J. had put together from their years in vaudeville.

My old friend Gene Merideth, with whom I had worked in Hollywood, was now married to Chic Johnson's daughter June and had a small bit in the show. Before the opening curtain he walked down the center aisle looking at his ticket. When he thought he had located his seat he proceeded to edge his way clear across the section, only to find that his seat was occupied. He then apologized to the people and again edged his way back to the aisle. He repeated this mistake two more times and by now everyone in the theater was watching him and snickering. Finally, an usher told him he couldn't find a seat to his ticket and took him up on the stage and gave him a camp stool on the corner of the stage. When the show started, Chic Johnson noticed him sitting there and brought him a newspaper. This caused a big laugh and Gene sat there reading that paper for the entire two hours or more of the show's duration. That must have been one of the most boring things any actor has ever done, but Gene hung in there for the entire length of the run of *Hellzapoppin!*

Ole Olsen, Jr., had probaby the funniest running gag in the whole show. About five minutes into the first act he walked slowly down the center aisle carrying a small potted plant and calling out "Mrs. Jones" in a hoarse whisper. He kept this up for several minutes walking up and down each aisle in his search for the illusive Mrs. Jones.

About halfway through the second act he reappeared, only now the plant has grown about two feet taller. Toward the end of the final act he emerged a third time. Now his plant was about eight feet tall and he still could not locate Mrs. Jones. When the show was over and the audience was filing out through the lobby, there was Ole, Jr., up in the branches of a full grown tree, still calling for Mrs. Jones in a plaintive voice.

On my last night in town Ole Olsen let me play six different stooge bits in the show. In one of these skits I jumped in bed with Chic Johnson's wife Catherine who played in several of the comedy routines. Before the skit was over there were six of us in bed with her and we all jumped out of bed and ran for the doors and windows when Chic burst into the room carrying a shotgun.

In my final bit I was one of about eight fellows sitting on a bench with our backs to the audience. We had numbers on our backs and looked like members of a football team. Ole Olsen was the coach and he gave us a highly emotional pep talk. When he was finished, he shouted, "All right men, now get out there and fight." We all jumped up and headed for the aisles—then the audience saw that we weren't football players but candy butchers. We all had trays filled with Crackerjack boxes and went up the aisles noisily selling our wares. The only deviation to the regular routine was, as I jumped up, Ole shot me in the seat of the pants with a blank pistol.

That was my only night on Broadway and my introduction to *Hellzapoppin!* and the world of Olsen and Johnson.

36

Gregory La Cava

Soon after my return from New York I had the experience of again working for the maverick filmmaker Gregory La Cava. This multitalented man started out as a newspaper cartoonist and then became a pioneer in the field of animated films. He broke into the motion picture industry in 1922 with C. C. Burr, writing the *Torchy* series for Johnny Hines and became a director soon after. Among his many credits is the classic *My Man Godfrey* which he directed for Universal in 1936, starring Carole Lombard and William Powell.

La Cava was such a fine writer and so fastidious a director that he ended up producing his films as well so he would have a minimum of front office supervision to put up with. I can see why he wanted a free rein because the way he worked would drive a studio bankrupt with today's costly budgets.

This particular experience with La Cava was at Universal in *Lady in a Jam,* which starred the lovely Irene Dunne, with Patric Knowles, Ralph Bellamy, Eugene Pallette, and Samuel Hinds in supporting roles.

Why I say he would bankrupt a studio is because La Cava would start a picture without a completed script and write as he went along. In the sequences that I worked in, Irene Dunne was down on her luck and working as the telephone operator of a big restaurant and I was the uniformed page who delivered her messages. When she answered the switchboard she sang, "This is the cafe Koh-i-nour; seven, eight, nine, two, three, four," or some series of numbers ending in four so it rhymed with Koh-i-nour.

We came to work in the morning and La Cava laid out the opening scene with Miss Dunne at the switchboard and me hovering in the background. Then he went into his trailer, parked just outside the sound stage and wrote our dialogue. This took about two hours. When he came back he handed out the pages he had written and we completed the scene. This happened each day I was on the picture and he must have spent four hours a day writing while the entire cast and crew cooled their heels.

In one scene Irene Dunne wanted to leave the switchboard and asked me to fill in for her. During her absence the phone rang and I answered it, repeating the restaurant name and the phone numbers as I had heard her do.

After rehearsing it a couple of times, I asked La Cava if I couldn't try to impersonate her musical telephone greeting, but sing it off-key as Alfalfa did in *The Little Rascals.* He pondered for a moment and then gave me a curt turn down.

I still think this would have given the scene an extra laugh but he would have none of it. I figured at the time that he didn't want my character to get a laugh, or maybe he turned it down because he hadn't thought of it himself.

37

ZaSu Pitts and Slim Summerville

One phase of the motion picture industry that is not well known about with the fans, but a welcome source of income for actors and crew members, is the industrial film. There are several production companies that specialize in this type of film and the product they turn out is top-notch. Through the years I have worked in several industrial films. Most were short subjects shown by the sponsoring company at sales meetings, conventions, and other promotional activities, and some are used for training.

In 1938 I was cast by Wilding Pictures Productions to work in an hour-long, feature-length film, *Uncle Joe,* for John Deere Tractors. This was as well made as a major studio production and is high in my memory as my parents in this little gem were the delightful pair, ZaSu Pitts and Slim Summerville. Can't you just imagine my pleasure playing in scenes with this great couple?

My girlfriend in this film was the lovely Gale Storm, who became famous in later years playing the title role in the "My Little Margie" television series where Charles Farrell was her father.

People always think of ZaSu Pitts as a zany, hand-wringing comedienne, but in her early films she created many different types of roles. Probably the strangest of all was when she played a miserly woman who was murdered for the money she hoarded in Erich Von Stroheim's *Greed,* released by MGM in 1924.

She played her last "straight" part at MGM that year, portraying the pathetic Broadway star whose husband left her for one of the show's younger beauties, played by a newcomer named Lucille le Sueur. Some of you film buffs might know Miss le Sueur better by the name the studio later selected for her, Joan Crawford.

I also had the pleasure of working with the lovely ZaSu in her first finger-twisting comedy role in *The Great Love,* written and directed by Marshall Neilan for MGM in late 1924 and later in two films at Warner Brothers, *River's End* in 1930 and *Penrod and Sam* in 1931.

Offscreen ZaSu was a very pretty woman. When she dressed for social occasions and fixed her hair and made herself up, she was a real knockout. She was another lady who must have thought I was a nice young fellow because, like Ruth Etting, she also invited me to her house for dinner where I met her very attractive daughter Anne. Here again I goofed. I should have followed up by asking Anne out, but I was tied up with a former high school girlfriend and missed another good opportunity.

38

The Dead End Kids

In 1935 playwright Sidney Kingsley's melodrama *Dead End* was brought to the New York stage. There were big parts for six tough kids from the ghetto in this dark Depression-era play. Extensive auditions were held to fill these roles. The producer's publicists led the public to believe that the six selected were right from the waterfront, but the majority of them were established actors who had already appeared in other New York plays or were accredited radio performers.

After the play had a successful run on Broadway, Samuel Goldwyn bought the screen rights and moved these kids to Hollywood to appear in the motion picture *Dead End* which he released through United Artists in 1937. Here these precocious kid actors joined Sylvia Sidney, Joel McCrea, Humphrey Bogart, Wendie Barrie, Claire Trevor, Allen Jenkins, Marjorie Main, and Ward Bond in this notable film which was directed by William Wyler. Even with this great cast, the kids stole the picture. Sam Goldwyn had no further use for them, so Warner Brothers placed all six of them under contract.

When these oddball kids hit the screen, all the established juvenile actors were affected. These guys were something like the screen had never experienced before and the following films, written expressly for their unusual talents, changed our lives for several years.

The first movie Warner Brothers starred them in was *Crime School* directed by Lewis Seiler and released in 1938. Warners added Humphrey Bogart to the cast to add box office clout.

Their second Warner Brothers motion picture was a real blockbuster. Here Warners took an original story by Rowland Brown and Michael Curtiz directed *Angels with Dirty Faces* into a memorable film. It also starred James Cagney, Pat O'Brien, Humphrey Bogart, Ann Sheridan, and George Bancroft.

The taut crime melodrama revolves around Cagney and O'Brien who play two poor city kids. O'Brien becomes a priest and Cagney a gangster. Much to the priest's surprise and chagrin, it is the gangster who wins the admiration of the neighborhood kids.

I played a very minor part in *Angels with Dirty Faces* where Bobby Jordan roughs me up in a pool hall when I ask him to pay me the money he owes me. I worked with the kids later in *Angels Wash Their Faces,* where they were joined by Ann Sheridan, Ronald Reagan, Bonita Granville, Frankie Thomas, Henry O'Neill, Eduardo Ciannelli, and Marjorie Main. Later I worked with Bobby Jordan in *Off the Record.* It was a newspaper story and one of his few films away from the other Dead End Kids.

Speaking of our past president Ronald Reagan, I worked in a second picture with him at Warner Brothers that year. It was *Brother Rat,* a story about life in a military academy. Its cast included Wayne Morris, Eddie Albert, Priscilla Lane, Jane Bryan, Jane Wyman (the former Mrs. Reagan), Johnny "Scat" Davis, William Tracey, and Henry O'Neill. I played a mischievous cadet in the film directed by William Keighley.

Most of this wild bunch made life miserable for Jack Warner and his publicity department. The tough job for the publicists was trying to keep their names *out* of the newspapers. Bernard Punsley and Gabriel Dell behaved pretty well, but Billy Halop, Bobby Jordan, Huntz Hall, and especially Leo Gorcey were frequently on the front pages.

Gorcey was once arrested for shooting at, but missing, the second of his five wives. He also served five days in the Los Angeles County Jail for driving 90 miles an hour within the city limits. Hall was arrested on marijuana charges. Both he and Halop were apprehended on separate drunk driving charges. Jordan was jailed for a few days when he couldn't keep up alimony and child support payments.

Their stormy stint at Warner Brothers lasted for six pictures over a two-year period. As their contract was ending, the kids began feuding among themselves as Billy Halop and Leo Gorcey both wanted to be considered the leader of the gang.

Halop went to Universal to star in a series called *The Little Tough Guys* with Huntz Hall, Gabe Dell, and Bernard Punsley. Bobby Jordan signed with Monogram to do a series called *The East Side Kids.* He was joined there by Leo Gorcey and Huntz Hall, and Gabe Dell followed when *The Little Tough Guys* ended at Universal.

Jordan, Gorcey, Hall, and Dell were later teamed with William Benedict, Stanley Clements, Bennie Bartlett, and Leo's father and brother, Bernard and David Gorcey, and that series became known as *The Bowery Boys.*

My pal William Benedict worked in about 80 of the combined *East Side Kids* and *Bowery Boys* films. He says things were pretty hectic at times on the set with Gorcey and Hall frequently ad-libbing and straying from the written script without warning.

Life was not always pleasant for the group. Bobby Jordan, the youngest of the six, was the first to die. He passed away in 1965 at the age of 42. His early demise was attributed to illness related to the heavy use of alcohol. I attended his funeral where the pallbearers were the remaining five and Frankie Darro.

Leo Gorcey retired to northern California where it was reported he made a small fortune in real estate. It didn't last, however, and he died in 1969 from cirrhosis of the liver.

The last time I saw Huntz Hall and Gabriel Dell was at Jackie Coogan's funeral where they both served as pallbearers. Since then Billy Halop and Gabe Dell have died and the last survivors are Huntz Hall and Bernard Punsley. It is strange that Bernard, the least recognized of the group as an actor is now by far the most successful of all. He broke away from the others and went to medical school. He is now Dr. Bernard Punsley and practices surgery and obstetrics.

In 1986 my friends William Benedict and Dick Wilson and I were the guests at the Memphis Film Festival. (If you don't recognize the name Dick Wilson, he played Mr. Whipple in the Charmin toilet tissue TV commercials for 25 years. He also played the drunk in "Bewitched" for nine years and the German sergeant in the prison camp in "Hogan's Heroes" for four years.) The sponsors of the Memphis Film Festival still talk about the year Huntz Hall was one of the guests. It seems that Huntz ran up a large tab at the bar and his wife charged many items from the hotel's gift shop to their room number. On the final day when checking out, they tried to sign off these items and were really miffed when the festival hosts refused to accept these charges.

Worst of all, as the festival sponsors told me, Huntz was also rude to the fans who attended. He was reluctant to sign autographs and as they said, "He really made a complete horse's ass of himself." I'm surprised Huntz would conduct himself in such a manner because when you accept an invitation to such a festival you are treated regally and should portray a good image for the film industry.

To this day the sponsors of the Memphis Film Festival jokingly award "The Huntz Hall Memorial Trophy" to the guest who does the wackiest thing at that year's event.

39

Mickey Rooney

Sidney Miller called me one day and asked if I would like to join him and Mickey Rooney in a vaudeville act. I first met Sid on *Penrod and Sam*. Then he played my pal in *The Little Red Schoolhouse* and in all of *The Frolics of Youth* series of comedies. Then he was the buddy of Jackie Cooper and myself in the serial *Scouts to the Rescue*.

Sid had been doing a very funny slow-motion wrestling act for a year or so with Frankie Darro and George Offerman, Jr. He told me it was his act and he wanted to drop Frankie and George because they were becoming unreliable due to their drinking. They were only about 20 years old but they were already showing signs of the alcoholism that eventually killed both of them.

Sid told me he wanted to star Mickey Rooney in the act and thought I would make a perfect "heavy." At that time I was, and still am, 5′ 6″ tall and weighed 150 pounds! Mickey had reached his peak altitude of 5′ 3″ tall and weighed in at about 130 pounds dripping wet.

In the hilarious impersonation of a championship wrestling match, we performed the entire act in extreme slow motion. I was the dastardly, eye-gouging villain, while Mick was the innocent, clean, good guy, and Sid was the referee.

Mickey was born Joe Yule, Jr., and walked on stage in his parents' vaudeville act when he was only two years old. After a few movies using his real name, he was cast to play Mickey McGuire in the *Toonerville Trolley* comedies based on the popular comic strip of the same name. He actually changed his name to Mickey McGuire and used it on screen for a few years.

I first met him on an interview when he was about five years old and I was about ten. I couldn't get over this precocious little kid. There were about eight boys of various ages on the interview. I think Mick was the youngest and he certainly was the smallest, but this little twerp kept us entertained for the entire half-hour or so that we were waiting together.

When Sid called, I had known Rooney through the years but never had the occasion to get close with him. By now he had already starred in *Boys*

Town with Spencer Tracy and was going strong on his *Andy Hardy* series. He was one of MGM's biggest stars and was among the top box office draws in the business.

Sid got the three of us together and taught us the act. Soon we were in big demand at benefits and other special performances around town. Unfortunately for me, we were never able to take the act on the road due to Mickey's demanding schedule at MGM. Mick and I got along great and soon I was among his inner circle of friends.

Ever since he had attained stardom, Mick was surrounded by a group of gofers who ran errands for him and bowed to his every wish. I was always able to stay out of this category and he liked and respected me as a true friend. In later years when I was head of the navy office in Hollywood and was seen in the studios in uniform, Mickey always gave me a warm greeting and would tell all in earshot that I was the only kid actor who ever really made anything out of himself. I think he really meant it when he said it. Why I say that is because Mick could say something one minute and then turn around and become a completely different person the next minute. He was jovial, joking, and pleasant and then in a flash would become moody and self-centered. However, as I said, we always got along great and never had an unpleasant moment.

Due to my association with Rooney I got to attend many special events. I double-dated with Mick a few times and even went out with him when he was squiring Ava Gardner. I think the young Ava was about the most beautiful woman I have ever known. If I had to pick one of equal beauty it would be the young Linda Darnell.

Ava was a sweet young girl and Mickey idolized her. She was 5′ 6″ tall, and in high heels she used to rest her chin on Mickey's head when they danced. It was strange, but this 5′ 3″ human dynamo had a fascination for taller women. His second wife, who had once been the Miss Alabama beauty queen, was nearly six feet tall.

He was a kick on a date and some of the tales he would tell his escorts were unbelievable. Once while sharing the back seat with him I heard him telling a gullible young chick about how his one true love had died and he knew he could never fall in love again. This girl, with stars in her eyes, believed every word; and to think this line was coming from a 17-year-old kid!

One day Mickey, Sid, and I were invited to a special charity day at the Del Mar Racetrack. It was in its first year and two of the founders and principal stockholders were Bing Crosby and Pat O'Brien. We got to sit with them in their owners' box and I've never enjoyed a day at the races more. Mick was a real sucker for the ponies and more than once I have heard him tying up the telephone on the set talking to a bookie while the assistant director was itching to use the phone for studio business.

Two years in a row our slow-motion wrestling act was the highlight of the Warner Brothers annual studio banquet. The climax of the evening each year was a reel of "blow-ups" by their stars. I know you are used to seeing various blow-up shows on television, the best of which I think is the one hosted by Ed McMahon and Dick Clark.

As funny as that show is, you can't imagine the inside humor when idolized Warner stars blew their lines in front of their coworkers. At that time blow-ups were kept secret by the studio film editors and never shown to the public.

I saw Bette Davis, beautifully made up as Jezebel, say, "I can't remember my next line with this goddamned wig slipping off my head." None of the Warner stars were spared. I saw Pat O'Brien, James Cagney, and even the stately Paul Muni as Louis Pasteur, turn to the camera and make funny faces as they went up in their lines. The lovely Joan Blondell and Claire Trevor came out with some surprisingly salty remarks while groping for their next line.

The crowning blow-up, because I saw it saved and repeated each year, was Dick Foran playing in a western. He tried unsuccessfully to mount his horse, then he turned to the camera and snarled, "Goddam it. I can't get my fat ass off the ground."

One night we were doing our act at a big benefit where Phil Harris was fronting his own orchestra. We were talking to him backstage and Sid was setting our music with him. He asked Phil to play "The Skater's Waltz" for us and hummed a few bars to let him know the slow pace we wanted. While we were waiting in the wings, the great George Burns, who was then still performing with his wonderful wife Gracie Allen, was regaling us with funny stories. He kindly told Sid he could use any of them if it would help him in introducing our act.

Just as we were about to go on, Phil Harris left the bandstand and ran up to us and said, "Sid, you didn't hum 'The Skater's Waltz,' you were humming 'Over the Waves.'" Sid realized his mistake and thanked him profusely as, for sure, it was "Over the Waves" that we really wanted for our music. Wasn't that nice? It just shows what a sweet guy Phil Harris is and he wanted us to have the right music.

Performing this act with Rooney paid off for me as it led to my having a good part in *Men of Boys Town* at MGM in 1941. I played one of the commissioners of Boys Town and was seen with Mickey throughout the picture. In the hospital sequence, when Larry Nunn is gravely ill and refusing all efforts to be cheered up, we decide to try to entertain him by doing our slow-motion wrestling act for him. Director Norman Taurog let us do about four minutes of the act and it came across very well on film.

I continued working with Mickey and played the character of "Red" in some of his *Andy Hardy* series. I appeared in four of them: *Love Finds Andy*

I was Mickey Rooney's buddy "Red" in four of the *Andy Hardy* films for MGM. I'm under his elbow to the right.

Hardy, *Andy Hardy Gets Spring Fever*, *Andy Hardy's Double Life*, and *The Courtship of Andy Hardy*.

In these films I had the pleasure of working with Judy Garland and Lana Turner in *Love Finds Andy Hardy*. I saw the 19-year-old Esther Williams make her screen debut in *Andy Hardy's Double Life*, and worked with a lovely newcomer named Donna Reed in *The Courtship of Andy Hardy*.

I look back with pleasure on my association with Mickey Rooney who I consider to be the greatest all-around talent to ever hit show business. At this writing, he's still working on stage in his riotous stage revue, *Sugar Babies*, with the ageless Ann Miller.

Rooney's parents, Nell and Joe Yule, were divorced when Mickey was only a child, but they remained friends through the years. On many occasions I attended barbecues at Mickey's five-acre estate in the San Fernando Valley to find his mother and stepfather, Fred Pankey, entertaining Joe Yule and his new wife.

As late as the mid–1930s, Joe Yule was still employed as the top banana at one of the burlesque houses on Main Street in downtown Los Angeles. He was a very funny little man and Mickey is now the spitting image of his father as he performs his "baggy pants" didoes in *Sugar Babies.*

When Mickey hit his peak at MGM the burlesque house started billing Joe Yule as "Mickey Rooney's father." The studio couldn't stand this sort of publicity so they placed Joe under long-term contract to get him out of the local burlesque theater.

We used to visit Joe Yule backstage before he left the burlesque house. I thought it was fun to stand in the wings and watch the strippers perform. In those days the limit of nudity in Los Angeles was tiny "pasties" over the nipples and the briefest of G strings. The girls would strip and bump and grind and really tease the audience without shame; however, when they completed their performance and came backstage, when they stood talking to you, they would cover themselves in complete modesty.

I guess girls will be girls in every walk of life.

40

1939

The year 1939 was so interesting for me that I'll have to cover it in more than one chapter. I'll describe some of the good movies I worked in that year; however, one separate film I will cover in a chapter of its own. I certainly think my small but very interesting role in *Gone with the Wind* deserves its own recognition.

A young Irishman named Douglas Corrigan startled the world in 1938 when he landed his small, single-engined plane unannounced at the airport in Dublin, Ireland. I don't think anyone really believed him, but with his toothy grin he tried to convince everyone that he meant to fly from New York to California and his compass must have been off by 180 degrees.

This crazy stunt tickled the funny bone of the nation and "Wrong Way" Corrigan became an instant hero. To show how he was idolized across the country, there were parades held in his honor in many major cities. When St. Louis toasted the little fellow, my late wife, whose maiden name was Corrigan, rode in a parade with her entire family, as did everyone else in the area named Corrigan.

The culmination of his triumph was the film *The Flying Irishman,* made by RKO in 1939. I played a small part in this film which boasted of an impressive cast, including: Eddie Quillan, Paul Kelly, Robert Armstrong, Gene Reynolds, Donald McBride, J. M. Kerrigan, Dorothy Peterson, Scotty Beckett, Joyce Compton, Dorothy Appleby, Minor Watson, Cora Witherspoon, Spencer Charters, and Peggy Ryan. That was quite a powerful cast playing in support of a crazy Irishman in his one and only film.

Another exciting film that year was *Golden Gloves* made at Paramount. This action-packed motion picture was directed by Edward Dmytryk in one of his earliest directorial assignments. Eddie had been one of Paramount's top film editors before becoming a director. I was really impressed with him and his handling of the actors in this difficult film. He later became one of the Hollywood Ten (more about him in more detail in a later chapter).

The lead in *Golden Gloves* was Richard Denning, and the fine character actor, J. Carrol Naish, was the nasty, unscrupulous fight promoter who took advantage of the young amateur boxers.

Our technical directors were Johnny Indrisano and "Mushie" Callahan, two former professional fighters who made a good living in the industry for years playing fighters, referees, and other related roles, in addition to their technical directing assignments.

"Mushie" Callahan was a former world's junior welterweight champion and my father was his doctor when he won his title at the old American Legion Stadium in Hollywood. ZaSu Pitts's husband, Tom Gallery, was the boxing promoter there at the time. For many years this famous Hollywood landmark was the favorite place to be each Friday night for the film crowd until it was torn down to make room for a bowling alley.

We young actors who played the amateur boxers in this film were carefully tutored by Indrisano and Callahan so we would really look like aspiring contenders for Golden Glove titles. Here again I played a kid with a bad heart and I died in the ring after being mismatched with a more experienced fighter by the villainous J. Carrol Naish. Strangely enough, Naish, who specialized in playing gangsters and other unsavory ethnic characters, was really a friendly, good-natured and very pleasant Irishman.

In Chapter 16 I related that in 1927 one of the films I worked in while under contract to Cecil B. DeMille was titled *The Country Doctor.* There I was featured with the marvelous Austrian actor Ruldoph Schildkraut. He played the kindly, overworked, and underpaid rural practitioner who made house calls in a horse-drawn buggy and more often than not took his meager fees in eggs and other bartered goods.

In 1936 Fox Studios released a film with the same title, but now it was the fine Danish actor Jean Hersholt playing the Canadian Doctor Dafoe, who delivered and cared for the famous Dionne quintuplets. In 1939, undoubtedly with a takeoff of this characterization in mind, RKO starred Hersholt in a series of films about another small-town doctor named Dr. Christian.

I had the good fortune of being cast in two films of the series. I played a hot-shot soda jerk who always had an eye out for the girls who frequented the drugstore where much of the action took place in the series.

In the opening film of the series, *Meet Dr. Christian,* my character was introduced in a spectacular scene where I build a sundae for Marcia Mae Jones by flipping three consecutive scoops of ice cream high in the air to land neatly into the dish. Then, as she watches in admiration, I flip a scoop over my shoulder, making it land perfectly into a cone just as I hand it to another cute girl at the counter.

For me to learn how to do this the studio sent me to the headquarters of Thrifty Drugs, where the man in charge of all their soda fountains gave me a crash course in ice cream dispensing. He was a genius at his art and showed me tricks he had learned in his 20 or more years in the business. At his suggestion, that night at home I practiced for two hours using a large pot of cold mashed potatoes that my mother prepared for me.

The next morning on the set our director, Bernard Vorhaus, had us "walk" through the scene without props to make sure we had the timing and dialogue right. Then he called for a complete rehearsal with ice cream before he would dare shoot the scene on film.

Would you believe, I went through the entire routine without an error and received shouts and cheers from the cast and crew when it was over! Now of course, Vorhaus was sick that he didn't have the courage to have the cameras rolling during that rehearsal.

On the first real take, about halfway through, I made a miss and I know the director was looking forward to a long day. However, my practice from the night before paid off and on the second take I again completed the routine perfectly. This time when the scene was successfully completed I received a standing ovation just as if I had scored the winning touchdown.

I should also mention that I was cleaning mashed potatoes off our kitchen ceiling for several days from the mistakes I had made at home while practicing for my big scene!

41

Gone with the Wind

In early 1939 I was called to my old studio in Culver City, once owned by Cecil B. DeMille. I was to be interviewed for a small part in what most film historians now consider to be the greatest motion picture ever made. I refer, of course, to *Gone with the Wind.*

The studio was now owned by David O. Selznick and I was pleased to report to Charles Richards who was the casting director there during the final years of my DeMille contract. Charlie was still located in the same corner office that I knew so well. He seemed really happy to have invited me back to my old home lot.

He walked me down to the sound stage where he introduced me to director Victor Fleming whom I had known from his many years at MGM. He approved me for the role but, like everyone else who appeared in *Gone with the Wind,* I had to receive the final blessing from David Selznick himself. After David gave his assent, I went to wardrobe to be fitted in the uniform of a ragged Southern soldier.

A few days later I received my call to report and was driven to the back lot of the main studio to the place we old DeMille players loving called "the Forty Acres." After dressing in my tattered uniform and being made up, I was met by Will Price who was the dialogue director for Southern accents. This charming young man was an expert on the various dialects of the South. At the time he was engaged to the lovely actress Maureen O'Hara whom he later married. He had a short career as a director at RKO following his work on *Gone with the Wind.*

Will Price worked with me for about 20 minutes teaching me to talk in a rich, backwoods Georgia accent. When he was satisfied that I sounded like a real "Cracker" he turned me loose. I checked in with assistant director Eric Stacey and told him I was ready. Then I watched for hours while Victor Fleming was lining up and shooting this important sequence of the film. My scenes came at the very end of the long night's work.

This was the part of the picture where Rhett Butler is driving Scarlett O'Hara, Melanie Wilkes with her new baby, and the slave girl Prissy away from Atlanta in a horse-drawn wagon. Soon after they pass the railroad

My wardrobe still as the collapsing Southern soldier in *Gone with the Wind.*

depot as it was burning and the munitions were exploding, their progress is halted while a straggling troop of retreating Southern soldiers plod past in front of them.

As he watches them, Rhett says to Scarlett, "Take a good look my dear. It's a historical moment. You can tell your grandchildren how you watched the South disappear one night."

Just then, one young soldier staggers in front of the wagon and collapses. A large soldier picks him up and slings him over his shoulder and continues the retreat. As Rhett watches this sad sight, he decides it is time for him to join the Confederate army.

This sequence took all night to shoot and the camera was located to give the same point of view that Rhett and Scarlett had from the wagon. As the larger man threw me over his shoulder, I protested groggily, "Put me down. Put me down damn ya. I can walk."

We worked until the sun was coming up. I was being paid $150 for my one day's work, but by the time I checked out, with all those extra hours at time and a half and then double time, my check came to $365. That was after all the deductions had been taken out and I thought that was pretty good earnings for one day's work in 1939.

I thought my association with *Gone with the Wind* was over, but six months later I was called back to the studio to repeat the entire scene. This time, however, we were on a sound stage and the camera was behind us to start with and then it moved in for close-ups of Rhett and Scarlett in the wagon. Also, by now, Victor Fleming had left the picture due to illness and another friend from MGM, Sam Wood, was directing. Sam had directed me in *The Girl Said No* at MGM in 1930.

I attended the local premiere of the film at the beautiful Carthy Circle Theater and was pleased at how well my small contribution to this great motion picture was received.

A few years later the film was rereleased with a highly publicized new and dynamic stereophonic sound track. I went to see it again and was just devastated to "hear" that my lines had been removed in this new recording system. I wondered why and years later I found out what had happened. You see, I had said "Damn" fully an hour and a half before Clark Gable as Rhett Butler shocked the audience with his final speech, "Frankly my dear, I don't give a damn."

That use of the then forbidden word caused real repercussions within the industry and David Selznick was fined $5,000 for his violation of the Motion Picture Producers and Distributors Code of Ethics.

Word later trickled down to me through the grapevine that Selznick had always regretted allowing my use of this word to slip past all the meticulous supervision on his greatest production. So, when he had this second chance to control the dialogue, my lines were "Gone with the Wind."

42

I Play a Ghost

Can you imagine working for weeks on a film and then only being seen as a ghost in the final scenes?

That's exactly what happened to me in *The Fighting 69th,* a fine World War I movie that I worked in at Warner Brothers in 1940. It was directed by William Keighley and starred James Cagney, Pat O'Brien, George Brent, Jeffery Lynn, Alan Hale, Frank McHugh, Dennis Morgan, Dick Foran, William Lundigan, Guinn "Big Boy" Williams, John Litel, and Henry O'Neill. That was nearly all the male members of the Warner Brothers "stock company" of the 1940s.

In the beginning I had scenes at the home parish where it was established that I was an altar boy, a good parishioner, and a friend of our pastor, Father Duffy, who was played by Pat O'Brien.

Later there was a sequence where I was a young soldier in the same training camp where Father Duffy was the Catholic chaplain. He meets me on the company street and tells me he has received a letter from my mother and she is worried about me because I have not been writing. He gives me a good fatherly counseling and extracts a promise from me that I will write to my mother on a regular basis.

In the trenches in France I am seen as a member of a company about to go over the top as part of an infantry charge. There is a huge explosion from an enemy shell and I am seen trapped under dirt and heavy timbers. Then I had a big close-up where the camera dollied in until my face filled the screen and I say the entire Act of Contrition and then die.

The final sequence of the picture shows the statue of Father Duffy as it stands in Times Square in New York City. Then all the principal players who died in the film are shown superimposed as images as they march by the statue and wave to Father Duffy.

To my chagrin, that was my only appearance in the film. Due to an overage in length, my character was one of several deleted from the motion picture, but my grinning ghost remained, marching, smiling, and waving to the statue of the good Father Duffy. Ah, the vagaries of show business!

I had another small part with Pat O'Brien at Warner Brothers that year

As a dying American soldier in the trenches in France in *The Fighting 69th.*

when I worked with him in *Knute Rockne—All American.* That was the famous film about the Notre Dame "Fighting Irish" football team where Ronald Reagan played the legendary George Gipp. His deathbed request to Rockne, "Win one for the Gipper," was frequently used by President Ronald Reagan in political speeches throughout the eight years of his presidency.

This film was directed by Lloyd Bacon and beside Reagan and O'Brien it also starred Gale Page as Mrs. Rockne and Donald Crisp as Father Hesberg. My part was very small but it was crucial to the story. I delivered a telegram to him when he and Mrs. Rockne were vacationing in Florida. The message in the wire invites him to attend an important meeting of coaches on the West coast. Mrs. Rockne asks him not to go, but he says he must and, as a result, he boards the airplane in which he crashed to his death on a farm in Kansas.

I worked in my second Charlie Chan movie at Twentieth Century–Fox that year. It was titled *Murder over New York.* Now instead of Warner Oland as the Chinese detective with the pithy Oriental observations, it was Sidney Toler as Chan and Victor Sen Yung was now the comedic "number two son," instead of my old friend Keye Luke who played the role of "number one son" with Warner Oland.

I played a bellboy in the swanky men's club where much of the action took place. I had some good scenes with Sidney Toler and Victor Sen Yung and the very funny Donald McBride. The big cast was rounded out by Marjorie Weaver, Robert Lowery, Ricardo Cortez, Melville Cooper, Joan Valerie, Kane Richmond, John Sutton, Leyland Hodgson, Frederick Worlock, Lal Chand Mehra, and the great black actor Clarence Muse. The director was Harry Lachman.

I again played the soda jerk in my second film of the *Dr. Christian* series with Jean Hersholt at RKO. This one was called *Remedy for Riches* and was directed by Erle C. Kenton. As in all the *Dr. Christian* series, this one had a fine cast that included Dorothy Lovett, Edgar Kennedy, Jed Prouty, Walter Catlett, Robert Baldwin, Warren Hull, Maude Eburne, Margaret Wade, Hallene Hill, Renie Riano, Barry Macollum, Lester Scharaff, Prudence Penny, Stanley Blystone, Tom Herbert, Maynard Holmes, Dick Rush, and Edward Hearn. It was a real pleasure working with such veterans.

My next film that year was *Men of Boys Town* at MGM. I've already mentioned quite a bit about that picture and, of course, it starred Mickey Rooney as the mayor of Boys Town and Spencer Tracy as Father Flanagan. I was one of the commissioners in the student government established by Father Flanagan. This was the film where Mickey Rooney, Sidney Miller, and I did about four minutes or so of our slow-motion wrestling act.

43

SHAZAM!

In the final week of my work in *Men of Boys Town* at MGM, I received a telephone call from my agent asking if I could get off for a few hours to go for an interview at Republic Pictures.

Republic is in Studio City in the San Fernando Valley and MGM is in Culver City, a good one hour's drive away. I asked Stanley Goldsmith, our assistant director, if I could leave the set for about three hours. It so happened I would not be needed for the required time so he let me off.

I drove frantically across town and over Laurel Canyon, which let me out right near Republic. At that time Republic was owned by Herbert Yates and was probably the best of the independents. They produced mostly westerns and serials but were considered tops in those fields. Their ace cowboy stars were Gene Autry and Roy Rogers and a group known as The Three Mesquiteers. This group fluctuated its cast from time to time, but in 1940 the principal players were Bob Livingston, Bob Steele, and Rufe Davis. Republic's other big star was a young fellow named John Wayne who had moved up from his spot as one of the Three Mesquiteers into higher-budget feature films.

My agent told me I was up for the costarring role of a kid named Billy Batson in a serial called *Adventures of Captain Marvel.* He said it was based on a running story in *WHIZ Comics* by Fawcett Publications and was well known among the younger set. I confessed I had never seen it and had no idea who Billy Batson or Captain Marvel were. I told him I had to go right from the set and would be in makeup and in the clothes I was wearing as a commissioner of Boys Town. He thought that would be all right and said to make the best of it.

At Republic I was ushered into the office of associate producer Hiram S. Brown, Jr., and met William Witney and John English who were to direct the serial. I had never met the three before. They were very friendly and seemed to know me from my past work. They were surprised I didn't know about the character I was interviewing for and suggested I buy a copy of *WHIZ Comics.* I did so on the way back to MGM.

My part in *Men of Boys Town* ended with the hospital sequence where

Mickey and Sid and I did our slow-motion wrestling act. I bid farewell to director Norman Taurog, Mickey, Sid, and Spencer Tracy, who autographed a nice 11″ × 14″ matte-finish portrait I had requested from the publicity department. I went on home where my mother gave me the good news that I had been selected for the role of Billy Batson and was to report to the Republic wardrobe department the following day.

From wardrobe I was sent to the office of assistant director Louis Germonprez who, I later learned, was considered the best in the serial business and he also doubled as unit production manager. Lou handed me the script of *Adventures of Captain Marvel* which I swear was as thick as the Los Angeles telephone directory. Then he handed me a second book, equally as thick, which he called the "breakdown book." This was Lou's "bible," which he used to control the production schedule of the 28 days we were to shoot. The serial actually took 32 days to complete due to inclement weather on days we had to work on location.

In Lou's office I saw the largest breakdown board I had ever seen. It ran the length of the room and across the top it was divided into the 28 days of production. Down the left side were the actors listed by the name of the character they were playing. Under each day there were movable strips that could be removed and shifted if need be. These strips listed the locations, the wardrobe changes, and other information pertinent to the day's work and also had a red "X" opposite the names of the cast members involved in that sequence.

The breakdown book that I mentioned coincided with Lou's breakdown board. For instance, on page one of the book it would say: Day 1, Billy Batson, 8:00 A.M. to 11:00 A.M., scenes 1–14 of episode 6, costume A, location C. So, on day one I would wear costume A and report to where location C was. The next entry would say: Day 1, Billy Batson, 11:00 A.M.–3:00 P.M., scenes 20–34 of episode 3, costume B, location E.

By using this breakdown book I knew which pages of script to study, what to wear, and where to show up to work in those scenes. If the location selected for the day was an exterior, there was always an interior cover set in case of inclement weather. As I said, Louis Germonprez was a genius at his job and this jovial man did his best to keep us on schedule. With all his good planning we still went four days over schedule. There were so many outside locations there was just no way he could cover them all with interiors. We were working in the months of December and January and the usual mild California climate rebelled against him.

In the story the unwelcome Malcolm archaeological expedition had traveled to a remote section of Siam seeking knowledge of the Scorpion dynasty. The local native tribes were concerned that we would desecrate the Valley of Tombs. If this desecration occurred it would be signified by the eruption of Scorpio, a long-dormant volcano.

The young radio reporter Billy Batson.

On the first day of the serial I reported to a sound stage at Republic where William Witney directed the scenes in the first episode in which members of the expedition are about to enter the tomb of the Scorpion to find and extract long-hidden treasures. When the leader makes it known they are going to violate the curse of the Scorpion by entering the forbidden crypt, Billy Batson refuses to accompany them. He says he doesn't feel it is right to break the sanctity and offers to go to another chamber to gather lesser artifacts.

When four members of the expedition break into the sacred tomb they find a golden scorpion, a metallic device with a lens clutched in each of its five adjustable claws. When one of the scientists aligns the lenses against a ray of sunlight shining into the tomb there is a flash of lightning and an explosion. All four men are knocked unconscious, and the shock wave causes a large stone monolith to fall across the entrance of the tomb sealing the scientists inside.

At the same time, in the separate chamber, Billy Batson is confronted by Shazam, a centuries-old, white-robed, bearded mystic who is the protector of the Scorpion. Because Billy has not broken the curse, Shazam gives Billy the right to utter his name and turn into Captain Marvel who, he says, will protect innocent people from any evil use of the Scorpion's lenses.

Billy looks skeptical, so Shazam points to a plaque on the chamber's wall that describes the powers Billy will receive by saying the magic name. They are:

Solomon:	Wisdom
Hercules:	Strength
Atlas:	Stamina
Zeus:	Power
Achilles:	Courage
Mercury:	Speed

In disbelief, Billy says, "Shazam." There is a clap of thunder and a puff of smoke, and there stands Captain Marvel, the world's mightiest mortal. Captain Marvel was portrayed in the serial by the western star Tom Tyler. Captain Marvel looks as surprised as Billy Batson did at this first transformation and he looks with approval at the cape and boots he is wearing and the uniform with the lightning bolt on the chest.

He bounds to the entrance of the sacred tomb where he finds the giant stone slab blocking the crypt. It weighs a ton or more but he easily lifts it aside and looks into the tomb, seeing the four scientists lying unconscious on the floor. Then he says, "Shazam" and is Billy Batson again. Billy now enters the tomb and helps revive the expedition members and leads them outside.

This sounds like pretty heady stuff, but it looked very realistic on film. Once outside the tomb, Tal Chotali, the expedition's Siamese scientist guide, demonstrates how, when the five lenses of the Scorpion are properly aligned, it becomes an atom smasher capable of destroying anything its rays are focused upon, or when lined up differently, it can turn objects into pure gold. The scientists now realize they can become the most powerful group on earth by proper use of the Scorpion.

They all agree that no one member should possess all five of the lenses.

Billy Batson meets the venerable mystic Shazam in the Republic serial *Adventures of Captain Marvel* released in 1941. Shazam gives Billy the right to utter his name and be transformed into Captain Marvel, "the world's mightiest mortal." Shazam!

They divide the lenses and the body of the Scorpion among themselves and entrust the scroll that tells of the device's many uses to Billy Batson.

Almost immediately one member of the group begins his nefarious scheme to acquire all the lenses and become the world's most powerful person. Twelve episodes later this man is exposed by Captain Marvel and the evil scientist is disintegrated by rays of the very Scorpion he had intended to use for his own greedy gains.

When the villain scientist is dead, Captain Marvel throws the body of the Scorpion with its lenses into the boiling cauldron of the volcano, declaring that its powers were now ended. At this point the ethereal voice of Shazam is heard from afar. This utterance of the magic name transforms Captain Marvel into Billy Batson. Billy stands there mystified that someone other than himself or Captain Marvel had spoken the name of Shazam to cause this change. In his confusion he asks, 'What happened? Who spoke?" Tal Chotali then explains to him that Captain Marvel had been the protector of the Scorpion and now that it has been destroyed, the power of Captain Marvel was at an end.

As I said earlier, on the first day of production we filmed the scenes

Billy Batson is about to be trapped in the mystic Shazam's private tomb.

at the entrance to the crypt. When the four expedition members entered the tomb their work for the day was over and they were excused.

Then we moved to the chamber where Billy meets Shazam. The ancient mystic was played by the distinguished actor Nigel de Brulier. He played many great roles in earlier years, including the crafty Cardinal Richelieu in *The Three Musketeers* with Douglas Fairbanks in 1921, and he repeated his Cardinal Richelieu performance with Fairbanks in *The Iron*

Mask in 1928. As serial schedules and the foibles of movie work go, this once revered actor was happy to receive one day of work in our serial and he was most impressive in his characterization of the venerable Shazam.

Republic filled the cast of *Adventures of Captain Marvel* with fine performers who were either on the way up or in the declining years of their careers. For instance, Bryant Washburn, who had once been a big star, played a supporting role, as did Jack Mulhall who had been a star in many movies dating back to the early 1920s.

Our leading lady was Louise Currie, making her debut at Republic. She later worked there playing opposite Gene Autry in *Stardust on the Sage* and in *The Masked Marvel,* a 12-chapter serial with a different kind of "Marvel." Louise is now a successful interior designer. Her husband is the antique dealer and importer John Good and they travel the world seeking art works and leading the good life.

My pal Whitey was played by William Benedict, one of filmdom's busiest actors. Bill came to Hollywood from Tulsa, Oklahoma, in 1934. He was under contract to the old Fox Studio for two years and had the pleasure of working there with the great Will Rogers in *Doubting Thomas* and *Steamboat Round the Bend.* His other serials include *Tim Tyler's Luck* and *Perils of Nyoka.* He played in a combination of 80 films with the former Dead End Kids in their later *Little Tough Guys, East Side Kids,* and *Bowery Boys* series. To this day Bill and I are still the best of friends.

Tom Tyler was doubled throughout the serial by the great stuntman David Sharpe. Dave was an absolutely fearless man who made even the most difficult stunt look easy. He had been a tumbler in gymnastic competitions, in vaudeville, and in circuses and played the lead in comedies for Hal Roach. He was a handsome man and he also played in many college-age feature films. When acting jobs thinned out he turned to stunting and some of his feats are still remembered with awe.

Though Dave was smaller in stature than Tom Tyler, their builds were similar and he looked most believable in the stunts he did for Tom. My favorite caper that Dave did in our serial was in the first chapter when he did a back flip, catching two of the native tribesmen under their chins with well-placed kicks.

Dave Sharpe was such a meticulous performer that he was rarely injured. I attribute this to his careful planning and his excellent timing and judgment of distance. He frequently brought a small trampoline to the locations and would use it to give him the proper bounce to make his incredible leaps. After he made contact with this device there was always a group of assistants holding a small fireman's net to catch him in his fall.

The tragic finish to Dave's career is that he died of the dreadful nerve disease ALS, referred to as Lou Gehrig's disease. I visited Dave in his final days at our great Motion Picture and Television Country Home. This outstanding specimen of manhood was now down to a shell of his former self and could hardly talk. He still tried to communicate with his eyes and made it evident that he was pleased that I had come to visit him.

One of the major contributing factors to the success of *Adventures of Captain Marvel* was the outstanding work of the Lydecker brothers, Howard and Ted. These young special effects experts made all the flight scenes of Captain Marvel completely believable. Part of this was accomplished by the use of a papier-mâché dummy of Captain Marvel that measured seven feet from head to toe. This dummy was used in several ways. I saw it suspended on a cable that must have reached 200 yards as the Lydeckers had it photographed "flying" down a location on Mulholland Drive in the Santa Monica Mountains. I swear, this cable didn't sag an inch as the dummy of Captain Marvel traversed its length. Close-ups of Captain Marvel flying were filmed on the process stage with Tom Tyler himself suspended in a harness with invisible wires, as clouds sped by him in the background in this process form of photography where cameraman Bud Thackery held forth.

The Lydeckers even had the dummy "fly" from ground level to the roof of the Biltmore Hotel in downtown Los Angeles in one exciting scene in the serial. First you saw Tom Tyler make his spring into the air, then a cut of the dummy, then a shot of Dave Sharpe making his landing, then a close shot of Tyler, supposedly landing on the roof. When the film editors put it all together it looked very plausible.

The transitions of Billy Batson turning into Captain Marvel were also very believable. While the transitions in the *Superman* serial were done by animation, ours were accomplished in live action on film. When Billy said "Shazam," there was always a puff of smoke. When the haze cleared, there stood Captain Marvel ready to protect the innocent. To do this there was always a trough of flash powder that was ignited electrically by a propman. When the smoke enveloped Billy, the cameraman would cut. Then Tom Tyler would take my place, the camera would turn, and the smoke charge would be set off again. As the air cleared this time, Tom would bounce off to do what was required of him. After the film editors did their splicing, the transformation was very credible.

There were times on outside locations, when the wind was blowing from an unfavorable direction, that I lost a few eyebrow hairs from the unexpected powder flash in my face. Oh well! That's a small complaint.

This was such a pleasant group of people to work with that Bill Benedict and I decided to give a present to everyone in the crew and the few actors still working near the close of production. About two days before the end we had a few hours off one afternoon and went into Hollywood to the Woolworth's five-and-ten that was then on Hollywood Boulevard.

We had a list of 40 names and we put together a budget of $40 of our own money. We bought a gag present for everybody on our list. We spent half the night wrapping these presents and gave them out in a little ceremony on the set the next day. It was a lot of fun and all appreciated our thoughtfulness.

We matched each recipient with a gift representing something in connection with his job. For instance, we gave Tom Tyler a jockstrap. That was not out of disrespect, but with his tight-fitting uniform, we thought it would be useful. We gave Dave Sharpe a blow gun that shot a toy man into the air and it wafted down safely to earth suspended by a little silk parachute. Louis Germonprez was always worrying about the weather and our schedule, so he received a miniature hourglass and a toy can labeled "Liquid Sun Shine." Our head driver was given an excellent road map. William Witney and John English each received little buggy whips, implying they were slave drivers, which of course they were not.

My final day of production was really a killer. It seems they saved all my water scenes for the last. In the morning I worked in a large tank where Witney had me photographed through a glass window while I was swimming underwater fully clothed.

That afternoon we went out to Lake Malibu, which was then a remote dammed reservoir, but is now surrounded by high-priced homes in the Westlake Village complex in Thousand Oaks. There we shot the scenes at the beginning of Chapter 11 in which I rescue the unconscious Louise Currie and tow her to shore. Louise had already completed her work in the serial, so I was really towing a stuntwoman who was doubling for her.

In this sequence I was wearing a heavy tweed suit and as helpful as the stuntwoman was, the sheer weight of this suit when wet was pulling me under as I tried to swim with one arm while my other arm was around the girl. After nearly sinking a few times I asked Witney if I could at least remove my heavy trousers and shoes. My lower body was not in view so Witney agreed to my request. So dear fans, when you watch the scenes where I am swimming Louise Currie to shore, I am actually barefooted and in my undershorts.

Adventures of Captain Marvel is now considered by most serial fans to be the best action episode film ever made. I attribute this to several contributing factors. First, it had an excellent, imaginative story line; it was forcefully directed by two of the best action men in the business, William Witney and John English; it had a fine and talented cast; David Sharpe's stunting was superb; and the clever special effects by the Lydecker brothers compares favorably with what you now see in Lucas and Spielberg films.

Also, Republic Pictures, the tops in the ranks of serial producers, gave it the appearance of a more expensive production than its limited budget would afford. They accomplished this by the inclusion of stock footage from several of their other motion pictures.

In the first episode, in the scenes of the native tribesmen raiding our camp and then the British cavalry charging to our rescue in Siam, the studio added footage from their 1938 feature film, *Storm over Bengal.* This gave our serial scenes that compared favorably with *The Charge of the Light Brigade* and *Lives of a Bengal Lancer,* both made at major studios with multimillion dollar budgets.

For the shipwreck scenes in episode ten, they incorporated clips from *SOS Coast Guard.* The volcano eruption and lava-flowing effects were from the Republic serial, *Hawk of the Wilderness.*

When I worked in *Adventures of Captain Marvel,* I just thought of it as another of the now more than 400 screen appearances I have made. Though I starred in silent and talking feature films and many comedy short subjects, most of my fans now consider this serial to be the most important and my best-remembered work.

Mainly due to this serial I am invited to film festivals here and around the country. As part of the film-cons, I am usually a guest on a question-and-answer panel where I am often asked about the making of *Adventures of Captain Marvel.* Since these fan groups nearly always ask me the same questions, I might as well repeat the most popular ones here.

I am always asked if I liked Tom Tyler and how was he to work with. I tell them that I first met Tom around 1926 when he was playing in a series of western films at FBO, before it became known as RKO. In those films he worked with Frankie Darro. The big chase scenes always had Tom on his horse, Frankie on his Shetland pony, and their German shepherd dog, running side by side. I related earlier it was the same mean little pony that tried to buck me off and then run me under a weeping willow tree when I was riding him in *Whispering Smith,* the first film on my DeMille contract.

All of the Tyler-Darro westerns were directed by Robert de Lacy, whose wife Leona was my mother's best friend. Many times when we had the de Lacys over for dinner, they would bring the tall, strapping, shy, handsome bachelor Tom Tyler with them. So, we were friends for a number of years before we costarred in *Adventures of Captain Marvel.*

It was strange that in the entire 12 chapters we never appeared in a scene together. This was, of course, because Tom never came into view until I said "Shazam."

Tom was born in New York in 1903 and, among other things, he was a coal miner, a seaman, a lumberjack, a prizefighter, a sculptor's model, and a champion weightlifter, before he broke into pictures in 1924 as an extra and a stuntman. He played good roles into the late 1940s and died in 1954 of a heart attack at the age of 50. He had been troubled by a crippling arthritic condition that forced him out of pictures and I fear he was in poor financial status when he passed away.

I'm always asked if it is true that William Witney directed all the action scenes and John English the ones with important dialogue. I always confess that I wasn't aware of this, but I do remember John was directing the day I had my heaviest dramatic sequence.

Truthfully I was not cognizant of any division of directorial assignments. It seemed to me there was action of some sort every day. On a serial the two directors alternated days because there was so much work on a six-week schedule that one man just couldn't work such long hours.

While one director was working from early morning into darkness, the other man was preparing the next day's shooting by checking script, locations for camera setups, and other important details. I have asked Witney about this. He said both he and English were capable of handling whatever the schedule called for, but if he did have a choice he always asked for the heavy action scenes.

The other question I am always asked is, how did I get selected to play the role of Billy Batson? I have always said I thought it was because I was the right size and age and was available at the time. Also that I probably resembled the character in *WHIZ Comics* more than most other young actors. I was talking to Bill Witney on the telephone recently and I asked him the same question. His immediate response was, "You were hired for the part because you were a damn good actor and we knew you could play the part the way we wanted it played." I decided to ask no further questions.

My most recent association with *Adventures of Captain Marvel* was when Leonard Maltin called and asked me if he could interview me for his TV show "Entertainment Tonight." Republic Pictures was releasing a tape of the serial on the home video market and Leonard, a real serial buff, interviewed me and I was seen on this show over NBC on March 21, 1988.

So there, a film thought to be just another job is still being remembered by the fans 50 years later.

SHAZAM!

44

War Hits Hollywood

Following my work in *Adventures of Captain Marvel,* things slowed down for me, as it did for many other young actors. We were now at war in Europe and many juvenile performers were already in uniform. Film was in short supply as the military needed it in the war effort and production in Hollywood was drastically curtailed. Because I was the sole support of my mother, I was granted a draft deferment and it looked like I would not be called up for a while.

During this period I worked in several training films for the army and even traveled to Fort Ord near Monterey, California, on one of them. I played a small role in *The Rear Gunner* which starred Burgess Meredith with Dane Clark.

One of the training films I worked in had to do with discipline and court-martials. In this one I played a young soldier jitterbugging wildly at a USO dance. In one of my reckless maneuvers I crash into the couple dancing next to me. That soldier is furious and decks me on the spot. He is apprehended by the MPs and has to stand courtmartial for striking another service man.

The trouble here was that I didn't know how to jitterbug. I was strictly a Glenn Miller– or Tommy Dorsey–type dancer and never did learn the Balboa or other fad dances of the era. I told Jackie Cooper about my problem and he had me over to his house where our good friend Buddy Pepper gave me a crash course in the latest steps. The next day on the set I gyrated as best I could in my newly learned movements. I felt foolish, but I must have pleased the director as he approved my work.

Also in this period I continued working in the *Andy Hardy* films until Mickey Rooney himself donned the khaki.

Later that year I had a small role in *The Man Who Came to Dinner* at Warner Brothers. This memorable film was based on the George S. Kaufman–Moss Hart stage play of the same name. It told of an acid-tongued radio celebrity who falls and breaks his hip while on a lecture tour and how he terrorizes the inhabitants of the suburban home where he must stay for several weeks as he recoups from his injury.

It starred Bette Davis, with Monty Woolley playing the Alexander Woolcott–type role of the vitriolic radio personality. Directed by William Keighley, it had a fine supporting cast with Ann Sheridan, Jimmy Durante, Reginald Gardiner, Richard Travis, Billie Burke, and Grant Mitchell.

In Chapter 25 I mentioned working with the then 25-year-old Bette Davis in *Hell's House,* one of her very first motion pictures. I was better known than she was at the time and was mentioned ahead of her in many reviews of the film.

After I had been working with her for three days, I did something daring. It was obvious that she remembered me from *Hell's House* since she had been very friendly to me. On my fourth and final day on the picture I brought the press book that Bennie Zeidman Productions had put out on *Hell's House* to the set of *The Man Who Came to Dinner.*

When she was not busy I brought the press book to Bette for her to look at. She smiled good-naturedly when she saw that the official studio billing read:

JUNIOR DURKIN
PAT O'BRIEN
bette davis – junior coghlan

She called director William Keighley over and showed it to him and he then walked around the set with it, showing it to everyone.

That evening as I was saying my goodbyes, she called me into her dressing room where she gave me a beautiful 11″ × 14″ matte-finish portrait photograph that she autographed for me.

So, the very classy lady was not offended at all.

45

Henry Aldrich

Back in Chapter 34, when talking about radio, I mentioned Henry Aldrich and told of working in that program with Ezra Stone when he came to Hollywood to star in *Those Were the Days* at Paramount in 1940. It was strange but Ezra, who made the character of Henry Aldrich a household name, never did get to play the role he created in a motion picture.

When Paramount bought the screen rights to the play, they overlooked Ezra, who was still playing Henry on radio, and cast Jackie Cooper as the ever-troubled teenager. Jackie starred in two films based on the Henry Aldrich character: *What a Life* released in 1939, and *Life with Henry* in 1941.

After the second film, Paramount thought Cooper was outgrowing the part, but they did want to continue the series. They again tested Ezra Stone but instead opted for Jimmy Lydon who had scored first-rate notices in the title role in *Tom Brown's Schooldays.*

Lydon was selected for the coveted part of Tom Brown out of a reported 1,500 other lads in a nationwide contest for the "typical American boy." Jimmy was well known in New York for his radio and stage work before his screen debut in *Back Door to Heaven* in 1939. Lydon was to play Henry Aldrich in nine films before the series ended in 1944.

I had a good part in *Henry Aldrich for President,* Lydon's first of the nine. I was Marvin Bagshaw, one of the high school kids who were trying to prevent Henry from being elected class president. I played a stooge for Kenny Howell, the rich kid villain, who was running for office against Henry. Here I was, Kenny Howell's good friend where he had been my hated enemy in *The Frolics of Youth* comedies at Educational in 1933 and 1934.

Henry's friend Dizzy was played by Charles Smith. Mr. and Mrs. Aldrich were Dorothy Peterson and John Litel and his sister was Martha O'Driscoll. His girlfriend was Mary Anderson and the school vamp was June Preisser. All nine of Lydon's films as Henry Aldrich were directed by Hugh Bennett.

While Dorothy Peterson played Mrs. Aldrich in *Henry Aldrich for*

President, Olive Blakeney portrayed the mother in the remaining eight films of the series. In a storybook-like romance, Lydon actually married Olive's real-life daughter Betty Lou in 1952 and they now have two grown daughters.

I made several lifelong friends while working on *Henry Aldrich for President.* Jimmy Lydon and I see each other on interviews for television commercials where we compete good-naturedly for grandfather roles. We also meet a few times a year for lunch. I see Mary Anderson at luncheons of the Pacific Pioneer Broadcasters. In 1987 I sat with Martha O'Driscoll and her husband at the annual reunion of "kid" actors who worked at Universal Studios in the 1930s and 1940s.

This marvelous afternoon affair is organized each year by Michael Fitzgerald, a fan I met at the Memphis Film Festival when I was a guest there in 1986. He and his friend Gary Bell call their parties the Jivin' Jacks and Jills Reunion and they hold it each year in August. The original date was selected to coincide with the joint birthdays of Donald O'Connor, Peggy Ryan, and Martha Raye.

In addition to the three mentioned above, the 1988 guest list included: Anne Gwynne, Martha Scott, Joan Leslie, Mary Anderson, Gloria Jean, Sybil Jason, Jane Withers, Jimmy Lydon, Bill Benedict, Dick Wilson (Mr. Whipple), Eddie Quillan, Billy Barty, Billy Lee, Leonard Maltin of "Entertainment Tonight," director Edward Dmytryk and his wife-actress Jean Porter, Rita Quigley, Frankie Thomas, Gene Nelson, Al Checco, Trudy Marshall, Bobs Watson, Marie Windsor, Martha Tilton, Marsha Hunt, John Howard, Margaret O'Brien, Virginia O'Brien, Vivian Austin, Diana Hale, Penny Singleton, Peter Coe, Rosemary DeCamp, Helene Stanley, Coleen Gray, David Holt, Buddy Pepper, Shirley Mills, Ann Rooney, Ruth Terry, Robert Shayne, Fayard Nicholas of the dancing Nicholas Brothers, Warren Stevens, Eileen Barton, Sidney Miller, and Tom Irish. Last year the list also included Debbie Reynolds, Cora Sue Collins, Allan Jones, Joy Hodges, and June Carlson, George Ernest, and Billy Mahan of the "Jones Family" cast.

Can you wonder why I look forward to attending this happy occasion each year?

The lovely Mary Anderson, who played Henry's girlfriend, came to Hollywood after scouts for David Selznick found her in Birmingham, Alabama, and cast her to play the part of Maybelle Merriweather in *Gone with the Wind.* Though she regrets that most of her footage was eliminated from the final cut of the film, the publicity she received from it started her on a fine career. The Selznick people even had her raise the rebel flag on the opening day of production with nationwide press coverage. (Mary and I were together at three separate functions in 1990 in connection with the 50th anniversary of *Gone with the Wind.*)

After subsequent film roles in *All This and Heaven Too* and in *Cheers for Miss Bishop,* Mary scored a major success on Broadway in *Guest in the House* and was rewarded with a contract at Twentieth Century–Fox. There she was cast in important roles in *Lifeboat, The Song of Bernadette,* and *Wilson.* She later traveled to Paramount where she was reunited with her *Gone with the Wind* costar Olivia de Havilland. Mary's pivotal role with her in *To Each His Own,* for which Miss de Havilland won her first Oscar, would be later remembered as the high point in Mary's screen career. However, as late as the 1960s Mary Anderson had a running part at Twentieth Century–Fox in the popular television series, "Peyton Place."

In 1953, at the age of 31, she married Academy Award winning cinematographer Leon Shamroy. Leon passed away in 1974 and Mary has lived alone in their beautiful canyon home ever since. On a special table in their home are Shamroy's four Oscars. They are for his camera work at Twentieth Century–Fox in *Black Swan* in 1942; *Wilson* in 1944; *Leave Her to Heaven* in 1945; and the spectacular *Cleopatra* in 1963.

Mary has told me of her several visits to visit Leon in Rome while he was photographing *Cleopatra.* She says she has never seen such time wasted on a set and of the almost unbelievable pampering lavished upon the then superstar Elizabeth Taylor.

June Preisser came to Hollywood from New Orleans and made a spectacular entry into motion pictures at MGM with her acrobatic dancing. She was featured there in *Babes in Arms, Dancing Co-ed, Strike Up the Band,* and also in *Judge Hardy and Son.* I'll never forget the amazing "face falls" that she used to perform. I still don't know how she kept from breaking her neck in those daring maneuvers. June passed away in 1984 at the age of 63.

My dear friend Martha O'Driscoll played Henry's sister in *Henry Aldrich for President,* but is not listed in the following films of the series. Martha worked in 37 motion pictures in her 11-year movie career, including *Mad About Music,* with Deanna Durbin at Universal. Her final film was *Carnegie Hall* in 1947. I gave her the nickname of Martha O'Drizzle and she loved it.

In 1947, at the age of 25, she married businessman Arthur Appleton and retired from active film work. Art, as she lovingly calls him, is president and chairman of the board of Appleton Electric Company and they now have four grown children. He also has interests in racetracks in Illinois and Florida. They share their time between a home on Chicago's prestigious North Shore and another on an island in Miami Bay. They also have a thoroughbred breeding farm where they raise horses for their own and other racing stables.

Martha says her life since leaving the movies has been very rewarding and for sure it has. As a young society matron she has been president of Chicago's Sarah Siddons Society, whose theatrical awards are comparable to the Tonys of the Broadway stage. She has served as chairman of the Ways and Means Committee of Chicago's Junior League, has been president of the Women's Board of the Chicago Boys Clubs, and on the board of the local chapter of World's Adoption International Fund as treasurer.

My wife and I sat with Martha and Art at the Universal Jivin' Jacks and Jills Reunion in 1987. They told us that on the following day they were flying to the Mediterranean to board their 145-foot yacht. It seems their busy schedule will not permit the time to cross the Atlantic on it, so they send it on ahead and fly to board it at the garden spot of their choice. I guess if you have a yacht that size, that's the only way to travel. With all their wealth, Martha and Art are just as old shoe as your next-door neighbors and I credit them for being such wonderful people.

Another dear friend I met because of the *Henry Aldrich* series is Rita Quigley. Though we didn't actually work together on the series, she had a featured role in *Henry Aldrich, Editor* and we met and dated a few times. Rita is the older sister of Juanita Quigley who has quite a track record of her own.

Rita broke into the movies in 1940 when, at the age of 17, she played Joan Crawford's neglected daughter in *Susan and God.* Some of her other credits include *The Howards of Virginia, The Human Comedy, Blonde Inspiration,* and *Women in Bondage.* Rita retired from the screen in 1944 and is now the happy mother of six children.

Juanita Quigley, born in 1930, entered films at the age of two and a half and continued until she was 18. Then she entered a convent and became a teaching nun. Thirteen years later she renounced her vows. She later met a former seminarian and they married and have two children. Juanita now teaches English at Delaware County Community College in Media, Pennsylvania, and her husband is professor of philosophy at nearby Villanova University. Juanita's best-remembered roles are probably those in *Born to Dance, Having a Wonderful Time, A Yank at Eton,* and *National Velvet.*

Two other friends from *Henry Aldrich for President* are Buddy Pepper and Lon McCallister. I have mentioned about Buddy being the piano player in Jackie Cooper's little band and how he taught me to jitterbug for the army training film. In all the years I have known him I have never heard him use any other name than Buddy. Oddly enough here, Lon, making one of his first films, was listed in the cast as Bud McCallister.

Lon, or Bud, went on to greater things after our picture together and he starred in such films as *Home in Indiana, Scudda Hoo! Scuddfa Hay!, The Story of Seabiscuit, The Big Cat,* and *The Boy from Indiana.* Lon is now living in retirement in a mountain home on Lake Tahoe.

Buddy Pepper was an exceptionally talented pianist and at various times he traveled as the accompanist for Judy Garland, Marlene Dietrich, and Margaret Whiting. He also wrote the title song for the movie *Pillow Talk* and, as I mentioned previously, he wrote the music for the popular standard

"Vaya con Dios." I saw Buddy Pepper for the first time in years at the 1988 Jivin' Jacks and Jills Reunion. I was devastated to see that he is now so crippled up with arthritis that he told me he hasn't been able to play the piano for over 20 years.

My girlfriend in *Henry Aldrich for President* was Noel Neill and we had many scenes together, although Dizzy beats me out for her affections in the end. By the time the picture was completed I had a real crush on her and we dated frequently for the next two years. Noel played in other films in the *Aldrich* series and it led to her receiving a Paramount contract. In addition to working in *Henry and Dizzy* and *Henry Aldrich's Little Secret,* she had featured roles in *Are These Our Parents?*, *Here Come the Waves,* and *Are You with It?* before her contact ran out.

When I was leaving for my navy flight training, Noel gave me an autographed photo which she signed, "Frank—Best to the best—Sprout 'em soon. Noel." By that she meant for me to "sprout my navy wings."

In that beautiful Paramount portrait gallery photo she was wearing a striking blue sequin formal gown that Edith Head had designed for Veronica Lake, who was then one of Paramount's top stars. Remember Veronica? She was the spectacular blonde actress known for always having her hair hanging over one eye.

That photo served me in good stead during my 18 months as a naval aviation cadet. I kept it framed on the inside of my locker door. During inspections, when the inspecting officer opened my locker and saw that stunning picture, he never even noticed my carefully stacked clothing and I always passed with flying colors.

Noel is now best remembered for playing Lois Lane in *Superman.* She worked in two, 15-episode motion picture serials, with Kirk Alyn playing the mighty man from Krypton. Then from 1953 to 1957 she played in 104 episodes of the "Superman" television series where George Reeves played Clark Kent, the mousy reporter on *The Daily Planet* in the city of Metropolis. That series would have gone on longer but for some unexplained reason Reeves took his own life and the series never resumed.

It is a good thing I didn't get too serious about Noel as, to my knowledge, she has been married four times already and I don't think she would have adjusted well to the life of a naval officer.

For years Noel traveled the college circuit with a presentation based on her role in the popular "Superman" series.

A few years back I asked her to consider doing a tour with me. I thought that Lois Lane and Billy Batson together would be a hit at the colleges, but she didn't want to tour anymore. She said it was a tough life of one-night stands and she had traveled enough.

I still think it would have been a natural and a very popular tour.

46

I Enlist, and *Follow the Band*

In late 1942 I was approaching my 27th birthday and was quite sure I would not have a draft-deferred status much longer. The war in the Pacific was raging and even as sole support of my mother I was sure I would have to serve eventually. There was only one way I wanted to go and that was as a naval aviator. My dear mother was afraid of flying and begged me to wait for the draft and take what she considered a safer route. I had already lost good friends on the beachheads in Europe and in the Pacific and decided if I was to go into the service, I wanted it to be the one of my choice.

On December 12, 1942, I passed the physical and was sworn in as a prospective naval aviation cadet. On the same day that I raised my hand and took the oath I was joined by two other actors, Robert Stack and Gene Reynolds.

Stack, best known later as Elliot Ness in the "Untouchables" television series, was a former national skeet-shooting champion and was immediately commissioned as a gunnery officer. Gene was accepted as an officer candidate and received his commission as an ensign after completing officers training.

Gene Reynolds was a fine young actor I had known through the years. He is now a very successful television director and producer and was the originator of the popular "M*A*S*H" television series and later produced "Lou Grant," which starred Edward Asner as the hard-nosed newspaper editor.

I was told there would be a six months' wait for my entry into flight training, so here I was, all signed up and no place to go. I hadn't been in school for five years and knew I had some tough sledding ahead on the subjects taught in aviation ground school. To make things easier for me, I enrolled in night courses at USC where I took 12 hours of college credits in aeronautics, meteorology, navigation, and aircraft engines. I really applied myself and was pleased to receive three As and a B in those demanding subjects.

Movie work was slow at the time, so I accepted a position as a ground school instructor at the Morton Air Academy at Blythe, California. This was a civilian-run school that instructed army air cadets on a field in the desert near the Colorado River. The flight instructors were all civilian aviators working under the supervision of U.S. Army Air Corps officers. The chief civilian instructor was my friend Roger Pryor, a well-known actor and band leader of the day, who once was married to the actress Ann Sothern.

After three months there I resigned to take a role at Universal in *Follow the Band*, which was to be my final motion picture before going into the navy. This was a good film, based on a story called *Trombone from Heaven*. It starred my dear old friend Eddie Quillan, who played a small-town musician who just could not play his finest numbers unless he took his shoes off. This led to many funny scenes where Eddie had to slip to stocking feet to render his sweetest solos.

I was the piano player in the band led by Skinnay Ennis, then a well-known singing band leader. This low-budget film, directed by Jean Yarbrough, had an impressive cast, including Mary Beth Hughes, Leon Errol, Leo Carrillo, and in specialty numbers, Alvino Rey and the King Sisters, Ray Eberle, Hilo Hattie, and Frances Langford.

There was another young fellow in this film named Robert Mitchum. He was working in his first production on a new contract with Universal Studio, after being picked up due to his work in westerns. He had played a scraggly bearded villain in four *Hopalong Cassidy* oaters that year and Universal scouts thought he had a future.

The then 26-year-old Mitchum was something else. He would come to the set each morning and astound us with tales of his exploits from the night before. I'll never forget one of those unbelievable stories. He claimed he drove a young waitress screaming from the restaurant when he told her he was going to hang her from the chandelier and go *up* on her.

Well, this young Mitchum fellow must have done a few things right through the years because he is now probably at his best in television productions like "War and Remembrance."

Eddie Quillan came from a vaudeville family and their act included Eddie and his three brothers, John, Joe, and Buster and their sister Marie. Eddie was picked up by Mack Sennett in 1926 and starred in a series of two-reel comedies for the next two years.

In 1928 he was placed under contract by Cecil B. DeMille and that's the first time I met Eddie. There he was featured by DeMille in his reform school classic *The Godless Girl* and starred in *Show Folks* and *Noisy Neighbors* with members of his own family.

Eddie is best remembered in Hollywood for his fine performance in the original version of *Mutiny on the Bounty* with Clark Gable as Fletcher Christian and Charles Laughton as the sadistic Captain Bligh. Eddie played the tragic seaman Thomas Ellison. He also played the errant young husband

Connie in John Ford's *The Grapes of Wrath,* and the accused murderer that Abraham Lincoln defended in *Young Mr. Lincoln.*

Eddie, who I don't think ever had an alcoholic drink in his life, was often seen on television in the 1980s playing a skid-row drunk. We used to meet for lunch several times a year and a nicer man you will never meet. I'm sorry to say that Eddie passed away on July 19, 1990, at the age of 83 from complications caused by a tumor on the brain.

47

The Eyes Have It

My day to enter flight training was approaching and I was called down to the selection board for a physical recheck after the six-month delay. To my complete horror, I failed the eye exam. I was ordered to report back two weeks later for another eye test. I failed that one too. Now I was beside myself, because I was told if I failed the third test, scheduled for two weeks later, my prospects of being a naval aviation cadet were over.

I had an old high school friend named Jeanne Jacques, whose father Louis Jacques, O.D., was a leader in the new field of eye exercises to improve visual acuity. I went to this marvelous man and he put me through a series of daily exercises to strengthen my optic muscles. Also for the next two weeks I went to bed early and drank quarts of carrot juice which was supposed to aid the vision.

On the day designated as my final test, Lieutenant Commander Dietrich, who had failed me on the two previous exams, called in Commander Joel Pressman, the chief doctor of the selection board. Commander Pressman wore the wings of a flight surgeon which meant he had gone through the School of Aviation Medicine at Pensacola and had the final say on acceptance or rejection at the board. Dr. Dietrich explained to me that he didn't want me to feel he was prejudiced against me, so he called in the chief doctor to make the decision in case I failed again.

Commander Pressman gave me the most demanding eye exam I had ever experienced. He not only made me read each line horizontally, but vertically as well. Then he made me read the chart diagonally. After I had successfully called out each letter perfectly, he turned to Dr. Dietrich and said he had never seen a prospective cadet with better vision and gave me the green light.

A side note here: Dr. Joel Pressman was the husband of superstar Claudette Colbert, but I did not know either of them and this had no bearing on his accepting me as a naval aviation cadet.

All through my life I had always thought my name was Frank Edward Coghlan, Jr. Otherwise, I never would have used the name Junior Coghlan and later, Frank Coghlan, Jr.

When I was enlisting in the navy I had to send to New Haven for a copy of my birth certificate. Then for the first time I learned that my father had been Frank Edward Coghlan, but the priest who baptized me insisted that I be named Francis Edward Coghlan in keeping with the Catholic tradition of naming all children with the name of a saint.

I presented a notarized affidavit from my attorney attesting that Francis Edward Coghlan and Frank Edward Coghlan, Jr., were one and the same person, but the chief petty officer in charge of paperwork at the selection board would not honor it. From then on, for the duration of my navy career, I was officially known as Francis E. Coghlan. If I knew then what I know now, I could have pressed the issue and gone over the chief's head, but I was afraid to cause a ruckus after all my eye problems.

When I reported for active duty on June 7, 1943, the naval aviation cadet program had five distinct phases of training. First there was Flight Preparatory School—a three-month stint at a university for ground school, heavy on math and lots of athletics to prove you were mentally and physically capable of completing the program.

Then came WTS, War Training Service, where the cadet received 35 hours of flight instruction from civilian pilots to prove you were able to solo and fly safely before going on to more demanding instruction from military pilots.

Next was Pre-Flight, where we poor guys were subjected to more ground training and unbelievable physical tests to prove we could survive if forced down on land or at sea. In our final tests on water we had to swim a mile and then tread water for 20 minutes. The navy wasn't about to let us graduate only to drown if we went down at sea.

This fitness training was great, but I really believe more good prospects were lost to naval aviation from separated shoulders in judo and broken knees in football than the program was really worth. Being a good swimmer from an early age, I was surprised to see how many good prospects from inland states could not meet the swimming requirements.

If you survived the arduous demands of Pre-Flight, you went on to Primary Training where for the first time you received flight instruction from naval aviators. After Primary you went either to Pensacola or Corpus Christi for Intermediate and Instrument Training before going to the final squadron of your choice. (It was of your choice if you were lucky in the draw!)

West coast NAVCADS, as we were called, usually went to colleges and naval air stations in California and ended up at NAS Corpus Christi in Texas. It so happened when I was called up the Dallas Selection Board was short of cadets and all 150 of us who reported that day were shipped to Dallas for further assignment. As a result, I was never stationed west of Fort Worth, Texas, in all my flight training.

The day before reporting to Los Angeles Union Station for transportation to Dallas, we were again processed at the Los Angeles Selection Board. By now I knew the leading chief petty officer real well, so I asked him if he thought it would be a good idea for me to take my tennis racket along. I knew we would have lots of athletics and thought having my own racket would give me the opportunity to get additional exercise in my spare time. To this day I don't know how the chief kept a straight face, but he agreed that taking my racket along would be a good idea.

Well if you can imagine, 150 prospective naval aviators and their well-wishing parents and friends gathered at Union Station and only old Junior was carrying a tennis racket.

I was a well-known and easily recognized actor at the time and all, or certainly nearly all present knew who I was. I guess most of them thought, here comes the spoiled, rich movie actor and what a drip he must be. I took my ribbing good-naturedly and soon everyone thought it was funny and we all laughed together. I was lucky I didn't also have my golf clubs with me because I seriously considered taking them along as well.

You know, we were kept so busy every hour of every day of the week that I never had time to use that racket once in the entire 18 months of my flight training!

48

You're in the Navy Now

I'm not going to bore you with page after page about my navy flight training and the 23 years wearing the blue uniform that followed. I'm sure many of you had equal or superior experiences than mine, but there are many occurrences in my navy life that were unique to me and so I'll try to narrate some of them.

The troop train we were riding in arrived at Austin, the capital city of Texas, late on the second night of our journey and we were bused to the University of Texas. We were issued bed linen and blankets and herded into a dormitory where we slept eight to a room in double bunks. We were exhausted and made our beds and went right to bed, or "hit the sack" as we later called it.

We were rudely awakened at 5:45 A.M. the next morning and told to muster outside at 0600. That's 6:00 A.M., but in the navy it is pronounced o-six-hundred. (The navy does not add the word "hours" after the time as they do in the army and the air force.) I had never brushed my teeth, showered, shaved, and dressed in 15 minutes before in my life, but I soon learned how.

We "fell in" outside and were marched off to "chow." I joined the line at the mess hall and took a metal tray. When I reached the steam table I was surprised to find that my first meal in the navy was wieners and beans. I mean, this was breakfast, and on my tray I found a big glob of baked beans with chunks of hot dogs looking up at me. Toast, milk, coffee and an orange was the rest of the meal. We were all starved so the "chow" tasted good and we wolfed it down.

I learned that our 150 cadets from Los Angeles were joined by an equal number from cities in Texas and Oklahoma. They thought we were city dudes and we thought they were hicks, but we gradually got to like each other.

The University of Texas has a beautiful campus with an impressive 307-foot-tall tower housing the administration building and general library. The summer in Austin was hot and humid and didn't cool off when the sun went down like it does in California. I was impressed at night by the seemingly millions of fireflies, or lightning bugs, flashing their presence for all to see. Also the area beneath the stands of the Longhorn's athletic stadium was the daytime home of thousands of bats. These winged mammals flew out at dusk seeking their nocturnal nourishment in the surrounding countryside. It took about 20 minutes for all of them to fly out and they made a picturesque exodus as they flew away. In the daylight I peeked into the opening they used for this departure and you could see and smell countless numbers of them hanging upside down as they slept during the daylight hours.

When my ten-week tour of Flight Prep was ending I received orders to Texas Christian University in Fort Worth for the WTS phase of training. They weren't ready for our group at TCU so I was granted a ten-day delay in reporting.

I hoped to get a ride home to California so I went to nearby Bergstrom Field to see if I could bum a ride home from the army. To my pleasure I ran into John Wyatt, a friend from high school days. He was a second lieutenant and wearing U.S. Army Air Corps wings. We had a good chat and he took me to Operations and had me placed on board a B-17 Flying Fortress that was departing for Edwards Air Force Base in the Mojave Desert. Edwards is now well known as the field where the astronauts land after cruising in outer space.

When I climbed on board the B-17 I was surprised and overjoyed to find that the copilot was Second Lieutenant Jimmy House, the youngest member of the House family from Hollywood. In Chapter 3 I mentioned Jimmy doubling for Dawn O'Day (Anne Shirley) in *The Spanish Dancer*. To recap, the House family had, at that time, the largest riding academy in the San Fernando Valley and rented livestock to the film companies. The oldest son, Newton House, became a western film star and my schoolmate Dorothy House married Andy Devine.

I was the only passenger on the flight and Jimmy gave me free rein of the big four-engined bomber. I'll tell you, if you have never seen our great country looking down from the nose gunner's turret of a B-17, you have missed one of the most open views of our landscape.

When we landed at Edwards I bid farewell to Jimmy and went to the front gate to hitchhike a ride into Los Angeles. I was picked up by a guy who, I soon found out, was three sheets to the wind from too much booze and he was very erratic in his driving. When he stopped at a bar for another drink, I left him on what proved to be the only dangerous leg of my cross-country trip.

I had a pleasant week at home, during which I visited several studios in uniform and was offered many good wishes from my former movie friends. At that time a cadet only earned $75 a month, so it was imperative that I sought help from the military for my return trip to Texas. I went to Long Beach Naval Base where I learned that a PB2Y Coronado was about to be ferried to NAS Corpus Christi, Texas. The Coronado was the giant, four-engined flying boat that Consolidated (later ConVair) was building for the commercial airlines and the navy was purchasing a group of them.

This plane was being flown to Corpus Christi by a Pan American Airlines pilot under contact to the navy. Again I was the only passenger on board. The pilot taxied the entire length of the takeoff route looking for hidden obstacles, then he turned the big flying boat into the wind and added power to the four powerful engines.

Though I was about to become a naval aviator, I was surprised that the seaplane was being flown overland once we took off from the water. In fact, I didn't see water again until we came to the Gulf of Mexico at Corpus Christi. The Pan Am pilot was a great guy and let me climb all over the giant flying boat.

From Corpus Christi I bummed another ride up to NAS Dallas and reported to Texas Christian University right on time for my War Training Service. Founded in 1873 and though only ten years older than the University of Texas, TCU was a private school and did not have the benefit of all the state funds and its campus was much smaller and its buildings less impressive.

The WTS was run by civilians and we flew at Singleton Field on the outskirts of Fort Worth. Most cadets in WTS at other bases received instruction in Piper Cubs and other light aircraft. I was fortunate as the operators of Singleton Field had a fleet of Waco UPF-7 biplanes with a 220-horsepower Continental engine. That was the same power I would later fly in the Stearman "Yellow Peril" at Primary training.

I received a total of 55 hours of instruction and solo flight time in the Waco before going on to Pre-Flight at the University of Georgia at Athens. I'll never forget my first solo flight when my instructor climbed out of the front seat and told me to take it around the field. When I got the Waco airborne I just couldn't believe how light it was on the controls. Then I realized that even though my instructor had seemed confident in me, he had been riding the controls all the time.

I was at TCU during the football season and we got into the college spirit with the civilian students with whom we shared the campus. I attended the game against the rival Southern Methodist University Mustangs in the Cotton Bowl and the game against the Texas A and M Aggies at the TCU Horned Toads' home field. Those Aggies were too much. The students wore military uniforms and made the freshmen stand up and cheer for the entire game.

While at TCU our group of cadets were joined by 20 marine enlisted men who were selected for flight training right from battlefield beachheads in the Pacific. Later at Primary our group was joined by some navy enlisted men who were carefully chosen for their aptitude and sheer desire to become naval aviators.

These marines were handpicked strictly for the the aggressiveness they exhibited in battle. Most of them were so happy to get out of the foxholes that they considered this chance at flight training to be a merry lark. They let it be known early that they weren't going to put up with any of the guff we cadets were forced to take. We were so afraid of being caught in misdemeanors that we wouldn't think of sneaking out of quarters after hours.

To us, lights out meant stop studying and get in bed. For our marine buddies it was the signal to go out the window and start living. They called it "hitting the beach." One of the toughest "jar heads" as we called them, was apprehended returning to the barracks about 0300 one morning with a snoot full. The young navy officer in charge of our detachment called him in for a lecture the next day. This battle-hardened veteran wasn't about to take a dressing down from some navy shore-based shave-tail. At the close of the lecture the marine called the young lieutenant a dry land sailor and told him in the Marine Corps he wouldn't make a pimple on a good officer's ass.

The next day the poor fellow was on his way to Camp Lejeune for further assignment and his chances of becoming a marine aviator were over.

49

Pre-Flight, Robert Taylor, and Jane Wyatt

After completing Flight Prep at Texas University, then WTS at TCU, I moved on to my third college, the University of Georgia for 12 weeks of Pre-Flight. The campus of the Georgia Bulldogs is located at Athens and was founded in 1785.

After proving we could retain knowledge at Flight Prep and that we could learn to fly at WTS, now we were to be conditioned into the best possible shape for the tough road ahead. From experience gained in combat, the navy was convinced that a physically fit aviator was less likely to be shot down due to superior endurance and coordination and that the downed pilot had a vastly improved chance of survival on a life raft or in the jungle if he was in superb physical condition.

The athletic program of Pre-Flight was first under the direction of Commander Tom Hamilton, the former football coach of the U.S. Naval Academy. He gathered the finest coaches and physical education instructors, men who had such athletic records that the cadets would respect them without question. When I was going through my training the officer in charge was Marine Colonel Bernie Bierman, the former great football coach of the University of Minnesota. His Golden Gophers were the national champions in 1940 and 1941.

One of my Pre-Flight coaches was Lieutenant Angelo Bertelli, the All-American quarterback and Heisman Trophy winner from Notre Dame. When men like that asked you to try a little harder you naturally complied. There were lots of injuries but we came out much tougher than when we went in. I'll always remember running the demanding obstacle course against time and doing push-ups in the snow on winter days.

I'm pleased to report that all through my flight training I was a popular member of the group. I think I was observed a little closer than most so I had to really dig in to show I could take it. On three occasions I was called upon to stage a big floor show at our graduation ceremonies. I wasn't really called on, rather I volunteered the idea. Each time I auditioned the cadets and enlisted the men at the school, wrote the script, and served as master of ceremonies.

I had my mother send my floppy shoes to me and I did my eccentric dance at each show. I also stole from my stock of Olsen and Johnson skits, like the Mrs. Jones gag with the ever growing potted plant. This was great fun for me and deeply appreciated by all my buddies.

Speaking of show business, one day we were told that Lieutenant Robert Taylor was to be the honorary inspecting officer at our weekly parade the following Saturday.

When I went through flight training there were two distinct groups of reserves working toward their navy wings. There were us, the NAVCADs, designated AV-N, who had to go through the entire 18-month program to graduate. Then there was the smaller group with the designation AV-T. Most of them owned their own airplanes and were required to have more than 300 hours of flight time in civilian aviation to qualify.

These candidates were given a direct commission and sent to NAS New Orleans for an accelerated three-month course. When they successfully completed training they received their wings and most were ordered to Primary training bases where they instructed in the N2S "Yellow Peril." A few of them, like my friend Charles "Buddy" Rogers, went into the ferry command.

The AV-T designator didn't bother us cadets, but I learned later at Primary that the AV-N instructors looked down on the AV-T group. They resented that they did not have to go through the cadet ranks and felt they had received privileged treatment.

Well, my good friend Robert Taylor had long owned his own airplane and qualified as an AV-T. He was on his way from NAS New Orleans to his first instructor duty assignment and was invited to inspect our battalion of Pre-Flight cadets. Everyone shined their shoes a little harder and shaved a bit closer for Lieutenant Taylor.

Bob was doing his best to act military and give a good inspection as he looked the cadets over very closely. As he came to me, he looked at my face for a clean shave and then at my shoes to see if they gleamed. He started to move on, then he did sort of a double take and stepped back to me. This time he gave me a closer look and in an almost incredulous tone of voice, he whispered, "Junior?"

I didn't dare move or speak, but I did smile with my eyes and gave my head a tiny nod. Bob then turned to our platoon officer and asked, "May I please have a word with cadet Coghlan?" The officer put me at ease and Bob and I chatted for about a minute. Then he wished me luck and continued on with the inspection. Needless to say, this occurrence tore through our battalion and my fame grew even more.

During my stay at the University of Georgia the campus was hit by an epidemic of catarrhal fever, which we quickly named cat fever. It started to strike me when I was going through one of our marathon swimming tests.

I came out of the shower room still sweating and felt real woozy as we were marching back to barracks in near freezing weather. That night I had a temperature of 104 degrees and was taken to the college infirmary. By now there were so many other cases that I was placed on a cot in the hall.

It was about two weeks before Christmas and I had one of my friends bring me the Christmas cards I had printed up and my list of card recipients so I could address them and mail them out while I was in the hospital.

On the second night, while still semi-delirious with a raging temperature, I was rudely awakened by an enlisted man who told me he was from Naval Intelligence. He had evidently gone through my belongings because he had my Christmas card list in his hand. His first question was, "Do you know Jane Wyatt?" I answered in a groggy condition that indeed I did know Jane Wyatt. Then he asked me when I had seen her last. I told him truthfully that I knew Jane from Hollywood but had not seen her since leaving for flight training. Then he showed me my card list and one of the names on it was J. Wyatt. This was my high school friend John Wyatt who I had met at Bergstrom Field and I intended to send him a card for his kindness in setting me up on the B-17 flight home.

I finally convinced this guy that J. Wyatt was my friend Second Lieutenant John Wyatt and that I did know the actress Jane Wyatt from my days in the movies. He then half-heartedly apologized for bothering me and explained there was a lady named Jane Wyatt who was under suspicion as a possible Nazi collaborator.

Can you imagine anyone confusing the real Jane Wyatt, so noted for her performance with Ronald Colman in Frank Capra's unforgettable original version of *Lost Horizon* of being a possible spy? This lovely lady later become the wife of Robert Young in the outstanding television series "Father Knows Best" for which she won the Emmy Award as best supporting actress for the three consecutive years of 1958, 1959, and 1960.

Oh well, as they sometimes say, truth is stranger than fiction.

50

On to Primary

Each week during Pre-Flight we were subjected to what was called the step test. Here we had to step up onto an 18-inch platform, then down again, 30 times a minute for five continuous minutes. Then a doctor would take our pulse and blood pressure at one-minute intervals for the next five minutes.

In the final week we were given what was considered to be the ultimate test of our physical fitness in a diabolical variation of the step test called the pack test. Each of us were required to wear a backpack containing one-third of our total weight. In my case that was an even 50 pounds.

They took our pulse and blood pressure before the test began, then we again stepped up and down on the 18-inch platform 30 times a minute for five minutes. I don't think I have ever been so exhausted in my life as I was at the finish of this fiendish ordeal.

Again they took our pulse and blood pressure each minute for five minutes. Those whose readings had not returned to normal at the end of five minutes were declared not physically qualified to continue in the flight training program. What a rude awakening this was for the unhappy cadets who might have excelled on the playing field, but were now eliminated and sent into the enlisted ranks. I was greatly relieved to squeak by this unforgiving examination.

From Pre-Flight I was ordered to report to the Dallas Naval Air Station for Primary training. We lived at the air station but Hensley Field, as it was called, was being used by North American Aviation for testing the P-51 Mustang and the AT-6 Texan trainer they were building there. (The navy calls the AT-6 the SNJ.) As a result, we were bused daily to Grand Prairie, halfway between Dallas and Fort Worth, where the navy had built two octagonal landing mats for us to use.

Now I was finally in the real navy—flying navy airplanes and being instructed by navy pilots. It so happened my first Primary instructor was a marine second lieutenant, but at least he was a graduate of NAS Pensacola who had chosen the Marine Corps after receiving his navy wings.

I know I promised not to bore you with the myriad of things we had to accomplish to become a naval aviator, but I'll bet there are things we had to learn that never entered your mind.

Nonflyers probably don't think of this, but the pilot is flying his plane in a body of air that is also moving and rarely in the same direction as the aircraft. You see the long runways at an airport but probably never realize that the pilot of your airliner hardly ever has the pleasure of an approach without crosswinds or gusts of air while making his landing approach.

We received five periods of instruction of one hour and 15 minutes duration, mainly to become familiar with the Stearman and to shoot landings. After a check ride, we were permitted to solo on the seventh flight. From then on we usually had a ride with our instructor and then a solo flight to practice what he had just demonstrated to us. We had lots of acrobatics, which we called aerobatics. There were loops: Chandelles, a quick simultaneous climb and turn in which the momentum of the airplane increases the rate of climb; and the Immelmann turn, a maneuver in which the plane is half looped to an upside-down position and then half-rolled back to normal flight, the purpose of which was to gain altitude while reversing direction. There were stalls, then tailspins out of a stall in which the aircraft spun wildly until the pilot straightened the plane with the rudder while lowering the nose to gain speed to overcome the stall. Then there was the frightening Falling Leaf. Here the throttle was eased back and the nose pulled up until the plane was about to stall from lack of flying speed. As the plane enters the stall with the stick pulled back to the pilot's stomach, he kicks in the rudder of his choice causing the plane to fall off violently in that direction. When the plane begins to stall again, the pilot kicks in the opposite rudder, causing a fall in that direction. This continues as long as altitude permits with the plane's progress making a path through the air resembling the name of the maneuver, a falling leaf. This was a truly frightening fall and one of our cadets got so carried away with the sheer thrill of it that he flew his Stearman right into the ground in the semi-stalled condition. The unlucky fellow survived, but after months in the hospital his permanent injuries forced him to leave the program.

At this early stage of training we had to become proficient in small field procedures, leading up to the ultimate goal—the landing at sea on a rolling and sometimes pitching deck of an aircraft carrier. For this we spent hours circling small fields where the instructor would cut the throttle and expect us to make a satisfactory landing, regardless of the position he placed us in.

Another demanding exercise was called pylon eights where we were expected to make a perfect figure eight pattern around two pylons in a crosswind condition. This was difficult as you had to ease into the wind on the first side and then bank sharply on the downwind side to make the perfect figure eight expected of us. Next we had slips to a circle, S turns to a circle, and other unusual landing exercises.

We were formed into groups of three for day and night formation flying and we alternated the lead in the air. Finally, the group of three made formation takeoffs and landings and then came the final check by the chief instructor. I'm happy to say I passed all the checks and was now on my way to Pensacola.

51

Pensacola: The Annapolis of the Air

As our bus drove over the long causeway crossing the Escambia River leading to the Pensacola Naval Air Station, I looked up and saw a formation of four OS2U Kingfishers, the single-engine, scout-observation float planes then operating off cruisers and battleships in the fleet. I said to myself right then, "Now that's real naval aviation and that's the plane I hope to fly some day." My wishes were not far off as the OS2U became the aircraft I flew in my final squadron before winning my wings.

My first stop at Pensacola was Ellyson Field where I received 20 hours in the Vultee BT-13 basic trainer, which we unkindly dubbed "The Vultee Vibrater." This was a single-engine, low-wing trainer with a 450- horsepower engine. For the first time we had hand-cranked flaps to deal with and the mysteries of what flaps do to the pilot in slowing the plane down on the landing approach. It also had an adjustable pitch propeller and three fuel tanks to deal with. This nearly led to disaster for several cadets, including me, on one night flight.

We were always supposed to take off on the reserve tank and then switch to the right and left tanks later in flight to equalize the load and then go back to the reserve tank for landing. On night flights we were taught to stay on the reserve tank for the entire period. Well, this one cadet forgot and changed tanks after takeoff. When it ran dry he had to make an emergency dead stick landing on a runway crossing the one we were using for touch and go landings. The "flying gods" were with us that night as the hapless cadet crossed right in front of me as I was settling down for what I thought would be a routine night landing.

During this Intermediate training in the Vultee I received my only down check. It was a routine check before we were to enter the formation phase at Ellington Field. The check pilot said I scared him by getting too low over the trees as I made my approach to the landing strip. As a result, I then had to fly two consecutive "ups" or I would be out of the program. I flew these next two check rides to the approval of two different check pilots and I see I wrote, "Whew" in my log book after the second successful check ride.

Also in the Vultee I experienced the most unusual event in my entire training. Our final night flight in Intermediate training was a monstrous ten-plane, step-down, formation flight of one hour's duration. That is, ten cadets flying solo in a step-down formation with an instructor flying in the eleventh, or last position. After a thorough chalk talk briefing in the ready room, we taxied out to the duty runway in a long procession and each of us were to take off on receiving a green light from the runway attendant. I was supposed to be the tenth and last cadet in the formation. I don't know what the instructor was thinking of, but he took my green light and went down the runway. I then took the next green light and began my climb to 1,500 feet and made the slow turn to join up on the plane ahead of me, which happened to be the instructor.

We finished this fiendish flight without incident and then made our landings. The instructor was amazed to find that one plane landed after he did. When we were all back to the line he called us in for his debriefing. When he learned I was the one who landed after he did, he asked me what had happened. I told him it was simple. He had taken my green light so I took off after he did and flew wing on him for the entire flight. He was nearly apoplectic with rage to learn that a cadet had him boxed in for the entire hour-long flight, but there was nothing he could do as it was his mistake.

It is not unusual that he didn't know I was behind him in the step-downed chain. You see, in formation flying, you never, and I mean *never*, take your eyes off the plane you are flying wing on. You stare at the rivets on his plane and make minor corrections with a combination of stick, rudder, and throttle to maintain the desired interval. It was very scary at first, but we became proficient at it after many hours of practice. From Ellington Field our group moved to Whiting Field in nearby Milton, Florida, for the instrument phase of training. Here we were introduced to the tricky Link Trainer where we spent ten hours practicing instrument procedures we would later fly in the air.

The plane we flew in was the SNJ, the North American trainer I had seen being built and tested at NAS Dallas. We never got to fly this pretty and feisty little critter, but instead spent 30 hours in the back seat, completely covered by a canvas hood. We had to perform various forms of radio controlled approaches and the instructor frequently put us in simulated emergency situations to see if we could cope with real emergencies later in our flying career. This was a very demanding and meticulous phase of training but important to our well-being in any form of inclement weather we might encounter when we were on our own.

In the last week of my stay at Whiting Field I received the welcome news that my choice had been granted and I would fly the OS2U Kingfisher, scout-observation plane in my final squadron at Pensacola.

52

Final Squadron and Wings of Gold

I reported to Squadron 7 at the Main Station of Pensacola where seaplanes were still being flown from the same ramps that had launched the NC-4, the first navy plane to successfully fly across the Atlantic.

My first seven hours there were in the N3N, a two-seat biplane built by the navy at its old aircraft factory on the Potomac River in Washington, D.C. This handy little aircraft was much like the Stearman "Yellow Peril," only on floats.

First we had to learn to "sail" our aircraft and how to maneuver it on the water before we were permitted to take it into the air. This was important because water handling was crucial to a seaplane pilot. We had to learn to moor it to a buoy and other things associated with yachting. We received three two-hour-long instruction flights, then a check ride, and from then on we flew solo.

Takeoffs were exciting. We would taxi on the water to the takeoff area, pull the throttle back, and the seaplane would weathercock into the wind. We would advance the throttle and keep the aircraft going straight on the water by using rudder to combat the torque created by the propeller that always tried to pull us to the left. The stick was held all the way back until sufficient speed was attained. Then the stick was pushed forward, which put the aircraft up on the step of the float. That attitude was maintained until the plane flew itself off the water.

Naturally, we didn't fly if the water was too rough, but a slight chop was desirable. Strangely enough, a completely slick water condition was the most difficult to take off from as the water adhered to the float in a suction-like phenomenon. Slick water was dangerous in landing too as it made it difficult to judge one's height above the water.

From the N3N I moved to the OS2U-Kingfisher, which was powered by a 450-horsepower, seven-cylinder, Pratt and Whitney air-cooled engine. It had a single float under the fuselage and two wing-tip floats for stability on the water.

We did just about everything possible with this great float plane. We performed glide bombing at a 30-degree angle where we dropped miniature bombs on float targets. Then we did actual dive-bombing where we flew over the target and did a chandelle, ending in a straight down dive to release our bombs and pull out at 300 feet. We did fighter-type high-side runs at a towed sleeve target, where the pilot fired his 30-caliber machine gun through the propeller and then the enlisted gunner in the rear seat fired at the sleeve as the pilot pulled away.

We spent countless hours on navigation flights where we left a fixed point, flew out for two hours, made a 90-degree turn, and after a predetermined period of time on that leg we would conduct an expanding square search pattern as though looking for a downed pilot. After supposedly finding the downed airman, we continued on the 90-degree course for a specified distance then turned back to the original point of departure. If we missed that point by more than two miles we were downgraded. We flew these missions at an altitude of 500 feet and became very proficient at reading the direction and velocity of the wind from the pattern it made on the water. Rarely did we miss the point of origin on the homeward leg.

My final flight as a cadet was the "heavy load takeoff" where I had to become airborne with two 325-pound depth charges under the Kingfisher's wings. I'm sure you can imagine that adding 650 pounds to the customarily easy flight characteristics of this plane was a new experience. The takeoff run was much longer and once into the air the usually maneuverable plane handled like a truck.

I flew to the target area where my instructor had dropped a smoke bomb and made my 30-degree approach to the target. When I released the first bomb, which was actually an oil-barrel-sized tank of water, I immediately noticed a change of balance in my airplane. I corrected for this by trim tabs and came around again to drop the real bomb. Well, if you have never seen the explosion that 325 pounds of TNT can make, it is very impressive. The bomb I dropped was set to explode after sinking to a depth of 30 feet. The plume of water that it caused rose about 150 feet above the surface of the water. It was exciting to see and I thought at the time that I'd hate to be in a submarine underneath that explosion.

On the day I was to receive my wings I suffered one of the biggest shocks of my life. A notice was sent to me at the cadet barracks telling me I was to report to the medical department before going to the commissioning ceremony.

I checked in there in a chipper mood as I knew absolutely nothing could be wrong as I had passed my final physical just the day before.

I was handed an official looking letter which I started to read with an air of bravado, but with the opening sentence my eyes began to bulge and I almost fainted. It started out by saying that I was disqualified from becoming a naval aviator because I was ⅛″ below the required height of 5″6″.

It went on and on and then in the last paragraph it stated that due to the urgencies of wartime I was being granted a waiver of 1/8″ and was therefore eligible to become a commissioned officer.

Can't you just imagine the glee the sadistic bastard in the Bureau of Medicine and Surgery had when he wrote that letter!

If the same letter had been written by a public relations man, the first words would have been, "Congratulations! We are happy to say you have been granted a waiver of a measly 1/8″ and you are now eligible to become a commissioned officer and wear those beautiful navy wings of gold." It sure depends which side of the table you are sitting on as how a letter can be written.

I received my wings on December 12, 1944, exactly 18 months and five days after I left Union Station in Los Angeles with the tennis racket under my arm. I had received 285 hours of flight instruction and felt ready to join the fleet and defend my country. There were about 300 other former cadets in the ceremony with me and finally I was Ensign Coghlan and as the saying goes, "an officer and a gentleman."

There was a tradition at Pensacola that the first person to salute a newly commissioned officer would receive one dollar as a token of appreciation. After the ceremony each new ensign had to report to the Personnel Office to receive his orders to the next duty station. When you walked out the back door of the building there was always a group of people waiting to give this first salute and receive the one dollar reward.

In the week I was waiting for my commissioning, I hid in the bushes of the building and received eight dollars from friends who were graduating before I did. I'm happy to say that the person who gave me my first salute was an enlisted man from our squadron who I found out had been waiting for me. As I gave him the dollar bill he said, "Good luck Mr. Coghlan. I've always liked you and I hope you have a fine career as a naval aviator."

Fortunately, I was able to complete the Operational phase of training right there at Squadron 7. This consisted of another 150 hours of training in the same type of aircraft. The most exciting flights of the Operational Training were the night catapult shots. The OS2U was flown off cruisers and battleships in the fleet and we had to first learn how to handle takeoffs from a shore-based catapult. My plane was lifted by crane onto an exact replica of a ship's catapult and aimed out over the water of Pensacola Bay.

I revved the engine up to full speed and held the throttle in the full forward position by grasping a hook-like device with the lower fingers of the left hand to ensure that the throttle would not be pulled back from the impact caused by the explosion of the five-inch artillery shell used to propel the plane into the air.

The evening I had my first night "cat shot" was a very unusual no-wind condition over the bay. I did everything I was supposed to. I held the stick pulled back into my stomach, I had the throttle held properly at full speed, and in spite of all this, my plane precariously skimmed the water before I built up flying speed. I tell you, the kick in the pants that catapult delivered and the second or two of complete disorientation that followed was very memorable.

When I completed Operational Training I was retained there at Squadron 7 as an instructor on the operational side of the squadron.

53

Instructor Duty

Being an Operational instructor was pleasant duty. I really hated to see my classmates depart for fleet duty, but I quickly established a camaraderie with the other new instructors. I now had my own permanent room in Bachelor Officers Quarters and led a good life.

My students were newly commissioned aviators and it was all chase work. I would demonstrate the required maneuvers of the day and then fly alongside their four-plane formation while they carried out the tasks I had assigned to them.

There was one unusual coincidence that occurred which I thoroughly enjoyed. Do you remember back in Chapter 47 where I told you about Lieutenant Commander Dietrich, the doctor who nearly kept me out of flight training when he failed me twice on eye examinations?

It so happened that a group of ten Navy doctors came through our squadron in their quest for flight surgeon status with the added benefits of flight pay and the other amenities associated with this desirable medical qualification. They all had been through a three-month-long course at Pensacola's School of Aviation Medicine and now were completing a course of 50 hours of flight training so they would be cognizant of the problems that a naval aviator faced in the line of duty. They didn't have to actually solo an aircraft, but many of them did. At our squadron they were to receive ten hours in the rear seat as a passenger to see at first hand the unique problems experienced by seaplane pilots.

It so happened, and I swear I had nothing to do with the scheduling, but LCDR Dietrich was assigned to me as a student. I met him in the ready room and introduced myself as his instructor. I took him on a tour of the squadron area and pointed out the complexities of scout-observation flying.

As we were about to go on our first flight together, I asked him if he recognized me. When he confessed he did not, I then told him I was the prospective cadet he had nearly kept from becoming a naval aviator.

I'm sure the poor man nearly choked when I said, "All right doctor, you get in the back seat and we'll see if my eyes are good enough for me to get you up into the air and back safely."

Dr. Dietrich was supposed to get ten hours of instruction from me, but I always stayed out longer with him and taught him many things I know the other members of the flight surgeon group did not receive.

At the conclusion of our final flight together, when I told him he had successfully passed, I said with a mischievous glint in my eyes, "Aren't you glad you finally approved me for flight training?" Touché!

Another most unusual coincidence occurred while I was instructing at Squadron 7. I was in the ready room talking to my officer students when the next group of cadets arrived to begin their first phase of instruction. I could hardly believe my ears when I heard, "Junior," shouted out. I looked up and saw one of my classmates from Fairfax High School, Eugene Bloodgood. I was delighted to see him, but I took him out in the hall and after throwing my arms around him, I said, "For gosh sakes Gene, please don't call me Junior here. These other instructors don't know about my old movie name, so if you don't mind, call me Ensign Coghlan, or Mister Coghlan until you receive your commission, but for crying out loud, don't call me Junior." He caught on immediately.

It so happened after Gene received his wings he was in a group of four students I was teaching when the only tragedy in my instructing career took place. It was on the simulated depth charge dropping that I wrote about earlier. I had led my four students about 50 miles out into the Gulf and dropped a smoke bomb for them to aim at as they dropped the 325-pound water-filled bombs they had under the wings of their OS2U-Kingfishers.

I led them through a practice run and told them to approach the target in a 30-degree glide, drop their bombs, and be pulled out by 300 feet, the altitude I would be circling at to observe their work. Each made a fine run and dropped the first of their bombs and formed up again to make the second and final approach on the smoke bomb.

All went well until the last of the four made his run. He was still in his glide when he passed my altitude and before I could reach for the microphone to warn him, I saw him fly right into the target. It looked like he tried to pull up at the last minute, but he hit the water in a flat altitude. Then his plane bounced off the water and turned over, landing nose first and upside down as it entered the water and disappeared from view.

I radioed to base telling that a plane had crashed. Then I told the three other students to circle so the rescue party would know where we were. I landed on the open sea and taxied around searching the water for evidence of my student. All I ever saw was one of the Kingfisher's wing-tip floats, a shoe, and a glove. Soon one of the senior instructors landed near me and we searched for a long time but found nothing more. The water was deep there, the currents strong, and the plane and the poor fellow's body were never recovered.

At the inquest that followed it was determined that he was so intent on making a good hit that he succumbed to a malady known as "target fixation." As a result, he just flew himself right into the target. The saddest part of all was that the young ensign had married soon after receiving his commission and his new bride had to return home from Pensacola alone and a widow.

54

I Get Married

Instructors at Squadron 7 were entitled to a cross-country navigation flight with an RON (remain overnight) once each quarter. Because we could not fly our seaplanes over land, we were permitted to go to nearby Barin Field and borrow one of their SNJs. I was due to have my first flight in this program and was planning to fly to Fort Worth to see the cute girl who kept the pilot's log books at Singleton Field while I was there for my WTS training.

There was another new instructor at Squadron 7 named Verlin E. Steffen with whom I had become friends. "Bud," as everyone called him, had once lived in Hollywood. He was a real movie fan and we frequently talked about motion pictures and our mutual friends. Bud asked me where I was going on my cross country. When I told him Fort Worth, he asked if I would change my mind and fly him to St. Louis.

He had just returned from there on his own cross country. He told me while there he had met a girl who had him in a tizzy and he wanted to see her again to see if it was true love. I hadn't written to the girl in Fort Worth. As long as she wasn't expecting me, I told Bud I would fly him to St. Louis if he promised I would be treated royally—and I was.

I landed at St. Louis's Lambert Field and taxied to the Naval Air Station that was then there. We were met by Steffen's heartthrob, a beautiful blond named Dorothy Rohan.

Dottie, as everyone called her, walked us to her father's Cadillac Fleetwood and drove us to the swanky bowling alley he owned where we had drinks and dinner. Then she drove us to the family home in Webster Grove where we changed into whites and went to a dance at the beautiful Knowllwood Country Club. Dottie explained that my escort for the evening was supposed to be Betty Corrigan, her best friend and classmate at Fontbonne Academy, an exclusive Catholic girls' school. Betty, however, had to beg off as she had a conflicting engagement.

As a result, Dottie arranged for my date to be Adele Kirkhoff whose family owned Pevely Dairy, the largest supplier of dairy products in St. Louis. Adele was a delightful companion and we struck it off real well. I was interested to learn she was going to enter Julliard School of Music the following year to study voice, hopefully leading to a career in grand opera.

That night Bud became convinced Dottie was the right girl for him and he popped the big question. When we returned to Dottie's house after the dance, Jack and Ethyl Rohan were just getting home from the bowling alley. We all stayed up most of the night talking and making wedding plans. The next morning after mass Dottie drove us to Pevely Dairy where Adele had ordered three gallons of ice cream for us to take back to Pensacola.

I flew the route at 8,000 feet and the cold air kept the ice cream in perfect condition. Bud kept talking to me on the intercom from his seat in the rear of the SNJ. As I said, I was flying at 8,000 feet, but he was flying much higher than our plane was that day.

In a few months the Rohans arrived at Pensacola in a three-car caravan with two other couples to make up the wedding party. They also brought Dottie's friend Betty Corrigan along to be the maid of honor. They checked into the San Carlos Hotel and called Bud to say they had arrived. When we got to their suite, Dottie opened the door and Bud gave her a huge hug and a long kiss. Though we had never met, when I saw what Bud and Dottie were doing, I put my arms around Betty Corrigan and gave her a big kiss. She was surprised, but she laughed so I knew I had not offended her.

Dottie wanted a real navy wedding, complete with the six groomsmen with sabers and the works. We were all reservists and not required to have sabers at that time. As best man it became my duty to go up and down the "Gold Coast" where the senior officers lived and borrow six swords and belts, which they all had from their days at Annapolis.

The wedding went off real well and it was followed by a reception at the clubhouse of the station's golf course. Bud and Dottie departed on their honeymoon that night and the Rohans and the two other couples drove out of town the next morning.

Betty Corrigan was on vacation from her job at the Darcy Advertising Agency and Bud told her she could stay the week in the bungalow where he and Dottie were going to live. He told me he had canvassed the bachelors in the squadron and had arranged a different date for her each night of the week. That was fine with me as I was going rather steadily with a lovely Wave officer and didn't want to upset that situation.

I don't know if Bud was kidding or not, because when I checked with Betty each afternoon she always told me she had no plans for the evening. So, to be polite, I took her out to dinner and usually dancing each night she was there. By the time I drove her to the plane for St. Louis a week later, I was really sad to see her leave. I couldn't get this cute Irish girl out of my mind. I was eligible for another cross country a few weeks later and darned if I didn't repeat Bud's performance. I flew to St. Louis and asked her to marry me and she accepted.

So, two and one-half months after the Steffen wedding, another three-car caravan drove down from St. Louis for our wedding. We were married on December 22, 1945. Betty's father, Virgil Corrigan, was in the men's retail clothing business and couldn't leave St. Louis until the Christmas shopping rush was over. We went on our honeymoon to the Edgewater Gulf Hotel in Gulfport, Mississippi. On Christmas Day we drove to New Orleans and met with Betty's folks and their St. Louis contingent who were spending a few days there before returning to Missouri. We had Christmas dinner with them in the Blue Room of the Roosevelt Hotel and after dinner we drove back to the Edgewater Gulf to continue our honeymoon.

55

Jacksonville, Michael, and the Blue Angels

After our happy honeymoon Betty and I drove back to Pensacola to take up residence in a small, one-bedroom cottage I had rented. At the time we thought it was marvelous, but I visited our first home on a subsequent trip to Pensacola about 30 years later and now realize it wasn't much of a house. Oh well, I guess newlyweds are easy to please!

In a few months we were able to move into a furnished apartment in Junior Officers' Quarters on the Main Station at NAS Pensacola and that was really nice. It was so close to my squadron that I could walk to work. Our apartment building was across the street and down the block from the admiral's quarters. Each morning at 0800 sharp (8:00 A.M.) the station band marched down the street playing stirring music on their way to the flag-raising ceremony in front of the admiral's home. It was a thrilling daily occurrence and we felt we were an important part of the navy.

We lived there for six months and then our squadron was transferred to NAS Jacksonville, Florida. By now we had received a contingent of the new Curtis SC-1 Seahawks, a sleek, high-powered, single-engine float plane. I had to ferry one of them to our new base on the St. Johns River. Betty drove over in our Ford convertible while I searched for temporary housing.

We spent our first few nights in Jacksonville in a large southern mansion on the river which had been converted into a rooming house by the old matron who owned it. In a week or so I qualified for government housing and we were still living there when our first child Michael was born in the navy hospital on the base just 11 months after our wedding.

It so happened I was weathered in on a cross-country flight to Orlando, Florida, on the night Michael arrived. He was born two weeks earlier than expected or I certainly would not have gone on the flight.

Betty's mother, Stella Corrigan, had flown down from St. Louis to be with Betty for this first arrival. Stella didn't drive and she was beside herself when Betty began having early labor pains. When the pains became five minutes apart and I was not home yet, Betty said, "Let's go," and she drove herself to the hospital.

We lived 15 minutes from the base and had several friends en route, but Betty made it to the hospital just in time. The first doctor to see her figured she would have a few hours before delivery, but as the pains came closer together they rushed her into delivery and Mike was born just before midnight on November 15, 1946.

The next morning when the weather cleared in Orlando, I flew back to NAS Jax, as we called it. I called home from the operations building to find no one was home so I bummed a ride to the squadron to go to work. When I walked in, my department head, Commander William Austin, seemed surprised to see me. He said, "You'd better get up to the hospital. Don't you know you're a new father?" Wow, what a surprise!

Our seaplane squadron was being decommissioned and I still had five months to serve before being eligible for release from the service. Then NAS Jacksonville was also the Headquarters of the Seventh Naval District and the Naval Air Operational Training Command. Two sharp young Waves in the headquarters office had written a nice radio script commemorating what is now called Armed Forces Day, but they didn't know how to get it on the air. (Remember, there was no television in 1947.)

I was invited into the office of Captain Walter Wingard, then the head of public relations for the Joint Command. He had me read the script and asked if I could get it produced for the two Waves. I made arrangements for air time from a local radio station, then I auditioned singers and band members, and put a good show together from the girls' script. Captain Wingard was impressed with my efforts and had me assigned to his office until my release date from the navy.

There was one very interesting thing that occurred while I was working for Captain Wingard. He told me the navy was forming a flight demonstration team and sent me down to the training squadron to interview the team members and write their first press kits. At that time they flew three F6F Hellcats in a Vee formation. Their first public air show was at Jacksonville, then they went on to fame in their first major performance in an air show in New York. There had been a contest at NAS Jacksonville to select a name for the team and the winning choice was "The Lancers."

While the team was in New York they had been entertained at a nightclub called The Blue Angel. They liked that name and when they were interviewed by the press following their spectacular performance, one of the team members said they wanted to change their name to "The Blue Angels." When they returned to Jacksonville the glowing press releases had preceded them and the new name stuck. I heard the wife of one of the captains on the base was furious as "The Lancers" had been her suggestion.

The team had its own permanent announcer/public information officer,

Lieutenant Jim Barnitz, but I was assigned to help and traveled with them on their first three shows in Florida. I would fly ahead as an advance man and set up press interviews and radio shows for them to appear on. At the time of the Gasparilla Festival in Tampa they also performed in St. Petersburg on the same day, so I announced one of those shows and Barnitz did the other one.

At Captain Wingard's suggestion I flew to Washington to see if I could be accepted into the regular navy. I was told I was one month too old in rank to become a regular navy officer, so I chose to be released from active duty on my eligibility date in May 1947.

I had built a reputation from my work in air shows, so on the way home I stopped over for a month in Birmingham, Alabama, where I assisted aviation pioneer Stedham Acker with the Birmingham Air Maneuvers that he used to stage each year. I suppose I could have become a professional air show promoter, but I wanted to return to Hollywood and the movies.

56

Back to Hollywood and Bill Lear

We drove across country all filled with hope and I just couldn't wait to get back to work as an actor. We moved in with my mother and I called on my agent the very next day. I spent the next week visiting all the casting directors to tell them old Junior was back and raring to get back in makeup.

I had been promised by people like Norman Taurog that Hollywood would be waiting for me, but even Norman didn't cast me in a part in the six months that I stayed available. I just couldn't believe what had happened to the motion picture business in the four short years I had been away. A whole new gang of young actors had cropped up in the absence of the old regulars and, due to the shortage of film, the studios were only making half as many movies as before the war. People who had been under contract when they entered the service were accepted back to complete those pacts but we freelancers were out in the cold.

My failure to land an acting job was a real shock to me. I had never gone six months without doing a picture before. I was now a married man with a family and bills to pay and I just had to be working. Our wonderful Screen Actors Guild granted me a full year of free dues because of my time in service but I just had to have a salary coming in.

I finally called on my first agent, Jerry Mayer, who by now had reconciled with his brother Louis B. Mayer and was head of production at MGM. I told him I was getting desperate for work and asked if he would give me a job in production behind the camera. This benevolent man looked at me with his cold eyes and asked, "What can you do?" In disbelief, I said, "Jerry, I spent 24 years in the industry. I was a star. I also produced 20 films while in the navy and I can adapt to any job you assign me to." I mentioned becoming a junior writer, an assistant to a producer, an assistant film editor, or a second assistant director. Jerry said he would think it over. I never heard from him again. This was the man who begged me to become one of his first clients when he was establishing his actors' agency. How soon they forget!

After exactly six months back in Hollywood, with no employment in the film industry, I called on my friend William P. Lear. Bill Lear was married to Moya Olsen, the daughter of Ole Olsen, of Olsen and Johnson. When I was leaving for flight training Bill had told me that if I received my navy wings he would give me a job when I left the service.

So, Betty, Michael, and I drove to Grand Rapids, Michigan, to go to work for Bill Lear. Moya Olsen Lear rode back with us from a visit she had been spending with her mother in California. Bill had a big home there and he put Betty, Mike, and me in a nice apartment on the upper level where we lived for several months. Bill used this home as a gathering place for his engineers to stay in when they came to Grand Rapids to report on Lear business.

First Bill placed me in the Lear hangar as assistant to the hangar manager where private pilots flew in to have Lear equipment installed in their aircraft. Soon he transferred his sales manager to Lear Cal, the firm that became Lear Seigler when he sold it off a few years later. Then I was moved up to become assistant to the new sales manager and placed in charge of advertising as well. All the time I was also doing test pilot work, the real reason for which I had been hired.

Being a test pilot is not always as glamorous as depicted in the movies where you climb to 30,000 feet and then nose over in a death-defying dive to earth. It is also many boring hours flying straight and level as I did with Bill as he was perfecting the Lear Orienter, a lightweight, low cost, automatic direction finder for civilian aircraft and the first autopilot ever designed for the use of private pilots.

Bill Lear was a true genius. It is reported he only had an eighth grade education, but I heard him correct MIT and Cal Tech graduates when he found errors in their work. Bill invented the first car radio, which he sold to Motorola, when he was barely out of his teens. He also invented the first eight-track stereo system and the Lear Jet. I believe Bill Lear is credited with more patents than Thomas A. Edison.

I was with Bill at one of the low periods in his business career as he struggled to move from his lucrative wartime production into the home radio and recording field along with his aims in civilian aviation.

He was obsessed with developing a wire recorder. His beautiful machine recorded high fidelity sound to a hair-thin wire, but was expensive to develop and so complicated that it didn't stand a chance against the cheaper tape recorders that soon took over the market.

My efforts in advertising were a farce as he really had nothing to advertise and no budget to buy space in the aviation publications. I saw the handwriting on the wall and when I was offered a chance to return to active duty in the navy, I jumped at it. That was the smartest decision I ever made and it led to a fine navy career and eventual retirement as a lieutenant commander.

57

Back in the Navy

I had been selected to become a member of the Naval Air Reserve Training Command which was definitely a plum assignment and the only real career opportunity for a reserve aviator. At that time the Command had 28 activities around the country where they trained the reserves known as "Weekend Warriors." I was ordered back to NAS Jacksonville where I had such success in my final wartime duty. This assignment was to last four years and while there at NAS Jax, our second son, Patrick, was born.

Probably the most interesting event to occur on this tour of duty was when I was assigned to coordinate a 60-plane flyover for the final scenes in the motion picture *Slattery's Hurricane,* being filmed at the Opa Locka Naval Air Station in Miami.

Here Richard Widmark, as Lieutenant Slattery, is being honored for his heroism during a disastrous hurricane that threatened the area. We flew 30 F4U Corsairs from Jacksonville to join with 30 F6F Hellcats from Miami to form this spectacular formation. I had never met Richard Widmark, but the leading lady in the film was my dear friend Linda Darnell.

The first day on the set while working on the ramp of the air station I told the assistant director I was a personal friend of Miss Darnell and I'd like to talk to her when she had the time. He gave me a skeptical look and was trying to impress me with just how busy she was when she stepped out of her dressing trailer about 30 feet away.

She saw me and in almost disbelief she shouted, "Junior," at the top of her voice. She ran over and gave me a big hug and the most enjoyable kiss I'd ever received from a major star. I turned to the assistant director and asked him if he had any questions. He just threw his hands up in the air, shook his head and said,"The set's yours."

Another interesting occurrence was when Ronald Reagan came to town promoting one of his films. I had worked with him twice at Warner Brothers in *Brother Rat* and *Angels Wash Their Faces* and knew him quite well. I called him at the theater where he was making his personal apperance and invited him to dinner at the air station. He accepted and I sent a car and driver for him.

I was technical adviser on *Slattery's Hurricane* in 1949. Richard Widmark was Slattery.

I set up a dinner with Betty and me and the commanding officer and executive officer of the base and their wives. Ronnie couldn't have been more charming and he made some new fans that night. We had pictures taken and after he became president I called a retired admiral on his staff and asked him if he would walk my photo into the oval office and have it autographed. He said he would so I had the photo mounted on an 11″ × 14″ white mat and mailed it back to the admiral. Within ten days it was back nicely autographed, "To Frank—With Very Best Wishes—Ronald Reagan." Naturally, it is now handsomely framed and has the place of honor on my trophy wall.

One day in late 1951 I received a distressing telephone call from Judge Otto J. Emme who was now married to my mother's dear friend, the former Leona de Lacy. He told me mother was in poor health and the apartment complex where she lived had been sold and mother had to move and was just not capable of handling this by herself.

I flew out to Los Angeles and put my mother's belongings together and had her flown back to Jacksonville. I went into the garage where I found boxes filled with hundreds of stills from my early motion picture days and many scrapbooks with clippings from the old days.

I put an ad in the newspaper and sold all of Mother's furniture. I settled her few bills, closed out her bank account, and shipped her personal belongings and the stills and clipping books back to Jacksonville. The stills have now been mounted in eight looseleaf binders by my present wife Letha and are an important asset for the publication of this book.

Soon I had Mother in the hands of navy doctors and her health began a steady climb back to normal. I'll relate more about Mother's medical problems in later chapters.

Another strange thing happened at NAS Jacksonville on this tour of duty. About 11:00 P.M. one night I received a telephone call from a man who told me he was an agent of the FBI. He asked me if I knew Jackie Moran. I told him I knew Jackie from Hollywood and that we worked together in *Meet Dr. Christian.* He asked when I saw him last and I told him I hadn't seen Jackie Moran since joining the navy in 1943.

He seemed surprised and asked if Jackie hadn't contacted me when he was in Jacksonville a week or so earlier. I assured him I didn't even know Jackie had been in town and I doubted if he knew I was stationed there.

I asked him what this was all about and he finally told me that Jackie was in town and had visited a rehearsal of the local little theater group. His presence there impressed this group of amateur thespians and they entertained him royally. The upshot was that he romanced one of the aspiring actresses and then borrowed her car. When he didn't return it she called the police and the car was found abandoned three days later in Charleston, South Carolina.

I happened to read in the local paper about three months later that Moran had been apprehended in Chicago on a bad check rap and one of the additional charges was car theft in Florida. This was one of many run-ins with the law by this fine young actor who I had always considered to be one of the best of the bunch. Sad.

In later years I got to know one of the chief FBI agents in Los Angeles and I told him of this Jacksonville story. He said, in no way was that an FBI agent who had called me. He said a true G-man would have come to the house and identified himself with proper credentials before interrogating me. His guess was it was an insurance adjuster trying to track down the stolen car for his company.

Probably the oddest thing that happened while I was at Jacksonville occurred in connection with an air show our reserve pilots were flying in at Tampa during that city's annual Gasparilla Festival. Tampa considers it to be their equivalent of Mardi Gras and it commemorates the days when the cutthroat José Gasparilla and his buccaneers held sway in the area.

Tampa is 195 miles from Jacksonville, so I decided to drive over the day before so I would be at the airport early the following day to make arrangements for publicity and for my announcing the show. Commander

Ben Welden and Dan Duryea were on location in Jacksonville, Florida. I invited them to cheer up patients at the naval hospital there.

"Red" Shrader, our operations officer, was to coordinate our flyover, so he and Mrs. Shrader drove over with Betty and me.

I saw in the Tampa newspaper that Sally Rand was there with her troupe and asked the Shraders if they would like to see her show. Sally had been one of the contract players while I was with DeMille. I remembered her as a 19-year-old, slightly overweight dancer that DeMille used in some of his spectacular epics. He seemed to feel she had promise, so he placed her under contract. When he sold the studio to Joseph Kennedy she didn't last long and went on to her own sort of fame with her fans and bubbles at the 1933 Chicago World's Fair.

When we arrived at the nightclub where she was performing I told the maitre d' I was a friend of hers and asked him to tell her we were in the audience. When she was through performing she joined us at our table while the rest of the show was continuing. She gave me a big kiss and told all at our table that Junior was her favorite child actor.

She rather stunned the ladies at the table when she pointed out one of her dancers and remarked how proud she was of her for returning to the act so soon after having just had an abortion the week before. I guess that should have prepared us for what was to follow.

Sally was telling me how tough it was for her to take a show like hers on the road and how demanding the unions were in imposing their hiring restrictions on shows in local nightclubs. Then Sally casually said, "Of course, I'm the only woman in show business who has ever told the unions to go fuck themselves."

My wife and Mrs. Shrader had never heard such language from the mouth of another female and their eyes bugged out and their mouths fell open.

Mrs. Shrader couldn't resist herself and she asked in almost disbelief, "What did you say?" Good old Sally had been asked a direct question, so she repeated her words verbatim, "I am the only woman in show business who has ever told the unions to go fuck themselves."

Well, what can you say? Sally spoke her mind and Betty and Mrs. Shrader were quiet for the rest of the evening.

58

The Pentagon

I had been at NAS Jacksonville nearly four years and things could not have been going better. My office was consistently rated in the top 10 percent of the 28 public information offices in the Command and I was considered to be the tops in staging open houses and air shows. After all, this was just another form of show business and came naturally to me.

I had received orders to move on to NAS Birmingham, the newest station in the Naval Air Reserve Training Command. I considered this to be a real challenge and, remember, I had spent time there on my way back to Hollywood helping Stedham Acker stage his Birmingham Air Maneuvers. I liked the area and already had friends there, so I was looking forward to this change of duty when a bombshell fell on my apple cart.

One day in February 1952, my commanding officer called me into his office and handed me a dispatch he had just received. A dispatch is what the navy calls a telegraph that comes in over the closed-circuit wire.

This dispatch said that Lieutenant Francis E. Coghlan is ordered to report to the office of the chief of information and gave me three weeks to get there. I couldn't believe my eyes and I checked out a TBM Avenger torpedo bomber and flew up to Washington, D.C., to see what this was all about.

It seemed that Lieutenant Commander Alan Brown who had been head of the motion picture section at CHINFO (chief of information) wanted to return to his production post with the "March of Time" and was leaving the service. So on this short notice I was to become the head of liaison between the navy and the Hollywood motion picture studios. *Wow!!!*

Fortunately, when I checked in Alan still had two weeks left before his departure so he was able to introduce me to the people I was to work with and there was a smooth transition.

In addition to handling script approval, arranging for the use of ships and shore locations, and assigning technical advisers on films that qualified for navy cooperation, Alan also produced about ten documentary public information films each year from the millions of feet of film stocked at the Naval Photographic Center across the Potomac River in Anacostia,

Maryland. I'm happy to say that my motion picture experience almost matched his and I was able to produce 20 films in my tour of duty at CHINFO.

Alan told me the first big challenge I would have in the new job was to coordinate cooperation on *The Caine Mutiny*. Stanley Kramer had bought the screen rights to Herman Wouk's book and was going to bring it to the screen at Columbia Studio. The navy was really worried about this film and for good reasons.

To begin with, up to then there had never been a mutiny on board a ship of the U.S. Navy, so the very title of Wouk's fictional book was displeasing. Producer Kramer was not considered to be a radical, but he was a known liberal as was the film's star Humphrey Bogart. The writer of the film's screenplay was Stanley Roberts, who admitted to being a former communist before the House Un-American Activities Committee. Edward Dmytryk who was to direct the film had been an unfriendly witness before this committee and had served time in federal prison for his confessed communist activities. It was only after Dmytryk was released from prison and recanted his former communist connections that he was able to return to directing motion pictures in the United States.

I'm sure you can see why the navy was worried about cooperating with this film. We finally decided it was better to cooperate with it so we could have some control over the production rather than have them go off on their own without our supervision.

I only insisted on one important change in the script. It was followed and I think made the story more believable. In Wouk's book, after the court-martial Captain Queeg was returned to duty as executive officer of a small navy depot in the Midwest. I insisted that in the film, after Queeg's breakdown on the witness stand, it be evident that he was a sick man and relieved of any further duty.

We didn't mind the character of Queeg being proven to be unstable, we just didn't want the entire navy to be portrayed in an unfavorable light.

After several rewrites a workable script was approved and full cooperation was granted. This was to include the use of ships at sea and permission for filming at navy bases in the Pacific.

We selected an outstanding officer to be the technical adviser. He was Captain James Shaw, a naval academy graduate with 17 battle stars on his Pacific area ribbon for action on destroyers during World War II. He was also a talented writer and had been one of Admiral Morrison's chief assistants when the admiral was compiling his series of books on the history of World War II.

The final step before the start of production was when Edward Dmytryk came back to Washington and had me take him to the Naval

Photographic Center to view stock footage to use in the film. When he was finished, I drove him up on a hill overlooking the Potomac and talked to him at length.

He had directed me in *Golden Gloves* at Paramount in 1939 and I felt I could talk to him straight from the shoulder. I told him the navy was concerned about its image being torn down if the film was directed with a derogatory slant. I told him Captain Shaw would be watching for such incidents and had the right to pull cooperation and leave the company stranded if he didn't like the way the film was progressing.

Eddie told me not to worry. He assured me that this was his big opportunity to return to top directing assignments and in no way would he jeopardize the motion picture with shady innuendos.

I believed him and he was true to his word. Captain Shaw reported daily that all was progressing in fine order and I think *The Caine Mutiny* turned out to be a good film for the public and the navy.

Do you want to hear a sideline to Captain Shaw's arguments on the set? The biggest dispute he had on the entire production was when he objected to the way Humphrey Bogart was buttering a piece of toast in a wardroom sequence. "Bogie" was making a big deal out of buttering and rebuttering this morsel of toasted bread as he harangued one of the men for a minor infringement.

Finally, Captain Shaw could stand it no longer and said,"Come on now. No Naval Academy graduate would ever display such poor table manners." Bogart stared at him and then said, "Oh yeah. Well that's the way we did it at Phillips Exeter." In other words he was telling Captain Shaw that he also attended a prestigious school and for Captain Shaw to confine his technical advice to navy matters.

During the two and one-half years I held this marvelous position, I always had more than one project in some phase of production. The major studios nearly always presented well-written scripts from their staff of highly skilled writers. The minor studios all too frequently submitted scripts that required lots of doctoring before we could extend cooperation. These stories were usually filled with unnatural conflicts that just don't exist in a well-functioning organization like the U.S. Navy.

Allied Artists sent a script they had the nerve to title, *The Annapolis Story*. It told of two competitive midshipmen who were both in love with the daughter of the officer who seemed to be the instructor of every class they attended. This doting man tried to tone down their ardor for his daughter, so naturally they hated him. Lo, when these two graduated from the Naval Academy, they both received orders to the same ship. Wouldn't you know, when they arrived there, that same instructor came on board as the ship's commanding officer!

After many critiques I submitted what was to be the final script to the commander of the Naval Academy for his approval. He wrote back, "If you can control the production of this turkey so it won't leave a bad taste in the public's mind, OK, but for heaven's sake, don't let them use the title, *The Annapolis Story,* as this does not tell the true story of our great institution." The studio took this under advisement and changed the title to *An Annapolis Story,* so we let them go ahead.

Too often the lesser studios wanted the very impressiveness of our beautiful ships to add stature to their productions and relied heavily on the miles of spectacular stock footage available to them at the Naval Photographic Center to augment their own photography to add credence to a minor film.

59

The Bridges at Toko-Ri

The next major motion picture I helped bring to the screen was one of which I am very proud. It was the prestigious *The Bridges at Toko-Ri*, produced by the fine team of Perlberg-Seaton for Paramount from the book of the same name by James A. Michener. It was directed by Mark Robson and the excellent cast included William Holden, Grace Kelly, Fredric March, Mickey Rooney, Robert Strauss, and Earl Holliman.

Much of this poignant story was filmed on an aircraft carrier operating in the icy waters off Korea at the height of that tragic war. It tells graphically of the task force's vital mission to destroy with jet bombers the heavily guarded bridges to stop essential supplies from moving to the communist front lines.

As the flyleaf of the book describes, "The center of the novel is one of the aircraft carriers and its key personnel—the Admiral in command, the jet pilots whose striking power the Admiral must direct and conserve, and the helicopter men who are on hand to try to rescue the pilots when they fall. These are extraordinary men with incredibly difficult and dangerous tasks to perform. The Admiral puts it very well: 'They leave this tiny ship and fly against the enemy. Then they must seek the ship, lost somewhere on the sea. And when they find it, they have to land upon its pitching deck. Where did we get such men?'"

William Holden plays one of the jet pilots—a reserve officer bitter about being recalled to active duty, causing him to lose his law practice and his home. Fredric March is Admiral Tarrant, an outspoken, embittered critic of the Korean War who had already lost two of his own sons in combat in naval aviation. Grace Kelly is Holden's wife and Mickey Rooney the enlisted helicopter pilot who dies with Holden when he tries to rescue him after his jet is shot down behind enemy lines.

Perlberg and Seaton presented Valentine Davies's beautifully written screenplay that factually followed Michener's best-selling novel. There was no doubt from the beginning that this production would qualify for full cooperation. The only question was how much assistance we could extend while we were engaged in this war.

The assistance granted was unique as we allowed a studio camera crew to film on board an aircraft carrier that was actually under combat conditions off Korean shores.

The script closely followed Michener's book and we requested only a few minor changes. The main objections were in the character of "Beer Barrel," the ship's landing signal officer, played by Robert Strauss.

"Beer Barrel" was an alcoholic who was in the habit of returning to the ship with many cans of beer smuggled aboard in the two oversized golf bags he always took ashore on each liberty from the carrier. We winked at this shortcoming as it only represented a flaw in one man's character and he always snuck the beer on board without the knowledge of the officer of the deck.

We did object, however, to Michener's description of the man when he wrote, "For he believed that if he had a can of cold beer in his belly it formed a kind of gyroscope which made him unusually sensitive to the sea and the sky and the heaving deck and the heart of the incoming pilot."

This we considered to be a gross injustice to the many fine landing signal officers, who in those days were responsible for directing the pilots safely back on board the carriers on the rolling and pitching decks in all kinds of weather at landing speeds of up to 140 knots. Especially as Michener intimated "Beer Barrel" could do a better job when half sloshed than the other LSOs could when cold sober. Michener added, "This was why Admiral Tarrant never bothered about the golf bags filled with cans of beer." Hogwash. Never would any task force commander knowingly condone such a practice.

The only other minor change we requested concerned Mickey Rooney's character of the enlisted helicopter pilot Mike Forney. Michener wrote of him as a real oddball who always wore a green top hat and scarf as he flew his copter off the carrier's deck. We enjoyed the rebellious, defiant personality of Mike Forney and the use of his green top hat. We only asked that he adorn himself with it after he was off the deck and on his way to rescue pilots downed at sea. This was such a trivial objection that it was readily agreed to by the producers.

Wasn't this strange? Here was I at the seat of government controlling a part played by my old buddy Mickey Rooney. I used to double date with him and Ava Gardner before their marriage; we did our slow-motion wrestling act for several years at benefits and other charity events; I played one of his commissioners of student government in *Men of Boys Town* where we performed our act on film in this MGM production; I played his pal "Red" in four of the *Andy Hardy* series; and now I was specifying what Mickey's character could, or could not do, in a film made many years later.

There was also another very unusual occurrence during the filming of *The Bridges at Toko-Ri*. All aircraft carriers are clearly identified by large painted numbers on both sides of the island superstructure and at the bow of the flight deck so returning pilots can identify their own ship when operating with other carriers.

When we allowed a second-unit camera crew from Paramount to go on board one of our aircraft carriers in Korean waters, the ship they worked on was the USS *Kearsarge,* number 34. A few months later the producers asked for permission to send another camera crew back to film additional scenes.

We granted this request, but to the studio's surprise, the carrier numbered 34 had been relieved of Korean duty and was now back in the United States for overhaul.

When the camera crew went on board the new carrier, they found to their dismay that it wore a different number and the earlier photography would not match what they were about to shoot. After many messages and dispatches back and forth, we granted permission to repaint the new carrier with the number 34.

This was a first in the history of naval aviation and caused some confusion at first. It also led to some good-natured messages back and forth between the two commanding officers. Finally, the skipper of the newly numbered 34 wrote to the CO of the real number 34 saying, "As long as I am now in command of my own carrier and also yours, I'll expect to receive your paycheck by return mail."

60

Mr. Roberts and Admiral John Ford

The final film I supervised from Washington was, I think, the best of all I worked on from my motion picture desk in the Office of Information. It was the memorable *Mr. Roberts.*

Thomas Heggen had his book *Mr. Roberts* published by the Riverside Press in 1946. Producer Leland Hayward brought it to the New York stage where Heggen and Joshua Logan collaborated on the stage play which Logan then directed.

After a long successful run on Broadway, Warner Brothers bought the screen rights and Joshua Logan and Frank Nugent wrote a dynamic screenplay which Leland Hayward again produced. Logan was not selected to direct the motion picture. That chore was assigned to the veteran four-time Academy Award winner John Ford.

The film cast had Henry Fonda reprising his role of Mr. Roberts in a part that many felt must have been written with him expressly in mind. The sadistic Captain Morton was played to perfection by James Cagney. The captain was depicted as a man who had worked his way up in the merchant marine, where he started as a galley steward and finally became the captain of a nondescript cargo vessel. On his way up the ladder he had grown to hate the put-downs he received from what he called "the college graduates," who ordered him around. Now when he finally had command of his own navy ship in wartime conditions, he wasn't going to take any more disrespect from the officers and men under his command.

For those of you who have seen the motion picture, can you ever forget the scene between Mr. Roberts and the captain where Mr. Roberts asks, "How did you ever get in the United States Navy? How did you get on our side?"

The part of the ship's doctor was played beautifully by William Powell. This fine actor began his motion picture career in 1921 after ten years or more on the New York stage. In his early film roles he often played oily villains, but was later best remembered for such performances as the butler in *My Man Godfrey* with Carole Lombard and his continuing role as the suave, whiskey-drinking detective Nick Charles in Dashiell Hammett's *The*

Thin Man series for MGM, where Myrna Loy played his devoted wife, Nora Charles. In *Mr. Roberts* an older William Powell was just marvelous as the compassionate ship's doctor.

The part of Ensign Pulver was assigned to a young actor named Jack Lemmon who was making only his third motion picture. Would you believe, this young performer ran away with the Academy Award for best supporting actor in his never-to-be-forgotten portrayal of Ensign Frank Pulver.

I had reviewed the movie script for *Mr. Roberts* that Warner Brothers sent back and because the story was so well known from the book and stage play there were no major objections to having it reach the screen.

There were some overly boisterous scenes when the crew was finally granted a much overdue liberty on the island and, of course, the skipper of the USS *Reluctant* was really obnoxious, but this was carefully explained in the buildup of his character. We were sure John Ford would handle these situations in good taste due to his love and respect for the U.S. Navy.

One of the big disappointments of my long movie career is that I never had the opportunity to work for two men I consider among the very best film directors of all time—Frank Capra and John Ford.

At least with Capra, I interviewed for the part of the jockey in *Broadway Bill,* only to lose out on the final reading to Frankie Darro. I never even went on an interview for a role in a John Ford production. Though I never worked for him as an actor, I performed many services for him while on active duty in the U.S. Navy. Our first meeting in person occurred in my Washington office in connection with *Mr. Roberts.*

John Ford was also a navy man; he went into the navy with the rank of commander soon after the start of World War II. He was assigned to the Office of Strategic Services as a direct assistant to Colonel William Donovan who headed the OSS. (This organization is now called the Central Intelligence Agency, or the CIA.)

He was placed in charge of the motion picture division and was responsible for many of our best wartime films, including the Academy Award winning *The Battle of Midway, December 7th,* and the unforgettable *The Fighting Lady.*

Ford was wounded in action during the filming of *The Battle of Midway* and left the navy with the rank of rear admiral. I met many admirals in my 23 years on active duty and none wore their stars with more authority than did John Ford.

One day I was told by the Warner Brothers Washington representative that Ford would visit my office to make the final arrangements for script approval, locations, use of a ship, and the assignment of a technical adviser for *Mr. Roberts.*

Well, Admiral Ford tore into my office with the same fervor as though he was storming a beachhead. It was the first time we had ever met, but the Warner Brothers representative had thoroughly briefed him on who I was. He gave me a warm handshake and said he was pleased that someone with my filmmaking know-how was in charge of the movie desk. Then he told everyone in the office that I was one of the original *Our Gang* comedy kids and that I played the role of Fatima.

I tried to explain to him that I had only been an extra in a few of the earliest *Our Gang* comedies and had never played a character called Fatima. It made absolutely no difference to him

Ford had just returned from Africa where he had directed *Mogambo,* starring Clark Gable, Grace Kelly, and Ava Gardner. He told everyone in earshot that we wouldn't like this film as "It's nothing but tits and tigers." Well this fine picture was much more than that, but he thought this was very funny. For the rest of the day everywhere I took him, including into the office of the chief of naval operations, he kept repeating the "tits and tigers" story and calling me Fatima.

Never before, or after, did I have to take a movie director into the office of the chief of naval operations, but with Admiral Ford it was different. Chief of naval operations at the time was Admiral Robert M. "Mick" Carney and they had known each other since Ford's film work in the Pacific during World War II. Admiral Carney welcomed us into his inner office and the two admirals chatted for a long time while I stood by rather uncomfortably. Needless to say, Admiral Carney heard the "tits and tigers" story and that in Hollywood I was known as Fatima.

Admiral Ford received everything he sought on that one-day visit. The U.S. Navy did not have any cargo ships like the USS *Reluctant* still in our active duty line, but we found one we had sold as war surplus to the Mexican navy and Warner Brothers rented it to use in *Mr. Roberts.*

Also due to John Ford's esteem in the Department of the Navy, his entire cast and crew were permitted to move onto Midway Island, which was then still considered off-limits to civilians. While they were working at Midway, John Ford became seriously ill. When he had to be flown home he was replaced by Mervyn LeRoy, who finished the picture and received codirector billing with Ford in the screen credits.

When I left the motion picture desk in the Office of Information and reported to my new assignment as a transport pilot in Squadron VR-7 in Honolulu, I was pleased to learn that the *Mr. Roberts* company was in town and having a farewell cast and crew party on the patio of the Officers Club at Hickam Air Force Base.

I dug out my only clean white uniform and my wife and I attended. I was met at the door by Mervyn LeRoy and he led Betty and me on a personally conducted tour to meet all the members of the cast and crew.

When he tried to introduce me to James Cagney I'm sure he was surprised when Jimmy threw his arms around me and said, "Hi Junior. You sure look great in that uniform." I guess Mervyn had forgotten I played Cagney's character as a boy in *Public Enemy.* When we came to William Powell I'm sure he was also surprised when Powell's wife, Diana "Mousie" Powell also threw her arms around me. Mervyn didn't know I had dated Diana many times long before she became Mrs. Powell.

This was a great night for me. I saw many crew members whom I had grown up with and they were so impressed and so pleased to see me as a navy lieutenant and a naval aviator out there on duty in Hawaii.

61

Washington, Admiral Gallery, and Arline Judge

Please forgive me. I got ahead of myself again, but I wanted to complete everything connected with *Mr. Roberts* in the same chapter.

I told you earlier about my mother's poor health and how I brought her back to Jacksonville to live with us. As long as I can remember, my poor mother suffered from severe sinus headaches. She had at least two painful operations for a deviated septum, hoping to relieve the pressures.

These were performed by a neighbor of ours who was reputed to be a qualified eye, ear, nose, and throat specialist. I remember this same doctor removing my tonsils and adenoids on my father's operating table in our home. I guess he wasn't very good at this either as before I could be accepted into the Navy I had to have my tonsil tags burned off by another doctor at my own expense.

Mother's painful pressures never did go away and finally she formed what looked like a boil on her eyelid. This finally burst and nearly a cup of pus-like fluid exuded from the opening. When it healed an adhesion formed and Mother was not able to completely close her eye again for years.

When I took her to navy doctors at the NAS Jacksonville hospital, the specialist who attended her said he had never seen such a condition. Because I was about to be transferred to Washington, D.C., he told us to wait until we were there for her to have her next operation. He had her wear an eye patch for two months so the ulcer forming on her open eye could subside.

Soon after our arrival in Washington she went into the great Naval Medical Center in Bethesda, Maryland, where they brought in the finest plastic surgeon in the area and he made Mother a new eyelid with skin from her neck. This operation and her subsequent miraculous recovery is in the annals of navy medicine.

Another big event during my tour of duty at the nation's capital was the birth of our first daughter, Mary Elizabeth, whom we have always called Libbey.

Each year while I was stationed in Washington the navy held a big fund-raising ball. The proceeds from this gala event went to Navy Relief, a fine organization that aids navy personnel in financial difficulties. It was held in the Sail Loft of the old Navy Gun Factory on the banks of the Potomac River.

The Gun Factory goes back to Civil War days and the Sail Loft at one time was used to hang the newly stitched sails to be used on our ships before we went to an all iron ship fleet. In later years the Sail Loft was converted to a large auditorium.

In CHINFO at that time was a wonderful man, Captain Walter Karig, who was considered by all there to be the dean of public information specialists. He was a well-published author and journalist and revered by all who knew him. Walter Karig wrote under several pen names, including Julia K. Duncan, James Cody Ferris, and Keats Patrick. Strangely enough, this big, strapping navy captain wrote the *Nancy Drew* books under the pseudonym of Carolyn Keene.

The year I was involved in the ball, Captain Karig wrote a fine script and asked me to appear in some of the skits. This was a banner year for the ball and the entire navy band and the midshipman choir from the Naval Academy were among the entertainment. Ed Sullivan came down from New York to be the master of ceremonies. The MGM swimming star Esther Williams was in New York at the time and Ed brought her down with him to be the guest of honor.

Ed Sullivan is well known for his many years as host of his outstanding television show. He was also a highly read columnist and his *New York Daily News* variety column "Little Old New York" was syndicated in hundreds of newspapers. This column brought him to Hollywood many times and we knew each other from interviews he had done with me.

When Ed arrived an hour or so before the start of the program, it became my task to brief him on the acts he was to introduce. He was pleased to see me and suggested we coemcee the program. Wow, what an honor!

The show was an outstanding success and at the close of the program, while we were standing together, Ed told the predominantly navy audience, "In Hollywood, Lieutenant Coghlan is known as Junior." I have several stills from that evening and my favorite is when Ed made that announcement and I show feigned embarrassment at his revelation.

One day I was called into the office of the chief of information, who was then Rear Admiral Lewis S. Parks, a highly decorated hero of submarine warfare in World War II. He told me that Rear Admiral Daniel V. Gallery, then the chief of Naval Air Reserve Training, had asked if he could borrow my services for a few days on a special detail.

Admiral Dan Gallery was becoming a well-known author and his "Cap'n Fatso" stories were being printed in the *Saturday Evening Post*. He was also a real hero of naval aviation. When he was a captain and in

Ed Sullivan has just told a navy audience that in Hollywood, Lieutenant Coghlan is known as Junior. I feign embarrassment.

command of the aircraft carrier USS *Guadalcanal* in the Atlantic, dive-bomber pilots from his ship dropped depth charges on a German submarine causing it to come to the surface. It was the U-505 and Captain Gallery had a boarding party on the sub before its crew could scuttle the disabled vessel. He took it under tow and brought it back to the United States. This was the first capture of a major enemy ship on the high seas since the Revolutionary War.

The U-505 was eventually towed to Lake Michigan where it is on permanent display at the Museum of Industry and Science in Admiral Gallery's hometown of Chicago.

The navy made a documentary film of the historical capture and Admiral Gallery wanted me to accompany him to Hollywood to show this film to movie producers, hoping to interest a studio in making a major motion picture based on this epic event.

I flew to the headquarters of his command at the Naval Air Station at Glenview, Illinois, to make myself available to the admiral. The next morning we boarded his private transport plane for the flight to movieland.

The only passengers on the four-engined R5D transport were the admiral, his chief of staff (a captain), his aide (a lieutenant), and of course, me, Lieutenant Coghlan. Soon after becoming airborne, the aide came back to me and said the admiral would like to play bridge and asked if I would make the fourth player. At that time I was a poor bridge player and should have said no, but as I was the only other person available, I reluctantly agreed to fill in.

As luck would have it, in the draw for seats I became the admiral's partner. In one of the early hands the admiral had a terrific fistful of cards and opened with a two bid. The next player passed. I only had two low cards in the admiral's suit and a total honor count of three, so I also passed. With this the admiral stood up and leaned across the table with his nose almost touching mine. Then he said, or rather snarled, "Coghlan, you can't pass." I reviewed my hand and as I had one suit with several cards and an honor in it, I bid in that suit and darned if the admiral didn't make a grand slam. Boy, I tell you, playing cards with admirals can be hazardous to your health.

We landed at the Los Alamitos Naval Air Station, one of the activities in the admiral's command, located in Orange County about 40 miles from Hollywood. They made a car available to us and we drove to the Hollywood Roosevelt Hotel to be near the studios for our visits the following day.

First we drove to Universal Studio, where producer Robert Arthur gathered a group of studio officials who viewed Admiral Gallery's film about the capture of the U-505. At that time Bob Arthur was preparing to produce *The Long Gray Line,* a story about West Point that John Ford was going to direct.

Arthur was interested in military films and later produced *Operation Petticoat,* the very funny movie where Cary Grant as the skipper of a damaged submarine rescued a group of navy nurses and brought them to safety from behind the Japanese lines during World War II. The sub needed a new coat of paint and the only color available was a bright pink, which resulted in lots of ridicule when the sub finally returned to Pearl Harbor.

This was also the film where Tony Curtis stole a pig from a farmer in the Philippines and snuck it on board to replenish the ship's food supply.

There were also some very funny scenes, such as when a nurse's girdle saved the day when it was used to replace a much needed broken part. There was also much visual humor when buxom nurses were forced to suck in their chests as they passed face to face with crew members in the narrow passageways. It all turned out well. Cary Grant married the chief nurse and Tony Curtis became CO of the sub before it was decommissioned at the close of the war.

Producer Robert Arthur told me the funniest story of all about this great motion picture. Additional scenes were needed and he went back to the naval base at Key West where they again painted one of our submarines pink to allow them to complete the movie. It so happened that the commander of the Atlantic Fleet was in the area on an inspection visit. When he saw this pink painted submarine leaving port he couldn't believe his eyes and ordered it back to the pier. It was finally explained to him that this was the submarine being used in a motion picture and he reluctantly rescinded his order.

Our final stop of the day was at Columbia Studio where Admiral Gallery had contacted producer Harry Joe Brown to have him see the U-505 film. He viewed it with interest but at the time Harry Joe Brown was mainly interested in making westerns. When the lights came on in the projection room, Brown said he was sorry but a film of this type was not in his plans. He then said, "Say Admiral, just so it won't be a total loss, why don't you join me tonight at a party I'm having at my home in Palm Springs."

We drove back to the Roosevelt Hotel in a rather gloomy mood. We checked out and then drove back to the Los Alamitos Naval Air Station. To the surprise of the aircraft crew we only flew about 70 air miles to the civilian airport at Palm Springs. When we landed there we were met by a limousine and driven to the house Harry Joe Brown lived in with his actress wife, Sally Eilers.

Brown opened the door for us and in we trooped. First, Admiral Gallery, then the chief of staff wearing the heavy gold aiguillettes that we always jokingly called "chicken guts," then came the aide with his thinner aiguillettes, and finally me, Lieutenant Coghlan.

As we entered the living room I looked over to the bar where I saw Betty Hutton and my old friend Arline Judge. Both of them were perched on bar stools and were feeling no pain. When Arline saw me she screamed, "Juuunnnior" at the top of her voice. Then she hopped off the bar stool and walked or rather lurched over to see me.

She threw her arms around me and gave me a big juicy kiss. Then she held me at arm's length and looked me over carefully. We were wearing khaki uniforms and she saw my gold buttons, my lieutenant's shoulder boards with a gold star and two gold stripes, my wings, and finally the four campaign ribbons I was entitled to wear.

After this close appraisal she tried to whisper, but in her condition I'm sure everyone in the room heard her say, "Junior, tell me the truth. Did you earn this all by yourself, or did you have to kiss somebody's ass?"

Admiral Gallery was standing right next to us and I though he would fall on the floor from laughter. That night as we were flying back to NAS Glenview, he called me up to his cabin where he was stretched out. He said, "Coghlan, I appreciated the way those Hollywood people treated you. Oh, they showed me all the respect they show to any admiral, but they reacted differently to you. I know they all felt you have accomplished something they have not and they gave you a distinctive type of respect and admiration. I thought it was great."

62

Orders to Sea Duty

I received a shock while running the motion picture desk at CHINFO when I was notified I had lost my status in the Continuous Active Duty program. Here I was performing a most important job for the navy, but I was an aviator serving in a billet supposed to be filled by a public information specialist. Now I was just a reserve officer competing against officers of the regular navy. This was not a favorable position for a reserve hoping to make the navy a career.

I discussed this with the Continuous Active Duty detail officer in the Bureau of Naval Personnel and he said the only way I could be reinstated as a CAD and also hope to be promoted to the rank of Lieutenant Commander was to leave CHINFO and serve on sea duty with the fleet.

I was now 38 years old and he said I would not be too welcome in a jet squadron, so carrier aviation was out for me. He advised that my best bets were to fly patrol bombers or transports.

Transports sounded better to me so he found openings in squadrons at Port Lyautey, Morocco; Naples, Italy; and in Hawaii. The advantage of being in a transport squadron as against being in patrol bombers was that my family could go with me.

Port Lyautey didn't sound too interesting and Naples had some good and some bad points. Friends who had been stationed there said you could rent lovely big homes at reasonable rates, but heating costs were astronomical and where the navy families lived was 40 miles away from the commissary and the military medical facilities. We had never been to the Hawaiian Islands and always wanted to go there, so I requested duty in VR-7, a navy transport squadron that flew out of Hickam Air Force Base on the main island of Oahu.

I was given a gigantic farewell party at the headquarters of the Motion Picture Association of America. All the Washington representatives of the major studios told me how much they had enjoyed working with me as a fellow who could understand their problems while representing the navy on the more than 30 films I had monitored in the nearly three years I was their Washington liaison. I thought it was a kind tribute to my fairness in bringing their films to the motion picture audiences while holding up the integrity of the navy in these productions.

When we left Washington I drove to St. Louis where I left Betty, my mother, and Libbey at Betty's folks' home. Then I drove across country with the boys, Michael, now seven years old, and Pat, who had just turned four. We had a great trip.

First I took them to Omaha, Nebraska, to see Boys Town which was tender in my memories from having worked with Mickey Rooney and Spencer Tracy in *Men of Boys Town.* I had never been there myself and I also wanted to see the establishment that Father Flanagan had made so famous. Then we drove through the Badlands of South Dakota and stopped to admire the spectacular Mount Rushmore National Monument. Next came Yellowstone National Park where we saw Old Faithful spout right on time. When we passed the Grand Tetons the boys saw their first moose grazing in a nearby meadow.

At Salt Lake City we heard the fantastic Mormon Tabernacle Choir and then we took a dip in the Great Salt Lake. We saw Zion and Bryce Canyon National Parks and spent one night at Lake Tahoe where we also dipped in that beautiful lake.

We reached our destination of San Francisco where we spent two nights with my dear friend the former navy chaplain Matthew F. Connolly. He was now a monsignor and serving as pastor of the Apostleship of the Sea, where he attended to the religious needs of visiting merchant seamen when their ships called at the port. He had a dormitory and a real ship's galley where these seamen stayed and were fed while their vessels were tied up in San Francisco Harbor. He had one of these sailors take Mike and Pat for a tour of the harbor and he took them on board several ships. They were just thrilled by their private tour of the port.

Betty and my mother and Libbey flew into town and we spent two nights in rooms at the Marines' Memorial Club while waiting to board the ship that would take us to Honolulu. It was the *General Shanks,* a former navy transport ship now being utilized in the Military Sea Transportation Service. There wasn't much high rank on board so we were provided with two large cabins right across from each other. Betty, Libbey, and I shared one of them and mother and the boys the other.

We had a pleasant five-day crossing and after leaving the rough water out of San Francisco it was smooth sailing. The MSTS ran a good ship. We had fine food and they showed movies each night and conducted games like regular cruise ships. During the day we played lots of shuffleboard and other deck games.

We were met at the pier in Honolulu by hula dancers and all the musical amenities received by passengers on Matson Line ships that docked at the same terminal. From the railing we saw a large poster with COGHLAN printed on it. We made our way to the sign where we met Roger and Betty Brown who, we learned, were our squadron sponsors. Roger was a pilot in VR-7 and is still one of my best friends.

We spent our first few days in Visiting Officers Quarters at Fort DeRussy, an old army fort located right on Waikiki Beach. From there we were assigned to a spacious Quonset hut where we lived for a month before receiving permanent housing in a nice three-bedroom duplex that was located above the navy-marine golf course. We lived there for a year and then I bought a really good home on the windward side of Oahu in Kailua. From there I had to drive over the old Pali road to get to Hickam Field. While living there we used the commissary and medical facilities of the Marine Corps base at Kaneohe Bay. Betty was even made a member of the Marine Officers' Wives Club where she joined their hula group. Betty became one of the best haole (white) hula dancers that I ever saw. Her teacher Caroline Tuck also took me on and I learned the Hukilau dance and the Cockeyed Mayor of Kaunakakai which Betty and I used to do together. We got so good at it that Caroline used to include us in her troupe when they danced professionally at big parties and luaus on the island.

Our Hawaiian dancing career came to a temporary pause when Betty found out she was pregnant again. So, less than a year after arriving in Honolulu, we had our second daughter, Cathleen Ann. She was born in the beautiful big Tripler Army Hospital high on the hills overlooking Pearl Harbor.

63

Flying the Pacific: Japan

The transition to becoming a transport pilot was not easy for me. When I arrived at Squadron VR-7 I was four months short of being a naval aviator for ten years and had 1,600 hours of flight time, all in single-engine aircraft. Now I had to learn to fly the Lockheed Super Constellation, a four-engine bird with many complicated systems that were completely foreign to me.

The R7V, as the navy called it, was loaded with complex hydraulics, air conditioning, refrigeration, pressurization, fuel transfer, emergency brakes, and an electrical system, to name a few, that I had to learn to perfection before being qualified as an aircraft commander. It was a real challenge for me, but I earned that distinction in my final months in the squadron. During the three years I was a member of VR-7 I added 2,400 more hours of flight time to my pilot's log book.

During training we had many hours of instrument practice and the instructors pulled countless emergencies on us. For instance, while flying along peacefully, he might ease back on two throttles and say, "We have just lost power on two engines. What are you going to do?" Or, "Wow, a lady has just delivered a baby in the passenger compartment. What are you going to do?" Or, "We have just lost all pressurization and must immediately descend 10,000 feet to keep our passengers alive." You can't imagine the fiendish situations these check pilots subjected us to in their efforts to mold us into complete transport pilots to equal the fine men who fly you in the commercial airlines.

I could go on for many chapters about my three years in Squadron VR-7, but I'd rather capsulize them into these next few pages as I don't wish to turn this into a travelogue.

My squadron, VR-7, and its sister navy squadron, VR-8, along with five air force squadrons, made up the Pacific Division of the Military Air Transport Service.

We respected our air force counterparts for being excellent pilots, but we always thought we were better trained than they were. To begin with, the air force transports always carried a nonpilot navigator. Shucks, we navy pilots were also completely trained navigators. We were taught all the existing navigational skills including dead reckoning, loran, pressure pattern, and, most important at the time, celestial navigation.

When we took off from Hickam Field the three navy pilots on board rotated all the duties. Besides the actual takeoff and landing, our most interesting hours were those spent at the navigation table.

Also the air force had what they called maintenance squadrons. When their planes came back from a trip they were assigned to this group for service. We had our own maintenance crew of well-trained aviation machinist mates and they took complete care of our aircraft.

The air force pilots did not have other jobs within their squadron and when they returned from a trip they were off until their next assigned flight. We all had collateral duties and after three days off for crew rest we went back to work on those assignments. We also took our turn as squadron duty officer, which was not required from our air force buddies.

Though I requested another assignment, as usual I was placed in public relations. My friend Roger Brown and I jointly filled this post and we had two enlisted journalists to keep things going when we were out flying the line. Among other things we put out a monthly eight-page newsletter. The two journalists did an outstanding job and one year our newspaper *The Seahorse* was named the best overseas publication in the navy.

We had two main routes to fly. One month we flew to Japan where we landed at Haneda Airport, then the main airport of Tokyo. The next month we flew to the Philippines where we landed at Clark Air Force Base about eighty miles from Manila.

When we flew to Tokyo we "staged" at Wake Island where another crew was waiting to take over our plane and passengers. We then laid over until the next scheduled flight arrived and we relieved that crew and continued their flight. The passengers were rarely on the ground for more than two hours while these transfers took place, but we were usually on Wake Island for three or four days in this "staging" arrangement.

Wake Island was an interesting place to visit. This strategic atoll located 2,300 miles west of Honolulu was captured by the Japanese a few days after Pearl Harbor. The conquering garrison remained there throughout the war in the Pacific. They had been bypassed by the Americans and left there to starve and only surrendered when the Japanese laid down their arms after signing the peace treaty on board the battleship USS *Missouri* in Tokyo Harbor.

When I flew in and out of there between 1954 and 1957 the island was still dotted with Japanese gun emplacements and a few rusted tanks. The battered hulk of one of the invader's ships was still being torn apart by the surf where it rested on the reef.

On one side of Wake was a gigantic pile of seashells, proving that the Japanese ate everything they could catch or dig up in their efforts to survive. We also heard they ate every rat and lizard and any other form of animal, plant, and bird life to hold off starvation.

When we landed in Japan we usually had a three- or four-day layover, but we were always on call so could not travel far from Tokyo. I did get to visit the nearby cities of Yokohama and Yokosuka and I did see the impressive Shrine of the Giant Buddha at Kamakura.

Shopping was great in Tokyo and I brought wonderful presents home on every trip. In addition to the fine stores, it was fun roaming through the Ginza where haggling was expected on every purchase. They also had good entertainment and I visited several of their night spots and tried to view all of their different theater art forms.

Nearly every bar in the Ginza area featured strippers. These shapely young ladies walked onto the dance floor and casually began disrobing to music played by a small combo. Some of these bars also had what we call B-girls. These well-dressed, attractive girls would circulate and ask if they could sit with you.

One night the group I was with welcomed this invasion of privacy and almost before I knew it there was a beautiful Japanese girl sitting next to me. She almost immediately asked if I would buy her a drink. I noticed when the waitress put down her drink she handed her what looked like a poker chip which my companion promptly tucked into her ample cleavage. While I was slowly sipping a single beer this lady had ordered four drinks which I had to pay for. I couldn't believe that four drinks would have such little effect on a young girl so when she wasn't looking, I took a sip of her drink. So help me, it was straight tea, or nothing much stronger.

Another popular form of diversion was the Tokyo Onsen, which we called the "hotsy baths." This was a large building with several floors, all devoted to cleanliness. I checked in as at a hotel and was assigned to a room. When I arrived there I found a lovely, scantily clad young lady waiting for me. She was wearing what resembled a brief white bikini. She indicated that I was to remove my clothing and diverted her eyes while I did so. Then she opened the double doors to a steam box and motioned that I was to be seated inside. After I was snugly enclosed with only my head visible. She wrapped towels around my neck and turned on the steam.

By the time my ten-minute steam bath was over, I was delighted to escape when she opened the doors. She led me to a sunken bathtub that was filled with extremely hot water and gestured for me to step in and be seated. I swear the water was almost as hot as the steam cabinet. Again with diverted eyes she modestly soaped me down and gave me a good scrubbing. When it came to the private parts she handed me the washcloth and the rest was up to me.

The bath was followed by a marvelous massage. At all times I was covered by a towel and she was respectful and discreet. Some of our squadron mates told of having the girls walk on their backs to relieve muscular tension but I never had such an experience.

Many of the squadron wives were furious when they heard their husbands had visited the Onsen, but their fears were unfounded as the "hotsy baths" were completely innocent of any indiscretions.

There was a great restaurant in downtown Tokyo that we visited often. It was a five-story building featuring a different cuisine on each level. We tried them all and preferred the top floor where they served Western-style food in an Oriental environment.

First we removed our shoes and jackets and were supplied with slippers and colorful cotton kimonos. We sat on cushions with our legs stretched out under the traditional low table. During the meal our private party was entertained by kimono-clad dancing girls. They were not the true Geishas, but were dancers who performed to the music of a samisen played by a member of their troupe. The samisen is the three-stringed musical instrument very popular in Japan and is strummed like a banjo. There were usually three dancers and they performed simple routines like the Baseball Players Dance and the Coal Miners Dance.

These dances were long in duration with much pantomime and had many repetitions as they progressed to a conclusion. Ham that I am, after watching the first two choruses or so, I just couldn't resist getting up and becoming a member of the line. It really cracked up these dancing girls to find an American naval officer following their movements, step for step, gesture for gesture, and not missing a beat. That's show biz.

In the center of the theatrical district of Tokyo is a large, circular building called the Nichigeki Theater. The structure holds several movie theaters and a really fine burlesque house.

I guess by the standards set by Minskys in New York, these shows are pretty amateurish but they were fun to watch. They had their equivalent of our baggy pants comics, but because they spoke in Japanese, I never really understood the punch lines. However, the natives roared with laughter, so I presume their double-entendre jokes were in keeping with Minskys' best.

The theater had a runway, as most burlesque theaters do, but here the girls started their walk from behind the audience on an elevated ramp. By the time they reached the stage they were already partially disrobed. Once on stage they continued shedding right down to the briefest of "G" strings. Strangely enough, these girls stripped in an almost dignified manner and did not resort to the bumps and grinds that we usually associate with burlesque.

The theater I enjoyed the most was the one featuring the Takarazuka

Dancers. If you have read James Michener's book *Sayonara* or seen the motion picture of it that starred Marlon Brando, you will recall that the girl he fell in love with was a Takarazuka performer.

These girls are carefully recruited and considered to be among the comeliest ladies in Japan. They train for years at the academy located in the city of Takarazuka from whence they are named. There are four troupes of the dancers, with one performing at the home theater, one in Tokyo, one on tour, and the other group in rehearsal.

The Takarazukas are an all-girl presentation with ladies taking the male roles as well. Their two-hour-long show compares favorably with anything Ziegfeld or Busby Berkeley ever staged and the finale with 115 girls dancing in unison reminded me of the famous Radio City Music Hall Rockettes.

The reverse of this is Kabuki where all the roles are played by men. Kabuki stems from the seventeenth century and is considered a modern version of No, or Noh, as it is sometimes spelled, which goes back to the Imperial Palace dance drama of the fourteenth century.

I went to the Kabuki-Da Theater one evening intending to see a complete performance. I must confess after five hours of watching Samurais in sword fights and those male actors portraying women carrying on in their peculiar sing-song voices, I just had to leave.

My wife tells an even more interesting story of her only visit to the Kabuki-Da Theater. She also sat for about three hours and then she noticed the Japanese around her began opening the traditional metal lunch boxes they carry. They began digging their chopsticks into the rice and raw fish they had brought with them. It wasn't long before the stench of fish became nauseous to her and she just had to leave the theater. In our country they say when an actor overemotes you can detect "the odor of pure ham." I guess in Japan the parallel would be "sensing the smell of sushi."

There was one other form of "entertainment" I observed in Tokyo that I'm almost ashamed to write about.

One night a group of us were walking down the street when we were approached by a well-dressed young man. This didn't surprise us as we were frequently stopped by hucksters pushing their particular store or restaurant. This fellow asked us if we wanted to see a "resbian show." We didn't quite understand him and asked him to repeat his question. Then we realized with the difficulty the Japanese have with the letters R and L, he was trying to say lesbian.

This didn't particularly appeal to us, but we had an hour to kill before our dinner reservation, so we agreed to go with him. We followed him for about a block when he led us into a dark alley.

After we had gone about 50 feet we became apprehensive that he might be steering us into a robbery or a mugging. However, right then he opened the back door of a building and ushered us into a well-lit room with a futon, the Japanese mattress-like form of bed, on the floor in the center.

We were met by a middle-aged man who bowed many times and then asked us for 2,000 yen apiece. At that time the yen was 360 to the American dollar, so whatever we were going to see was going to cost each of us about $5.50.

When he had our money he clapped his hands and two pretty girls entered the room. They were both in their twenties and were wearing loose fitting kimonos. They walked to the futon and dropped the kimonos to the floor and stood there stark naked.

They both laid down on the futon and began kissing and fondling each other. They changed positions frequently and we saw what I assumed to be lesbian lovemaking being performed in many erotic attitudes.

Finally the girl who was the obvious aggressor of the pair got up and left the room. Then the other girl asked one of our group to hand her his lighted cigarette. When she had it in her fingers she slid her heels back until they touched her buttocks. Then she spread her knees wide apart and inserted the cigarette into the most surprising place you can think of.

With quick contractions of her stomach muscles she was actually able to inhale on the cigarette and exude little puffs of smoke from this unexpected location. After several puffs she withdrew the cigarette and handed it back to the fellow who had supplied it. I don't know if she expected him to smoke it or not. He told her she could keep it and she snuffed it out in an ashtray.

Now the other girl returned and she was carrying what looked like a large, rubber, two-headed penis about 12 inches long. She inserted one end of it into her vagina and stood there looking just like a woman with an erection.

The other girl submissively laid back and put her feet up into the air and spread her legs wide apart. The "butch" of the two then mounted her like they were man and wife. For the next few minutes they had what looked like violent intercourse in positions I didn't know were possible. Finally with many moans and groans they both had what appeared to be a very fulfilling and satisfying orgasm and laid there exhausted, panting, and whimpering.

That was the end of the "show" and we were ushered out into the alley. As we walked to the restaurant, I felt more like going back to the BOQ and taking a shower than wanting to eat dinner.

On the return flight from Japan we stopped at Midway Island for fuel and a hot meal for our passengers. In the winter, if the winds were favorable, we could overfly Midway, but this was a rare occurrence. Though we didn't have to stage at Midway I knew the island well. I had been there many times on the weekly Midway turnaround flight by which we brought in the mail and replenished the island's food and medical supplies. I thought the most beautiful of all the atolls I landed at was Midway.

Midway is also famous as the nesting place of the black-footed albatross. Each year hundreds of these handsome birds fly into Midway to nest and they do their best to take over the island. Because of their comical antics they are known throughout the navy as "gooney birds."

Much of this nickname is earned from the most unusual mating dance these odds birds go through before they breed. It is believed that after many months at sea they tried to seek out the same mate and even the same nesting site they used on previous visits to Midway.

When they finally pair off they commence a breeding ritual that is very humorous to watch. It starts with the two birds doing what is called beak snapping, which is the first stage of the acceptance process. Here the male extends and lowers his long neck while walking around the lady gooney bird, flapping his wings, stomping his feet, making groaning and croaking noises, and emitting high-pitched whistles, beak snapping all the while. She responds by preening her neck feathers to make herself more attractive to her swain. This curious courtship display goes on for hours.

Once they decide this must be true love they conclude the ritual by both birds tapping their beaks at the same spot on the ground. This is called "showing the nest site" and is where copulation takes place and where they build their nest.

Eventually, a single egg is produced and both birds take turns incubating it for the necessary 65 to 79 days that this process has been observed. Another curious habit here is that the male usually takes the first four to six days on the nest without a break. I saw the mud- and grass-mounted nests they build all over the island, including some on the front lawn of the base commander's home.

After the egg hatches both parents take turns feeding the chick when they return from long flights out to sea gathering food. We all have seen birds feeding their young in the nest by dropping food into their open beaks. The gooney bird, of course, does it differently.

When the adult returns to the nest it opens its beak to the limit and the chick places its entire head into the opening. Then the adult regurgitates the partially digested squid and other forms of seafood from its craw and the young bird greedily gulps it down. This it not a pretty sight to see, but the fuzzy-downed youngster thrives on it. After about three months the baby is almost as large as the parents and just as nasty.

The first time I saw one of these nestlings it looked so cute that I tried to pet it. To my surprise I came away with a bleeding finger when it took a chunk out of my hand with its sharply hooked upper beak.

The black-footed albatross has a near 11-feet wing span which is not more than nine inches wide over its entire length and it tapers to a point at the tip. This efficient wing structure enables it to soar effortlessly for hours in favorable wind conditions. The wing can be compared to that of a fighter plane in that it requires high speed to become airborne and also mandates a fast landing. At takeoff on a calm day the bird may have to run for 100 yards while flapping its wings to get into the air. On the water it has even more difficulty. There it starts swiming rapidly and finally lifts itself out of the water and actually runs across the surface using its webbed feet for propulsion until it flies into the air.

Due to its high-speed approach on landings nearly every one ends up in a crash with the poor gooney bird tumbling over two or three times. This doesn't seem to faze it as the bird gets up, shakes itself off, and struts away while maintaining its dignity. Watching one of these birds landing in the slipstream of an airplane is a real comedy.

These birds, so graceful in the air, become a real menace when the chicks begin to fly. At that time of the year we were ordered to land at Midway only at night when they were back at the nest sites. When we had to take off in daylight hours we made what was called a maximum speed climb out. In other words, we took off and raised the landing gear while skimming the water at about 20 feet of altitude. After we had cleared the island and had gained about 175 knots of air speed, we abruptly pulled back on the yoke to zoom through the area where the young birds were circling.

They usually stayed below 500 feet, so we were through the danger zone in a matter of seconds. I'm happy to say I was never in a plane that contacted one of these 25-pound birds, but there are reports of cracked windshields and dented wings from other pilots who had this misfortune.

We were flying propeller-driven aircraft and if one of them hit a prop it was messy but no real harm was done. Today's jet aircraft with their large air intakes suffer more serious damage if they ingest a large bird.

I was flying the plane on the day a group of avian experts descended on Midway with the express purpose of trying to discourage the gooneys from disrupting flight operations on this strategic island. They told me of their plans and I checked with their progress on subsequent flights.

They were not permitted to harm any of the birds or destroy any eggs in their efforts. They did have free rein, however, in other devious schemes. On one area of the atoll they painted eggs in outrageous colors like red, yellow, orange, green, and blue. In another section they switched eggs from one nest to another. They also set off smoke bombs and firecrackers. The birds may have been annoyed at first but in the long run it didn't phase them much as they still produced a bumper crop of fledglings. I mentioned earlier about the birds' most unusual mating dance. I got pretty good at doing an imitation of it and used to perform it on demand at parties.

I never did try it in front of a real live lady gooney bird because I was not quite sure what she might expect from me at the conclusion.

64

Flying the Pacific: The Philippines

During the month we flew to the Philippines, we staged first on the atoll of Kwajalein in the Marshall Islands and then at Agana, the capital of Guam in the Marianas. Of all the Pacific islands we stayed at, Kwaj, as we called it, was my favorite. I said Midway was the prettiest, but Kwaj was the most interesting.

When we drove the Japanese off Kwajalein our SeaBees dredged out a gigantic portion of the reef to obtain coral. This was used in rebuilding the airstrip to support the heavy bombers used in the final assault on the home islands of Japan.

This hollowed-out area was the size of two complete football fields and was about ten feet deep. The reef protecting Kwajalein is very wide and this dredging hardly made a dent in it. As each new tide came in this pit was filled with a new supply of exotic sea life that was trapped there until the next high tide. We used to snorkel in it and many times I came face to face with unbelievably beautiful fish.

At times we stayed clear of some that were dangerous like the angelfish, so pretty to see, but one you wouldn't want to tangle with as its bite can be fatal.

One day several of us spent half an hour dislodging a good-sized octopus from its hiding place in the rocks. It sure is a strange feeling when one of its tentacles wraps around your arm. Yuck!!

Regarding the ocean life around Kwaj, it was interesting to watch them dump garbage into the ocean each evening. When this refuse from the mess hall hit the water you wouldn't believe the turmoil as many large sharks fought each other for their share of the goodies. On the outskirts of this conflict were rays who kept out of the ravenous thrashing and waited for their gleanings from what was left over. These rays were so interesting to see. They were about the size of a bridge table and it looked like they were flying through the water instead of swimming.

This brings to mind a real tragedy that occurred there during the Korean War. We were sending a detachment of navy nurses to serve in the war zone and the plane they were in went down right after takeoff from

Kwaj. The plane broke up and there was evidence that some of the nurses and crew members made it into life rafts but there were no survivors. They later found torn and blood-stained rafts on the reef. It is a foregone conclusion that sharks took this terrible toll. What a way to go! Imagine—to survive a plane crash and then be eaten alive by sharks while trying to reach shore.

One day while staging at Kwaj I checked out some fishing gear and was dunking a line off the pier near the pilot's station. As I was sitting there the port pilot saw me and engaged me in conversation. I later found out he was a real movie fan and had recognized me from my film work.

He was a chief boatswain, the highest of the four ranks of warrant officer in the navy. This interesting man had nearly 30 years in the service and was about to retire to civilian life.

A boatswain, or bos'n, as they usually are called, is the real workhorse of the navy. They are the mainstays of the deck force at sea where they handle the anchors and mooring lines among many other things. They are also the small boat handlers and some end up in charge of tugboats. Most readers should have heard of bos'ns' pipes and bos'ns' chairs and they also come under their control.

This man had worked his way up through the enlisted ratings and when he made chief he was placed in command of a large fleet tug. Due to all his experience with tugs, he finally became a qualified port pilot.

The atoll of Kwajalein has several narrow outlets through the reef and it was his duty to safely guide ships in and out of these treacherous passages. When a ship was departing Kwaj he was on the bridge advising the captain on a safe passage through the reef and out to the open ocean. When a ship was approaching the atoll, his launch took him several miles out to sea where he climbed aboard to then guide the ship through the dangerous inlets to a safe mooring.

He had a fine, fast motor launch and a crew of three enlisted men and this boat was put to use every time he worked a ship. With an outbound ship it followed and brought him back. With an incoming ship it took him out to sea and then returned to port.

One day he asked me if I would like to ride his launch and fish from it while it was on this mission. He told me this launch was used by base personnel for recreation and had a good selection of fishing gear in its locker. Each round trip took about an hour and a half and I trolled with various feathered lures while the launch was performing its required task. I got to enjoy this privilege four times and it led to the finest fishing I have ever experienced.

Twice I caught about ten skipjacks that weighed about five pounds apiece. The skipjack is the smallest of the tuna family and is a real fighter on the line. Once I hooked three 30-pound onos. Ono is the Polynesian word for good, so you can imagine how well my catch was received at the mess hall that night.

On the last trip I made on the launch, while waiting for my friend to climb down from the ship, I hooked the first marlin swordfish ever known in those waters. I was using light gear, expecting fish like the skipjacks and to hook a marlin was completely unexpected. When this great fish hit my line I was beside myself with joy, but with the light gear I was using there was no way I could ever hope to land this heavy fish. Also when trying to catch fish of this size, the serious angler wears a shoulder harness with a leather pocket in which to place the end of the fishing rod. I had none of these. I was wearing khaki pants and a tee shirt and was forced to stick the end of the rod right into my stomach.

I saw the marlin break water three times before he parted the light line. I only had him hooked for about ten minutes and I sure hated to see him break loose. When he was gone and the excitement was over I realized I had a very sore tummy. I dropped my pants and found that my gut looked like hamburger. It wasn't really bleeding, but was the next thing to it. Where the rod had been held against my stomach it had the same effect as someone rubbing my belly with sandpaper. There was no serious damage but it sure smarted for a few days.

The wide reef was an interesting place to visit at extreme low tides. You could walk out on it for about 200 yards to where it dropped off and the surf pounded against the sheer exposed coral. The reef, now bare of water, was filled with tidepools containing all sorts of odd ocean life.

We used to gather beautiful shells to take home. I still have a very pretty cowry and a conch shell that I brought home from there. These shells still had their occupants on board and you wouldn't dare pack them into your luggage due to the unpleasant odors that would soon begin to be noticed. We used to bury them in the sand behind the BOQ and dig them up two months later on our next trip to the island. By that time the ants had done their work and our shells would be clean of any form of ocean life. After we washed them off, they were treasures to take home.

I was staging on Kwaj the night one of the atomic bomb tests were held on Bikini atoll. We were just leaving the outdoor movie theater at about 10:30 P.M. when suddenly the sky lit up as if it were noon. Bikini is located nearly 300 miles from Kwaj and it was frightening to realize that an atomic blast could illuminate the sky from so far away. We had been in total darkness and then for about 30 seconds you could have read a newspaper in the light that was produced by the blast from such a far distance.

The next morning the plane we had been waiting for arrived from Guam and we flew it back to Hickam Field. It had been cruising at 19,000 feet when it passed nearly 300 miles south of Bikini, yet a routine check at Hickam found contamination in its oil sumps.

Because of this we were called in from our crew rest and given a series of tests. Fortunately, none of us were found to be suffering from excessive radiation and we were given a clean bill of health. What a relief! If we had tested "hot" all of our passengers would also have to be rounded up for tests. Most of them had already progressed on to the United States and that would have been a difficult task.

When we staged on Guam the officers were billeted in a large Quonset hut and our enlisted crew moved into the barracks with the base personnel. In the officers club there was a sign over the bar that declared, "Guam is good."

We used to hold contests to see how many different ways we could interpret this message. Such as: "GUAM is good"; or, "Guam IS good"; or, "Guam is GOOD???" One night over many drinks one fellow won the contest with 17 separate renditions of this poignant statement. After all, there wasn't much else to do while waiting for the next plane to arrive.

Clark Air Force Base was then one of our most important overseas bases. We also had Sangley Point near Manila and I was there during the years we were building the gigantic fleet base and air station at Subic Bay. There we leveled three mountains to fill in the required area and I heard it described as the largest land-moving project since the building of the Panama Canal.

A few miles from Clark Air Force Base is the city of Angeles where we used to visit and do lots of shopping. One day while staging at Clark I hired a jeepney and went into Angeles. The jeepney is a unique, multi-colored vehicle converted from the traditional jeep into the taxi used by the Filipinos for hired transportation.

There was a fine factory in Angeles where I ordered a complete set of living room furniture made of five-rung rattan. It was beautifully made and we used it for years. One of my married daughters still has it in her home.

When I left the factory I noticed my crew chief sitting in a bar and I joined him and ordered a beer. To my surprise a cute little Filipino girl climbed on the stool next to me and immediately placed her hand on my crotch and began squeezing me in a very tender area.

I was startled by this direct approach and asked her what she wanted. She unabashedly said, "I want you, señor." Then I asked her what she wanted of me and she said if I would go back to the base and buy a bottle of whiskey and a carton of cigarettes and bring them to her house she would show me a wonderful time. I told her I had a very busy day lined up and doubted if I could make it back. I later learned that my crew chief heard her make that offer to me so he followed up on it. He said it was a wonderful time as she promised it would be.

Also while in Tokyo we never had too many days available to really enjoy the area. I did get into Manila on one long layover and saw as much of that beautiful city as possible. I toured the Intramuros, the walled city that once was filled with churches and convents. It was completely burned out by the Japanese when they were sacking the area and killing its occupants as they retreated from Manila when General MacArthur's forces were approaching. It was still in the slow process of being rebuilt when I was there.

I also visited the beautiful Santo Tomas University, one of the top institutions of learning in the Pacific. Little did the Dominican friars who founded it in 1611 ever expect that it would later become the infamous prison where the Japanese held many civilian and military personnel while they were occupying the Philippines!

This brings to mind the story one of my navy friends told me. After he was captured and forced to be a member of the infamous 200-mile Bataan Death March, he had to pull out all of his own teeth when they became rotten and his gums went bad due to malnutrition while he was imprisoned.

Once our crew was able to visit Bagio, the summer capital of the Philippines. We had a three-day layover so we hopped the mail plane that was going there on its daily mission. First we checked in to the BOQ and then went into town for sightseeing and some excellent shopping. The Philippine people are very artistic and I brought home some beautiful wood carvings among other artifacts.

The BOQ bordered on the spectacular mountainous golf course which we intended to play the next morning. Would you believe, while on the first tee we received word that the crew who took the plane we brought in the day before had to return to base for mechanical problems and we were now the backup crew! Then they told us there was already a plane en route to return us to Clark Air Force Base. So much for my only visit to Bagio.

The runway at Bagio Airport is unique. There is a mountain at one end and a steep drop-off at the other end. So an incoming pilot had to make his approach over this drop-off, heading right toward the mountain at the end of the runway. Takeoffs were made only in the other direction.

I'll never forget the impressive view the passengers receive on takeoff. You are thundering down the runway just praying to become airborne before reaching the end. Then suddenly you are in the air staring straight down about 2,000 feet at a most striking view of steeply terraced rice paddies—a really spectacular sight.

During the years from 1954 to 1957 when I was flying into Clark Air Force Base, parts of the surrounding area were still subject to raids from the Hukbalahaps, or Huks as they were called. They were bands of armed, landless peasants, urged by the communists to cause as much trouble as possible to disrupt the peace. Once while there I heard of a car filled with American sailors from Sangley Point who were ambushed and killed while driving from Sangley into Manila for what they expected to be a routine trip to the capital city while on liberty.

Just outside the fence of Clark Air Force Base, in a remote canyon, lived a tribe of Pygmy Negritos. These dark-skinned, hairy people are under five feet tall and are probably descendants of the original inhabitants of the Philippine Islands. They still were living a most primitive existence with limited farming and at the time still did most of their hunting for food with spears and bows and arrows.

They were fearless warriors in their day and admired by the Filipinos because they were never completely captured by the Japanese invaders. There are many tales of their bravery when they served as scouts in helping area residents in guerrilla-style raids against the Japanese.

I visited their compound one day and found them to be very friendly people who were eager to sell us their handiworks. I bought some of the spears and bows and arrows as souvenirs for my den.

They still lived in huts that they constructed from wood and bamboo. Their primitive living quarters were on stilts about three feet above the ground and were covered by nipa fronds and palm leaves to protect them from the elements and the heavy seasonal rains.

They cooked with wood or charcoal and I saw that during inclement weather they cooked inside these huts, protecting the flooring with sheets of metal they had scrounged from the air base. I presume this indoor cooking also gave them warmth during the cold months and I guess they never worried about carbon monoxide and other fears we have about indoor charcoal cooking.

On my final trip into Manila I was granted a special tour of the Malacanang Palace. It is the Philippine equivalent of our White House. At that time this exquisite mansion located on the Passig River was the home of President Ramon Magsaysay and his family.

The Malacanang Palace has received much publicity in recent years as the place where Imelda Marcos stored her 30 fur coats, her boxes of 200 black bras, and, of course, her 3,000 pairs of shoes.

I wonder if she ever had to tell President Ferdinand Marcos that she just didn't have a thing to wear?

65

The Embassy Flight

Four times during my three years in Squadron VR-7 I was a crew member on an embassy flight. This extended journey started out like a regular Japan turnaround. However, after the normal staging time in Tokyo, when we left Japan we flew in the opposite direction and our passengers were mainly embassy staff members and couriers. Some even had briefcases handcuffed to their wrists.

The first day out of Tokyo we stopped for fuel at Kadena Air Force Base in Okinawa and spent the night at Clark Air Force Base in the Philippines. The next day we fueled at Saigon in Vietnam and then proceeded to Bangkok, Thailand, for an overnight stop. The third day we gassed up at Calcutta, India, and spent the night in New Delhi.

The last day our gas stop was Karachi, Pakistan, and we ended the embassy flight at Dhahran, Saudi Arabia. There we met an air force plane that had originated their section of the embassy flight in Charleston, South Carolina. After spending the night in Dharhan, we took over their passengers and started back and they began their return trip with our former passengers.

When we were in Saudi Arabia we were exactly halfway around the world from our home base in Honolulu. We made all the same stops on our return flight with the bonus of enjoying a three-day crew rest in New Delhi if we were on schedule.

From the time we left Clark Air Force Base until we returned there eight days later, we were very careful where and what we ate and drank. We stayed at hotels where the food and water met our rigid medical standards by contractual agreement. When we went out for dinner it was only to approved restaurants. In the plane we carried a large supply of bottled water and ate nothing but C rations.

Those readers who served in the ground forces may have unpleasant memories of those canned foods that were introduced during World War II. I guess along with Spam there are more jokes about C rations than any other food imaginable.

For the few days I had to eat them I didn't think they were so bad.

Maybe in the trenches they had to be eaten cold, but at least we had the nicety of steam cookers and ate hot meals while airborne. There was a large variety of entrees available, such as chicken and noodles, beef stew, franks and beans, to name a few and all in all I didn't think they were too bad for a temporary substitute diet.

When we landed at Ton Son Nhut Airport in Saigon it was still occupied by the French who were slowly being driven out of Vietnam. It was still considered a war zone and we weren't allowed to leave the confines of the airport. The French didn't feel too secure there and the entire airport was enclosed by an eight-feet-high brick wall with jagged broken bottles set in concrete all along the top.

The flight from Saigon to Bangkok was very interesting. We crossed Cambodia and flew over the capital city of Phnom Penh and the picturesque Tonle Sap, or the Great Lake. We also passed over the striking ruins of the Angkor Wat, once the largest religious building in the world. It was then nearly hidden by a dense forest of giant teak and rubber trees.

Bangkok was a great city to visit. The people were friendly and the architecture was strikingly beautiful. We landed at Don Muang Airport and had about a 30-minute bus ride into town where we stayed at the Princess Hotel.

On our ride we passed along many canals, or klongs, as they are called. The Thais are very clean people and we saw evidence of this as we drove along. The houses all had little boat docks jutting out into the klongs. On one you might see a man kneeling down washing his face. On the next one would be a man brushing his teeth using the water to rinse his brush. Next might be lady bathing her baby in the water, but on the next dock could be a man urinating into the same water. Oh well, they were all using the klong for their own specific purpose.

At cross intersections of these klongs we saw floating markets where the natives were selling their abundant produce from sampans in their version of a floating farmers' market. Water buffaloes were the most frequent animal that we saw. The people used them for plowing the rice paddies and also rode them for short distances.

The Princess Hotel was selected for us to stay in because our assigned rooms had window air conditioners for relief from the hot and humid climate. They also promised to serve us boiled water in carafes to protect us from dysentery and other digestive disorders. I always wondered when we ordered drinks from the bar if the ice cubes had the same safeguards.

Bangkok, due to its many canals, is sometimes referred to " the Venice of Asia." In addition to its more modern buildings, the city is said to contain more than 400 ornate gilded Buddhist temples. I believe this and visited many of the most famous ones. My favorites were the Emerald Pagoda and the Temple of the Reclining Buddha. Here was a 150-foot-long replica of

Buddha lying on his side and he is completely covered in gold leaf. At today's prices I wonder what that statue is now worth.

The Thais are very religious and nearly all are Buddhists. It is considered the duty of each young man to spend three months of his life as a monk. They enter the monastery, or wat, where they live a very restricted life. Their heads are shaven and they wear saffron-colored robes for the three-month period. They live a life of complete poverty and even have to beg for their food. It is a common sight to see these young monks in the orange-hued robes roaming the streets carrying their begging bowls. The populace is generous to them and each family feels obligated to put out food for them. After all, their own sons might be next. After they have finished filling their bowls they return to the wat to eat their single meal of the day and to study the scriptures and pray.

I liked the night life in Bangkok. We rode for short distances in bike-driven rickshaws called samlors. I admired the stamina of those skinny little guys as they toted us from one stop to another. I really enjoyed the entertainment in the best restaurants where lovely girls performed the classical dances in glittering costumes with tall, pointed head-dresses with much grace and elegance in their stylized gestures.

Bangkok is filled with many family-run businesses. I visited one where an entire family was engaged in making Niello ware, the unique, beautiful form of Thai jewelry. The parents smelted the alloys of silver, lead, copper, and sulfur and poured it into silver molds to harden. These molds usually featured Thai dancing girls in various classic positions. Then the children spent hours rubbing the hardened, black-colored enamel inlay into a highly polished sheen.

Another family enterprise was the construction of an attractive tableware that has a brass alloy for the blades of the knives, forks, and spoons, and handles made of water buffalo horns. At these homes I saw many water buffalo horns under the stilted houses waiting to be used.

Bangkok has many jewelry stores where we used to shop for attractive items at what seemed like bargain prices. On one trip I bought a five-carat topaz ring for my wife that she just adored. I decided to have it appraised back in Honolulu and the jeweler there informed me that instead of being a real topaz, I had bought a large hunk of tan quartz crystal. You never know when you shop for bargains in the Orient!

One item that was legitimate there was the truly beautiful Thai silk that we all bought at the shop run by the Englishman Jim Thompson. He established a factory where his weavers combined many shades of silk thread to produce fabrics of great beauty and originality.

I bought many yards of it and brought it home where Betty had it made into attractive dresses. A few years later I read that this Britisher, who started a new and prosperous enterprise in Bangkok, went out into the jungle on a hunting trip one day and was never seen again. There is much speculation on the cause of his disappearance, but jealousy from competing merchants is considered topmost.

I saw something else in Bangkok that was interesting but also very depressing. I believe it is now outlawed by the government, but in those days there were many opium dens in the city. While they were not highly advertised, they were available to visit for a fee.

One night my rickshaw driver asked me if I would like to see one. When I said yes, he dropped me off in front of a popular restaurant and told me to climb the stairs to the second level. There I was surprised to see a family environment with several young children running around.

After I had paid a fee, the man in charge took me back to an area that was filled with crude bunks curtained off from each other where the addicts were smoking their pipes or sleeping. I saw the lady in charge assign billets to her customers and then she produced long-stemmed pipes for them to smoke. As I best remember it, she first deposited a pea-sized object that looked like a glob of tar and then tamped it down with tobacco before she lit it for them. After the poor addict had taken a few puffs, he was away in peaceful dreams and left to sleep off his drug-induced euphoria.

When we flew out of Bangkok we headed for Rangoon, the capital city of Burma. This spectacular city is located at the mouth of the Irrawaddy River on the Gulf of Martaban. Our flight took us right over the spectacular Shwedagon Pagoda, the nation's most famous landmark. It rises 300 feet high and is completely covered with layers of gold leaf and topped with a jeweled orb. We could see it reflected in the sunlight from miles away. To the north of Burma is the city of Mandalay, made famous by Rudyard Kipling in his writings and the song that followed.

Next we crossed the Bay of Bengal and landed for fuel at Calcutta, India's second city. It is the nation's major port to Asia and located at the mouth of the mighty Ganges River. After refueling at Calcutta, we continued on to New Delhi to spend the night. We landed at Palam Airport, now renamed Indira Gandhi Airport for the late prime minister.

We had a near hour-long bus ride to the Maidens Hotel. Delhi is really two cities, Old Delhi and New Delhi. New Delhi is the present capital of India and this modern city was planned and constructed by the British when they ruled India. In contrast, Old Delhi is a mixture of gorgeous palaces and mosques built by earlier rulers, and slums where squalid houses huddle along mean, crooked streets.

Both cities have grown and become overcrowded since the partition of India and Pakistan in 1947. Old Delhi receives hundreds of thousands of Hindu refugees fleeing from religious persecution in Pakistan. New Delhi swelled as the functions of the republican government called for thousands of new officials.

Our drive from the airport took us through parts of both cities and the contrast was striking. In the old section I saw women in colorful garb filling earthen water jugs at the village well. When the jug was filled they balanced the heavy object on their heads and walked back to their home with it. In some of the narrow streets I saw craftsmen squatting cross-legged while working in open stalls under what looked like a single 20-watt light bulb. Cattle roamed everywhere completely unrestricted as they are considered to be sacred. Also along the road outside of town I saw many herds of monkeys running loose.

The Maidens Hotel was a beautiful old building and one of the main hotels of the Oberoi chain. The food was excellent, but I'm convinced the Indians don't know how to make curry. That is a joke, of course, as curry is the national dish. Their curry is not as creamy as we know it, but thin and runny and it really burns the back of your throat from the huge amounts of curry powder, cumin seeds, and a few other pungent spices.

Delhi is a wonderful city for sightseeing. In the center of town is the Red Fort, a most impressive edifice built in 1650 by the Shah Jahan, the great Mogul ruler who also built the magnificent Taj Mahal. The Red Fort was originally known as the Red Palace. When in its splendor, within its walls were gardens and fountains and a harem of pure white marble. Much of this was wrecked in later years by the British to make room for barracks for their troops.

Other interesting, but eerie sights were the burning ghats along the Jumna River. Here on concrete slabs I saw mourning family members place the bodies of deceased loved ones on large piles of wood and then the eldest son or senior male family member would set the wood on fire to cremate the remains. I was told they usually used sandalwood because its incense-like aroma when burning helps disguise the stench of burning flesh.

When the pyre cooled all the ashes were then scattered into the river. I have read that in earlier days it was customary for the grieving widow to throw herself on the burning logs feeling that her life should end with that of her deceased husband. This rather unusual ritual is now discouraged in modern-day India.

I have another rare memory of India. There was a young fellow about 18 years old who used to come to our rooms in the Maidens Hotel and show us samples of the wares he was selling. He would take our orders and then deliver our purchases the next evening. On one of these visits he told us he was to be married the following week to a 15-year-old girl he had never met. He said the two families had made the wedding contract and the couple had been engaged since he was eight years old and she was only five.

He also told us that after the wedding she would come to live in his parents' home and they would sleep in a bed in the same room where his mother and father and his two married brothers slept with their wives. Each couple would have their own bed but all would share the same bedroom. He said this was the normal arrangement in small houses in India.

Weddings were holy rites among the Hindus and I saw several processions where the wedding party was going to or from the ceremony. They were all led by the bride and groom riding side by side on horseback. The groom always wore a turban and the bride a sari of red or pink silk. She was also heavily bejeweled and always had a red dot, called a tilak, between the eyes on her lower forehead.

On one of our three-day crew rests I was able to take a chauffeured trip to Agra to see the absolutely beautiful Taj Mahal. It was a four-hour drive and we passed through many small villages. We passed several camel caravans and usually walking close behind would be women picking up camel dung and forming it into large pancakes. I noticed they stacked the flattened cakes into neat piles every half mile or so and I was told these stacks were their main source of fuel for heating and cooking.

In a small park alongside the road I saw a fakir, or holy man, giving his blessing to the passersby. He was completely nude except for the briefest of loincloths and had covered himself from head to toe with ashes. Our driver told us this was a sign of piety.

Ten hours later, after we had seen the Taj Mahal and were returning to Delhi, we again passed this same park. Darned if the holy man wasn't still standing in the same spot and still receiving bows and kudos from those he blessed.

In one small clearing we saw a roadside stand with a group of people waiting in line to be served. We asked our driver to stop so we could see what was being sold. Here we saw a potbellied merchant sitting in the usual cross-legged position. He was surrounded by trays and baskets of various spices and other condiments. There were also some jars filled with cooking oils and other mysterious-looking liquids. Everything in the shop was literally covered with flies.

When a customer made a selection, the fat merchant would first shoo the flies away from that particular tray, then he would scoop some of that commodity onto a small scale and weigh it. Next he would take a sheet of waxed paper and roll it into a cone-shaped receptacle and pour the purchased item into the cone. He was so adept at this that I even saw him ladle cooking oil into one of these paper cones and not spill a drop.

Alongside was a man with an open-air stand and he was selling our equivalent of fast foods. When a customer placed an order, the proprietor selected a large leaf from a stack of mulberry leaves. First he wiped the dust off the leaf on the leg of his dirty pants and then loaded it with a pile of curry and rice or some other local delicacy. The buyer would then walk away eating the runny mixture with his fingers. They all looked happy as jaybirds so their systems must have been inured to foods served in that fashion.

I am sure all my readers have seen pictures of the magnificent Taj Mahal, which has been called the most perfect structure in the world. What surprised me was that the entrance building is also very attractive and on both sides of the Taj Mahal are other striking buildings where the Shah Jahan used to entertain his guests.

A short distance from the Taj Mahal is another massive structure, also called the Red Palace. This is where Shah Jahan lived and held court while he was having the Taj Mahal constructed.

I took a guided tour through this former palace and it is opulence to the highest degree. I saw the giant pool where the shah's harem used to bathe. Each of his wives had their own private niche around the pool where they used to sun themselves between dips in the crystal-clear water.

Shah Jahan spent 20 years building the Taj Mahal to be a shrine for his beloved empress Mumtaz Mahal who died in 1631. It was his intention to build an identical structure across the river out of black marble as a shrine to hold his own remains. History tells us that the Shah Jahan was dethroned by his eldest son in a palace coup and the poor old man spent his final years as a prisoner in the dungeon of his own Red Palace. As a result, the black taj mahal was never built. Boy, speaking of an ungrateful son, I guess that one takes the cake!

When we left Delhi we took a fuel stop at Karachi, Pakistan, and then flew to Dhahran, Saudi Arabia, our final destination on the embassy flight. When we departed from Karachi we flew over parts of the Arabian Sea and the Gulf of Oman along the southern border of Iran. Though at the time we were Iran's biggest supporter, we were forced to remain at sea and not fly over their territory.

Dhahran was undoubtedly the least interesting city we visited. It was on the bank of the Persian Gulf and the airport we landed at had the most stringent customs regulations I had ever seen. Even we crew members had our belongings searched as if we were unwelcome tourists.

I don't know if this was really true or not, but we were warned to never have a copy of *Time* magazine in our possession as it had recently committed the unpardonable sin of running an unflattering article about the Saudi ruler King Ibn Saud. It didn't happen on one of my flights, but I heard the tale of an air force colonel who had a pistol in his luggage and the poor fellow spent a few days in a Saudi jail as punishment.

Saudi Arabia was an absolutely dry nation and the Koran, the bible of their Muslim religion, forbids the eating of pork and the consumption of alcoholic beverages.

King Ibn Saud formed the nation of Saudi Arabia when he defeated the hostile tribal chiefs of the area and brought them under his command. Ibn Saud was especially opposed to alcohol as one of his sons took to drinking and shot and killed a British vice consul while in a drunken rage. Ibn Saud had him committed to life in prison and he was only released when his brother granted him amnesty after the death of their father.

On my final visit to Dhahran I met some officials of the Arabian American Oil Company and was invited to a party at one of their homes. Aramco, as it is called, is a consortium of oil companies who developed the petroleum industry in Saudi Arabia and made it one of the world's leaders in the field. It is still the dominant member of OPEC.

To my surprise, I found that the occupant of the house had a still working in a closet under his stairwell. Then I learned that this was a well-kept secret and all the Aramco executives made their own booze.

The host asked me what I wanted to drink and mentioned scotch, bourbon, gin, rum, brandy, and a few other choices. Then I found out, no matter what I asked for, it was all straight alcohol laced with a few drops of the flavoring agent of my choice.

It reminded me of the funny scene in *Mr. Roberts* where the doctor adds a few drops of iodine to make the ship's alcohol taste like Scotch whiskey.

66

Air Evacs

One of the most demanding type of flights a transport pilot is called on to make is an Air Evacuation, or Air Evac, as we called them. Here the aircraft is converted into a flying hospital. I made six of these flights while in VR-7 and was the aircraft commander on the final one.

The Super Constellation is well suited to this conversion. This four-engine, three-tailed transport was called the Lockheed 1049 at the factory in Burbank, California. In the navy we called it the R7V and the air force named their model the C-121.

Trans World Airlines (TWA) and the other airlines that flew the Super Constellation had 105 permanent seats. The military version that we flew had four bunks and a navigation table in the flight compartment and our maximum seating capacity was 78 passengers. Our seats were less plush than the civilian planes and our seats always faced aft. The military considers this to be the safest way to sit, but the airlines fear their paying customers resent facing to the rear. While their seats were permanent, ours were removable and slid out easily, making a plane suitable for cargo or, in this case, for medical evacuation.

When we were in the air evac configuration we kept the required number of seats for ambulatory patients and had portable litters along the side of the passenger compartment in a double-bunk arrangement.

The air evacs that I piloted originated either at Clark Air Force Base or at Haneda in Tokyo. We were flying servicemen or their dependents home for treatment in Honolulu or in the United States. I say in the States because at that time Hawaii was still a territory and had not yet become the fiftieth star in our nation's flag.

On each of these air evacs there were always two or more flight nurses on board. We called them the "angels of the skies" and they certainly earned this accolade. Sometimes there were navy flight nurses on board, but usually they were air force nurses from the detachments based at Haneda or at Clark.

What concerned me on these flights was the number of patients returning home from overseas assignment with tuberculosis. With all our modern-day medicine and the good nutritional foods available to our servicemen and their dependents, I thought this disease would be uncommon. Maybe they caught it from the local citizens they came into contact with on foreign shores. The other most depressing memory of these flights was the number of psycho cases we carried.

You may have heard the term "rock happy" as applied to those in the military who couldn't stand the monotony of months of assignment on a small island. Well, this form of psychosis also occurred among some servicemen and their dependents stationed at larger bases as well.

The last air evac I flew was by far the most memorable. It was an all-psycho flight load. I was the aircraft commander and we only had a total of 14 passengers and they were all considered dangerous. There were eight patients in the double-deck bunks on one side of the aircraft in the aftermost section of the passenger compartment and then six patients sitting facing to the rear of the plane in a single row of seats, three on either side of the center aisle. The rest of the plane was empty as no passengers were allowed to ride in psycho air evacs.

The eight in the bunk beds were shackled hand and foot and the six in the seats were strapped in with restraints. One of the seated patients was the very pretty 24-year-old daughter of an air force colonel who just cracked up for some unknown reason.

The man in the lowest bunk aft was a real mean SOB. He kept ranting and raving and was very profane in his outbursts. After level off I went back to see how the nurses were making out and this bird spotted me. He said, "Commander, I want to come up front and help you fly this airplane." I told him I didn't need his help right then but I'd come for him if I had any problems. This seemed to satisfy him for the moment and he quieted down.

After several hours in the air one of my male navy enlisted flight attendants came up to the pilot's compartment to tell me about the latest escapade this weirdo had indulged in. As I stated earlier, all the bed patients were shackled hand and foot. When this fellow had to urinate, instead of asking a nurse to bring him a portable urinal, he purposely went all over the deck of the aircraft and then laid there ridiculing my flight attendant while he was swabbing up the mess this man had caused.

I came back two other times during the eight-hour flight and each time this character made the same request that he wanted to come up front and help me fly. I was always able to pacify him by telling him I would come and get him when I really needed some help.

I had picked up this flight on Guam and our leg would end at Kwajalein where another crew was waiting to take over. After I had secured the cockpit and was ready to disembark, I heard a very strange dialogue between the colonel's daughter and the troublemaker.

She was sitting there, still shackled, while they were serving her lunch and she had finally endured enough of his profane ranting and raving and she started telling him what a mean, contemptible person he was. She called him just about every dirty adjective she could think of. Her choice of words were unbelievable and it was hard to imagine such foul language coming from the mouth of this lovely, angelic-looking young lady.

What was almost humorous about this verbal exchange was that the formerly belligerent weirdo just laid there listening to her in almost amazement. Then after each of her tongue lashings he would meekly reply, "That's your opinion Ma'am."

As I was walking away shaking my head, I wondered how the incoming shift of flight nurses were going to endure the next leg of the flight.

67

Hopalong Cassidy

One day I read in the *Hawaiian Advertiser,* the area's leading newspaper, that William Boyd, now lovingly known to the motion picture and television audiences as Hopalong Cassidy, was vacationing in the Hawaiian Islands. It stated that Bill and his lovely wife, the former actress Grace Bradley, were presently staying at the Royal Hawaiian Hotel.

This was my dear friend Bill Boyd with whom I had worked in five films in the silent era. I first met him in 1922 when he was the leading man opposite Wanda Hawley in the unusual film, *Bobbed Hair.* Then during my five-year contract with Cecil B. DeMille we worked together in *The Road to Yesterday, Her Man o' War,* with Jetta Goudal, then in my favorite film, *The Yankee Clipper,* and finally in the fine western, *The Last Frontier.*

Bill was married five times. First to a Boston heiress he met while working as a chauffeur, then to actresses Ruth Miller, Elinor Fair, Dorothy Sebastian, and Grace Bradley. The first four marriages ended in divorce, but he and Grace Bradley had been married for 35 years when he died in his Palm Springs home in 1972 at the age of 74.

Ruth Miller bore him his only child, a son who died at the age of nine months. When we were so friendly at DeMille Studio I always felt he treated me like the son he wished he had. I truly adored the man and wanted to see him if at all possible.

I called the Royal Hawaiian and, of course, they wouldn't put me through as they were protecting his privacy. I wasn't at all surprised at this, so I left the following message with the hotel operator. "Your old friend, Junior Coghlan, now Lieutenant Commander Frank Coghlan, is stationed here in the navy. May I come by the hotel and bring my two sons to meet you?"

In about ten minutes I heard his friendly voice say, "Jujie," which he always called me when we were working together. He told me he and Grace would be sunning themselves in front of the Royal Hawaiian and he would be most happy to see me and meet my two boys.

My sons Mike and Pat were now ten and seven years old. As they both were born while I was in the navy, they really didn't know I had once been a child actor. So, I wasn't a film hero to them, but when I told them I was going to take them to meet their idol, Hopalong Cassidy, my stock really went up in their eyes.

We drove to the Royal Hawaiian Hotel and soon found Bill and Grace. We had a great reunion and my boys were overjoyed to see that Hopalong Cassidy was truly an old friend of mine.

We had been chatting a while when a brash young local kid spotted us. He barged up and said to Bill, "Hey, aren't you Hopalong Cassidy?" Bill responded politely that yes, that was what they now called him in movies and on television.

Then this brat asked, "What are you doing here?" Bill kindly replied that he and his wife were vacationing. At this the kid blurted, "Did you bring your horse Topper with you?" Bill said, "No, I don't take my horse on vacation with me."

The kid then asked, "Does your horse do any tricks?" Bill kept his patience and said, "No, I don't want to be upstaged by a smart animal." Then the brat said, "Roy Rogers's horse can do tricks. He can even count to ten."

Bill thought for a minute and then said, "That may be true, and do you know, Roy can't count much higher."

Sorry Roy. Please forgive Bill. I know he really liked you and this was just said as a joke.

68

Aloha to Hawaii

My three-year tour of duty in VR-7 was coming to a close and all the good things my detail officer in the Pentagon told me about came true. By becoming a member of a MATS squadron I had satisfied the requirement of fleet duty and was promoted to the rank of lieutenant commander. I also was reinstated in the TAR, or Continuous Active Duty program for career reserve officers.

After I had been in VR-7 for a year, Roger Brown, my best friend and my senior officer in the Public Relations Office, received orders to NAS Patuxent River, Maryland. The navy was forming airborne early warning squadrons and was using a version of the Super Constellation for this task. They were known as the WV-2, or Willy Victors as we called them. This was the regular R7V with a gigantic radome on top of the fuselage and it was a flying radar station loaded with exotic electronic equipment.

Because of Roger's experience in the R7V, he was assigned to Pax River, as we called the base, to be a senior instructor to train pilots in this new concept of early warning warfare. After a year of this instructor duty, Roger volunteered to be a member of the first squadron to be based at NAS Barbers Point, on the coast of Oahu, about 15 miles north of Pearl Harbor. Roger and Betty Brown loved the Hawaiian Islands and they couldn't wait to return to their favorite spot for his new assignment.

We had kept in touch and he wrote telling me they would be arriving on the Matson liner *Lurline* in a few days. By that time, because of my squadron public relations activities, I had met many executives in the Matson organization. As a result, I was able to pull the best practical joke of my life.

A Matson public relations man allowed Betty and me to board the pilot's boat and we met the *Lurline* out at sea a few miles from Diamond Head where we both climbed the Jacob's ladder the ship dropped down for the pilot. It was a rough climb in the rolling sea but we both relished this unusual experience.

When we were on board, the dining room steward directed us to the table where the entire Brown family of Roger and Betty and their now five children were having breakfast. He provided us with two extra chairs and we sat down with them. Roger and Betty just couldn't believe their eyes. After many hugs and kisses we told them we had a really rough swim to meet the ship off Diamond Head. Then we all went up on deck to line the rail with the other passengers to watch the hula show at the Matson terminal.

Now that I had been reinstated in the TAR program, I was pleased to see that they appreciated my public information experience and had me ordered to the staff of the chief of Naval Air Reserve Training at his headquarters at NAS Glenview, Illinois, about 30 miles north of Chicago.

This was a plum assignment for me, but also presented a problem. After three years in the best climate in the world, we were gong to a locale where the weather was much more severe. On my last trip to Tokyo I spent $1,000 buying overcoats and other cold-weather items for my family. Can you imagine my kids going from Aloha shirts and bare feet to snow-oriented equipment?

In the last year of my Hawaiian duty my mother began failing badly. She began having very poor balance and was in danger of falling when she walked. We took her to Tripler Army Hospital for a series of tests and the first doctor treated her as if she was merely becoming senile. I knew it was more than that and finally had her examined by a fine neurosurgeon who said he was sure Mother had a brain tumor. He operated on her and found she did indeed have a tumor but it was in such a position that he could not remove it.

He did one thing, however, and installed tubes in her cranial cavity that bypassed the pressures to her spinal column and much of her balance and mobility returned. She still remained a partial invalid and only moved about with the aid of a walker for the rest of her life.

When we finally left Honolulu Betty was eight and one-half months' pregnant with our fifth child. Military Sea Transportation Service would not move us for that reason and neither would Military Air Transportation Service, my own MATS squadron. The commercial airlines did not have this restriction and we all enjoyed first-class air accommodations on United Airlines.

We had a 17-year-old Portuguese girl named Shirley Ann living with us for our last six months in the islands and we received her parents' permission to take her to the United States with us to help Betty. Naturally, I had to pay for her airline ticket as she was not one of my military dependents. Due to my mother's condition, she followed us a day later by military air evac.

There was no way we could handle Mother with the new baby due so soon so Judge Otto J. Emme arranged for Mother to be moved into a really comfortable convalescent home. We met her air evac plane and saw her nicely settled into the rest home. We then flew to Betty's home in St. Louis to await the arrival of the stork. Three days after we arrived in St. Louis, Betty gave birth to our fifth child, our third daughter, Judith Rose, who has always been known as Judy.

I arranged for a student to pick up our car at the Matson terminal and he drove it to St. Louis. I found a pleasant apartment in St. Louis where Betty and now the five children and Shirley Ann could stay while I was house hunting in Glenview, Illinois.

I checked into my new duty station and soon found a great old two-story house located on a corner of a tree-lined street. Like all homes in this climate, it was complete with attic and basement. For the first time in my life, and for the next three years, I had to put up screens on the porches in summer, rake leaves, put up storm shutters in autumn, and shovel snow in the winter.

The Naval Air Reserve Training Command at that time had 28 naval air stations located across the country. Our admiral used to inspect these stations and the reserve squadrons who trained there each year. The first two years I was on the staff I was a member of the inspection team. We usually covered three stations on each trip so I was away from home for three and four days at a time, nine times a year, on these inspection trips. We also conducted a public information and recruiting seminar for those specialized station members at NAS Pensacola each year. For these reasons I was glad to have the big, comfortable house and that we had Shirley Ann to help Betty while I was away.

My title on the staff was Industrial Liaison Officer. Our command was also responsible for the procurement of naval aviation cadets. In our efforts to keep the pipeline to Pensacola filled it was my task to tour the aircraft industry, urging them to assist in our advertising. They were pleased to accommodate us as they could not sell airplanes if there weren't new pilots to fly them.

One other rewarding project I handled was the promotion of the outstanding Naval Aviation Cadet of the Year. I had this assignment twice and really hit the jackpot on my second effort. That year the honoree was a graduate of helicopter training and the Sikorsky Aircraft Company people were eager to exploit him.

I met him in Washington, D.C., and escorted him to the office of the secretary of the navy where he was introduced to the media. Then I took him to the convention of the Daughters of the American Revolution where I introduced him at their main luncheon.

Then we flew to New York where we were met at the airport by Sikorsky representatives who led us to a waiting helicopter and flew us to their plant at Bridgeport, Connecticut. We had lunch and a tour of the plant and then they rotored us back to a special heliport on the bank of the Hudson

River. I'll tell you, to fly at slow speed across the heart of New York City at an altitude of 1,500 feet is a thrill and the view is spectacular.

Due to my show business connections I had my cadet introduced from the audience at the Bert Parks Show. I was also able to take him backstage to meet and pose for pictures with my old friend Ed Sullivan. Then Ed kindly introduced him during his then outstanding, top-rated television show.

I knew that another old friend, Joe Franklin, had a film business–oriented television show called, "Joe Franklin's Memory Lane." I got a message to Joe and asked if he would interview my cadet. He said he would be happy to do so if he could also interview me. I figured, what the heck, if that was the only way to get my cadet exposure on television, why not.

At the show the next morning Joe Franklin sat between us and talked to the cadet about Pensacola and flight training for about one minute. Then he turned to me and we spoke for about five minutes while he questioned me about my movie career and why I was now a naval aviator.

When this discussion was over he then said, "And now Commander Coghlan, I want to take you down Memory Land and have you meet a nice little kid named Junior Coghlan." Then to my complete surprise he ran two scenes from the silent film, *The Yankee Clipper*. When Joe's show was over he gave me the little reel of 16mm film that contained those two scenes. That was the first film of my early movie days that I owned at the time.

Years later I saw in a catalogue that Blackhawk Films was selling 16mm prints of *The Yankee Clipper* and I ordered one. When I screened it I was surprised to find that the two scenes Joe Franklin gave to me were missing from my brand new print. What must have happened is Joe Franklin clipped the scenes from a print of the film. When he presented those two scenes to me, someone spliced the print back together without these two scenes. That print then must have become the master print that Blackhawk used for their distribution.

I wrote to the president of Blackhawk telling him about the missing scenes. I even offered to lend them to him so he could then distribute a complete print to his customers. He wrote back saying he was afraid those scenes might be copyrighted, but I am sure he just didn't want to mention them as he might have to make new prints for those who had bought the incomplete product from him earlier.

In 1985 David Goldin, the president of Video Yesteryear, contacted me saying he was going to distribute VHS tapes of *The Yankee Clipper* and asked if I would permit them to make a five-minute taped introduction as a lead-in to the tape. I told him I would be pleased to do so and would even have my son tape the introduction here at the house with his minicam. Then I told Dave about my little film and offered to lend it to him to include in the new tapes. He was delighted and now the tapes distributed by Video Yesteryear of Sandy Hook, Connecticut, are complete versions of *The Yankee Clipper.* Since then Grapevine Video of Phoenix, Arizona, has also come out with a complete version of my favorite motion picture.

One day I read in a box on the front page of the *Chicago Tribune* that a former *Our Gang* comedy kid was down and out and needed blood. It told that David Durand was found face down in a pool of his own blood and near death from bleeding ulcers. It went on to say he was now a part-time bartender living on welfare and all his earnings as a child star had dissipated. It told of the sleazy apartment he was found in and that he apparently had no friends to supply the needed blood.

This was a real shock to me as I had known David since we were kid actors. I mentioned earlier that David had a little crippled mother who used to drive him to the studios and he was not a popular chum to the other kid actors as he always seemed to feel sorry for himself.

On the serial *Scouts to the Rescue,* Jackie Cooper and Sid Miller and I didn't pal around with him as he always seemed to resent playing a lesser part to Cooper and we thought he always carried a chip on his shoulder. Also Dave was no more an *Our Gang* comedy kid than I was, but that is explainable, as newspaper writers called all child actors who worked in the 1920s, "former *Our Gang* comedy kids."

Despite the fact that Dave and I were not the best of friends from the old days, I certainly wasn't going to have him in need of blood when I had some to spare. I went to Cook County General Hospital in downtown Chicago where I found Dave on a charity ward. He was really pleased to see me and very much surprised that I had come out of nowhere to donate blood for him. After I had supplied a pint of blood I returned to his ward to wish him the best of luck and a speedy recovery. Some newspaper photographer heard I was on the ward and took a photograph of us together. I was really upset about the story that accompanied the photo. The writer played up the fact that one former kid actor was now a successful officer in the navy and married with five children where the other one was a down-and-out failure. I thought it was dirty pool, but I guess that's the way they sell newspapers.

My three-year tour of duty on the Naval Air Reserve Training Command staff was coming to an end and I received orders to be the public information officer at NAS Point Arguello, just south of Vandenberg Air Force Base near Lompoc, California. Point Arguello was a satellite station of the Pacific Missile Range which had its headquarters at NAS Point Mugu near Oxnard, California. My old friend from CHINFO days, Commander Bob Barracks, was the PIO of the Missile Range and he had selected me for this position. It was a plum assignment and satisfied the TAR program as I would be in a flying category and within their jurisdiction.

I hitched a ride on one of our inspection flights and left the group at NAS Oakland where I had a friend fly me to NAS Point Arguello so I could house hunt. In just one day there I found a good home and put a down payment on it. I also visited the local parochial school and enrolled my boys there. Then I had another friend fly me to NAS Los Alamitos where I rejoined the inspection party and flew back to NAS Glenview with them. Can you imagine, in just one day I had put my family into a perfect move to the new duty station!

The very next day I was at my desk in Glenview when the telephone rang. I picked it up and to my surprise on the other end was Admiral Kirkpatrick, the chief of information. I mean it wasn't his secretary or his aide, it was the admiral himself. He said, "Good morning Coghlan. What are you doing?" I told him I was getting ready to be transferred and just the day before I had placed a down payment on a home in Lompoc, California.

He then said, "Well Frank, I hope you didn't put too much down on it as I have other plans for you." Then he told me he wanted me to be officer-in-charge of his Hollywood office. I told him I was afraid this would again cost me my status in the Reserve Continuous Active Duty Program as it was not an aviator's billet. He asked me to think it over and call him back the following morning.

I went home in a daze and told Betty all about my out of the blue telephone call from the chief of information himself. After a near sleepless night I finally decided; how in the world could I possibly turn down the chance to be the navy representative to Hollywood where I would be in charge of all navy cooperation with the motion picture and television industries?

I called him back the next morning and told him I was thrilled at his selection of me for this great position and he had made me an offer I just could not refuse.

I won't bore you with the details, but we put the big house in Glenview on the market and it sold in just two weeks. Shirley Ann had married a nice young fellow the year before, so we didn't have her with us any longer. I dropped Betty and the three girls at her folks' home in St. Louis and again I drove across country with the two boys who were now 14 and ten years old. I put them in a summer camp and used the rest of my leave and travel time house hunting.

I found a nice four-bedroom house with a swimming pool in Sepulveda in the San Fernando Valley and it was to be my home for the next 16 years.

69

I Command the Hollywood Navy

When I assumed command of the Navy Public Relations Office in Hollywood on August 10, 1960, all the armed forces had spaces in the same building near the corner of Sunset Boulevard and Gower Street. It was a great location. We were right across the street from Columbia Studio and CBS, and about two miles from RKO and Paramount Studios. We were about a 30-minute drive from MGM in Culver City, about the same distance from Warner Brothers, Disney, Four Star, and NBC in the San Fernando Valley, and Twentieth Century–Fox was about a 20-minute drive away.

On my staff I had two lieutenants, a Wave enlisted journalist, and a civilian secretary. I wasn't surprised to learn that I was the junior of all the other service commanding officers. The army and air force had full colonels in charge and the marines and coast guard were led by a lieutenant colonel and a commander. Though I was the junior of the group, it wasn't long before I found all the other COs coming to me when they had a question or a problem. My lieutenants were both public information specialists and I was the first and only naval aviator to ever be in charge of the Navy Hollywood Office.

There were many navy admirers in the area and the most supportive group was the Beverly Hills Council of the Navy League of the United States. In the first week I was in Hollywood they gave me a gigantic welcome aboard reception in the Beverly Hills mansion of Marion Davies. It was a marvelous evening for me and her home was filled with old friends. All evening long I was greeted by the likes of Pat O'Brien, Jack Oakie, Dick Powell and his then wife June Allyson, Glenn Ford, and many other old associates from my earlier film days.

It was a kick for me when the master of ceremonies, Jack Oakie, said, "And now we introduce the new officer-in-charge of the Hollywood Navy office. I sure hope he knows his way around the studios." There was much laughter at his remark and it was evident that my assignment to Hollywood was a popular one.

When I was in charge of the motion picture desk in the Office of Information in Washington, this Hollywood office did not yet exist. At that time the producers had to send their scripts and representatives directly back to the Pentagon. Now there was a convenient liaison office right in their home area. When a producer had a story idea he thought would merit navy cooperation, he would have me to the studio to listen to his story line. Sometimes I would work with him and the writers for weeks and even months getting a script in workable order. When I thought it was ready I would send it back to my old desk in CHINFO for final approval.

The first motion picture I handled in my new assignment was *All Hands on Deck* for Twentieth Century–Fox in late 1960. At that time each of the major studios had a man assigned to governmental liaison as films about the military, the FBI, and other Washington agencies were very much in vogue. The person with this position at Twentieth was then Frank McCarthy.

Frank was a retired army brigadier general and was serving as aide to General George Marshall at the close of World War II. He later became a producer and his film *Patton* won four Academy Awards in 1970. It was voted the best picture of the year, George C. Scott was declared the best actor, and Franklin Schaffner received the Oscar as best director. The fourth Oscar it earned was for best screenplay and the writers honored for this award were Edmund North and a new, young writer named Francis Ford Coppola. He, of course, went on to his own fame in later years for, among other achievements, *The Godfather*, for which he wrote the screenplay and directed. McCarthy's other most notable film was *MacArthur* in 1977, where Gregory Peck played the venerable general who made good his promise, "I shall return."

Frank McCarthy invited me to the studio for a meeting with my old high school friend Stan Hough, then head of production for studio chief Richard Zanuck. Richard's father Darryl F. Zanuck founded Twentieth Century–Fox and Richard earned his stripes later when his film *Driving Miss Daisy* won the Academy Award as best picture in 1989.

All Hands on Deck starred Pat Boone, Barbara Eden, Dennis O'Keefe, and the very funny Buddy Hackett. Pat Boone was a charming young man and treated me with much respect on the set. Those who thought Barbara Eden was cute as the cuddly sprite on her television show "I Dream of Jeannie," should have seen her in person as a 24-year-old newcomer to films on the set of this film. She was really breathtaking.

Buddy Hackett is considered a real clown and I hear his nightclub act at Las Vegas and other spas is as blue as a comedian can get. This surprises me as on the set he was a very quiet and reserved person. Despite his portliness, he is very knowledgeable about physical fitness and diet and expounded on the subject frequently. However, when questioned, he would regale us with hilarious stories about his breaking into show business in the borsht-belt circuit in the Catskills.

This lightweight comedy about navy life was directed by my old friend

Director Norman Taurog tells Elvis Presley he has known Commander Coghlan "since he was this tall."

Norman Taurog and that brought back many memories of my days at Jackie Cooper's house. Norman had directed me in *Men of Boys Town* and I reminded him that he had first directed me in a Larry Semon comedy for Vitagraph when I was only four and he was a brash young director, no more than 19 or 20 years old.

From then on he told everyone on the set that he had known me since I was "this high," holding his hand at waist level. So my first film assignment in the new job was a very happy one.

70

"Hennesey"

I could go on for countless pages relating anecdotes about the many motion pictures and television series I became involved with in my five years in charge of the Navy Hollywood Office. In order to keep this book down to a single volume I will only mention the ones I consider important, or those that were somewhat unusual.

My good friend Jackie Cooper was coproducing and starring in a fine television series, "Hennesey," where he played a young navy doctor. Roscoe Karns was the captain in charge of the base hospital and Abby Dalton was the lovely navy nurse that Dr. Hennesey had a crush on.

Jackie's partner in this production venture was Don McGuire, a former actor who had turned to writing and directing. Don knew that Cooper and I were good friends but he would never permit my office to have anything to do with script preparation. "Hennesey" was made without navy cooperation, but because of the positive way it depicted navy life, we did give them the right to visit the Long Beach Naval Base to film shots of Cooper and others driving on the station and walking in and out of the naval dispensary and other needed fill-in scenes.

I always thought that McGuire really hated the military for some reason or other because he was one of the writers who got real pleasure from making the high-ranking officers look stupid. In the second year of the series he had Roscoe Karns promoted to the rank of admiral. I begged him not to do so, as at that time, the only admiral in the medical branch was the chief of the Bureau of Medicine and Surgery. Don ignored my suggestion as I assume he thought it would be much funnier for an admiral to make silly mistakes than a mere captain.

At the close of the second year Jackie bought out Don McGuire. Then I asked him if my office could at least read his scripts each week to ensure accuracy. In the very first script of the new season they featured Sammy Davis, Jr., as an errant sailor. In one scene he gets in trouble on board his ship and they had a member of the shore patrol place him under arrest and lock him in the brig.

I went to Cooper and said, "Come on now Jack. You were in the navy and you know there are no members of the shore patrol on board a ship. That task at sea is handled by the master at arms. Jack thought it over and agreed with me. He told the writer to make the change, but would you believe, I guess his ego was hurt as he complained that everyone knew about the shore patrol, but no one had ever heard of a master at arms. Jack chided him and insisted he make the change. This proved to Cooper that our office could be of help to him and for the rest of the series we checked each script before it went into production.

Jack began directing on his earlier series, "The People's Choice," and I admired the way he directed on "Hennesey." In rehearsal Jack directed from the camera operator's seat and he was an expert at visualizing action through the lens.

With Don McGuire now gone Jack could not possibly handle the chores of producer and star and still direct each episode of the series. He made a wise move when he brought our mutual friend, the former kid actor Gene Reynolds in to make his directorial debut on some of the "Hennesey" segments.

Gene had a natural talent for directing which was confirmed a few years later when he became the executive producer and director on probably the biggest hit television series of all time, "M*A*S*H."

Here again, Gene couldn't possibly direct all the "M*A*S*H" segments, so he reciprocated by bringing Jackie Cooper in to direct several in the first year. I hear that Jack could have directed many more segments of the series, but he and Alan Alda had a personality conflict and Gene Reynolds had to drop Jackie from the show to appease Alda.

71

Unusual Navy Cooperation

I promised I would relate the details of some unusual and unexpected motion pictures and television productions my office was called upon to help. I hope you don't mind if I hop from movies to television, and please understand that these projects are not necessarily in order by date but rather in their degree of unusualness.

Would you believe that I provided assistance on the great film, *The Sound of Music*? In early 1964 my old friend Robert Wise called me from Twentieth Century–Fox to say he was planning to produce and direct a movie on the experiences of the legendary Von Trapp family. His film was to be based on the musical by Rodgers and Hammerstein which had its book by Lindsey and Crouse.

I had known Bob Wise since the 1930s when he was an assistant cutter at RKO. A cutter is now called a film editor. Bob was a fine one and earned his first Academy Award nomination as film editor on Orson Welles's all-time great film, *Citizen Kane*. In 1961 Bob's production *West Side Story* was voted best picture of the year by the Academy and he shared the best director Oscar with the film's choreographer, Jerome Robbins.

Bob told me the part of Baron Von Trapp would be played by Christopher Plummer. He was to be a retired captain in the Austrian Navy and when he wanted an immediate appearance from his seven unruly children he would call them on a bos'n's pipe.

Wise then asked me if I could provide help with the bos'n's pipe. That was no problem. I called friends at the Long Beach Naval Base and they sent me a first-class bos'n. He came to the studio and showed Plummer how to hold and finger the pipe while making the various calls. He also went to the studio music department where he recorded a number of calls that were actually used in the film's sound track.

The Sound of Music was a blockbuster with Julie Andrews playing the trainee nun assigned to be governess to the Von Trapp children. She falls in love with the baron and finally helps the family escape the Nazis.

Again, a Robert Wise production was voted the best film of the year for 1965 and Wise also received the best director Oscar. For years *The*

Sound of Music stood as the highest gross-earning film until it was later surpassed by the comparatively lightweight John Travolta film *Grease.*

I learned a bit of trivia from the bos'n's mate on *The Sound of Music* that I never knew before in all my years in the navy. Being an aviator I wasn't aware of such things. The bos'n told me that most of his compatriots "tuned" their pipes to their own liking. Most of them accomplish this by pouring melted beeswax into the bell of their pipe until they have the tone they desire. Beeswax is chosen because it will not melt at normal temperatures while they hold the pipe in warm weather. He said some bos'ns instead distort the shape of the bell with pliers, but this is looked down upon by real connoisseurs. So you see, even bos'n's mates can be virtuosos in their own craft.

In 1940 Cary Grant and Irene Dunne costarred in a memorable film, *My Favorite Wife.* It was directed by Garson Kanin and featured Gail Patrick and Randolph Scott. By coincidence, Robert Wise was the film editor on *My Favorite Wife.* In the story Irene Dunne as the wife was lost at sea. Seven years later she is found on a deserted island by the U.S. Navy. They rescue her and when she returns home she is dismayed to find that her husband, Cary Grant, is now remarried to Gail Patrick.

Twentieth Century–Fox was about to remake this film, now titled, *Move Over Darling.* It was to be directed by George Cukor and would costar Marilyn Monroe and Dean Martin. I was called to the set on the very day that the lovely Marilyn was swimming nude, and I mean completely nude, in the family pool. Marilyn didn't know who I was but she didn't object when Cukor escorted me to the side of the pool and introduced me as the navy technical adviser on the film. Unfortunately, Marilyn fell out of grace with the studio and the project was canceled.

The following year the studio reactivated it, this time starring Doris Day and James Garner with Mike Gordon directing. I was asked to provide a submarine to the location site at the Long Beach Naval Base. There were no subs stationed at Long Beach, but the San Diego Submarine Base kindly arranged for the visit of one so we could be seen in this pleasant film.

The submarine came into Long Beach the night before filming and I wanted to be the first to meet the movie crew. I asked the skipper if I could spend the night on board and he kindly agreed. I was assigned to a space in the executive officer's quarters and he placed me in a bunk right underneath his own. I felt like I was sleeping on a shelf. After being an aviator for all my years in the navy, I really feel for the submariners who are inured to living in such close quarters.

In the movie the sub docks and Doris is escorted out of it in the tattered clothes she was wearing on the Pacific island. She goes to a nearby telephone booth and asks one of her navy benefactors if she can borrow a nickel to call home. Then she is told that in her seven years of absence the rate for a telephone call has gone up to a dime. (Wouldn't it be nice if we could still make a call for ten cents!)

One of the navy officers drives her to her home, where she finds that her children don't recognize her but her dog does. Then she learns that she has been declared legally dead due to her seven-year absence and her husband has just that day remarried, to Polly Bergen, and the newlyweds were at that very time checking into a hotel to begin their honeymoon.

Well, she wasn't about to stand for this so she goes to the hotel where they are registered. By accident, the husband sees her in the elevator and just can't believe his eyes. They meet and he checks her into another room and for the rest of the night the poor guy moves from one room to the other. He doesn't want to tell the new wife about the first lady, and is trying to hide the new marriage from his first wife.

It all works out in the end. She is declared legally alive and the second marriage is annulled by a mystified judge played comically by Edgar Buchanan.

One day during the production of *Move Over Darling* we were working at a mansion in Beverly Hills and I was called to the telephone. It was my office calling to tell me the producers of Garry Moore's television show "I've Got a Secret" were trying to reach me and they wanted me to appear on the show. I wasn't really needed for a few days, so I flew to New York.

Garry was very friendly and the company put me up in a good hotel room. The next morning I appeared on camera in my navy-blue uniform, complete with gold braid, wings, and ribbons. The secret they wanted me to admit to was that I used to appear in the *Our Gang* comedies and usually played the sissy. Panelist Henry Morgan was getting close, but they never did guess my "secret."

Back at *Move Over Darling,* on the day they shot the scenes where Doris Day disembarks from the submarine, she causes whistles and racy comments from a group of sailors on the ship next to where the submarine docked. I was pleased to see that director Mike Gordon had cast former Dead End Kid Billy Halop to play the wisecracking sailor.

Billy recognized me and was surprised to see I was now a navy officer. We talked about the old days, but I felt he was embarrassed for me to see him playing such a small part. As the day wore on, many of the real sailors came up to him to ask questions about his old films. He was friendly and patient at first, but he finally stormed at them saying he didn't want to talk about, or even think about, the Dead End Kids ever again. I thought it strange and rather pathetic that he had become so bitter and didn't even want to discuss the very thing that brought him his greatest fame and recognition.

Another unusual television show that I became involved with was a segment of "Dennis the Menace." Mr. Wilson's nephew was about to graduate

My son Pat, left, played Jay North's pal Herman in 15 episodes of "Dennis the Menace."

from the Navy Recruit Training Station at San Diego and he invited Dennis and his family to join him at the big ceremony.

At that time, on every Friday afternoon, the recruit station held a graduation ceremony where about 2,000 recruits marched in review. I had cleared everything with the base commander, so they were ready for us. Right in the most important part of the ceremony Dennis's dog Ruff gets loose and Dennis runs out to retrieve him. This, of course, completely disrupts the ceremony.

Of interest here is that the man who arranged for all the navy cooperation was Frank Capra, Jr., the son of one of the greatest directors of all time. Young Capra was then production manager on "Dennis the Menace" and he has gone on to greater acclaim in his own right as a motion picture producer.

Regarding "Dennis the Menace"—when we moved to Hollywood for me to take over the navy office, my children really found out for the first time that I had once been a child star. Then they begged me to let them get into motion pictures. I really didn't want to encourage this, but they persisted. It was easy for me to get them an agent and soon all of them had appeared in a few films, television programs, or in commercials.

One day my son Patrick, then ten, was called to an interview for a Wrigley's Spearmint gum commercial. For some reason Betty couldn't take him, so I took off and drove him to the studio. Mike, then 14, was at home, so I took him with us. When Pat returned from having his audition, he said the director recognized the name and asked if he was my son. When he said he was, the director, Charles Barton, said "I know your father, please have him come to see me."

I couldn't leave Mike there alone, so I took him with me. I had known Charlie Barton for many years and he gave me a big welcome. As it turned out, Barton thought Pat was too young for the Spearmint commercial and he had Mike try out for it. Mike won the assignment and made about $3,000 in residuals over the next two years. The other good result here was that Barton was impressed with Pat and cast him to play Herman, the third friend of Dennis, and Pat played in 15 segments of the series over the next few years. To this day Pat is still receiving small residuals from his participation in this series. We even saw him on television once when we were vacationing in the Caribbean.

Wouldn't you consider "The Real McCoys" to be a television series that would never require navy cooperation? I did until the producers brought a cute script to my office and asked if we would extend assistance.

It told the story of the McCoy family: Grandpa Amos McCoy (Walter Brennan), his grandson, Luke McCoy (Richard Crenna), and Kate "Sugar Babe" McCoy, Luke's wife (Kathleen Nolan). They all drive from "West Virginie" to California in their battered jalopy and settle in the San Fernando Valley to start a new life.

They heard there was a destroyer at the Long Beach Naval Base named in honor of the only real navy hero from West Virginia, so they decide to visit the ship. When they arrive they are appalled to see a sign stating that on the very next day contractors are going to commence tearing the ship apart and the metal will be sold for scrap. That night they decide this sad event just cannot take place.

Early the next morning the three of them sneak aboard the ship before the demolition crew. When the workers arrive, old Amos keeps them from boarding by holding them at bay with a high velocity fire hose.

This causes much consternation at the navy base. Soon reporters and television crews arrive to film this unusual occurrence and word of it quickly arrives at the office of the secretary of the navy. This fine gentleman admires their spunk and sends word to Amos that if he will allow the demolition to continue, he promises that the very next destroyer to be launched will bear the name of the West Virginia war hero and the McCoy family will be special guests at the commissioning ceremony.

This sounds easy doesn't it? Well, I escorted the location manager to the base and we both agreed on a certain destroyer and the pier where it was docked. I cleared all of this with the base commander and saw no conflict.

As usual, I arrived about an hour before the movie people and to my horror I found a civilian construction team about to cut off all water to this particular pier.

I asked the man in charge what this was all about. He told me that his firm was shutting off the water to this pier on a contract signed at least six months ago. I tried to explain that water to this particular pier, on that very day, was crucial to a commitment I had made to the producers of "The Real McCoys." This kind fellow made a few telephone calls and was able to move his crew to another pier which was also involved in his plumbing contract.

Isn't it weird, after I had made what I thought were all the required arrangements, we nearly came to disaster? I guess you can also say, "That's show business."

What about "McHale's Navy"? Do you think we gave them cooperation? No, the producers of this zany comedy about Lieutenant Commander Quinton McHale and his crew of misfits on PT-73 went it all on their own. They wanted to make a wild farce about navy life and didn't even bother to submit scripts.

Strangely enough, "McHale's Navy" evolved from a very dramatic, hour-long program seen on "The Alcoa Premiere." Here Ernest Borgnine was the commander of a PT boat that was sunk in Japanese waters and his crew took refuge on a deserted island. Late in the story they have the opportunity to storm a Japanese PT boat, kill the enemy crew, and make their escape. At first Borgnine does not want to risk losing any more men, so he decides against the raid. His crew outvote him and they eventually make good, stealing the Japanese vessel and making their way to freedom with many thrilling moments as they take the enemy craft into American waters.

When producer Edward Montagne and his stable of writers at Universal Studio got through with their version of "The Alcoa Premiere" story you wouldn't recognize the original concept.

Borgnine was still the PT boat skipper, but now his executive officer was the comical Ensign Charles Parker, played to perfection by one of television's funniest clowns, Tim Conway. PT-73 was based at the Pacific island of Taratupa. The CO there was Captain Binghamton, played by Joe Flynn, who raged to his aide, Robert Hastings, that Quinton McHale was trying to turn his island into the Las Vegas of the Pacific.

Though we did not provide technical advice, I used to drop by the set frequently just to check their uniforms, ribbons, and other things. When I would walk on the set, Ernie Borgnine or director Sidney Lanfield would playfully shout, "Oh, oh. We must be in serious trouble. Here comes Commander Coghlan."

Officially, Washington frowned on this farcical and disrespectful series, but really 99 percent of the people in the navy loved it. Soon I was being asked to invite Ernest Borgnine and Joe Flynn to ceremonies at various navy bases. Being great guys, they cheerfully accepted. I remember one night Betty and I were sitting with Ernie on our way to the commissioning of a new naval activity in the San Diego area. At that time he was going through a nasty divorce settlement with his former wife, the great entertainer Ethel Merman. It was obvious that he was upset with his own personal problems, but this kind man then told me he would still be available for any event the navy wished to have him attend.

I'll tell you here that Ernest Borgnine is just as fine a person as he is a performer. He won the Academy Award as best actor for his portrayal of *Marty* in 1955 and he is just as kind a person in regular life.

In the fourth year of "McHale's Navy," the entire group moved from Taratupa to the Italian village of Voltafione to assist in the European war. Here the mayor of the village was played by Jay Novello and his silly aide was my dear friend, Dick Wilson.

"McHale's Navy" ran from 1962 to 1966 and there were 138 episodes aired during this time. In the third year there was a spinoff called "Broadside" that ran for 32 episodes.

Here producer Montagne brought a detachment of Waves to the island. They eventually ended up on their own island of Ranakai where the star, Kathleen Nolan, was constantly in trouble with the base commander, played by Edward Andrews. It was really "McHale's Navy" in skirts. Again, we did not extend cooperation to the series.

However, I did escort the lieutenant in charge of Wave recruiting in the Los Angeles area to the set to help the wardrobe department get the uniforms and stripes correct. We figured if the girls looked neat and had their uniforms on properly their funny antics would not be resented too much by the very fastidious directors of the Waves in Washington. Some of the senior Waves just couldn't stand being kidded and I was criticized for extending them even this small amount of assistance. Oh well, you can't please everyone.

Edward Montagne was a genius at casting. He had to be to put McHale's nutty crew together. In addition to McHale and Ensign Parker, PT-73 was manned by such characters as Carl Ballantine, Billy Sands, John Wright, Edson Stroll, Gary Vinson, and even Gavin MacLeod, before he later became skipper of his own ship, "The Love Boat."

72

Television and the Navy

In addition to Jackie Cooper's "Hennesey," there were a few other television series that received full cooperation on an as needed basis.

There was a clever public information officer in the navy named William J. Lederer who was really a unique individual. Bill Lederer was uncommon in several respects. He was a graduate of the Naval Academy, he was Jewish, and he spoke with a stutter. (Some who knew him better than I did claimed he only used his stutter when he wanted to attract attention.) In spite of these possible handicaps to promotion, Bill had a distinguished career. He became a highly published author and after his retirement from the navy he became a Far East correspondent for *Reader's Digest* magazine. Of his many books, the most recognized is *The Ugly American* which he coauthored with Eugene Burdick. It was later made into a motion picture of the same name starring Marlon Brando.

In one of his early books he humorously described the events of the only time he was in charge of a ship of the line. He was a brand new ensign and was the duty officer on the bridge while a battleship was being moved from its anchorage to a berth in Norfolk Harbor. He claims it was not his fault but, due to changes in the tides, the ship ran aground on an uncharted sandbar with much embarrassment to the navy. He then decided that ship handling was not his forte, so he requested a change of designator to public information specialist.

His book, *Ensign O'Toole and Me* was purchased by Four Star as a possible television series. The producers were Hy Averback and Bob Claver. Averback was a former radio announcer. He gained recognition while in the service on Armed Forces Radio and when he returned to Hollywood, Bob Hope hired him to announce some of his shows. Bob Claver gained his production experience under Jackie Cooper on "Hennesey."

Averback called me to his office to ask if we could cooperate on the proposed series. The scripts were humorous, yet not disrespectful, so we decided to go along. They really did not need much assistance. They built the interior of a destroyer in the studio so did very little filming on board our ships. They did pickup shots around ships at Long Beach Naval Base and the rest was in the studio. We provided a technical adviser and allowed them to use lots of navy stock footage and that was about all they requested in the way of cooperation.

The story told of life aboard the destroyer USS *Appleby* and, unfortunately, this series only lasted one season with 32 segments of 30 minutes each. Ensign O'Toole was played by Dean Jones who later became a mainstay for Walt Disney Productions in such films as *The Love Bug.* There was an oddity in the series as you never did see the commanding officer of the *Appleby.* However, the executive officer was very much in evidence. He was played by the fine actor Jack Albertson, who received the Oscar for best supporting actor in 1968 for *The Subject Was Roses* and later starred with Freddie Prinze in the television series "Chico and the Man."

The leading chief petty officer on the *Appleby* was the old-time actor J. C. Flippen. This comical fellow once described his face as being a cross between a tomato and a Pekingese. The *Appleby* had a crew of fine young actors including Harvey Lembeck, Robert Sorrells, and a new fellow named Beau Bridges. Does that name sound familiar?

In 1960 Columbia Studio produced a film, *The Wackiest Ship in the Army.* My office had provided limited cooperation on it before my arrival. This interesting movie starred Jack Lemmon and the supporting cast included Ricky Nelson, John Lund, Chips Rafferty, Tom Tully, Joby Baker, Warren Berlinger, and Richard Anderson. It told of a small navy crew assigned to army intelligence, to be the crew on a small two-masted, vintage 1871 schooner. They posed as neutral Swedish sailors and their mission was to sail in Japanese waters to observe and report on enemy shipping.

In 1965 Screen Gems, Columbia's TV arm, decided to produce a television series based on the story lines of the motion picture. It too was titled "The Wackiest Ship in the Army."

It featured Jack Warden as Major Simon Butcher, the army intelligence officer, and Gary Collins as Lieutenant "Rip" Riddle, who was in charge of the navy crew. The navy men were horrified when they saw the ancient schooner and had many misgivings about having to serve under an army officer. They nicknamed their rickety old tub the USS *Kiwi* and had many close scrapes in their clandestine operations behind the enemy sea lanes.

This series did not require much actual navy cooperation, but we did let them sail the *Kiwi* around navy ships and gave them technical advice and lots of U.S. and captured Japanese stock footage. It was an hour-long show produced by Danny Arnold and unfortunately only ran for 29 episodes.

In 1964 producer Frank Price invited me to Universal Studio to read the proposal of a television series to be called "Convoy." This story told of the many problems and heroics of a convoy of 200 heavily armed American ships slowly heading for Europe during World War II.

The star of the series was John Gavin, as Commander Dan Talbot, the commanding officer of escort DD-181. John Larch was the convoy commander, Captain Ben Foster, who led the group from his freighter flagship. His top assistant was Linden Chiles, playing Chief Officer Steve Kirkland. (Of interest here: they chose number 181 so they could use stock footage showing the ship going in either direction by reversing the film.)

We liked the story outline and granted them full cooperation. I escorted the entire company on board the repair ship USS *Hector,* based at the Long Beach Naval Base. They filmed on board the *Hector* for several days, shooting countless scenes of operations at sea. As much as we rooted for this fine 60-minute dramatic series, showing the best of navy life under stress in wartime conditions, it only ran for 13 episodes.

I'm sure my readers are familiar with the handsome John Gavin who was later our ambassador to Mexico. Frank Price became head of production at Columbia Studio, then at Universal, and is now again president of Columbia Studio. Frank Price's associate producer on "Convoy" was Jo Swerling, Jr., whose father Jo Swerling received an Academy Award nomination in 1942 for his work on the screenplay of the great film, *The Pride of the Yankees.* Jo, Jr., is now the executive assistant to Stephen J. Cannell on his many television series.

There were two other TV series that required my assistance on the set for one time only. First was "Ben Casey," which starred Vince Edwards as the chief resident of neurosurgery under Sam Jaffe and later Frachot Tone, who both played the chief of neurosurgery in this fine medical series.

In "Ben Casey" there was one episode where a naval aviator needed Dr. Casey's help after a plane crash.

"The Lieutenant" was a series of life with the marines at Camp Pendleton in Southern California. This series had Gary Lockwood as the marine captain and Robert Vaughn as his assistant, Lieutenant Steve Franken.

I only mention these two series because they were the only times I was treated rudely by the stars of productions while I was on the set giving technical advice. Both times I was on the set for the entire day, available to the director and crew whenever needed. Both Edwards and Vaughn saw me, knew what I was there for, and completely ignored me. Maybe they were having a bad day. On other sets people like John Wayne would come right up to me and offer their hand in greeting, while these two superstars treated me like I was an intruder. Maybe they thought I would ask them for an autograph.

The only other time I was treated rudely during my entire five years in charge of the Hollywood office was one day at Universal when I dropped in on a set where Yul Brynner was starring in a film. I was probably between calls on "Convoy" or "McHale's Navy." I was in full uniform and was usually welcome on any set as I was the man whose advice was sought after, and my presence on a set was usually considered a compliment.

I was standing way back behind the camera crew talking quietly with friends when a young assistant director came up and said that Mr. Brynner would like me to leave as he didn't want any visitors. When I told this story later, everyone who knew Yul said in no way was this directive coming from him. They all said he was a charming man and this must have been the whim of an overeager assistant director.

I'm sure my readers know who Fess Parker is. He came to fame playing Davey Crockett in several films for Walt Disney. From 1964 to 1970 he starred in the television series "Daniel Boone" for Twentieth Century–Fox. In this exciting series Ed Ames played the Indian chief and other supporting players were Burl Ives and Albert Salmi. It was a thrilling 60-minute show and ran for 165 episodes on NBC. The series was produced by my high school friend Aaron "Rosey" Rosenberg and his assistant producer was a young fellow named Aaron Spelling. His name has become very familiar from his other productions in later years, such as "Hart to Hart," "Starsky and Hutch," and the long-running super hit "Dynasty." The publicity director on "Daniel Boone" was my friend Will Fowler, son of the great writer, Gene Fowler.

In 1965 the navy was due to commission the nuclear submarine USS(N) *Daniel Boone* at the Mare Island sub base in San Francisco Bay. I don't know whether Will Fowler thought of it first or I did, but it was easy to convince the navy and Twentieth Century–Fox to invite Fess Parker to be a special guest at the commissioning ceremony.

The commander-in-chief of the Pacific Fleet, Admiral Ulysses S. Grant Sharp, accepted the submarine for the U.S. Navy and Fess Parker was present in all the photos. This kind man stayed at the base all day and attended the banquet that night where he willingly signed autographs for all who asked. Fess is now a multimillionaire with vast real estate holdings in the Santa Barbara area. He has just completed a giant hotel complex there and I wish him well as he is truly an outstanding man and a credit to the television industry that brought him fame.

In addition to the series I have described, there were a number of variety-type television shows where the navy was called on to provide support.

On several occasions the producers of "Queen for a Day" called to say the wife of a navy man would be a guest on the next program. This show ran on NBC from 1956 to 1960 and then on ABC from 1960 to 1964. Jack Bailey was the host and Jeanne Cagney his cohostess.

Women from all over the country were asked to write in telling of their hardships and what they needed most in their lives. The writers of the most heartrending letters were invited to be contestants. Each week four ladies were guests and they bared their souls describing their problems. At the close of the show the audience selected the one they considered the neediest and she was declared "Queen for a Day." She then received her most sought-after object and was showered with other gifts as well.

Why we groaned whenever a navy wife was a contestant was because of the bad image it gave to navy life. We knew that some families suffered hardships with the husband at sea, checks late in arriving, sick kids, and forced moves to unfamiliar locations. We just hated to hear Jack Bailey dramatize these conditions and make them seem even worse. The only reason I liked to visit the program was I got to see my dear friend Jeanne Cagney.

I had a very exciting experience in connection with "Truth or Consequences." This long-running program started on CBS and during its 15-year run moved to NBC. In 1967 it returned to the air in syndication. The way we got involved was that a young lady marine was to be reunited with her mother whom she had not seen for several years. The meeting as it was set up was to be a complete surprise to both of them. The Ralph Edwards people brought the mother out from her home in the East and I was to get the lady marine to the show under a false pretense.

The trouble was, everything went wrong. Due to inclement weather the navy plane the girl was flying in as a passenger had to overshoot where we were waiting for her. It landed at a remote airport and I had to send a helicopter to pick her up. Again, due to low clouds, the chopper put down on the front lawn of the Ambassador Hotel where the producers had a police car drive her to the television station with sirens blaring so she could make the air time.

She arrived at the very last moment, just as the director was about to give the order to scratch the surprise meeting. Through all the suspense, Bob Barker was charming, good-natured, and humorous. Whew!

There was an entertaining variety show called "The Lively Ones" that ran on NBC for the two seasons of 1962 and 1963. It was produced and directed by Barry Shear and the host each week was the singer Vic Damone. The hour-long program was filled with music, singing, and dancing. The sponsor was the Ford Motor Company and the account executive for the J. Walter Thompson advertising agency was Tom DePaolo. Tom was the son of the famous auto race driver Peter DePaolo who had won the Indianapolis 500-mile race in 1925 in a Dusenberg Special. His average speed was 101.13 miles per hour and he was the first winner to surpass 100 mph in the history of Indy.

When I went to Tom's office at J. Walter Thompson's I was pleased to see that my old friend Philippe de Lacy had the next office to him. I mentioned Philippe back in Chapter 20 and he was now a successful advertising executive.

Tom DePaolo told me "The Lively Ones" would like to do a show with one of the musical numbers taking place on a navy ship. The next day I escorted Tom, Barry Shear, Vic Damone, and a few production assistants to the Long Beach Naval Base. I took them aboard an aircraft carrier, a cruiser, and a destroyer. Darned if they didn't select a minesweeper, the smallest combatant ship in the navy!

We were leaving the base when we passed by the pier where 12 MSOs were tied up, bow to stern and two abreast. The MSO (Mine Sweepers Ocean) is the largest class of minesweepers in the fleet at 224 feet long and 39 feet wide. They are compact little ships and foot-for-foot are the most expensive ships in the navy.

The hull and superstructure are all wood. The engine and all metal fittings are made of nonmagnetic metal alloys to protect them from the magnetic and electronically controlled mines they may pass over while clearing hostile waters for our ships.

The dance director Ward chose these ships as he could visualize a good musical number using the entire top deck of the rugged-looking MSO.

On this particular show, Vic Damone's guest star was the rotund Allen Sherman who was very popular at the time for the very funny parodies he was writing and singing. Sherman was a former television writer and producer who began writing parodies to well-known songs and singing them at parties to entertain his friends.

His wit became so well known that Jack Benny, George Burns, and Milton Berle encouraged him to record them. His first album, *My Son the Folksinger,* was a runaway hit and he became the hottest performer in the record industry that year. He soon released two more albums, *My Son the Celebrity* and *My Son the Nut.* He even went on tour and I saw him one night at the Hollywood Bowl where he performed in front of the Los Angeles Symphonic Orchestra and set an attendance record.

Most of his songs were filled with Jewish humor. One reviewer said his singing was "Manhattan delicatessen style" and another called his voice "pure nasal Brooklynese."

His parodies were incredibly funny and clever. For instance, he sang one called "Harvey and Sheila" to the tune of "Hava Nagilah"; the classic "Aura Lee" became "Every Time You Take a Vaccine, Take It Orally"; and "Won't You Come Home Billy Bailey" became "Won't You Come Home Disraeli."

To the tune of "The Battle Hymn of the Republic" he sang "Glory, Glory, Harry Lewis." This poignant ditty told the story of a cutter in Irving Roth's garment factory who stood fast during a catastrophic fire. It concluded with the cutter, Harry Lewis, "Trampling through the warehouse where the drapes of Roth are stored."

Sherman's biggest hit single was "Hello Mudda, Hello Fadda," which told the story of a child writing a complaining letter home from camp. If you can imagine, this was written to the music of "Dance of the Hours," from the opera *La Gioconda.* To Allen Sherman nothing was sacred.

Songwriters really suffered when he parodied their popular works. Richard Rodgers called him a devastator when he parodied his "There Is Nothing Like a Dame" into "There Is Nothing Like a Lox."

Meredith Wilson probably suffered the most when Sherman parodied his "Seventy-Six Trombones." With new lyrics he turned it into an ode to a Jewish country club by singing "Seventy-six Sol Cohens in the country club, and a hundred and ten nice men named Levine."

Dance director Ward staged an excellent number where Vic Damone and the pear-shaped Allen Sherman, both in ill-fitting sailor suits, sang and danced all over the MSO to the accompaniment of offstage prerecorded music. The number sounds rather ridiculous, but it was well received and we were glad we allowed them to use our ship.

There was another popular variety show of the era called "Hollywood Palace" that ran on ABC for six years. It was presented before a live audience in the Hollywood Palace Theater on Vine Street and was produced by Nick Vanoff and William Harbach who are still big names in the production of large specialty shows on television.

It featured different performers each week who were backed up by the Ray Charles Singers and the Buddy Schwab Dancers with Mitchell Ayres as musical director. The producers' representatives came to our joint military office to ask if all the services would band together on a special show to commemorate Armed Forces Day. We all agreed and then each of us went to our headquarters to request the very best form of entertainment we could supply for this special event.

The army provided a band with a fine vocalist. The air force sent a spectacular drill team of black enlisted men who excited the audience with their double time, off-beat cadence in close order drill maneuvers. The marines brought a good drill team who thrilled the spectators with their daring use of rifles with bayonets attached.

The navy sent me the spectacular trampoline team from NAS Pensacola. The four young sailors and two Waves on the team jumped so high during rehearsals that the stagehands had to raise the overhead lights backstage.

The single best memory I have of the show was the lovely young lady making her first entry into show business as the Card Holder. This stunning creature wore a very skimpy outfit as she walked across stage with her sign announcing the name of the next act. Her name was Raquel Welch and I can best describe her walk as "titillating."

Through the years Tennessee Ernie Ford has had several fine television series. From 1960 to 1965 when I was in charge of the Hollywood office he had two different series. When I first met him he aired his folksy variety show over NBC. Then he moved his operations to San Francisco and broadcast over the ABC network.

I'm pleased to say my office provided assistance on both of these series. On the latter group over ABC I placed the Naval Aviation Cadet Choir from NAS Pensacola in a show that was taped on the deck of the aircraft carrier *Antietam* while it was anchored in San Francisco Bay with the bridges in the background. As good as that program was, it was my first association with Ernie Ford that endeared me to this man.

When the show was being broadcast from NBC one of his production assistants called to ask if they could do a show on the deck of an aircraft carrier at the Long Beach Naval Base. I made some telephone calls and reported back that the USS *Princeton* was based there and they would welcome the show to be staged on board.

A few days later I escorted the producer Selwyn Touber and some of his aides to visit the *Princeton.* With the group was Ward, the dance director who had done such a fine job on the MSO for "The Lively Ones."

On this series Ernie had a musical group, The Top Twenty, composed of ten men and ten women who all were talented singers and dancers. On that visit Ward took down the measurements of *Princeton*'s flight deck. When I went out to NBC a few days later I saw he had measured off the flight deck on the NBC parking lot and was rehearsing The Top Twenty just like they were on the deck of the carrier.

On the afternoon before the show, Ernie Ford and his group came on board to spend the night so they could get an early start on the show's preparations. The ship was at anchor in the harbor and when Ernie came on board he was carrying the largest ham I have ever seen. He told me it was a gift from the governor of Tennessee and was the prize-winning ham at the Tennessee State Fair.

Ernie asked me to check with the ship's personnel officer and to tell each man from Tennessee that he was invited to a special breakfast at 7:00 A.M. the following morning. I did so and then took Ernie to the ship's galley to meet the chief cook so he could make his special arrangements.

The next morning 23 enlisted men and two officers who were natives of the Volunteer State arrived at the mess hall we had reserved. They didn't know why they were ordered to be at this particular mess hall, but to their complete surprise and great pleasure they saw Tennessee Ernie Ford at the head of the serving line wearing a chef's hat.

Breakfast that morning for this special group was a large slice of the prize-winning ham, scrambled eggs, grits, honey, and biscuits, and a special redeye gravy that Ernie had made himself. He also served the gravy, spooning out a generous amount over the ham and pressing a ladle full into the grits. Also beside each place setting at the mess table was a quart of buttermilk to go along with the coffee. Throughout the meal Ernie circulated among the gathering and spoke kindly to everyone present.

That was a breakfast that those who were invited will never forget. I'm happy to say that I was among the special guests.

Up on deck the ship's crew chipped in to help the NBC people in setting up a stage and backdrops. They also set up 600 chairs so many of the crew could sit and watch the show.

In addition to Ernie, The Top Twenty, and the NBC orchestra, there were to be skits with Ernie and Joe Flynn from "McHale's Navy" and another skit between Ernie and Minnie Pearl. When Minnie arrived the morning of the show she was already dressed in her trademark gingham dress with white cotton hose, black Mary Jane shoes, and the straw hat with the price tag hanging from the brim. It was quite cool and windy, so while Minnie was dressed in her usual hillbilly wardrobe, she was also wearing the most beautiful calf-length mink coat I had ever seen.

Things progressed fine during the day. Ward rehearsed The Top Twenty and the girls made out all right in their high heels on the rough flight deck. However, about an hour before show time the wind kept getting stronger until it was blowing at a speed of 30 knots. It finally blew the set down and when the girls in The Top Twenty twirled, their pretty knee-length fluffy chiffon dresses blew up over their heads. This brought appreciative whistles from the crew but was causing Ward and the dancers lots of consternation.

I checked with the ship's meteorologist and he told me the wind would hold steady at 30 knots for the rest of the day. When I relayed this information to producer Selwyn Touber he told Ernie Ford that we were on the brink of disaster as there was no way they could tape the show in those heavy wind conditions. This was serious as it meant there would not be a new Tennessee Ernie Ford show that week and the network would have to resort to a rerun of an old show.

The captain of the *Princeton* heard these remarks and said, "If you give me one hour I can save your show."

With that he ordered the anchor up and we steamed out to sea right into the wind for a very rough hour. Then he turned the big ship around and steamed with the wind at the exact speed it was blowing. Now it was like a calm on the flight deck.

The crew quickly turned the set around and moved the chairs. You see, at anchor a ship weathercocks with its bow into the wind. Now the way the carrier was sailing downwind, it was blowing at the ship's stern. At anchor the sun was shining on the bow. Now it too was shining from our stern.

In this no-wind condition the show went off without a hitch and the 30-minute program came to a close just as the carrier was approaching back to Long Beach Naval Base. Ernie Ford could not have been happier.

When the NBC company was leaving the *Princeton* that evening, Ernie told the captain he would never forget his thoughtfulness and kindness.

The captain said, "Well, I told you the show could be performed on our flight deck. I just wanted to make good on my promise."

73

Feature Films

In the last three chapters I have detailed the various forms of cooperation received from my Hollywood office. While there were many others I dealt with during my five years, there are six motion picture feature films that I most remember.

My good friend George Wells, who led to my becoming a radio actor in 1936 when he wrote "The Lux Radio Theater," was now a very successful writer-producer at MGM. He wrote the screenplay and was producer of *The Honeymoon Machine* and had me out to MGM to discuss cooperation and technical advice. This film was to star Steve McQueen, a hot new prospect after his big hit in the television series, "Wanted Dead or Alive."

The movie also featured Jim Hutton, Paula Prentiss, Brigid Bazlen, Dean Jagger, and Jack Weston. It told the story of two young navy officers who figured out a way to break the bank at Monte Carlo by sending messages from the casino which his partner then entered into the ship's computers while it was at anchor in the bay nearby. We allowed them to photograph one of our cruisers anchored in San Diego Harbor. The studio then made it look like the Mediterranean by special effects.

My most vivid memory of this film was when George Wells took me to the set to make sure McQueen was properly attired as a naval officer while he was seated at a gaming table.

In real life Steve had been abandoned by his parents at an early age and spent some of his youth in reform school. Despite this upbringing, he wanted to become an actor. He studied under Uta Hagen and Herbert Berghof and later at the famous Actors Studio. As a result of this training he became one of the early "method actors."

This day Steve was sitting at the gaming table and director Richard Thorpe asked him to read a simple line. Steve, in his desire for perfection, asked Thorpe, "What is my motivation for this scene?"

I was standing next to George Wells when he heard McQueen's request. Wells turned to me in disgust and muttered, "For Christ's sake. Why doesn't he just read the line the way it was written and forget what in hell the motivation is?" I guess that pretty well sums up the feelings of an author when an actor questions the meaning of one of his carefully written lines of dialogue.

A producer at Warner Brothers called me in to talk about a most unusual film that would combine live action and animation. It was *The Incredible Mr. Limpet,* which starred Don Knotts, with Jack Weston, Elizabeth MacRae, and Andrew Duggan.

In this strange film Don Knotts was a timid soul as a human being who became a dolphin in animation. He aids the U.S. Navy during World War II and finally finds true love with a pretty lady fish in the animation scenes. Silly as it sounds, we spent many days on the set to help the live action and give advice on the animated sequences.

Probably the most time-consuming film for me was *PT-109,* the motion picture that Warner Brothers made about the World War II exploits of John F. Kennedy when he commanded at PT boat in the Pacific.

The producer of *PT-109* was Bryan Foy, the eldest child of vaudevillian great Eddie Foy. The story of his family was brought to the screen when Bob Hope played the legendary Eddie Foy in *The Seven Little Foys.*

Despite all the jokes told about Bryan Foy, he was a very talented man. He is credited with writing the words and music for the song, "Oh Mr. Gallagher, Oh Mr. Sheen," which was the timeworn introduction to the famous vaudeville act of Gallagher and Sheen.

Bryan Foy was famous in the film industry for his string of moneymaking, low-budget motion pictures. His nickname at Warner Brothers was "The King of the Bees." He bragged that he could read a lurid headline in the newspaper and have a film on the subject before the cameras within a week.

Bryan had me to the studio often during his preparations and he thought he could have anything he asked for from the navy due to the subject of his motion picture. What he didn't know was that I had a copy of a letter the chief of information had received from Pierre Salinger, President Kennedy's press secretary, telling us that the president insisted we were not to provide any more cooperation on this film than any other script of comparable value the navy would receive.

There was one important request Foy made that I was unable to provide. The script called for a squadron of six PT boats. The PT boat of World War II (Motor Patrolboat–Torpedo) was like a very large speedboat. The PT-109 was in the largest of the class. It was 80 feet long and carried four torpedo tubes. It was powered by three 12-cylinder, 2,000 horsepower Packard aircraft engines, the same used in the P-51 Mustang and it burned 100-octane aviation gasoline.

There were many PT boats sold as war surplus at the close of the war, but no small boat owner could afford to burn the expensive aviation gasoline, so all were converted to the more sensible diesel engines. Now instead of churning 45 to 50 knots, they cruised at around 18 knots maximum.

I learned there were still two PT boat hulls in the navy powered by the three aviation type engines, but neither of them could be made available to Warner Brothers. One was used in the submarine service to retrieve high-speed torpedoes and the other was loaded with exotic electronic gear in a super-secret project.

When the film company went on location in the Florida Keys, they rented some air-sea rescue boats from the air force and converted them to resemble the wartime navy PT boats.

An interesting and embarrassing sidelight here was when the producers of "McHale's Navy" were searching for a PT boat, they found the only other one in existence that was still powered by the three aviation engines. Can you imagine where it was? It was in the hangar in Long Beach Harbor nestled alongside Howard Hughes's all wood seaplane, the Spruce Goose. It was to be his personal rescue boat when he took the great plane off the water on its short flight.

Some smart person at Universal Studio knew about this boat and arranged a purchase through executives of the Summa Corporation, the Hughes holding company. When Howard Hughes, now in his dotage, heard of the sale he was furious and ordered that the boat be bought back. Universal was not about to relinquish their own PT boat, so Howard was ignored. If you take the Universal Studio tour you can still see the PT-73 tied up in a lagoon on the studio back lot.

At the time the *PT-109* company went on location in the Florida Keys with Cliff Robertson playing the late president, the film was supposed to be directed by Lewis Milestone, still famous for directing the original version of *All Quiet on the Western Front.* The aging "Millie," as he was lovingly called in Hollywood, soon proved he was not up to this strenuous location filming and was replaced by Leslie H. Martinson, who had worked his way up on the Warner Brothers television side for his credits on such TV series as "77 Sunset Strip."

PT-109 was not highly acclaimed at the box office, but Warner Brothers gave it their best shot. I was present on the day they filmed the exciting scene when the Japanese destroyer Amagiri rammed the PT-109 in the Blackett Strait of the Solomon Islands.

This scene was filmed on the studio's large tank stage. When the bow of the enemy destroyer cut the PT-109 in half it threw the crew members into the flaming water when the aviation gas tanks exploded. I was most impressed with the excellent job done by the special effects people who staged this most realistic simulation of the crash at sea.

There was a full-sized bow of the Amagiri on wires and the torpedo boat was pulled in front of it as the cameras rolled. The crash and the ensuing flames were really frightening to watch. In real life, after the PT-109 was torn apart and Kennedy and his surviving crew members were finally rescued, he was placed in command of another PT boat, the older and slightly smaller PT-59.

While in command of PT-59 Kennedy actually rescued 65 marines whose landing craft was stranded on a reef of Choiseul Island. The rendition of this rescue caused the biggest flap we had between our technical director and the film company.

Director Les Martinson ordered Cliff Robertson to back the torpedo boat up to the reef so the marines could climb over the stern. Then Cliff was to shove full forward on all three throttles so the boat would make a heroic spume as all three propellers made a froth in their wake.

Our technical adviser, an active-duty navy captain who had commanded a PT boat squadron in the Solomons said, "No way." He said no PT boat skipper in his right mind would back his three churning screws into unknown rocks. He tried to explain that one ding on a propeller and the boat would be crippled and a sitting duck for the enemy. He insisted that the boat be carefully nosed into the coral reef and the marines were to climb over the bow as they actually did.

Martinson objected that this would be far less dramatic, but our technical adviser won out. He had placed a call to me to tell me of this impasse, so the production people knew he meant business. As filmed, the boat carefully nosed into the reef, the marines climbed to safety, then the boat backed away, turned around, and then gave the cameras the desired plume of water. Common sense won again.

One day during the production of *PT-109* Bryan Foy took me to lunch in Jack Warner's private dining room. This was an elite place and only the top executives ate there. Warner sat at the head of the table and I guess he felt like King Arthur with his Round Table. Jack was really a crude person and took great pleasure in needling the people who worked for him. This day he welcomed me to his private enclave. During the fine luncheon he looked at me and said, "You know, when you were a kid actor I called you Junior. Now I have to call you Commander. Maybe next I'll be calling you a bum." It was a pretty typical crack from Warner. I never really did understand what he meant, but I chuckled good-naturedly along with the others who were also embarrassed by the rather uncalled-for remark.

There was another rather unusual movie that I helped Walt Disney bring to the screen. It was *Lt. Robin Crusoe, U.S.N.* It starred Dick Van Dyke as a naval aviator forced down at sea on a Pacific island where he became involved in the women's lib movement on the atoll. The leader of the lady uprising was Nancy Kwan and the tribal chieftain was played by Akim Tamiroff. Before Van Dyke meets the ladies of the island, he takes up refuge in a wrecked Japanese submarine with a chimpanzee.

I made all the arrangements for one day's filming at sea with the commanding officer of the aircraft carrier *Kitty Hawk*. When filming finally began, *Kitty Hawk* had been transferred away and we then did the carrier scenes on its replacement carrier, the USS *Constellation*.

My most memorable memory of this film was that we flew the principals out to the *Constellation* in a COD (Carrier On-board Delivery) aircraft. We let Walt Disney sit in the right front seat with the pilot when they came in for the landing on the carrier. We also let him sit there the next morning when we were catapulted off the carrier's deck.

When we landed back at the Naval Air Station on Coronado Island near San Diego, Walt declared that this experience topped anything he had to offer at Disneyland. I think that is a pretty good endorsement from the master of all illusions.

Producer Joe Pasternak started out in Hollywood as a busboy in the Universal Studio commissary. He then made his way to fame as a producer when he "discovered" the talented young singer Deanna Durbin and starred her in *Three Smart Girls*. That was the year 1936 when the lovely soprano from Winnipeg was only 14 years old. Over the next few years he continued with a series of blockbuster hit musicals with Deanna that saved Universal from the brink of bankruptcy.

It was now 1963 and Deanna had long since retired from the screen and was living in France with her writer husband. Pasternak had moved to MGM where he continued to be a successful producer. This kind, mild-mannered man invited me to his corner office in the Thalberg Building and handed me a copy of the old *Collier's* magazine and asked me to read a story titled "Moon Walk."

It told of an attractive young widow with three sons who since the death of her naval aviator husband had shunned all advances from other men. She was still living in the family home on Point Loma, across the channel from the North Island Naval Air Station. Most of her admirers were also navy pilots and she just didn't want to place herself in jeopardy of becoming a widow for the second time.

The unusual title of the story stemmed from the fact that her brother, an airline pilot, used to bring large weather balloons home from his trips. He would inflate them with helium gas and attach them to a harness and tow the youngest son around the property while he was suspended several feet above the ground. The youngster loved this game and called it "moon walking."

When I finished reading it, Joe asked me what I thought about it and did I think the navy would cooperate with it if he bought the screen rights. I told him I thought it was a delightful story and on my recommendation he had MGM make the purchase.

He assigned Ruth Brooks Flippen to write the screenplay and she did

In 1963 I was the technical adviser on *A Ticklish Affair* at MGM. From the left: Red Buttons, Carolyn Jones, Lieutenant Commander Coghlan, Shirley Jones, and Gig Young.

a very good job. Ruth was married to J. C. Flippen whom I knew so well from having worked with him on the television show "Ensign O'Toole." Pasternak also brought George Sidney back to his home studio to direct.

I thought the casting was great. They signed Shirley Jones to play the young widow and Gig Young to be the naval aviator with whom she finally fell in love and married. The airline pilot brother was Red Buttons and the next-door neighbor that he later marries was the fine actress Carolyn Jones, no relation to Shirley Jones in real life. At that time Carolyn Jones was married to the now super-producer Aaron Spelling and Shirley Jones to the actor Jack Cassidy.

Shirley Jones's crotchety old father was the delightful actor Edgar Buchanan who is probably best known from the television series, "Petticoat Junction," where he was Joe Carson, manager of the Shady Rest Hotel in Hooterville. "Buck," as we called him, was once a practicing dentist and worked at that craft for several years. He finally tired of the drills and went into acting.

This little film was loaded with talent on both sides of the camera. Shirley Jones won the Academy Award for Best Supporting Actress in 1960 for her role of the prostitute in *Elmer Gantry*.

Red Buttons won the Oscar for Best Supporting Actor in 1957 for his portrayal of the tragic air force enlisted man in *Sayonara.*

Carolyn Jones received a nomination for Best Supporting Actress in 1957 for her role in the arty Bohemian swinger in *The Bachelor Party.* Strangely enough, she lost out for the award to Miyosi Umeki that year for her equally tragic part as Red Buttons's Japanese lover in *Sayonara.*

Gig Young went on to win the Oscar for Best Supporting Actor in 1969 for his performance as the dance marathon master of ceremonies in *They Shoot Horses Don't They.* Also, Shirley Jones's eldest son in the film was the then 12-year-old Kurt Russell, who has gone on to bigger and better things since then.

The veteran cameraman on *A Ticklish Affair,* as the film was finally titled, was Milton Krasner, who received Academy Award nominations for his work in 1950 for *All About Eve,* in 1957 for *An Affair to Remember,* in 1963 for *Love with a Proper Stranger,* and again in the same year for his participation on *How the West Was Won.* He was also nominated in 1964 for his work on *Fate Is the Hunter.* I'm pleased to report that he won the Oscar on his own for his artistry in 1954 on *Three Coins in the Fountain.*

The art director on the film was Edward Carfagno who received credit for his work on *Gone with the Wind* and shared the Oscar in 1959 for his contributions to the spectacular *Ben Hur.*

I had now been in charge of the Hollywood office for three years and had already served more than 20 years on active duty as a reserve officer and I did not know just how much longer I would be allowed to stay in the navy. I liked the story of *A Ticklish Affair* so much and, as it was about naval aviation, I decided to serve full time as its technical adviser. I was assigned a desk in the office of the MGM location manager Howard "Dutch" Horton and spent seven weeks on this pleasant assignment.

First, "Dutch" Horton, George Sidney, Ruth Brooks Flippen, and I cruised the entire harbor at San Diego and the Coronado Island area seeking location sites before production actually commenced.

In the story the youngest son had a hobby of going up into the attic and sending out messages on the ship's blinker light his father had given to him. One night, while bored, he started sending out the message SOS.

This international distress signal was interecepted at the nearby naval air station and the command duty officer, Gig Young, led an armed boarding party to investigate the urgent message.

When Gig and his boarding party arrived, they were met by the lovely Shirley Jones, who just could not imagine what the excitement was all about. This first meeting and the love story that follows becomes *A Ticklish Affair* for Shirley.

Gig keeps dropping around, at first on the premise of seeing how the kids are, but it is soon evident that he is interested in her as well. The children really like him and urge her to become serious with him. She fears she is falling for him so she tells the boys she just isn't going to see him anymore.

At this news the youngest boy decides to take matters into his own hands. The next time Red Buttons returns home, the kid begs him to inflate six balloons, instead of the usual three, so he can soar higher and faster in the "moon walking" game. When Red is distracted, the kid unties the tether and begins drifting over the countryside. Shirley and Red watch in alarm and climb into the family convertible to follow him.

This leads to many funny scenes as the youngster drifts silently along. Startled golfers can't believe their eyes when the kid passes over them just as they were making the crucial putt. People walk into each other on the sidewalk and cars crash at intersections as drivers crane their necks to see the young fellow drifting by suspended from his weather balloons.

By now Shirley and Red are leading a procession of about 30 cars as they try to follow the boy. When it becomes evident he is going to drift out to sea, Shirley stops at a pay telephone and calls Gig at the naval air station to tell him of the situation. He alerts an aircraft carrier and it steams to stay under the kid. The coast guard sends about 25 privately owned boats from the coast guard reserve to join in the search.

Finally, Gig goes up in a navy blimp and is lowered down in a harness to try and snag the kid with a boat hook. As a last resort he has a rifle lowered to him and with great care he shoots four of the balloons until the boy is no longer gaining altitude. When the child's progress is stable, he snags him with the hook and they are raised up into the gondola of the blimp. When the blimp lands there is a happy reunion between Shirley and her son.

Well, after all these heroics, she realizes Gig is the man for her and she accepts his offer of marriage. So *A Ticklish Affair* has a happy ending, as all good movies should.

I was pleased to see that MGM hired Busby Berkeley to direct the second unit on the film. Berkeley, of course, is best known for his great dance direction on such movies as *42nd Street* and his spectacular musical numbers with waterfalls and other eye-catching ensembles. I was impressed with him and found he had not lost his mastery after several years of inactivity. I was present when he held his predirection meetings with the stunt drivers for the auto chase and again with the coast guard reserve contingent who were to work at sea around the aircraft carrier.

The 30-car chase was led by Carey Lofton, who was the best of the auto crash experts at the time. I was amazed as Carey and his group piled up the 30 cars in a massive rear-ender-type collision. For instance, one car towed an unseen ramp. When that car stopped, the following vehicle went up and over it and crashed on the side of the road. It was really frightening to watch, but those stunt drivers said it was just part of the job. One of the drivers was a fellow I had known at high school. I asked him what he did when he knew a car was going to crash into him in a few seconds. He said he set his feet on the floorboard, rested his head on the back of the seat, and just relaxed. He said the shock was absorbed by his whole body and he never got hurt. It sure sounds scary to me.

In my capacity as technical adviser I became involved in many phases of filmmaking I had never experienced as an actor. One of these was the production meeting. The day before *A Ticklish Affair* was to start filming, the MGM chief of production called a meeting where the script was gone over, page by page. Present around a large table were director George Sidney, his assistant director, the unit production manager, Ruth Brooks Flippen, Howard "Dutch" Horton, art director Edward Carfagno and his set dresser, director of photography Milton Krasner, the master of properties, the chief grip, the head makeup man, the chief hairdresser, the head driver, and other key craft members.

When my turn came I reported on what I had accomplished to make the navy participation factual and accurate. For instance, I stated I had borrowed the real license plates, decals, and gate passes needed for entrance into North Island Naval Air Station. I also stated that in the sequence where Gig Young leads the armed boarding party into Shirley's home after receiving the SOS message, we were completely covered. I had available the actual helmets, arm brassards, and white cotton–laced leggings that the shore patrol at the North Island Naval Air Station wore at that time.

I also stated that I had six of the actual khaki utility belts, complete with the unique brown leather-flapped holsters and the standard navy issue 45-caliber automatic pistols that the shore patrol wore. This was to show we were authentic, as against the open-holstered 38-caliber six-shooter revolvers worn by cowboys in the old west. They were pleased with my report and it showed I had done my homework.

A Ticklish Affair went real well on the set and I was complimented by navy friends later for having done a nearly complete job as technical adviser. There was one error that snuck through that wasn't really my fault, but sharp-eyed navy friends caught it anyway.

In one scene Shirley Jones told Gig Young that she was also a "navy brat," meaning she had been raised in a navy family. Well, in the navy we call our offspring "navy juniors," and the term "brat" is used among army and air force families to describe their children. This error crept in one night after I had left for the day. Director George Sidney was afraid to have Shilrey say she was a "navy junior" as against "navy brat," without Joe Pasternak's permission. Joe had also left for the day, so my one technical grinch appeared in the film.

Well, nobody is perfect, as Joe E. Brown once said, so I felt I had performed a pretty good job as technical adviser.

74

The Art Director

In the last chapter I described being present at production meetings and working closely with craft experts whom I had never experienced in all my years as an actor.

Looking back at this, I feel that the most vital talent not completely understood by the casual filmgoer is the art director. I remember back in my five years with Cecil B. DeMille, seeing his art director, Edward Jewell, coming on the set with sketches under his arm while he supervised the construction of a room we were soon to work in. Little did I know of the countless hours he had spent making these sets workable for the producer, the director, the cameraman, and the actors.

It wasn't until I worked from day to day with Edward Carfagno on *A Ticklish Affair* that I fully realized what the art director went through to put his artistry on the screen.

For example, in the scene where Gig Young received the SOS message from the young son of Shirley Jones, Ed Carfagno and I went to the real operations office of the North Island Naval Air Station so he could see it. There he made many sketches and took photographs of the office so he could reproduce it later on a sound stage at MGM. While there I was given copies of the actual charts and photos seen on those walls and Ed used them to make the office completely accurate. When he was finished building this set, I assure you any military pilot would feel right at home in his rendition of an air station operations office.

Working with Ed Carfagno on this film reminded me of another time I worked closely with a well-known art director, Hilyard Brown, and this movie was the Doris Day, James Garner picture, *Move Over Darling.* I was most impressed when Hilyard came on the set one day with a large white cardboard panel about 4′×5′ in size. In the very center of the panel was a clip of Miss Day's own blond tresses. Surrounding this bit of hair were samples of everything she would be associated with in the scenes to follow. Over the curly lock was a piece of felt from the hat she was to wear. Her very earrings were pinned beside the hair. Next was a swatch of velvet from her collar and a bit of silk from her dress.

Farther down was a strip of leather from her shoes and above that a sample of the hose she would wear. At the very bottom was a piece of the carpeting those expensive pumps would tread. Down each side of the panel were strips of the wallpaper of the room and they were complemented by splashes of paint from the doors and moldings. Between the wallpaper and clothing samples were strips of the drapes and even bits of brocade from the sofa her lovely frame would rest upon. All this was to ensure that Doris Day would be surrounded by a color scheme that enhanced her natural beauty.

From *Move Over Darling* Hilyard Brown went to Rome where he spent the next two years designing and supervising the construction of all the barges and ships used in the battle scenes in *Cleopatra.* Who can forget the impressive scenes where Elizabeth Taylor as Cleopatra makes her entrance into Rome, seated on her throne, cradled between the arms of a gigantic replica of the Sphinx? This too was a Hilyard Brown creation.

For his artistry on *Cleopatra* Hilyard Brown shared the Academy Award with six other art directors who all combined to make this classic film the most beautiful production of 1963.

I also feel sure that many people are confused with the title of production designer. Basically, an art director is a combination architect and interior decorator; a production designer has greater responsibilities. He also supervises the work of the costume designer and works with the producer, director, and later the cameraman in setting the visual style of the entire production.

The first time I heard of this title was when David O. Selznick awarded it to William Cameron Menzies for his work on *Gone with the Wind.* To quote Selznick: "What I want on *Gone with the Wind,* and what has been done only a few times in picture history is a complete script in sketch form." This demanding task took more than a year and by the time filming started Menzies had submitted 1,500 colored sketches. These were assembled into a giant story board. From them the set builders, costume designers, and the other crafts people went to work. Menzies's right-hand man on the production was the talented art director, Lyle Wheeler.

William Cameron Menzies was a pioneer art director and in the first year of the Academy Awards he received the Oscar for two films he had completed the previous year, *The Dove* and *The Tempest.* The following year he received a nomination for his work on the Douglas Fairbanks thriller, *The Iron Mask.*

There was no award for production designers in 1939, so Lyle Wheeler won the Oscar for art direction in *Gone with the Wind.* For his artistic effort, William Cameron Menzies was presented with a special award for "Outstanding Achievement in the Use of Color for the Enhancement of Dramatic Mood" in the production of *Gone with the Wind.*

For several years there were two awards presented for art direction, one for films made in black and white and another for those filmed in color. Now the award is shared between the art director and his assistant, the set decorator.

Another famous person to receive production designer status was Cecil Beaton for his overall contribution to the success of the Warner Brothers production of *My Fair Lady,* with Rex Harrison and Audrey Hepburn.

Beaton had complete artistic supervision of the Lerner and Lowe stage presentation when it appeared on Broadway and was brought to Hollywood to be given this same distinction on the filmed version of the hit show. It is said he personally designed more than 1,000 costumes for the motion picture.

When Academy Award time came around, Beaton received his own Oscar for costume design and shared the award for art direction with my friend from high school days, Gene Allen. Gene was elected president of the Academy of Motion Picture Arts and Sciences for the years 1984 and 1985 and is presently executive director of the Society of Motion Picture and Television Art Directors.

Another veteran art director who has received production designer status is John De Cuir for his work on *Hello Dolly* at Twentieth Century–Fox in 1969.

De Cuir shared the 1956 Academy Award for art direction with his coworker Lyle Wheeler for *The King and I,* and with six other art directors for *Cleopatra* in 1963.

On *Hello Dolly* De Cuir also received the Oscar as art director with his assistants, Jack Martin Smith and Herman Blumenthal. This is probably the only time in Academy history where a production designer also took credit for art direction.

75

John Ford

Back in Chapter 62 I mentioned John Ford and how he just about took over the Pentagon when he stormed into my office to set up the navy cooperation on *Mr. Roberts.* That was when he told everyone I was the original *Our Gang* comedy kid Fatima and then regaled all with his corny "tits and tigers" joke about his latest film, *Mogambo.*

Soon after Pearl Harbor, John Ford joined the U.S. Navy with the entry rank of lieutenant commander. President Roosevelt appointed Colonel William "Wild Bill" Donovan to be the director of a new government agency called the Office of Strategic Services (OSS) (later renamed the CIA). Donovan selected John Ford to head the Field Photographic Branch. Ford put together a fine unit, including many who had worked for him in Hollywood.

United States Intelligence discovered the Japanese fleet was planning an attack on Midway Island in May 1942. Ford asked to go there and film the attack. His request was approved and he and cameraman Jack McKenzie flew to Midway.

The Japanese fleet attacked and was defeated by the combined efforts of the U.S. Navy, Air Force, and Marines. It was the first major victory for the U.S. forces and a turning point in the war in the Pacific. Ford was wounded and awarded the Legion of Merit, an Air Medal, and the Purple Heart.

In 1945, while Ford was still on active duty, he arranged a leave of absence to direct a motion picture the navy wanted made. It was *They Were Expendable,* the saga of the PT boats that were doing such dangerous work in the Pacific.

He took the project to MGM where he told Louis B. Mayer he would direct the film and get John Wayne to star in it if Mayer would give him the highest salary ever paid to a director up to that time, $250,000. There was another proviso, that Mayer would also make an equal personal contribution of $250,000. He told Mayer he would use the $.5 million to purchase property for a permanent tribute to men who served in his film unit and would call it the Field Photo Farm.

When Mayer asked, "What's the Field Photo Farm?" Ford told him that while he (Mayer) was making movies and money, others, including himself and his OSS film unit, had been fighting the Nazis and the Japanese. Mayer accepted Ford's terms and *They Were Expendable* was made.

My dear friend Robert Parrish writes about the Field Photo Farm in his book *Growing Up in Hollywood* which I think is the best book ever written about the early days in the movie business.

Bob Parrish and I were kid actors in the 1920s and then he became a top-level film director. He joined Ford's OSS unit and was film editor on *The Battle of Midway* which won the Academy Award as best documentary in 1942.

After the war he returned to Hollywood and won his own Academy Award for film editing on *Body and Soul* in 1947. He then turned to directing and has many credits in that field. His favorite is *The Wonderful Country,* starring Robert Mitchum.

True to his word, Ford purchased eight acres in the San Fernando Valley from Columbia Pictures' executive Sam Briskin. It was typical of the many small ranches then located in the valley. It contained a five-bedroom house, a swimming pool, a stable, and a tennis court. Ford converted the stable into an nondenominational chapel. He retained the hitching post, as he said, "In case someone wants to stop and pray when they come in from riding."

One of Ford's dreams was to have a wedding or a funeral at the farm. His first opportunity came when Harry Carey died. When Ford was a novice director of 22, he directed westerns with Carey. They had remained friends ever since.

Although Carey was too old to join John Ford's unit, his son Dobie (Harry Carey, Jr.) served under Ford. As far as John Ford was concerned, Harry Carey deserved a memorial service in the farm's new chapel. Throughout the service, Harry Carey's horse was tied up to the hitching post.

That chapel has now been moved to the grounds of our Motion Picture and Television Country House and Hospital. A few years ago I attended the memorial services there for my friend Viola Dana with whom I had worked at MGM in 1924 in *The Great Love.*

Ford used to gather members of his OSS film unit together at the farm to hold ceremonies on such occasions as Memorial Day and Armistice Day, now called Veterans Day. Each time he did this he asked me to provide a four-man color guard and a bugler. I only had one enlisted man in my office, so I had to call around to my four sources capable of sending me such a special group.

I didn't want to wear out my welcome with local base commanders, so I staggered these requests between the Long Beach Naval Base, the Naval Reserve Training Center in Chavez Ravine, the Naval Air Reserve Station at NAS Los Alamitos, and the Pacific Missile Range at Point Pugu. I was always granted my request when I explained it was for Admiral John Ford.

What Ford didn't think about, or care about, was that five specialized sailors and a car were required at a time when gasoline money was short and that these people were working on a holiday. I also had to see that the men were fed and more than once I had to pick up the tab for their meals.

I'll never forget one night when John Ford himself called me at home around 9:30 P.M. and casually said, "Well Fatima, I suppose everything is all set for the color guard and bugler for our ceremony at the Farm tomorrow morning?"

I told him I knew nothing about any special ceremony and no one had called me to arrange for such an event. Then he stormed, "Didn't that dumb SOB" and then named some poor member of his unit who was probably never told to call me in the first place. John Ford was something else.

I'd better explain one thing before I tell this next story. Ford had very poor eyesight and always wore dark glasses. For the last years of his life he also wore an eye patch over his left eye.

Now to continue. One day the colonel in charge of the army unit in our building asked me to invite Ford and John Wayne to a ceremony where the army would present a plaque to Ford for the many films he had made about the army. This was for *The Long Gray Line,* which honored their academy at West Point, *She Wore a Yellow Ribbon,* and many other army-related classics he had made with John Wayne.

I made the required calls and met John Ford and John Wayne at the front gate of Paramount Studio where the presentation was to take place. As we were walking to the award site, I stepped between them while explaining who they would meet at the ceremony. We had only gone a few paces when Ford turned to me and asked, "Commander, do you always walk on the right side of admirals?"

I was surprised at his unkind remark and said, "I'm sorry Admiral, I just wanted to be on the side where you could see me better." I looked to Duke Wayne for help and he raised his eyes to heaven and said, "Commander, you just said the wrong thing." Wow, that was the only time I ever had an admiral pull rank on me.

While serving as technical adviser on *A Ticklish Affair* at MGM in 1963, Shirley Jones told me a story about John Ford that I am sure has never been printed before. She was on location in Bracketville, Texas, on *Two Rode Together* which also starred James Stewart, Richard Widmark, and Andy Devine.

For years one of the stalwarts of the Ford acting group had been Ward Bond. Ward was not available for this film because he was starring in his own television series, "Wagon Train." While on location in Texas, Ford heard about Ward Bond's death. He shut the film company down for two days while he flew to Los Angeles to attend Bond's funeral.

Shirley told me that she, Jimmy Stewart, and Andy Devine walked Ford to his car to be driven to the airport. She says as Ford was entering the limo, he turned to Andy Devine, looked him straight in the eye and growled, "Now you're the biggest shit I know."

I'm sure poor Andy never forgot this "compliment."

76

"And Darn Well Worth It"

In early 1965 I was notified by the Bureau of Naval Personnel that I would be retired from active duty at the close of the fiscal year on June 30, 1965. This was not a surprise because I had just been passed over for the fifth time for promotion to the rank of commander.

What was disappointing for me was that here I was in the best possible job assignment in the navy for me but I had to go. As I stated earlier, I was an aviator in a nonflying billet. The men on my promotion board were all aviators. They not only would not vote to promote me, but they wanted me to go as they thought I was keeping another aviator from serving on active duty.

When I was passed over the first time I called the chief of information who at the time was Rear Admiral Dan Smith, also a naval aviator, and told him my problem. His personnel people suggested that if I would give up my flight status and become a public information specialist I could remain on active duty to complete 30 years of service and retire with the rank of captain, equal to colonel in the other services.

I considered his offer, but I had five children living at home, all in orthodontia, and the additional $240 a month flight pay was more than I could afford to give up, so I decided to take my chances. I have no regrets. It was a wonderful 23 years and I retired at home at age 49 and was able to get right back into the movie business.

I had been so honest and conscientious in my dealings with the film producers that I did not have a job lined up when I took off my blue uniform.

The first thing I did in civilian life was to serve as technical adviser on a segment of "The Beverly Hillbillies." It was an episode called "Admiral Jed Clampett." Due to its comedy approach to navy life, my former office denied them cooperation and the use of a destroyer that the story called for.

I thought it was not detrimental to the navy, so I offered my assistance and received a handsome fee. I found a destroyer at a drydock in the harbor area about to be scrapped. They painted it up to look like new and it served its purpose. I supervised the construction of the ship's bridge at the studio and, with the help of stock footage, I'm sure the viewing public didn't notice that "Admiral Jed Clampett" never really went to sea.

I noticed there was a small part of the helmsman in the script that had not yet been cast. I asked the director Joe Depew if I could play the part and he gave his okay. Joe and I had been kid actors together and he was happy to give me my first acting role in my new career. Here I had been a navy officer for 23 years and in my first performance I was to play an enlisted man of the lowest rank! Buddy Ebsen has since told me that "Admiral Jed Clampett" is his favorite of all the 216 segments of "The Beverly Hillbillies" that ran on CBS from 1962 to 1971.

At that time "The Addams Family" was being filmed in the same studio. That was the comedy television series where Carolyn Jones played the mother Morticia, John Astin was her husband Gomez, and Jackie Coogan was the ghoulish Uncle Fester, complete with white makeup and a shaved head.

My old friend Jackie Coogan had seen me through the years while I was head of the Navy Hollywood Office and knew that I had a successful second career in the navy. On this day when he saw me in the sailor's uniform and in makeup, he asked, "Junior, are you back in the business?" When I told him I was, he asked me how long it had been since I had made a movie. When I told him 23 years, he said, "God, what a layoff!"

If you don't get the humor here, layoff is the term vaudevillians use meaning the time off between jobs. Jackie, with his razor-sharp wit, was being facetious, of course.

Next, Robert Wise gave me the small part of a nasty American businessman in the auction sequence in the brothel in *The Sand Pebbles* and my new acting career was off and running.

This was where Steve McQueen and Richard Attenborough go to the brothel to claim the Chinese girl being held there in bondage. They have scrimped to save the needed $400, yet when they offer it to the crafty man who ran the place, he tells we three Americans drinking there that we can bid on the girl.

This leads to a big fistfight, and would you believe it, now in my second new performance, I end up fighting Steve McQueen who was an American sailor in the film. I could have been court-martialed for such an offense if it happened while I was on active duty.

While things were looking up for me and I was able to get a good agent right away, I didn't want to depend on acting jobs with all the expenses I had at home. I had the benefit of my navy retirement, but I also wanted a steady paycheck coming in each month.

I went to work for the public relations firm that represented Coca-Cola and my job was to have the then familiar Coke bottle and their vending

My first motion picture after retirement from the navy. I was one of the three nasty American businessmen bidding for the services of the Chinese slave girl in *The Sand Pebbles* for Robert Wise at Twentieth Century–Fox in 1965. I'm at the left in the funny glasses. That is Richard Attenborough in the lower right.

machines seen in films. It was a pleasant assignment. I toured the studios and encouraged the producers, directors, and especially the propmen, to make sure it was Coke on camera when soft drinks were required.

After a year the agency lost the Coke account and I was on my own again. I liked this work and built up a list of clients for my own agency. One was Kentucky Fried Chicken and I received a $6,000 fee for getting Colonel Harlan Sanders a part in a Jerry Lewis film. I also earned $5,000 for getting the original horse-drawn Bekins moving van on camera in *Hello Dolly.*

This venture came to a sad demise because of an illness to Elizabeth Taylor. The lovely Liz was booked to make a film, *The Only Game in Town,* where she was to costar with Frank Sinatra. The locale of the film was Las Vegas, but at the time Richard Burton was making a movie in Europe and Liz didn't want to be too far from him as their marriage was getting shaky. As a result she insisted that the movie be filmed in Paris.

I was granted the product placement on the film and went to Las Vegas where I arranged for all the storefronts seen in the shopping center featured in the film to be shipped to Paris.

Poor Liz became deathly ill and ended up needing a tracheotomy to save her life. Liz was incapacitated for six months. When she was ready to resume work on the motion picture, Frank Sinatra was no longer available. As a result, Liz made this film in Las Vegas with Warren Beatty as her costar because Burton was now in the United States and she wanted to work where Richard was.

I had spent six months working up this film and had made several costly trips to Las Vegas lining up my clients. I was promised $17,000 in comissions from them, but when Miss Taylor decided to make the movie in Las Vegas, all my efforts went down the drain. I decided right then that this was too risky a profession, so again I went looking for a steady job.

I liked the security of government work, so I took and passed the exams for public relations positions with the city of Los Angeles and went to work for the Department of Water and Power. After a year there I left to accept a good paying position at the Los Angeles College of Optometry. I spent a year there, but the college was moving to a new campus in Fullerton and I didn't want to move there. I enjoyed the PR part of the job and being editor of their quarterly alumni magazine, but I didn't like the fundraising, so I left.

There was a student there who was working in television commercials to pay his way through school. He got me interested in television commercials and introduced me to his agents. I signed with them and darned if I didn't get a job after my first interview and made my first TV commercial for Champale Malt Liquor. This was a new approach to show business for me. I worked for one day on the commercial and then the mailman delivered residual checks to the house for the rest of the year.

When I left the college I accepted a fine L.A. city job as special events coordinator at the Port of Los Angeles. This was a dream assignment for me. I was the liaison between the port and the city of San Pedro on such events as the annual Fisherman's Fiesta, the Christmas Parade of Lighted Boats, and all other activities where the port assisted the local community. One of my favorite tasks was handling the arrival of new ships to the harbor. I was there to present the first arrival plaques and as a result, Betty and I had tours and meals on all new ships on their first call at L.A. Harbor.

While in this marvelous position, tragedy struck our house when Betty died in her sleep on the night of February 24, 1974, from a massive internal hemorrhage. After the funeral some of the ladies that Betty played golf with told me she had been seeing a doctor for extreme high blood pressure, but the poor dear never told me about her problem.

I was shattered by her death, but worst of all I was working at the harbor, 46 miles away from home and I still had five children living in my valley home. Fortunately, the position of director of public relations at the Los Angeles Zoo was open and I moved into that slot which was miles closer to home. I could even drive home at lunchtime if an emergency arrived. This was a happy assignment and I jokingly told my friends I had a nice warm cage near the entrance and people patted me on the head and fed me bananas and peanuts as they walked by. I used to sit in on the board of directors' meetings where the lovely Betty White and Jimmy Stewart's wife Gloria were active members.

As usual, I coordinated any visit of a film company on the many times the zoo was a location site. Rock Hudson and Susan Saint James came to the zoo for a segment of "McMillan and Wife," among many others.

One day Arthur H. Nadel, the producer-director of a new television series, "Shazam," came to my office to arrange filming in our zoo. This was the 30-minute show that ran on CBS where Billy Batson was played by Michael Grey and the famous radio actor Les Tremayne was his mentor, the retired Captain Marvel.

Nadel could hardly believe his ears when I told him I had played the original Billy Batson in the Republic serial *Adventures of Captain Marvel* where by uttering the word "shazam," I became "the world's mightiest mortal," Captain Marvel.

Nadel was quick to write a small part in this show for me where I played an animal keeper who drove Michael Grey and Les Tremayne through the zoo in a golf cart while they were searching for some bad boys who needed the help of Captain Marvel.

No doubt the strangest television show I helped with was when producer Ross Hunter wanted to film scenes in the zoo for the pilot film of a new television series, "The Lives of Jenny Dolan," which was to star Shirley Jones.

Hunter's people came to me for suggestions on where best to film. To my surprise, the day before production was to start, the assistant director told me the director had toured the zoo on his own the previous Sunday and he wanted to film in front of a certain cage in the aviary section of the zoo.

It so happened he had chosen the open area in front of the cage that held the only female Philippine monkey-eating eagle in captivity in the entire world.

When I related this to the zoo's curator of birds he nearly had a stroke. He screamed, "Do you realize the excitement caused by the lights and sound equipment and a million other distractions might cause this bird to kill itself by flying into the sides of its cage?"

I passed his decision on to the assistant director and he reported the refusal to Ross Hunter. Hunter's immediate response was, "Buy the bird." Can you imagine, this flamboyant, egotistical producer actually thought we would sell him the only bird of its kind in any zoo in the world if the price was right!

I didn't have the nerve to relay his remark to the curator of birds and just told the assistant director flat out that they would have to find a different spot for their filming. As a result they settled for the fenced-in area of the children's petting zoo where the most valuable animal was a baby goat.

This led to a pleasant experience for Shirley Jones. We were having a happy reunion after the seven weeks I had spent with her on the set at MGM on *A Ticklish Affair*. I asked her if she would like to visit inside the zoo's nursery. I took her in where the public was not allowed and while there she had the pleasure of bottle-feeding a two-month-old baby gorilla whose mother had abandoned it at birth. She was overjoyed at this unique experience.

One day I was sitting at my desk in the zoo when I received a telephone call from Val Sulima, a U.S. Customs executive I had known from my time at the Port of Los Angeles. We chatted for a while, then he asked me how I was getting along and if I had started dating yet. I told him I had not, but was starting to think about it. He knew Betty had passed away eight months prior to this conversation and asked me if I would like to meet a truly lovely lady. He told me his wife's sister Letha was recently divorced and now living in the area and asked if I would like to meet her.

It so happened that Betty and I had sat at the same table with Val and his wife Edwina at harbor functions on three separate occasions. He said he always admired the way I treated Betty and thought I would be a nice fellow for his sister-in-law to meet. This sounded like a good endorsement so I agreed to meet them for dinner the following Saturday night. We met at a restaurant in Long Beach and then went to his house to play bridge after dinner.

I really enjoyed Letha's company, so on Monday I called Val and asked if we could repeat the pleasant evening. We did so, and then I asked her if she would see me again on our own. She agreed and six months later we were married.

Letha had been married to an air force navigator for 26 years and was blessed with five sons. Two of her children were killed in accidents, but at this writing our children have produced 11 grandchildren and I am sure there will be more as three are still unmarried.

From the zoo I had the opportunity to return to the public relations office at the Port of Los Angeles where I moved up to director status. By that time all our children had moved out of the house and Letha and I settled in the home we now occupy in Orange County. We have four bedrooms, three baths, and a pool. Now our grandchildren are in the pool more than we are!

There are two more things I would like to narrate before I close this journal.

In 1977 Norman Lear, who produced such fine television series as "All in the Family," "Maude," and many others, bought the rights to the *Our Gang* comedies and intended to produce a daily 30-minute television series to run five days a week at the 4:00 P.M. time slot aimed at the after-school kids. He is supposed to have interviewed 5,000 children across the country before he finally selected the eight who were to appear in the series.

He found a boy to play Spanky, but never did find anyone who could fill the shoes of the great Alfalfa, so he dropped that name from the cast. None of the white boys or girls chosen, to my knowledge, ever appeared in anything of importance again, but the leading black boy was Gary Coleman, who Lear later starred in his own series, "Diff'rent Strokes."

After many interviews, I was picked to play the role of Officer Witowski, the friendly neighborhood cop. He was a good man who loved the kids even though they drove him nuts at times. This part was played through the years by such fine comedians as Johnny Arthur, Jimmy Finlayson, and the great Edgar Kennedy.

Lear had ten scripts written and we rehearsed them on the actual sets, beginning with script number one and going on to the tenth script. We spent an entire day roughing out the stories from the first scene to the ending. Then we commenced shooting the scripts in the reverse order, from number ten to the first one.

To everyone's dismay, the two scripts that we actually filmed took three days each to complete. This was because the children could only work four hours a day on the set. Due to the strict California child labor laws, they had to have three hours of school and one hour of recreation each day, leaving only four hours for filming. With the limited time the children were available, and also because there was always a dog involved, a daily half-hour show was out of the question. Lear went to the networks and changed his plans, opting to make the series a once-a-week show aimed at the Saturday morning audience. Even this did not please them and his show, "The New Little Rascals," never did come to television.

This was a shame, because the *Little Rascals,* as the two-reel films were called after MGM bought the rights to the Hal Roach–produced *Our Gang* comedies, are still being seen almost daily on television around the country. Our proposed series was so much better. They were modern stories, in color, and not nearly as "slapstick" as the old reruns seen on television today.

Wouldn't that have been the perfect wrap-up to my career? From playing an extra in some of the original *Our Gang* comedies made in 1922, to being the lovable cop in the new television series 55 years later.

My final entry for a happy ending to this book is what is now keeping me gainfully employed. In 1975 I went for an interview and won out over 87 other actors to become the spokesman for Curtis Mathes, a Texas-based television manufacturer. From 1975 to 1981 I was seen in 30 TV commercials for them.

Two years ago I played in an eight-minute film made to recruit franchised dealers back to the newly reorganized company. This film, titled "Frank's Back," tells how in those years while I was their spokesman, sales rose from $32 million to $207 million. I have to feel I was partly responsible for them gaining their share of this highly competitive market.

The company mushroomed and Ray Harvey, who was director of advertising when I was hired, was promoted to become director of manufacturing. In their expansion they brought in the former vice president of advertising for General Electric. This highly qualified man just could not stand to work with the local Dallas advertising agency who had made the company famous. He began a search of other agencies and finally selected Young and Rubicam, one of the nation's largest.

The first thing Y and R did was have me back to Dallas where they reshot the last five commercials I had worked in for the local agency. They were under pressure to make this reshooting as the original five commercials were due to be released on the air in two weeks.

They accomplished this by filming all five commercials in one continuous session. I went to work at 9:00 A.M. and we completed the fifth commercial at 3:00 A.M. the following morning. I was on my feet performing for 18 continuous hours, the longest session I have ever been subjected to in all my years in the business. As you know, the camera does not understand what time it is, so I had to be just as convincing and as exuberant at 3:00 A.M. as I had been 18 hours earlier.

The shame of it was, these five new commercials didn't look any better than the original five the small Dallas agency had made. The people from Young and Rubicam cost Curtis Mathes about $250,000 for this reshoot and the improvements were negligible.

While I was in Dallas, the Y and R people told me I was in their plans for at least the next two years which made me feel very good. However, I

Here is an unusual photo. I'm in front of my own TV set at home while one of my Curtis Mathes television commercials is running. On top of the set is one of the life-sized point of purchase displays that are seen in most of the Curtis Mathes dealerships around the country. The photo on my wall at the upper right is from when Ronald Reagan visited me at NAS Jacksonville in 1951.

soon learned that the bigwigs in the home office of Y and R had already convinced Curtis Mathes, Jr., that he, and only he, could properly represent the company on the air. This appealed to his ego, so he agreed to do the commercials himself.

With all respect to Curtis, he did a fine job on the air and was very convincing in his role as chairman of the board. Curtis was killed in an airline crash three years later. New people came in to manage the company and in less than three years the firm was near bankruptcy.

Now for the good news, and to give my book a really happy ending. Ray Harvey, who was in charge of advertising when I first joined Curtis Mathes, is now president of the company. The first thing he did was to seek out Ron McQuien and Dave Lawson, the two advertising men who had conceived the campaign that had been so successful. They found me and now I am the spokesman again and going into the third year of my new contract.

When I travel around the country attending film festivals, I find that fans are surprised to learn that the Curtis Mathes spokesman they see on the air is really the old kid actor Junior Coghlan.

Curtis Mathes is not represented in every city, but the commercials appear in 43 of our 50 states, so it is as good as network as far as my earnings are concerned.

If you have not seen the commercials, at the end of each I say, "Curtis Mathes, the most expensive television sets in America and darn well worth it."

I'll tell you, it sure has been "darn well worth it" for Letha and me and we are enjoying every minute of it.

Epilogue

It seems strange to me after a now 72-year career in motion pictures and on television, with 425 on-camera appearances, the thing I am best remembered for is my work in serials.

Remember, I starred in silent feature films while under contract to Cecil B. DeMille, then was starred in other feature films for independent producers. I costarred as Sam in *Penrod and Sam,* then starred for two years in the series of comedies, *The Frolics of Youth,* where Shirley Temple played my young sister before going on to her own stardom.

Yet is is mainly my performances in three action serials that is now the prime reason I am being invited as a guest to film festivals around the country.

At the party preceding the release of the fine "Republic Pictures Story," Charles Durning came up to me, held out his hand and said, "You were one of my heroes when I was growing up." Can you imagine receiving such a tribute from that great award-winning actor?

In his fine book on serials, *In the Nick of Time,* William C. Cline tells how in 1966, his then six-year-old daughter asked him, "What's a serial Daddy?" That made him realize if his own daughter knew nothing about his favorite subject, there must be many others in the same boat.

Strangely, I was asked this same question by a 28-year-old man during a panel I was conducting at the Atlanta Film and Memorabilia Fair in September 1991. This was a festival honoring the stars of serials. This young man had paid to attend, yet he had never seen a motion picture serial. We all assumed the closest thing to a filmed serial he had ever seen was watching "Dallas" and other soap operas on television.

Now I am doing my best to interest a new generation in the serials and the "cliffhangers." They are my own grandchildren. When they come to the house, instead of wanting to watch cartoons on television, they always ask to see a chapter or two of one of my serials.

They have seen me wearing war paint as Uncas in *The Last of the Mohicans* with Harry Carey; as Jackie Cooper's pal Ken in *Scouts to the Rescue,* but their favorite is watching me transform into Captain Marvel, "the world's mightiest mortal" by uttering that magic word "Shazam." When the smoke clears, there stands Captain Marvel, who then flies off to protect the innocent.

My daughter Cathy had her children here recently and after viewing a chapter of *Adventures of Captain Marvel,* she said her five-year-old whispered in her ear, "Can Grandpa really fly?" She smiled and answered, "Yes dear, but he can't fly as fast as he used to."

As they say, "Out of the mouths of babes."

Filmography

Since starting in the movies in 1920 when I was still only three years old, I figure I have appeared on camera in 425 motion pictures, television segments, and television commercials. Assembling a complete filmography of all these credits will be most difficult.

From those first appearances in 1920 until I became a featured player a few years later, there must have been at least 75 performances where I was an extra and there is just no way I can gather those titles.

When my five-year contract with Cecil B. DeMille and Pathé ended in 1930 I began keeping a journal that listed every appearance I made up until I entered the navy in 1943. There must have been at least 150 films entered by date, studio, director, and the most important cast members.

Unfortunately, this running record was lost when I had to close out my mother's home in 1952. At best I can recall only about half of those titles. With the help of libraries and reference books like *The American Film Institute Catalog of Feature Films; The Motion Picture Guide;* David Ragan's *Who's Who in Hollywood, 1900–1976* (Arlington House); *The Film Encyclopedia* by Ephraim Katz (Thomas Y. Crowell); and also from loyal fans, I have been able to put together a respectful list of credits. However, I am pleased to report that each appearance made since my retirement from the navy in 1965 to the present has been carefully listed for tax purposes.

One more item worth mentioning is the order of the appearances listed in this filmography. If they seem to vary from the text of this book it is because in the book I list the films in the order that I actually worked in them. Most filmographies are listed by studio release dates as that is the way film historians keep track of them.

For example, I worked for Marshall Neilan in *The Skyrocket* in 1924, but its release date was September 1926. I can easily explain the variance: Neilan directed this film starring Peggy Hopkins Joyce at his own studio in Edendale. Unfortunately, the flamboyant "Mickey" Neilan ran short of money and he could not come up with the post-production costs, so the production was dormant for two years. Then he went to MGM where he wrote and directed *The Great Love* and *Mike.* With the funds he earned from these he went back and completed the post-production on *The Skyrocket* so it could be released to the theaters. Also you will note that *Mike* was released in 1926. It was made in early 1925 and I had moved to my Cecil B. DeMille contract and completed three motion pictures there that were released before *Mike* left the confines of the MGM studio vaults.

So, with that in mind, I will list the following films by their studio release dates so as to not be at variance with the Library of Congress. To avoid repetition I have left my name out of these cast listings, but I assure you, I appeared in each of these productions. The names immediately following the direction and or production credits are the cast members.

1920 *Mid Channel.* Garson Studios/Equity Pictures Corporation. Director Harry Garson. Cast: Clara Kimball Young, J. Frank Glendon, Bertram Grassby, Eileen Robinson, Helen Sullivan, Katherine Griffith, Jack Livingston.

1920 *To Please One Woman.* Paramount. Producer-director-writer Lois Weber. Claire Windsor, George Hackathorne, Edith Kessler, Edward Burns.

1920 *The Suitor.* Short subject. Vitagraph. Directors Larry Semon and Norman Taurog. Larry Semon.

1921 *Rookies.* Short subject. Century Studio. Released through Universal November 1922. Director Alf Goulding. Buddy Williams.

1921 *The Poverty of Riches.* Goldwyn. Director Reginald Barker. Richard Dix, Leatrice Joy, Louise Lovely, John Bowers, Irene Rich, De Witt Jennings, Frankie Lee, Dorothy Hughes, Roy Laidlaw, John Cossar.

1922 *The Sin Buster.* Short subject. Universal. Director R. N. Bradbury. Tom Santschi. This must be a working title as it is not listed in the Library of Congress.

1922 *Bobbed Hair.* Relart Pictures. Released by Paramount. Director Thomas N. Heffron. Wanda Hawley, William Carleton, William Boyd, Adele Farrington, Leigh Wynant, Jane Starr, Ethel Wales, Robert Kelly.

1922 *Bow Wow.* Mack Sennett–First National. Director Fred W. Jackman. Louise Fazenda, John Henry, Jr., Teddy the dog.

1922 *Our Gang* comedies. Short subjects. Hal Roach. Director Robert F. McGowan. I played as an extra in three of the comedies in their first year of production including *Giants vs. Yanks,* Pathé, 1923.

1923 *Our Alley.* Comedy by Arrow Film Corporation. Producer Eddie Lyons. Director Eugene De Rue. Bobby Dunn, Glen Cavender.

1923 *The Fourth Musketeer.* R.C. Pictures–FBO. Director William K. Howard. Johnnie Walker, Eileen Percy, Eddie Gribbon, William Scott, Edith Yorke, Georgie Stone, James McElhern.

1923 *Little Old New York.* Goldwyn/Cosmopolitan. Director Sidney Olcott. Marion Davies, Stephen Carr, J. M. Kerrigan, Harrison Ford, Courtnay Foote, Sam Hardy, Spencer Charters, Harry Watson, Louis Wolheim, Charles Judels.

1923 *The Spanish Dancer.* Famous Players–Lasky. Distributed by Paramount. Producer Adolph Zukor. Director Herbert Brenon. Pola Negri, Antonio Moreno, Wallace Beery, Adolphe Menjou, Kathlyn Williams, Gareth Hughes, Edward Kipling, Charles A. Stevenson, Robert Agnew, Dawn O'Day—who was known later as Anne Shirley.

1923 *The Darling of New York.* Universal. Director King Baggot. Baby Peggy Montgomery, Sheldon Lewis, Gladys Brockwell, Frank Currier.

1923 *A Woman of Paris.* United Artists. Producer and director Charlie Chaplin. Edna Purviance, Adolphe Menjou, Carl Miller, Lydia Knott.

1923 *Cause for Divorce.* Distributed by Selznick Distribution Corporation. Producer and director Hugh Dierker. David Butler, Fritzi Brunette, Charles Clary, Helen Lynch, Pat O'Malley, Peter Burke, Cleve Moore, James O. Barrows, Harmon MacGregor.

1923 *The Law of the Lawless.* Famous Players–Lasky. Director Victor Fleming. Dorothy Dalton, Theodore Kosloff, Charles De Roche, Tully Marshall, Fred Huntley, Margaret Loomis.

1923 *Garrison's Finish.* Jack Pickford Productions. Director Arthur Rosson. Jack Pickford, Madge Bellamy, Charles A. Stevenson, Tom Guise, Frank Elliot, Clarence Burton, Audrey Chapman, Dorothy Manners, Ethel Grey Terry, Herbert Price, Charles Ogle, Lydia Knott.

1924 *Winning His Way.* Short subject. Universal. Jack Dempsey, Hayden Stevenson.

1924 See above regarding *The Skyrocket* and *The Great Love* chronology.

1925 *The Great Circus Mystery.* A Universal serial in 15 chapters. Director Jay Marchant. Joe Bonomo, Louise Lorraine.

1925 *The Great Love.* MGM. Director-writer Marshall Neilan. Robert Agnew, Viola Dana, Frank Currier, ZaSu Pitts, Chester Conklin, Malcolm Waite, Norma the elephant.

1925 *The Road to Yesterday.* Producers Distributing Corporation. Producer and director Cecil B. DeMille. Joseph Schildkraut, Jetta Goudal, Vera Reynolds, William Boyd, Julia Faye, Casson Ferguson, Trixie Friganza, Clarence Burton, Josephine Norman, Charles West, Iron Eyes Cody, Walter Long, Dick Sutherland, Chester Morris, Sally Rand.

1925 *Whispering Smith.* Released by Metropolitan. Producer Cecil B. DeMille. Director George Melford. H. B. Warner, John Bowers, Lillian Rich, Will Walling, Lilyan Tashman, Eugene Pallette, Robert Edeson, James Mason, Richard R. Neill.

1926 *Her Man o' War.* Producers Distributing Corporation (PDC). Producer Cecil B. DeMille. Director Frank Urson. Jetta Goudal, William Boyd, Grace Deslys, Frank Riecher, Grace Darmond, Robert Edeson, Jimmie Adams, Michael Vavitch.

1926 *Mike.* MGM. Director-writer Marshall Neilan. William Haines, Sally O'Neil, Charles Murray, Ford Sterling, Ned Sparks, Frankie Darro, Muriel Francis Dana.

1926 *The Skyrocket.* Celebrity Films. Director Marshall Neilan. Screenplay by Associated Exhibitors Benjamin Glazer from the book by Adela Rogers St. Johns. Peggy Hopkins Joyce, Charles West, Gladys Brockwell, Owen Moore, Muriel McCormack, Gladys Hulette, Paulette Duval, Lilyan Tashman, Earle Williams, Bernard Randall, Bull Montana, Arnold Gregg, Ben Hall, Nick Dandau, Eddie Dillon, Hank Mann.

1927 *Rubber Tires.* Cecil B. DeMille–PDC. Director Alan Hale. Bessie Love, Harrison Ford, May Robson, Erwin Connelly, John Patrick, Clarence Burton.

1927 *The Yankee Clipper.* Cecil B. DeMille–PDC. Director Rupert Julian. William Boyd, Elinor Fair, John Miljan, Walter Long, Stanton Heck.

1927 *The Country Doctor.* Cecil B. DeMille–PDC. Director Rupert Julian. Rudolph Schildkraut, Virginia Bradford, Frank Marion, Gladys Brockwell, Sam de Grasse, Jane Keckley, Ethel Wales.

1927 *Slide, Kelly, Slide.* On loan out to MGM. Director Edward Sedgwick. William Haines, Sally O'Neil, Harry Carey, Karl Dane, Paul Kelly, Guinn (Big Boy) Williams, Warner Richmond, and Johnny Mack Brown in his first motion picture.

1927 *The Last Frontier.* Cecil B. DeMille–PDC. Director George B. Seitz. William Boyd, Marguerite de la Motte, J. Farrell MacDonald as Wild Bill Hickok, Jack Hoxie as Buffalo Bill, Gladys Brockwell, Frank Lackteen.

1927 *A Harp in Hock.* Pathé. Director Renaud Hoffman. Rudolph Schildkraut, May Robson, Bessie Love, Joseph Striker, Elise Bartlett.

1928 *Marked Money.* Pathé. Director Spencer Gordon Bennet. George Duryea, Virginia Bradford, Tom Kennedy, Burt Woodruff, Maurice Black, Jack Richardson.

1928 *Let 'er Go Gallegher.* Pathé. Director Elmer Clifton. Harrison Ford, Elinor Fair, Ivan Lebedeff, Wade Boteler, E. H. Calvert.

1929 *Square Shoulders.* Pathé. Director E. Mason Hopper. Louis Wolheim, Anita Louise, Philippe de Lacy, Montague Shaw, Johnny Morris, Clarence Geldert, Maurice Black, Kewpie Morris, Erich Von Stroheim, Jr.

1930 *The Girl Said No.* MGM. Director Sam Wood. William Haines, Leila Hyams, Francis X. Bushman, Jr., William V. Mong, Phyllis Crane, William Janney, Clara Blandick, Polly Moran, and Marie Dressler who stole the picture with her short sequence as a drunken millionairess.

1930 *River's End.* Warner Brothers. Director Michael Curtiz. Charles Bickford, Evalyn Knapp, J. Farrell MacDonald, ZaSu Pitts, David Torrence, Walter McGrail, Tom Santschi.

1931 *Penrod and Sam.* Warner Brothers. Director William Beaudine. Leon Janney was Penrod and I played Sam. Matt Moore, Dorothy Peterson, Helen Beaudine, ZaSu Pitts, Johnny Arthur, Wade Boteler, Charles Sellon, Nestor Aber, Billy Lord, Margaret Marquis, Betty Graham, Robert Dandridge, James Robinson, Duke the dog.

1931 *Public Enemy.* Warner Brothers. Director William A. Wellman. James Cagney, Edward Woods, Jean Harlow, Joan Blondell, Beryl Mercer, Donald Cook, Mae Clarke, Leslie Fenton. I played James Cagney as a boy in the prologue and Frankie Darro was Edward Woods as a boy.

1931 A Bobby Jones golf short. Warner Brothers. Director George Marshall.

1931 *It Pays to Advertise.* Paramount. Director Frank Tuttle. Carole Lombard, Norman Foster, Richard "Skeets" Gallagher, Eugene Pallette, Louise Brooks, Lucien Littlefield.

1932 *Union Depot.* Warner Brothers. Director Alfred E. Green. From a screenplay by Gene Fowler. Douglas Fairbanks, Jr., Joan Blondell, Alan Hale, Frank McHugh, George Rosener, Guy Kibbee, David Landau.

1932 *Hell's House.* A Bennie F. Zeidman Production. Director-writer Howard Higgin. Junior Durkin, Pat O'Brien, Bette Davis (I received equal billing with Miss Davis), Charles Grapewin, Emma Dunn, Morgan Wallace, Hooper Atchley, Wallace Clark, James Marcus, Mary Alden.

1932 *Racetrack.* James Cruze–World Wide Pictures. Director James Cruze. Leo Carrillo, Kay Hammond, Lee Moran, Huntley Gordon, Wilfrid Lucas, Joseph Girard. I rode my first race as a jockey in this film.

1932 *The Last of the Mohicans.* A serial in 12 chapters by Mascot Productions. Directors Ford Beebe and Reeves "Breezy" Eason. Harry Carey, Hobart Bosworth, Edwina Booth, Lucille Brown, Walter Miller, Walter McGrail, Mischa Auer, Nelson McDowell, Bob Kortman. I played Uncas, the last of the Mohicans.

1933 *Drum Taps.* KBS for Tiffany Studios. Director J. P. McGowan. Ken Maynard, Kermit Maynard.

1933 *Fireman Save My Child.* Warner Brothers. Director Lloyd Bacon. Joe E. Brown, Evalyn Knapp, Lillian Bond, Guy Kibbee, George Ernest, Dickie Moore.

1933 *This Day and Age.* Paramount. Produced and directed by Cecil B. DeMille. Charles Bickford, Judith Allen, Richard Cromwell, Harry Green, Eddie Nugent, Ben Alexander, Oscar Rudolph, Billy Gilbert, Lester Arnold, Fuzzy Knight, Wade Boteler, Bradley Page, Harry C. Bradley, Louise Carter, Guy Usher, Charles Middleton, Warner Richmond, Arthur Vinton, Nella Walker, Mickey Daniels, Samuel S. Hinds, Donald Barry, Michael Stuart, George Barbier, Onest Conly, Howard Lang.

1933 and 1934 *The Frolics of Youth.* Educational. Director Charles Lamont. I played the lead in nine comedies of this high school–age series. See Chapter 29 regarding the fluctuating cast members. The titles of the four shorts in which Shirley Temple appeared are *Merrily Yours, Pardon My Pups, What's to Do,* and *Managed Money.* The title of the short that featured the Poodles Hanneford Family equestrian act is *The Little Big Top.*

1934 *In the Money.* Invincible. Director Frank Strayer. Richard "Skeets" Gallagher, Lois Wilson, Warren Hymer, Sally Starr, Arthur Hoyt, Erin La Bissonler, Harold Waldridge, Louise Beavers.

1935 *Kentucky Blue Streak.* C. C. Burr Productions. Director Raymond K. Johnson. Edward Nugent, Patricia Scott, Roy D'Arcy, Margaret Mann, Cornelius Keefe, Roy Watson, Joseph W. Girard.

1935 *Happiness C.O.D.* Chesterfield. Director Charles Lamont. Donald Meek, Maude Eburne, Irene Ware, William Bakewell, Polly Ann Young, Lona Andre,

Malcolm MacGregor, Edwin Maxwell, Robert McKenzie, Fred Sumner, Richard Carlyle, John Dilson.

1935 *Stranded.* Warner Brothers. Director Frank Borgzage. George Brent, Kay Francis, Patricia Ellis, Donald Woods, Robert Barrat, Barton MacLane.

1936 *Make Way for a Lady.* RKO. Director David Burton. Anne Shirley, Herbert Marshall, Gertrude Michael, Margot Grahame, Taylor Holmes, Mary Jo Ellis, Clara Blandick, Murray Kinnell.

1936 *Melody in May.* Short subject. RKO. Director Ben Holmes. Ruth Etting, Margaret Armstrong, Ken Howell, Robert Meredith, Joan Sheldon.

1936 *The New Average Man.* Short subject. RKO. Director Les Goodwins. Edgar Kennedy, Rosita Butler, Jan Duggan, Tempe Piggott, Pat O'Malley, Vivian Oakland, Harry Bowan.

1936 *Charlie Chan at the Racetrack.* Twentieth Century–Fox. Director H. Bruce Humberstone. Warner Oland, Keye Luke, Helen Wood, Thomas Beck, Alan Dinehart, Gavin Muir, Gloria Roy, Jonathan Hale, G. P. Huntley, Jr., George Irving, Frankie Darro, John Rogers, John Hallen, Harry Jang, Jack Mulhall.

1936 *The Little Red Schoolhouse.* Chesterfield. Director Charles Lamont. Ann Doran, Lloyd Hughes, Dickie Moore, Sidney Miller, Richard Carle, Ralf Harolde, Frank Sheridan, Ken Howell, Mathew Betz, Corky the dog.

1937 *Blazing Barriers.* Monogram. Director Aubrey Scotto. I starred and was billed as Frank Coghlan, Jr., for the first time. Edward Arnold, Jr., Florine McKinney, Addison Randall, Milburn Stone.

1937 *Saturday's Heroes.* RKO. Producer Robert Sisk. Director Edward Killy. Van Heflin, Marian Marsh, Richard Lane, Alan Bruce, Minor Watson, Frank Jenks, Willie Best, Walter Miller, Crawford Weaver, George Irving, John Arledge, Dick Hogan, Al St. John, Charles Trowbridge, Jack Mulhall.

1937 *Red Lights Ahead.* Chesterfield. Director Roland Reed. Andy Clyde, Lucile Gleason, Roger Imhoff, Ben Alexander, Paula Stone, Ann Doran, Addison Randall.

1938 *Scouts to the Rescue.* A serial in 12 chapters. Universal. Producer Henry MacRae. Director Ray Taylor and Alan James. Jackie Cooper, Vondell Barr, Bill Cody, Jr., Sidney Miller, David Durand, William Ruhl, Ivan Miller, Edwin Stanley, Ralph Dunn, Jack Mulhall, Jason Robards, Sr., George Regas, Jim Hussey, Emmett Vogan, Sam Bernard, Dick Botelier.

1938 *Angels with Dirty Faces.* Warner Brothers. Director Michael Curtiz. James Cagney, Pat O'Brien, Ann Sheridan, The Dead End Kids.

1938 *Brother Rat.* Warner Brothers. Director William Keighley. Ronald Reagan, Priscilla Lane, Jane Wyman, Wayne Morris, Eddie Albert, William Tracy.

1938 *Love Finds Andy Hardy.* MGM. Director George B. Seitz. Mickey Rooney, Lewis Stone, Judy Garland, Cecilia Parker, Fay Holden, Ann Rutherford, Betsy Ross Clarke, Lana Turner, Marie Blake, Don Castle, Gene Reynolds, Mary Howard, George Breakstone, Raymond Hatton, Frank Darien, Rand Brooks, Erville Alderson.

1938 *His Exciting Night.* Universal. Producer Ken Goldsmith. Director Gus Meins. Charles Ruggles, Richard Lane, Stepin Fetchit, Maxie Rosenbloom, Marian

Martin, Ona Munson, Frances Robinson, Regis Toomey, Georgia Caine, Benny Baker, Eddie Acuff, Raymond Parker, Stanley Hughes, Virginia Sale, Mary Field, Frank Sully.

1938 *Service de Luxe.* Universal. Producer-director Rowland V. Lee. Constance Bennett, Vincent Price, Charles Ruggles, Helen Broderick, Mischa Auer, Joy Hodges.

1939 *Angels Wash Their Faces.* Warner Brothers. Director Ray Enright. Ann Sheridan, Ronald Reagan, Bonita Granville, The Dead End Kids, Frankie Thomas, Henry O'Neill, Eduardo Ciannelli, Burton Churchill, Minor Watson, Margaret Hamilton, Jackie Searle, Bernard Nedell, Cy Kendall, Dick Rich, Grady Sutton, Aldrich Bowker, Marjorie Main, Robert Strange.

1939 *Off the Record.* Warner Brothers. Director James Flood. Pat O'Brien, Joan Blondell, Bobby Jordan, Alan Baxter, William B. Davidson, Morgan Conway, Clay Clement, Selmer Jackson, Addison Richards, Pierre Watkin, Douglas Wood, Armand Kaliz, Sarah Padden, Howard Hickman, Mary Gordon, Lottie Williams, David Durand, Norman Phillips, Jr., Tommy Bupp, Wade Boteler, Sibyl Harris, Stanley Fields, Emmett Vogan, Al Hill, Jr., William Gould.

1939 *Andy Hardy Gets Spring Fever.* MGM. Director W. S. Van Dyke II. Mickey Rooney, Lewis Stone, Cecilia Parker, Fay Holden, Ann Rutherford, Sara Haden, Helen Gilbert, Terry Kilburn, John T. Murray, George Breakstone, Charles Peck, Sidney Miller, Addison Richards, Olaf Hytten, Erville Alderson, Robert Kent.

1939 *Lucky Night.* MGM. Director Norman Taurog. Myrna Loy, Robert Taylor, Marjorie Main, Douglas Fowley, Henry O'Neill, Charles Lane, Bernardine Hayes, Lillian Rich, Edward Gargan, Frank Faylen, Irving Bacon.

1939 *Meet Dr. Christian.* RKO. Director Bernard Vorhaus. Jean Hersholt, Dorothy Lovett, Robert Baldwin, Enid Bennett, Paul Harvey, Marcia Mae Jones, Jackie Moran, Maude Eburne, Patsy Lee Parsons, Sarah Edwards, John Kelly, Eddie Acuff.

1939 *Boy's Reformatory.* Monogram. Producer Lindsley Parsons. Director Howard Bretherton. Frankie Darro, Grant Withers, David Durand, Warren McCollum, Albert Hill, Jr., Bob McClung, George Offerman, Jr., Ben Weldon, Lillian Elliot.

1939 *Daytime Wife.* Twentieth Century–Fox. Director Gregory Ratoff. Tyrone Power, Linda Darnell, Binnie Barnes, Joan Davis, Wendy Barrie, Warren Williams.

1939 *Second Fiddle.* Twentieth Century–Fox. Producer Gene Markey. Director Sidney Lanfield. Sonja Henie, Tyrone Power, Edna May Oliver, Rudy Vallee.

1939 *Golden Gloves.* Paramount. Director Edward Dmytryk. Richard Denning, J. Carrol Naish, Jeanne Cagney, Robert Paige, William Frawley, Edward S. Brophy, Robert Ryan, George Ernest, David Durand, James Seay, Sidney Miller, Alec Craig, Pierre Watkin, Leona Roberts, Lorraine Krueger, Thomas E. Jackson, Johnnie Morris.

1939 *East Side of Heaven.* Universal. Director David Butler. Bing Crosby, Joan Blondell, Mischa Auer, C. Aubrey Smith, Irene Hervey, Jerome Cowan, Baby Sandy.

1939 *The Flying Irishman.* RKO. Director Leigh Jason. Douglas Corrigan, Eddie Quillan, Paul Kelly, Robert Armstrong, Gene Reynolds, Donald McBride, J. M. Kerrigan, Dorothy Peterson, Scotty Beckett, Joyce Compton, Dorothy Appleby, Minor Watson, Cora Witherspoon, Spencer Charters, Peggy Ryan.

1939 *Two Bright Boys.* Universal. Director Joseph Santley. Jackie Cooper, Freddie Bartholomew, Melville Cooper, Dorothy Peterson, Alan Dinehart, Willard Robertson, J. M. Kerrigan, Eddie Acuff.

1939 *Chicken Feed.* A comedy short subject. RKO. Director Jean Yarborough. Billy Gilbert, Dick Elliott, William Benedict.

1939 *It's a Wonderful World.* MGM. Writers Ben Hecht, Herman J. Mankiewicz. Director W. S. Van Dyke II. James Stewart, Claudette Colbert, Guy Kibbee, Nat Pendleton, Frances Drake, Edgar Kennedy, Ernest Truex, Richard Carle.

1939 *Gone with the Wind.* Selznick-International, released by MGM. Directors Victor Fleming, Sam Wood. (George Cukor started directing but was replaced by Victor Fleming. Sam Wood came in for a period when Fleming became ill.) Vivien Leigh, Clark Gable, Leslie Howard, Olivia de Havilland, Thomas Mitchell, Barbara O'Neil, Evelyn Keyes, Ann Rutherford, George Reeves, Fred Crane, Hattie McDaniel, Butterfly McQueen, Ben Carter, Victor Jory, Everett Brown, Zack Williams, Howard Hickman, Alicia Rhett, Rand Brooks, Carroll Nye, Marcella Martin, Marjorie Reynolds, Laura Hope Crews, Eddie Anderson, Harry Davenport, Jackie Moran, Jane Darwell, Mary Anderson, Ona Munson, Cliff Edwards, Ed Chandler, Roscoe Ates, John Arledge, Eric Linden, Tom Tyler, William Bakewell, Lee Phelps, Paul Hurst, Ernest Whitman, William Stelling, Louis Jean Heydt, Isabel Jewell, Robert Elliott, George Meeker, Wallis Clark, Irving Bacon, Adrian Morris, J. M. Kerrigan, Olin Howland, Yakima Canutt, Blue Washington, Ward Bond, Phyllis Callow, Cammie King, Mickey Kuhn, Lillian Kemble-Cooper, Tommy Kelly, Patrick Curtis, Ricky Holt.

1940 *Free, Blonde and Twenty-One.* Twentieth Century–Fox. Director Ricardo Cortez, Lynn Bari, Mary Beth Hughes, Joan Davis, Henry Wilcoxon, Robert Lowery.

1940 *Remedy for Riches.* RKO. Director Erle C. Kenton. Jean Hersholt, Dorothy Lovett, Edgar Kennedy, Jed Prouty, Walter Catlett, Robert Baldwin, Warren Hull, Maude Eburne, Margaret Wade, Hallene Hill, Renie Riano, Barry Macollum, Lester Scharaff (Sharp), Prudence Penny, Stanley Blystone, Tom Herbert, Maynard Holmes, Dick Rush, Edward Hearn.

1940 *Love Thy Neighbor.* Paramount. Producer and director Mark Sandrich. Jack Benny, Fred Allen, Mary Martin, Eddie "Rochester" Anderson, Verree Teasdale, Virginia Dale, Richard Denning.

1940 *Murder over New York.* Twentieth Century–Fox. Director Harry Lachman. Sidney Toler as Charlie Chan, Marjorie Weaver, Robert Lowery, Ricardo Cortez, Donald MacBride, Melville Cooper, Joan Valerie, Kane Richmond, Victor Sen Yung, John Sutton, Leyland Hodgson, Clarence Muse, Frederick Worlock, Lal Chand Mehra.

1940 *Star Dust.* Twentieth Century–Fox. Director Walter Lang. Linda Darnell, John Payne, Roland Young, Charlotte Greenwood, Mary Beth Hughes, Donald Meek, William Gargan.

1940 *Those Were the Days.* Paramount. Producer and director J. Theodore Reed. William Holden, Bonita Granville, Ezra Stone, Judith Barratt, Vaughn Glaser, Lucien Littlefield, Richard Denning, Alan Ladd, James Dodd, Janet Waldo, Rod Cameron, Cyril Ring.

1940 *The Fighting 69th.* Warner Brothers. Director William Keighley. James Cagney, Pat O'Brien, George Brent, Jeffery Lynn, Alan Hale, Frank McHugh, Dennis Morgan, Dick Foran, William Lundigan, Guinn (Big Boy) Williams, John Litel, Henry O'Neill.

1940 *Knute Rockne—All American.* Warner Brothers. Producer Hal B. Wallis. Director Lloyd Bacon. Pat O'Brien, Gale Page, Ronald Reagan, Donald Crisp, Albert Basserman, John Litel, Henry O'Neill, Owen Davis, Jr., John Qualen, Kane Richmond.

1940 *Double Alibi.* Universal. Director Philip Rosen. Wayne Morris, Margaret Lindsay, William Gargan, Roscoe Karns, Robert Emmet Keane, James Burke, William Pawley, Frank Mitchell, Eddy Chandler, Cliff Clark, Robert Emmett O'Connor, Wade Boteler, Mary Treen.

1941 *Uncle Joe.* John Deere industrial film. Wilding Pictures Productions. ZaSu Pitts, Slim Summerville, Gale Storm, Maynard Holmes, Dick Hogan, Jimmy Butler.

1941 *Men of Boys Town.* MGM. Producer John W. Considine, Jr. Director Norman Taurog. Spencer Tracy, Mickey Rooney, Bobs Watson, Larry Nunn, Darryl Hickman, Henry O'Neill, Mary Nash, Lee J. Cobb, Sidney Miller, Addison Richards, Lloyd Corrigan, George Lessey, Robert Emmet Keane, Arthur Hohl, Ben Welden, Anne Revere.

1941 *Adventures of Captain Marvel.* A 12-episode serial by Republic Pictures. Associate producer Hiram S. Brown, Jr. Directors William Witney, John English. Captain Marvel was played by Tom Tyler and I was Billy Batson, the young radio reporter who was transformed into Captain Marvel, "the world's mightiest mortal," by uttering the magic name "Shazam." Other cast members were William Benedict, Louise Currie, John Davidson, Reed Hadley, Robert Strange, Harry Worth, Peter George Lynn, George Pembroke, Nigel de Brulier, Jack Mulhall, Augie Gomez, Al Taylor, Eddie Dew, Carl Zwolsman, Marten Lamont, Major Sam Harris, Leyland Hodgson, Bryant Washburn, Sr., Curley Dresden, Kenne Duncan, John Bagni, Carlton Young, Stanley Price, Dick Crockett, Loren Riebe, Duke Taylor, Jerry Jerome, Tetsu Komai, Francis Sayles, James Fawcett, Ken Terrell, George Suzanne, Earl Bunn, Frank Marlowe, Frank Wayne, Edward Cassidy, Chuck Morrison, Ted Mapes, Al Kikume, Ernest Sarracino, Paul Lopez, Armand Cortez, and Gerald Mohr as the voice of the Scorpion.

1941 *Out of the Fog.* Warner Brothers. Director Anatole Litvak. Ida Lupino, John Garfield, Thomas Mitchell, Eddie Albert.

1941 *Henry Aldrich for President.* Paramount. Director Hugh Bennett. Jimmy Lydon, Charles Smith, June Preisser, Mary Anderson, Martha O'Driscoll, Dorothy Peterson, John Litel, Rod Cameron, Luciene Littlefield, Kenneth Howell, Buddy Pepper, Vaughn Glaser, Dick Paxton, Lon (Bud) McCallister, Irving Bacon, Sidney Miller, Noel Neill, Jean Porter, Helen Westcott, Carmencita Johnson.

1941 *Unfinished Business.* Universal. Producer and director Gregory La Cava. Irene Dunne, Robert Montgomery, Eugene Pallette, Preston Foster, Walter Catlett.

1941 *The Man Who Came to Dinner.* Warner Brothers. Director William Keighley. Bette Davis, Monty Woolley, Ann Sheridan, Jimmy Durante, Reginald Gardiner, Richard Travis, Billie Burke, Grant Mitchell, Ruth Vivian, Mary Wickes, George Barbier, Elisabeth Fraser.

1942 *Pardon My Stripes.* Republic Pictures. Director John H. Auer. William Henry, Sheila Ryan, Edgar Kennedy, Harold Huber, Paul Hurst, Cliff Nazarro, Tom Kennedy, Edwin Stanley, Dorothy Granger, George McKay, Maxine Leslie.

1942 *Andy Hardy's Double Life.* MGM. Director George B. Seitz. Mickey Rooney, Lewis Stone, Cecilia Parker, Fay Holden, Ann Rutherford, Sara Haden, Esther Williams, William Lundigan, Robert Pittard, Bobby Blake, Susan Peters.

1942 *The Courtship of Andy Hardy.* MGM. Director George B. Seitz. Mickey Rooney, Lewis Stone, Cecilia Parker, Fay Holden, Ann Rutherford, Sara Haden, Donna Reed, William Lundigan, Steve Cornell, Frieda Inescourt, Harvey Stephens.

1942 *Rings on Her Fingers.* Twentieth Century–Fox. Director Rouben Mamoulian. Gene Tierney, Henry Fonda, Laird Cregar, Spring Byington.

1942 *Footlight Serenade.* Twentieth Century–Fox. Director Gregory Ratoff. Betty Grable, John Payne, Victor Mature, James Gleason, Phil Silvers, Jane Wyman.

1942 *Girl Trouble.* Twentieth Century–Fox. Director Harold Schuster. Don Ameche, Joan Bennett, Billie Burke, Frank Craven, Alan Dinehart.

1942 *To the Shores of Tripoli.* Twentieth Century–Fox. Director Bruce Humberstone. John Payne, Maureen O'Hara, Randolph Scott, Nancy Kelly.

1942 *Lady in a Jam.* Universal. Producer and director Gregory La Cava. Irene Dunne, Ralph Bellamy, Patric Knowles, Eugene Pallette, Samuel Hinds.

1942 *The Court Martial.* An army training film.

1943 *The Rear Gunner.* An army training film. Warner Brothers. Director Ray Enright. Burgess Meredith, Dane Clark.

1943 *This Is the Army.* Warner Brothers. Producer Hal B. Wallis. Director Michael Curtiz. George Murphy, Joan Leslie, Irving Berlin, George Tobias, Alan Hale, Ronald Reagan, Kate Smith, Joe Louis, Rosemary de Camp, Frances Langford, Gertrude Niesen.

1943 *Youth on Parade.* Republic. Producer Albert J. Cohen. Director Albert S. Rogell. John Hubbard, Martha O'Driscoll, Bruce Langley, Ruth Terry, Charles Smith, Nana Bryant, Ivan Simpson, Chick Chandler, Paul Fix, Lynn Merrick, John Boyle, Jr., Marlyn Schild, Eddie Acuff, Sue Robin, Ruth Daye, Edward Earle, Betty Atkinson, Harry Hayden, Walter Soderling, Yvonne de Carlo, Boyd Irwin, Walter Fenner, Alfred Hall, Elmer Jerome, Maurice Cass, Barbara Slater, Ben Lessy, Warren Ashe, Jack Boyle, Ivan Miller.

1943 *Corvette K-225.* Universal. Producer Howard Hawks. Director Richard Rosson. Randolph Scott, James Brown, Ella Raines, Barry Fitzgerald, Andy Devine, Richard Lane, Fuzzy Knight, Noah Beery, Jr., Thomas Gomez, David

Bruce, Murray Alper, James Flavin, Walter Sande, Holmes Herbert, John Frederick, Oscar O'Shea, Robert Mitchum, Milburn Stone, Addison Richards.

1943 *Follow the Band.* Universal. Director Jean Yarbrough. Eddie Quillan, Mary Beth Hughes, Leon Errol, Leo Carrillo, Robert Mitchum. There were also specialty numbers by Skinnay Ennis and his band, Alvino Rey and the King Sisters, Ray Eberle, Hilo Hattie, and Frances Langford.

1946 *One More Tomorrow.* Warner Brothers. Director Peter Godfrey. Ann Sheridan, Dennis Morgan, Jack Carson, Alexis Smith, Jane Wyman, Reginald Gardiner. (My records show that I worked in this film in early 1943. I can't explain the delay in release date unless it was caused by problems in connection with World War II.)

1943–65 I served on active duty in the U.S. Navy as a naval aviator and public affairs officer. Due to my film background from 1952 to 1954 I was head of the motion picture desk in the Office of Information. While there I helped set up the first two television programs with a navy theme. They were "Navy Log" and "Victory at Sea," with the prestigious musical arrangement written by Richard Rodgers. Also, while in charge of the motion picture program I set up the navy cooperation on three of the finest navy feature films ever made: *The Caine Mutiny, The Bridges at Toko-Ri,* and *Mr. Roberts.*

1960–65 I was in charge of the Navy Office in Hollywood. While there I was liaison officer on the television shows "Hennesey," with Jackie Cooper; "Ensign O'Toole," with Dean Jones; "Convoy," with John Gavin; and "The Wackiest Ship in the Army," with Gary Collins.

Among the many feature films I handled were *All Hands on Deck* with Pat Boone, Barbara Eden, and Buddy Hackett; *PT-109,* the John F. Kennedy story where Cliff Robertson played the late president. My final film was *In Harm's Way,* which starred John Wayne, Patricia Neal, Kirk Douglas.

1965 My first job as an actor after retiring from the navy was in a segment of "The Beverly Hillbillies," titled "Admiral Jed Clampett." It was directed by Joseph Depew and starred Buddy Ebsen, Irene Ryan, Max Baer, Jr., Donna Douglas, Raymond Bailey, Nancy Kulp.

1966 *The Sand Pebbles.* Twentieth Century–Fox. Producer and director Robert Wise. Steve McQueen, Richard Attenborough, Richard Crenna, Candice Bergen, Mako, Marayat Andriane, Larry Gates, Charles Robinson, Simon Oakland, Ford Rainey, Joseph Turkel, Gavin MacLeod.

1966 *Mr. Terrific.* Universal. TV pilot. Producer Edward Montagne. Director Don Weis. Alan Young. This was the pilot film and when the series aired on CBS for only 13 episodes in 1967 it was produced by David J. O'Connell and directed by Jack Arnold. It starred Stephen Strimpell, Dick Gautier, John McGiver, Paul Smith, Ned Glass, Ellen Corby.

1966 "The F.B.I." "The Defector." An episode of the television series. Producer Quinn Martin. Director Christian Nyby II. Efrem Zimbalist, Jr., Philip Abbott, Stephen Brooks, Lynn Loring, Tom Reynolds, Shelly Novack, Anthony Eisley, with the narration by Marvin Miller.

1966 *Dragnet 66.* Universal. Produced and directed by Jack Webb. Starring Jack Webb and Harry Morgan, Virginia Gregg.

1966 *Love Thy Customer.* An industrial film made for the Ford Motor Company. Rampart Productions. Director Dave Bowen.

1966 *A Garden of Cucumbers.* Goldwyn-Mirish. Director Delbert Mann.

1966 "12 O'Clock High." ABC. A television series. Producer Quinn Martin. Director Frank Glicksman. Robert Lansing, John Larkin, Frank Overton, Lew Gallow, Barney Phillips, Paul Burke, Chris Robinson, Andrew Duggan. This episode had a guest appearance by Ralph Bellamy.

1967 *Valley of the Dolls.* Twentieth Century–Fox. Producer David Weisbart. Director Marc Robson. From the novel by Jacqueline Susann. Barbara Parkins, Patty Duke, Susan Hayward, Paul Burke, Sharon Tate, Martin Milner, Tony Scott, Charles Drake, Alex Davion, Lee Grant, Robert Morris.

1967 *The Love Ins.* Columbia. Producer Sam Katzman. Director Arthur Dreifuss. Richard Todd, James MacArthur, Susan Oliver, Mark Goddard, Carol Booth, Marc Cavell, Janee Michelle, Ronnie Eckstine, Michael Evans, Hortense Petra, James Lloyd, Mario Roccuzzo, Joe Pyne, The Chocolate Watch Band, The UFOs, The New Age, Donnie Brooke.

1967 *The Shakiest Gun in the West.* Universal. Producer Edward Montagne. Director Alan Rafkin. Don Knotts, Barbara Rhodes, Jackie Coogan, Dick Wilson, Don Barry.

1968 "The Outcasts." Screen Gems. A television series. Producers Hugh Benson, E. W. Swackhamer. Director Jon Epstein. Don Murray, Otis Young.

1969 *The Love God.* Universal. Producer Edward Montagne. Director Nat Hiken. Don Knotts, Edmund O'Brien, Anne Francis, James Gregory, Maureen Arthur.

1972 A Champale Malt Liquor television commercial. Director Rick Levine.

1967 *Fitzwilly.* United Artists. Producer and director Delbert Mann. Dick Van Dyke, Barbara Feldon, John McGiver, Edith Evans, Harry Townes, John Fiedler, Norman Fell, Cecil Kellaway, Stephen Strimpell, Anne Seymour, Helen Kleeb, Paul Reed, Sam Waterston, Albert Currier, Nelson Olmsted, Dennis Cooney, Noam Pitlik, Billy Halop.

1973 "Here's Lucy." Universal. A television series. Director Coby Ruskin. Lucille Ball, Gale Gordon, O. J. Simpson, Cliff Norton, Al Checco.

1973 A Toyota television commercial.

1975 "Shazam." CBS. Producer-director Arthur H. Nadel. Les Tremayne, Michael Grey, Jackson Bostwick, John Davey.

1975–81 Thirty television commercials for Curtis Mathes.

1977 "The New Little Rascals." T.A.T. Productions. Producer Norman Lear. Director James Field. We rehearsed ten scripts and filmed two pilot films. Unfortunately, the proposed series never reached the networks.

1978 "Dinky Hocker." A television film. Robert Guenette Productions. Director Tom Blank. Wendy Sperber, June Lockhart.

1982 A Ben Hogan Golf Products television commercial.

1982 Twenty-six television commercials for Oles Home Centers. I played a character called "The Little Wimp." In this series I worked with sports personalities Jack Youngblood, Nolan Cromwell, Steve Sax, John Matusak, and the lovely Angela Cartwright.

1983 "Newhart: New Faces of 1951." MTM Productions. Producers Barry Kemp, Sheldon Bull. Director John Tracy. Bob Newhart, Mary Frann, Tom Poston, Julia Duffy, Steven Kampmann, Ernie Brown, John Bluto.

1984 A La Quinta Motor Inns television commercial.

1986 "Scrabble." NBC. I was a contestant on the show, and host Chuck Woollery talked to me about my part in *Gone with the Wind.*

1988 "Frank's Back." A television film for the Curtis Mathes dealers.

1988 "Wheel of Fortune." NBC. I was a contestant on the show and when I won, game show host Pat Sajak stood beside me and said "Shazam!"

1988 Twelve television commercials for Curtis Mathes.

1988 Four television commercials for Curtis Mathes.

1989 "Entertainment Tonight." NBC. I was interviewed by Leonard Maltin in connection with the release of the Republic serial *Adventures of Captain Marvel* to the home video market.

1990 Three television commercials for Curtis Mathes.

1990 "Harold Lloyd." A television spectacular by Thames Television of London, England. I was interviewed by Kevin Brownlow for having known Harold Lloyd through the years.

1990 "Entertainment Tonight." NBC. I was again interviewed by Leonard Maltin at a reunion of the "kid" actors who worked at Universal Studios in the 1930s and 1940s.

1991 "Entertainment Tonight." NBC. Leonard Maltin interviewed me and other Republic Pictures' performers who would be seen in the forthcoming AMC special, "The Republic Pictures Story."

1991 "The Republic Pictures Story." A two-hour special on the American Movie Classics cable television network honoring the greats who performed in motion pictures and serials made at Republic Pictures. I was pleased to be included along with John Wayne, Gene Autry, Roy Rogers and Dale Evans, Gabby Hayes, Smiley Burnette, Linda Stirling, Kay Aldridge, Maureen O'Hara, Victor McLaglen, Barry Fitzgerald, Tom Tyler, Tom Steele, Richard Webb, William Benedict, Louise Currie, Peggy Stewart, Don "Red" Barry, Vera (Hruba) Ralston, Judy Canova, The Three Mesqueteers, Edmund O'Brien, Mickey Rooney, Orson Welles, Catherine McLeod, Ruth Terry, Ralph Byrd, Olsen and Johnson, Ann Jeffreys, Crash Corrigan, the Weaver Brothers, Maude Eburne, Rita Hayworth, Leonard Nimoy, Robert Stack, Peggy Ryan, Gail Russell, John Carroll, Clayton Moore, Ramon Navarro, Walter Brennan, Richard Dix, Joan Fontaine, Bela Lugosi, Duke Ellington, Barbara Stanwyck, Richard Lane, Martha O'Driscoll, John Hubbard and directors William Witney and George Sidney.

1992 "Shirley Temple—America's Little Darling." A PBS special. Wombat Productions. Writer and producer Gene Feldman. Also featured are: Jane Withers, Dickie Moore, Darryl Hickman, Marcia Mae Jones, Delmar Watson, Gloria Stuart, Cesar Romero, and Alice Faye.

Index